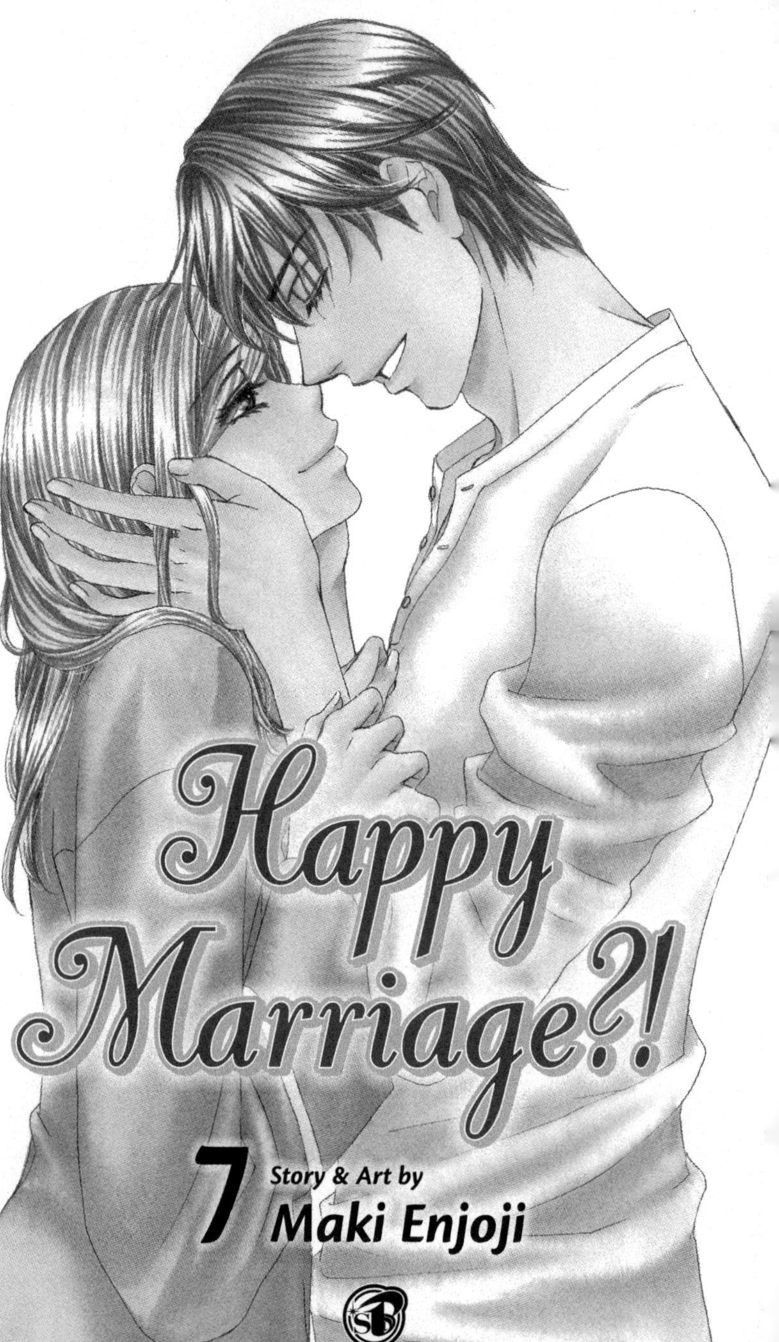

Happy Marriage?!

7

Story & Art by

Maki Enjoji

Shojo Beat

Happy Marriage?!

Characters

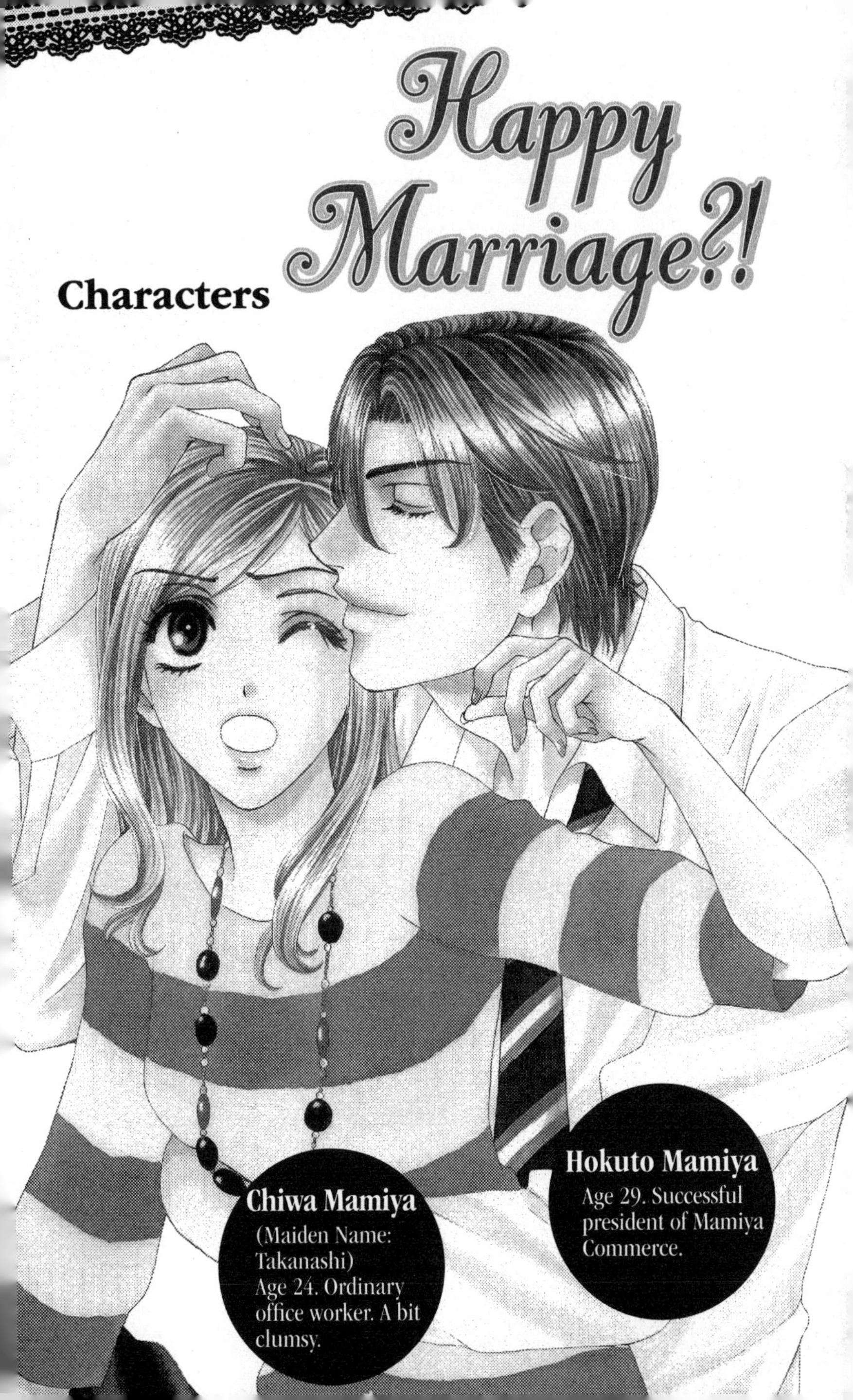
Hokuto Mamiya
Age 29. Successful president of Mamiya Commerce.
Chiwa Mamiya
(Maiden Name: Takanashi) Age 24. Ordinary office worker. A bit clumsy.

Misaki Shitara

President of a famous brand. In the past she was in a relationship with Hokuto...?

Kaname Asahina

Two years older than Chiwa, he was an upperclassman at her university. He is now her boss at work.

Story

Chiwa Takanashi has no girlish fantasies about finding Prince Charming, and she wanted nothing but to lead a normal life until she found herself marrying company president Hokuto to pay off her father's debts. Though the marriage is in name only, Chiwa has fallen in love with her husband. Chiwa starts to study up on Hokuto's industry to understand his work better. But she is still having problems with her boss, Asahina. While trying to balance her studying and job, Chiwa collapses from overwork...?!

Happy Marriage?!

Contents

Step Twenty-Five: Will I Be Tied Down to You?

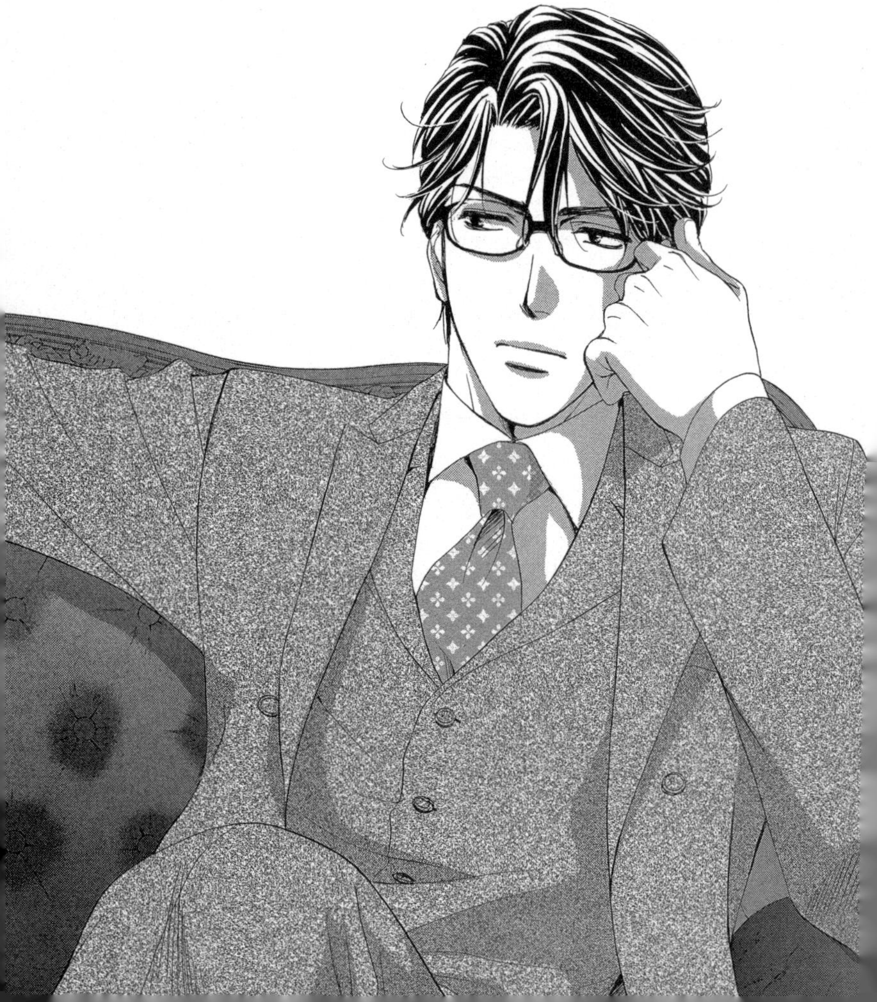

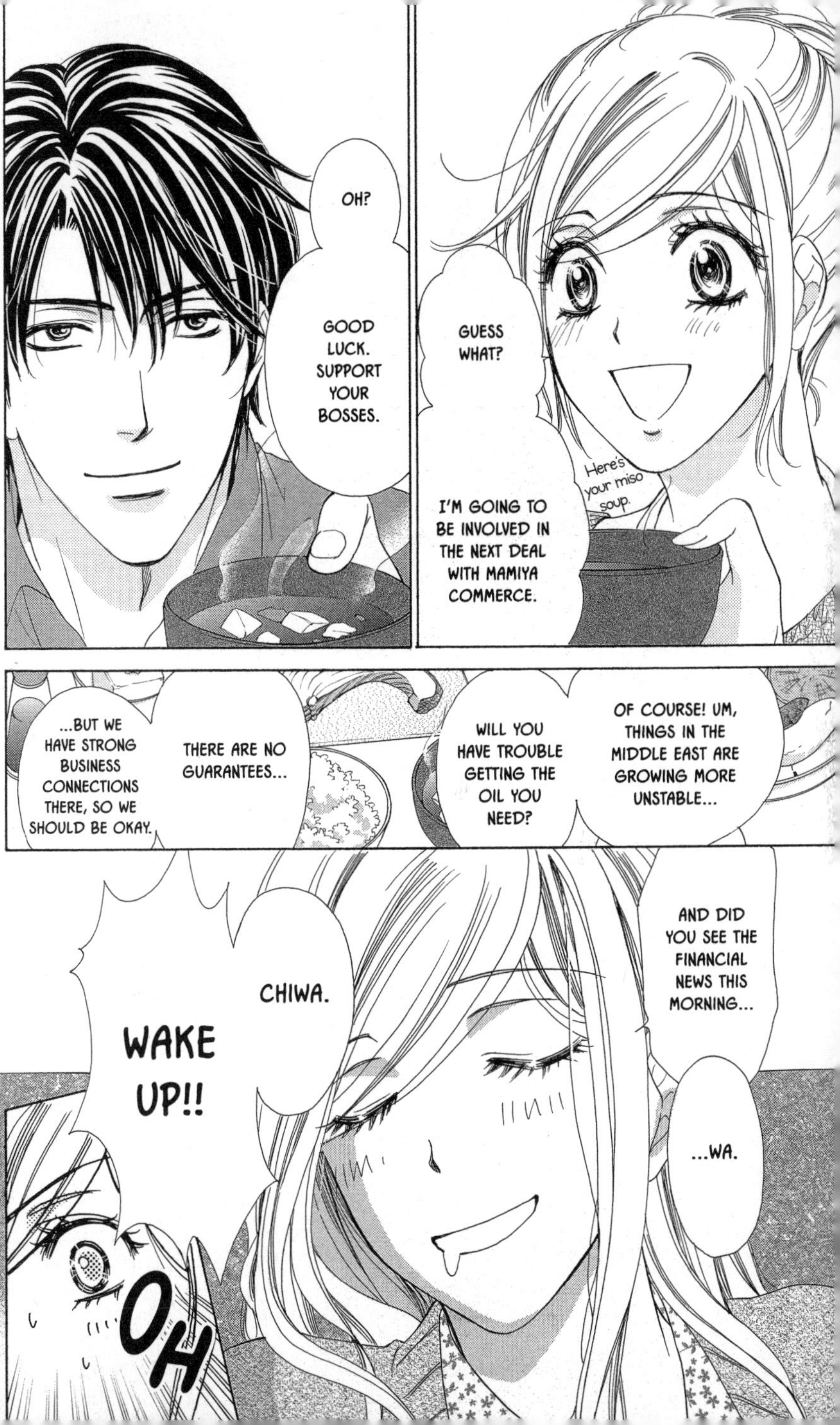
GUESS WHAT?
Here's your miso soup.
I'M GOING TO BE INVOLVED IN THE NEXT DEAL WITH MAMIYA COMMERCE.
OH?
GOOD LUCK. SUPPORT YOUR BOSSES.
OF COURSE! UM, THINGS IN THE MIDDLE EAST ARE GROWING MORE UNSTABLE...
WILL YOU HAVE TROUBLE GETTING THE OIL YOU NEED?
THERE ARE NO GUARANTEES...
...BUT WE HAVE STRONG BUSINESS CONNECTIONS THERE, SO WE SHOULD BE OKAY.
AND DID YOU SEE THE FINANCIAL NEWS THIS MORNING...
...WA.
CHIWA.
WAKE UP!!
OH

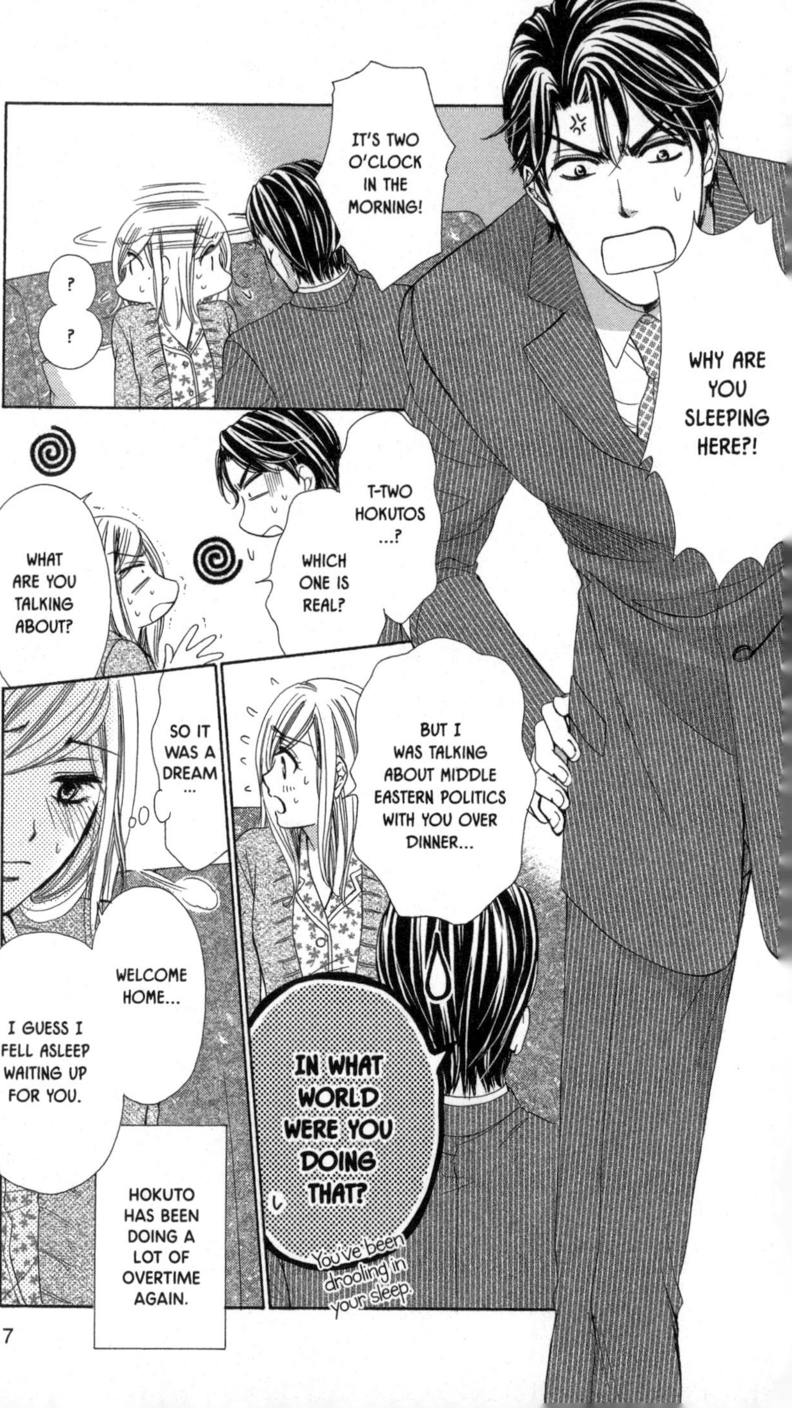
WHY ARE YOU SLEEPING HERE?!
IT'S TWO O'CLOCK IN THE MORNING!
?
?
T-TWO HOKUTOS ...?
WHICH ONE IS REAL?
WHAT ARE YOU TALKING ABOUT?
BUT I WAS TALKING ABOUT MIDDLE EASTERN POLITICS WITH YOU OVER DINNER...
IN WHAT WORLD WERE YOU DOING THAT?
You've been drooling in your sleep.
SO IT WAS A DREAM ...
WELCOME HOME...
I GUESS I FELL ASLEEP WAITING UP FOR YOU.
HOKUTO HAS BEEN DOING A LOT OF OVERTIME AGAIN.

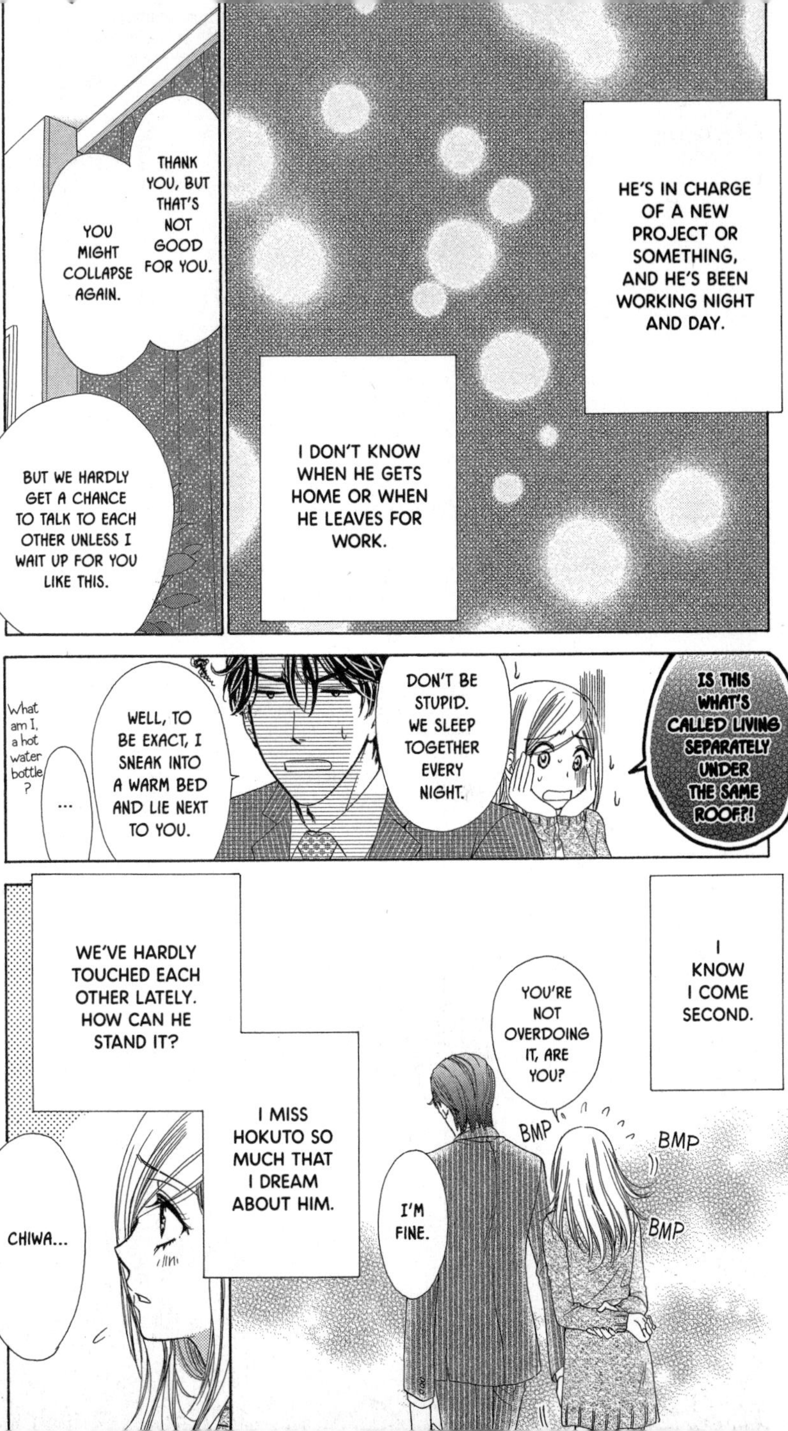
HE'S IN CHARGE OF A NEW PROJECT OR SOMETHING, AND HE'S BEEN WORKING NIGHT AND DAY.
I DON'T KNOW WHEN HE GETS HOME OR WHEN HE LEAVES FOR WORK.
THANK YOU, BUT THAT'S NOT GOOD FOR YOU.
YOU MIGHT COLLAPSE AGAIN.
BUT WE HARDLY GET A CHANCE TO TALK TO EACH OTHER UNLESS I WAIT UP FOR YOU LIKE THIS.
IS THIS WHAT'S CALLED LIVING SEPARATELY UNDER THE SAME ROOF?!
DON'T BE STUPID. WE SLEEP TOGETHER EVERY NIGHT.
WELL, TO BE EXACT, I SNEAK INTO A WARM BED AND LIE NEXT TO YOU.
...
What am I, a hot water bottle?
I KNOW I COME SECOND.
YOU'RE NOT OVERDOING IT, ARE YOU?
BMP
BMP
BMP
I'M FINE.
WE'VE HARDLY TOUCHED EACH OTHER LATELY. HOW CAN HE STAND IT?
I MISS HOKUTO SO MUCH THAT I DREAM ABOUT HIM.
CHIWA...

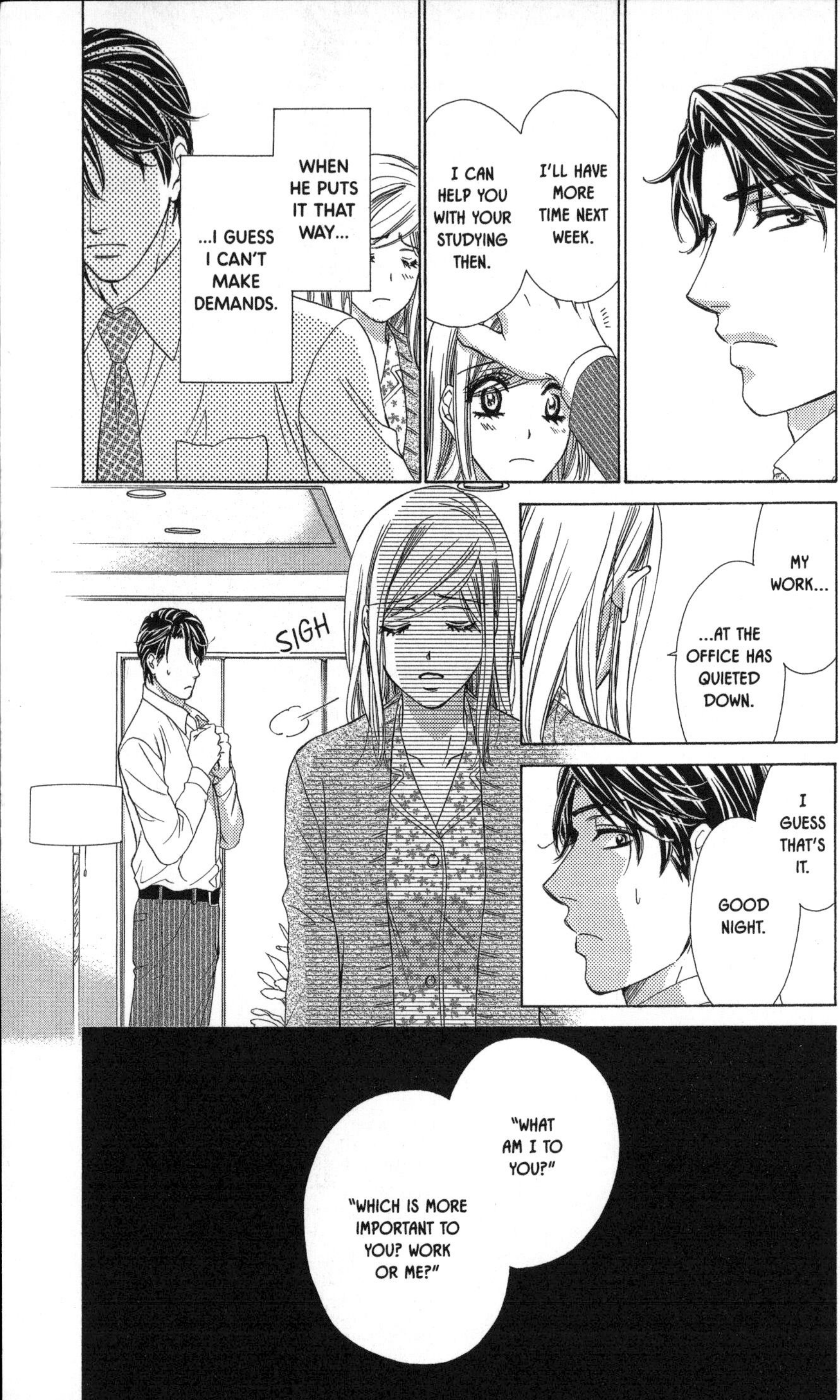
I'LL HAVE MORE TIME NEXT WEEK.
I CAN HELP YOU WITH YOUR STUDYING THEN.
WHEN HE PUTS IT THAT WAY...
...I GUESS I CAN'T MAKE DEMANDS.
MY WORK...
...AT THE OFFICE HAS QUIETED DOWN.
I GUESS THAT'S IT.
GOOD NIGHT.
SIGH
"WHAT AM I TO YOU?"
"WHICH IS MORE IMPORTANT TO YOU? WORK OR ME?"

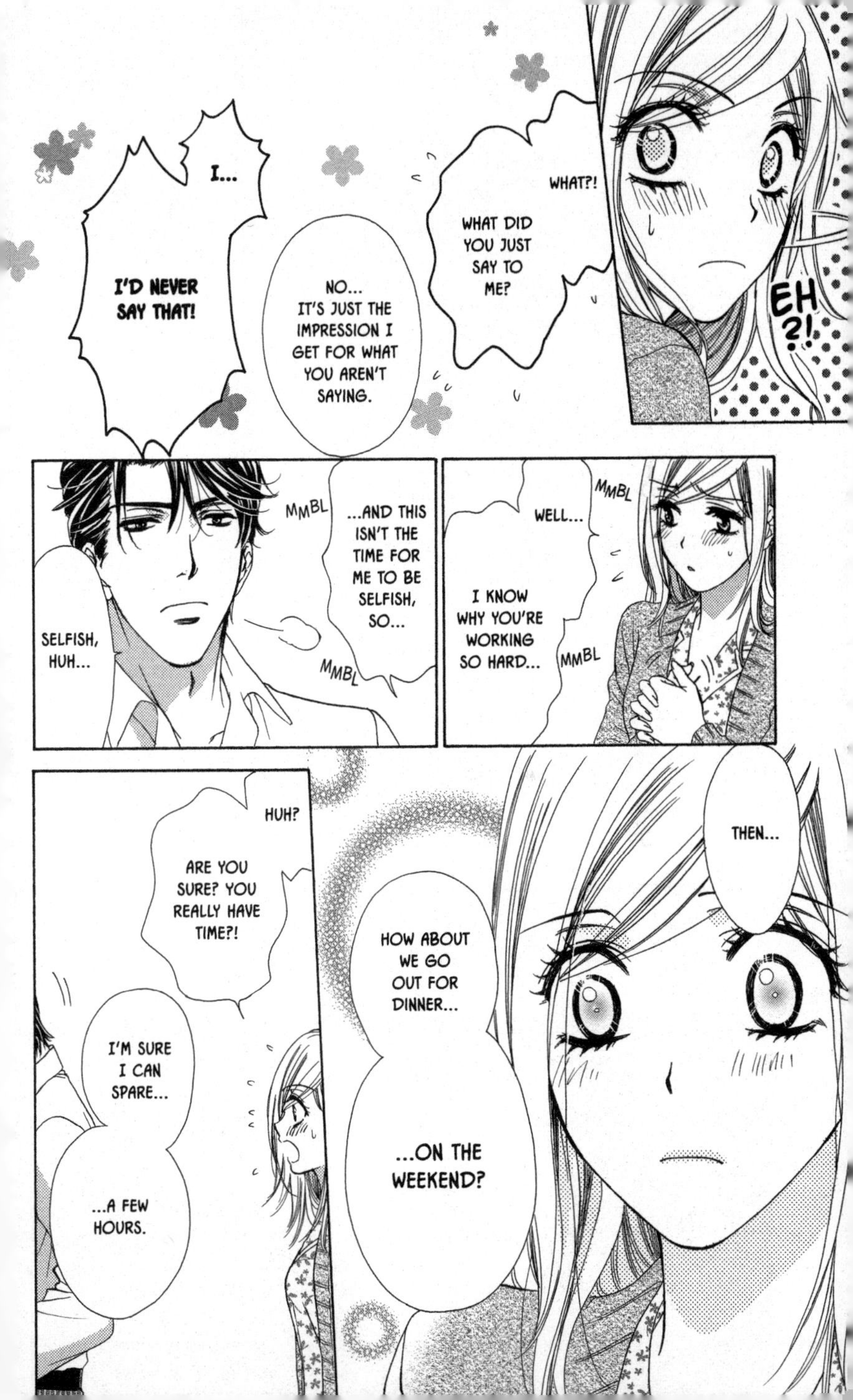
EH?!
WHAT?!
WHAT DID YOU JUST SAY TO ME?
NO... IT'S JUST THE IMPRESSION I GET FOR WHAT YOU AREN'T SAYING.
I...
I'D NEVER SAY THAT!
MMBL
WELL...
I KNOW WHY YOU'RE WORKING SO HARD...
MMBL
MMBL
...AND THIS ISN'T THE TIME FOR ME TO BE SELFISH, SO...
MMBL
SELFISH, HUH...
THEN...
HOW ABOUT WE GO OUT FOR DINNER...
...ON THE WEEKEND?
HUH?
ARE YOU SURE? YOU REALLY HAVE TIME?!
I'M SURE I CAN SPARE...
...A FEW HOURS.

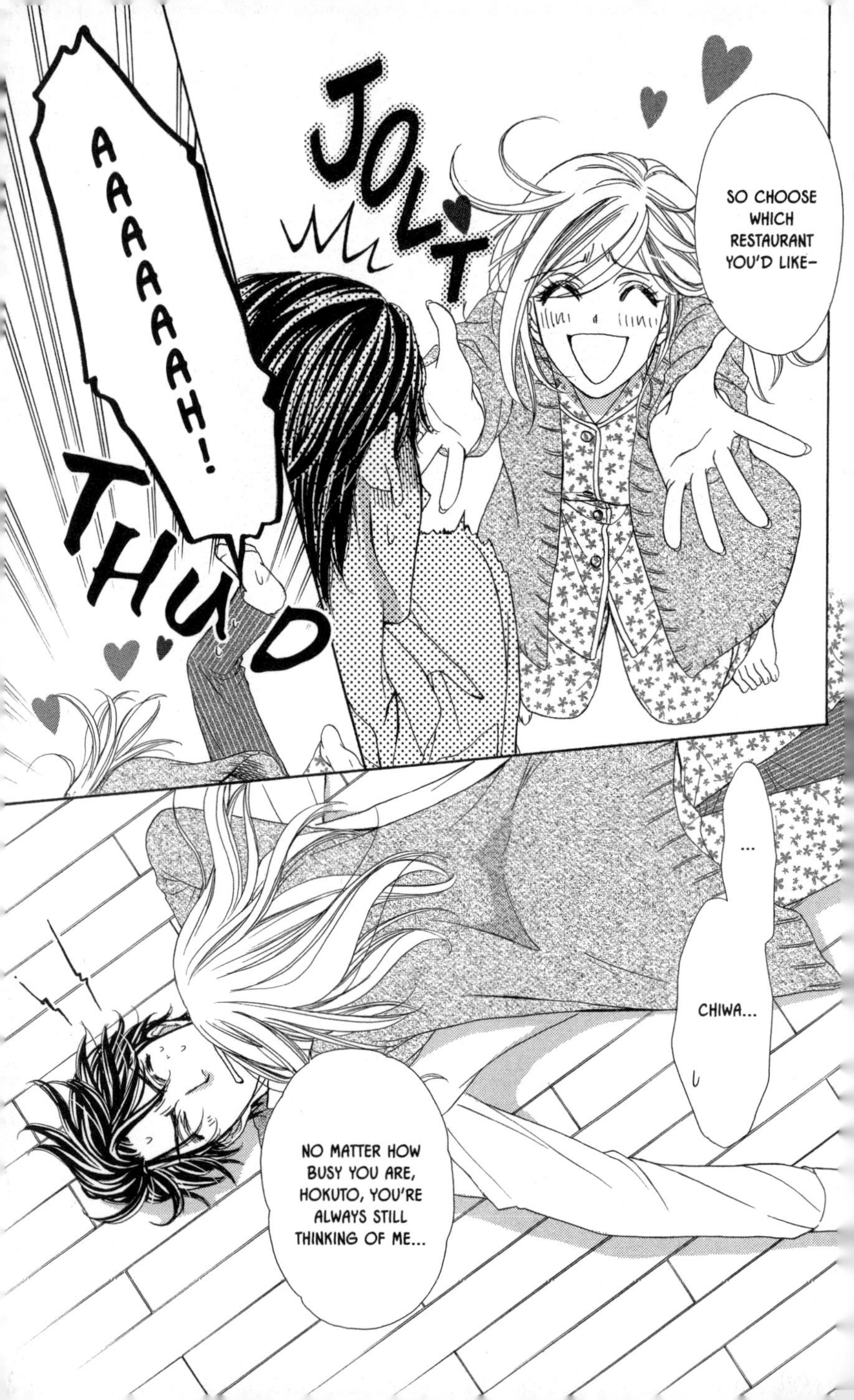
SO CHOOSE WHICH RESTAURANT YOU'D LIKE–
JOLT
AAAAAAAH!
THUD
...
CHIWA...
NO MATTER HOW BUSY YOU ARE, HOKUTO, YOU'RE ALWAYS STILL THINKING OF ME...

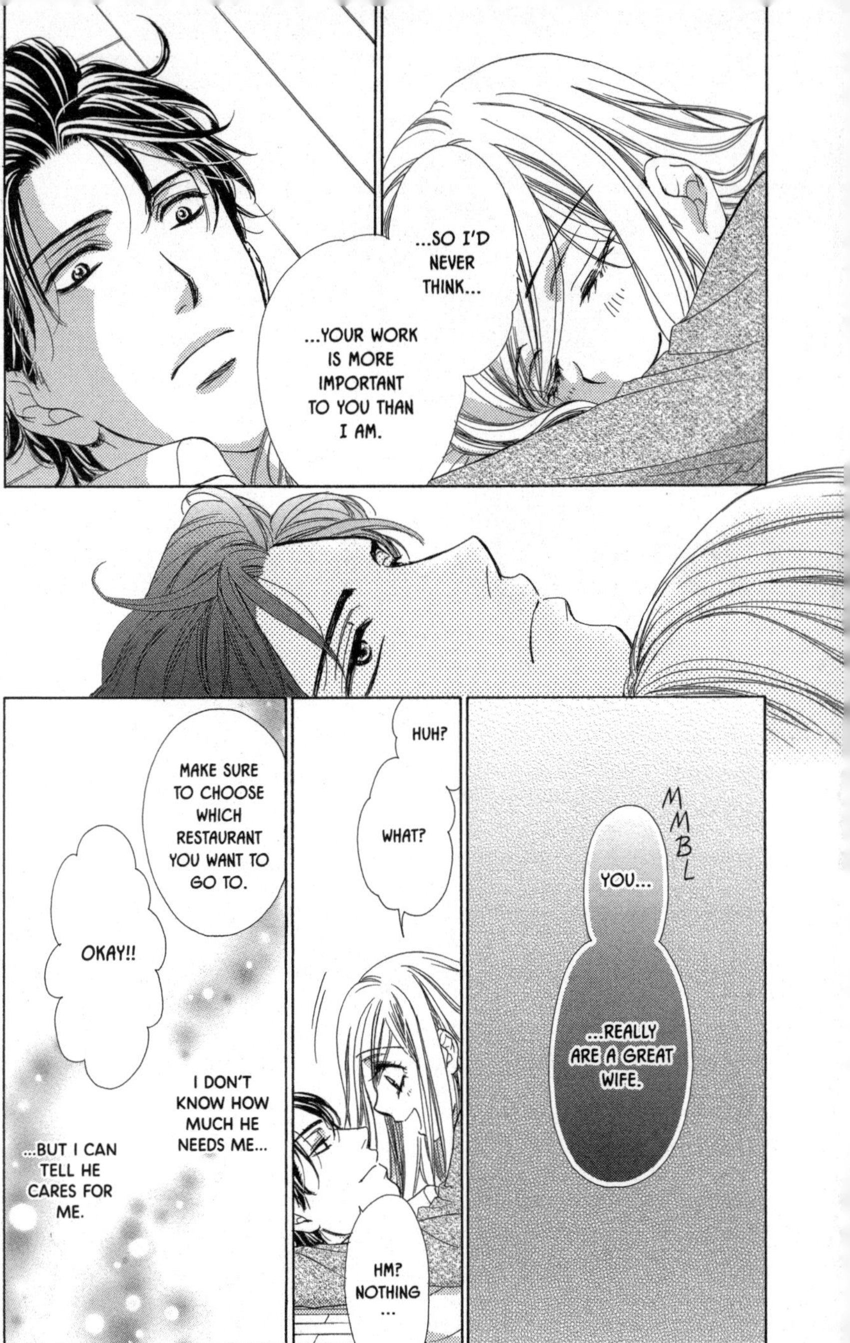
...SO I'D NEVER THINK...
...YOUR WORK IS MORE IMPORTANT TO YOU THAN I AM.
MMBL
YOU...
...REALLY ARE A GREAT WIFE.
HUH?
WHAT?
HM? NOTHING...
MAKE SURE TO CHOOSE WHICH RESTAURANT YOU WANT TO GO TO.
OKAY!!
I DON'T KNOW HOW MUCH HE NEEDS ME...
...BUT I CAN TELL HE CARES FOR ME.

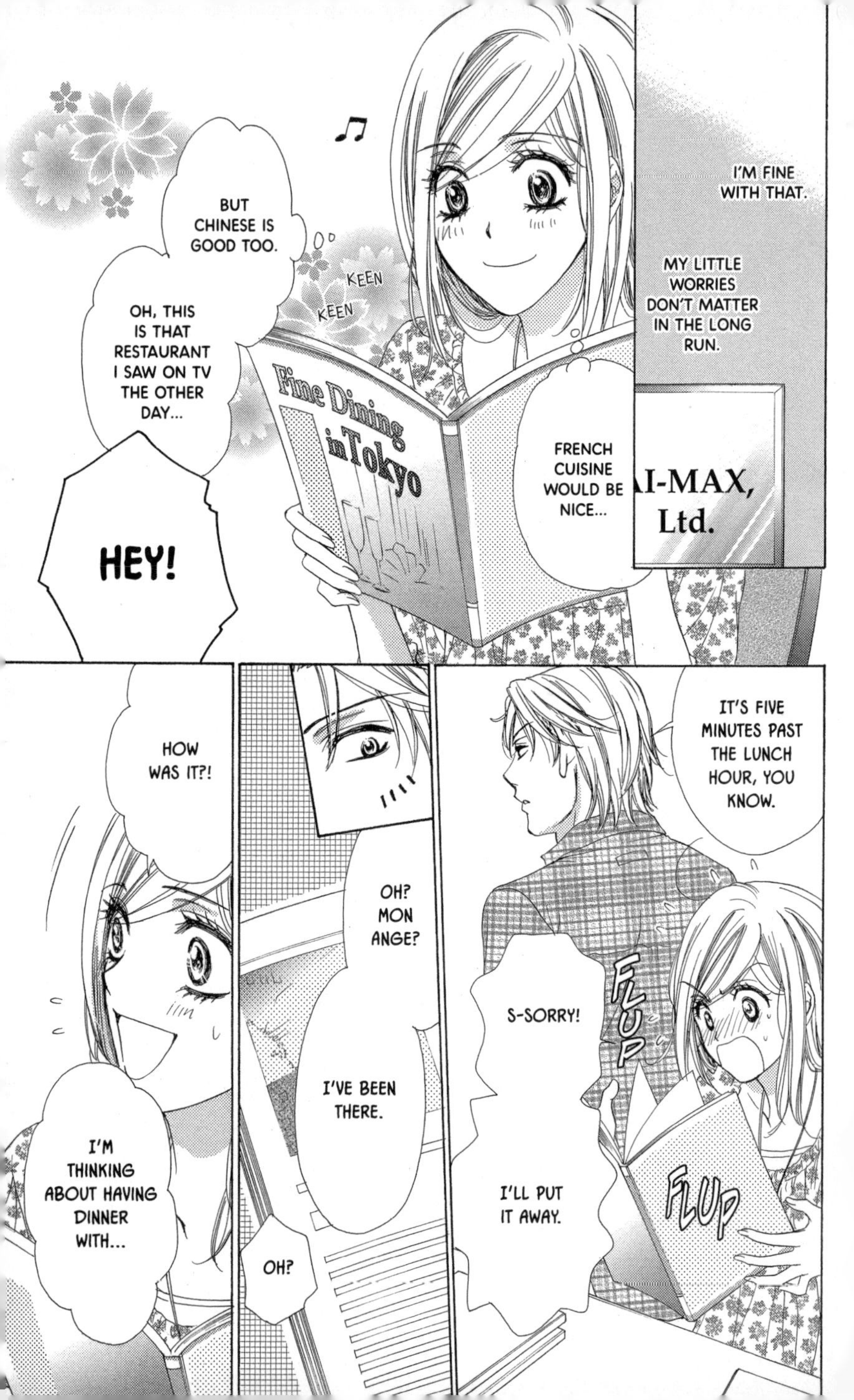
I'M FINE WITH THAT.
MY LITTLE WORRIES DON'T MATTER IN THE LONG RUN.
AI-MAX, Ltd.
♫
FRENCH CUISINE WOULD BE NICE...
BUT CHINESE IS GOOD TOO.
KEEN
KEEN
OH, THIS IS THAT RESTAURANT I SAW ON TV THE OTHER DAY...
Fine Dining in Tokyo
HEY!
IT'S FIVE MINUTES PAST THE LUNCH HOUR, YOU KNOW.
S-SORRY!
FLUP
I'LL PUT IT AWAY.
FLUP
OH? MON ANGE?
I'VE BEEN THERE.
OH?
HOW WAS IT?!
I'M THINKING ABOUT HAVING DINNER WITH...

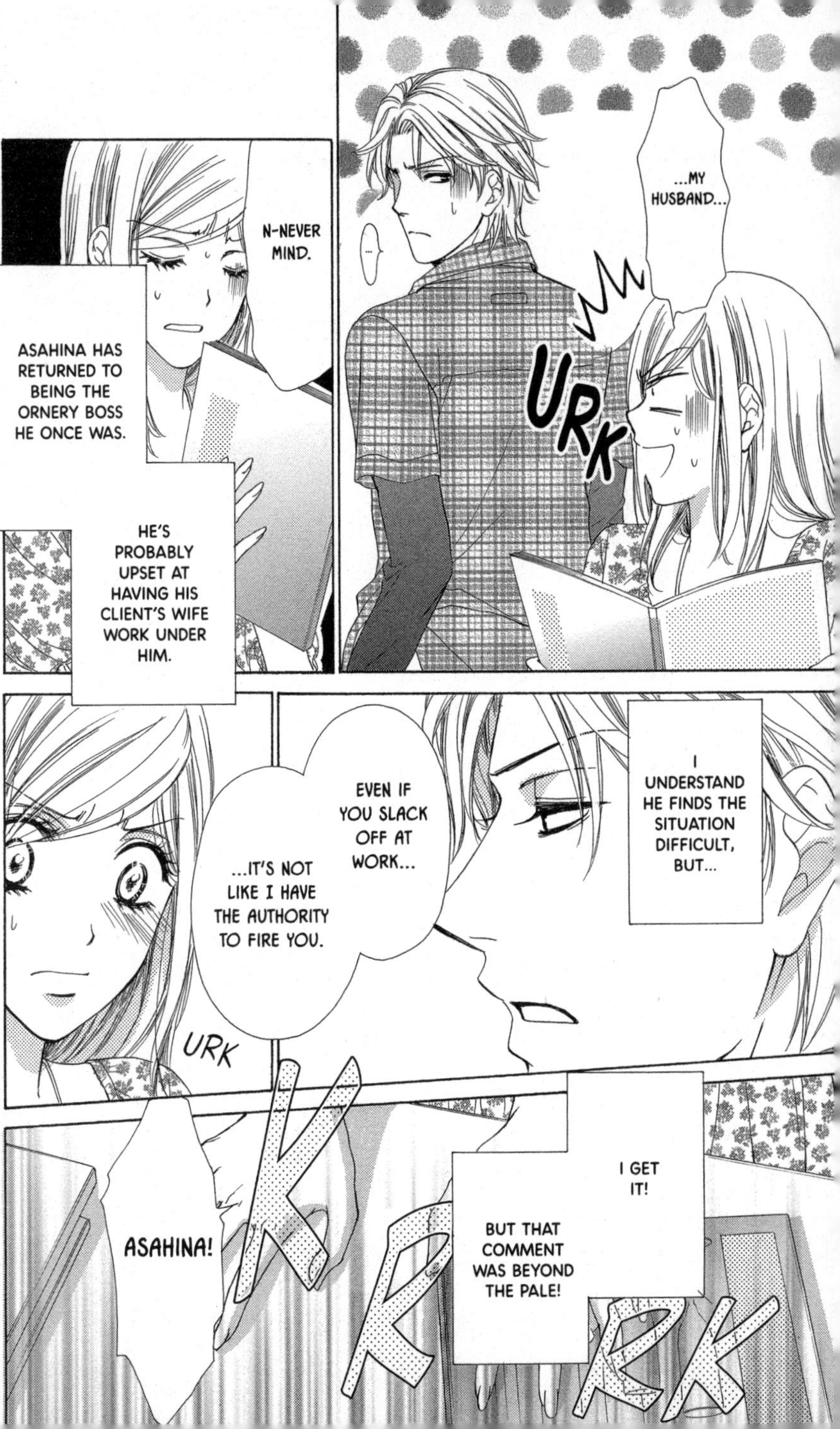

...MY HUSBAND...
URK
...
N-NEVER MIND.
ASAHINA HAS RETURNED TO BEING THE ORNERY BOSS HE ONCE WAS.
HE'S PROBABLY UPSET AT HAVING HIS CLIENT'S WIFE WORK UNDER HIM.
I UNDERSTAND HE FINDS THE SITUATION DIFFICULT, BUT...
EVEN IF YOU SLACK OFF AT WORK...
...IT'S NOT LIKE I HAVE THE AUTHORITY TO FIRE YOU.
URK
I GET IT!
BUT THAT COMMENT WAS BEYOND THE PALE!
ASAHINA!

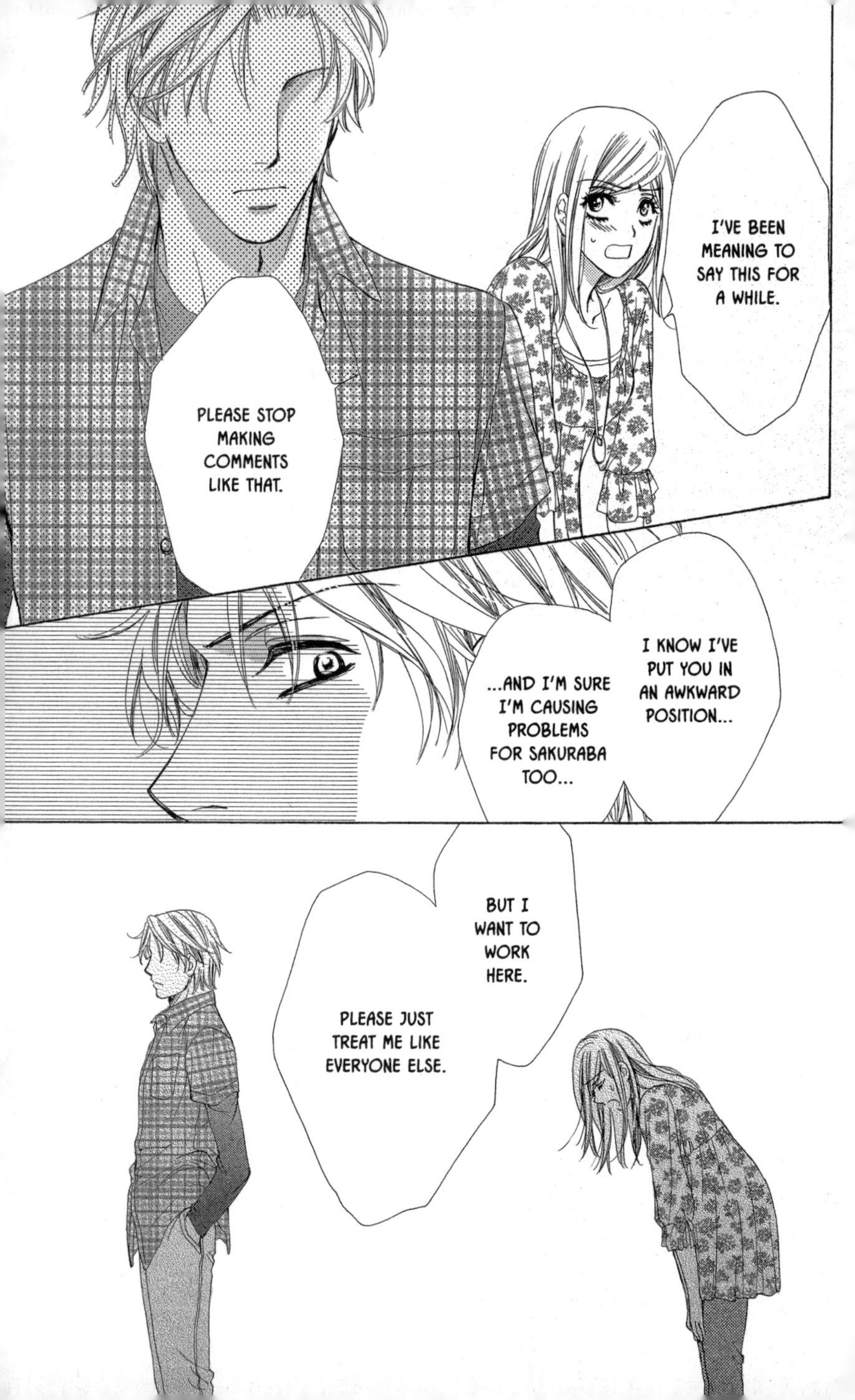
I'VE BEEN MEANING TO SAY THIS FOR A WHILE.
PLEASE STOP MAKING COMMENTS LIKE THAT.
I KNOW I'VE PUT YOU IN AN AWKWARD POSITION...
...AND I'M SURE I'M CAUSING PROBLEMS FOR SAKURABA TOO...
BUT I WANT TO WORK HERE.
PLEASE JUST TREAT ME LIKE EVERYONE ELSE.

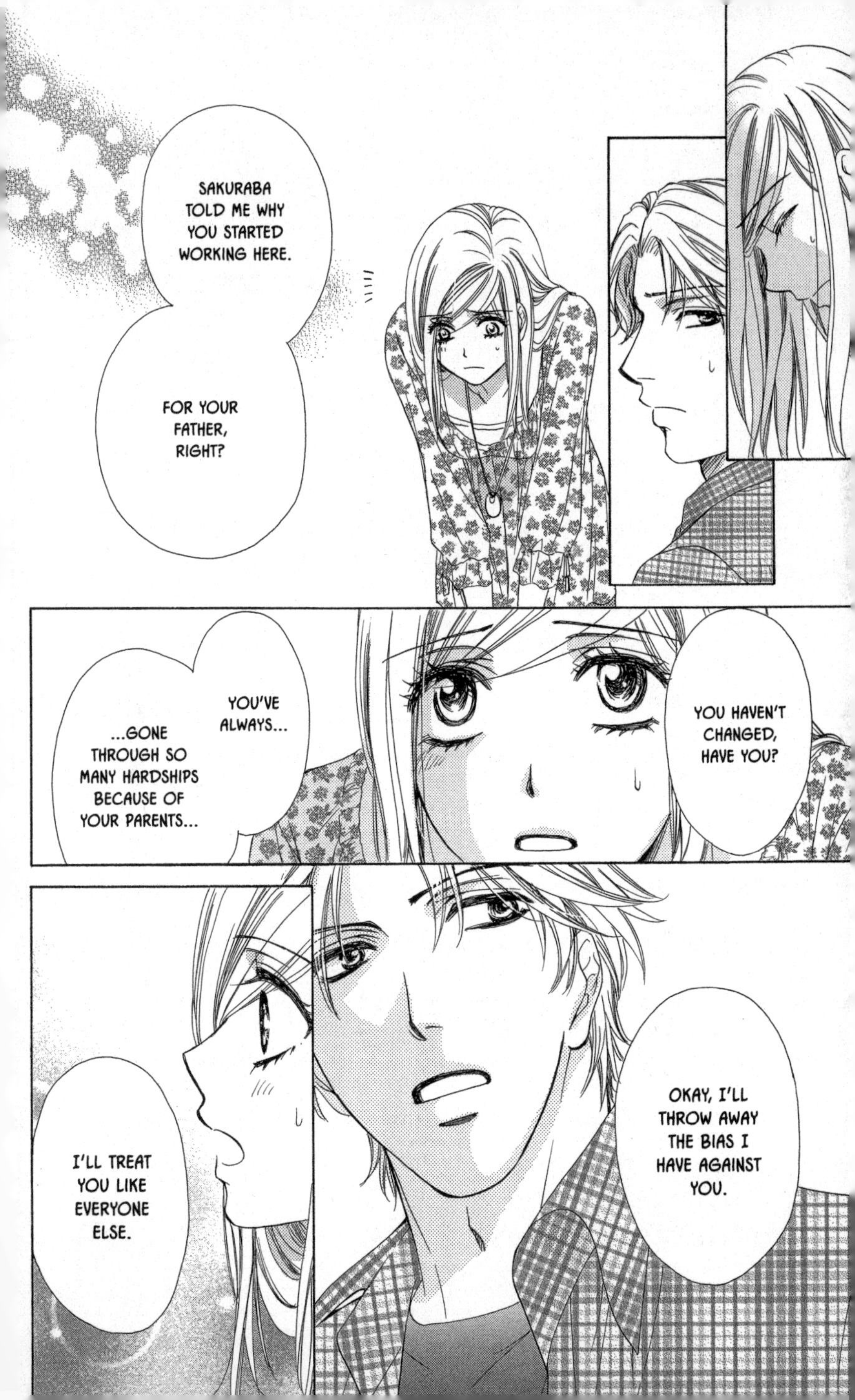
SAKURABA TOLD ME WHY YOU STARTED WORKING HERE.
FOR YOUR FATHER, RIGHT?
YOU HAVEN'T CHANGED, HAVE YOU?
YOU'VE ALWAYS...
...GONE THROUGH SO MANY HARDSHIPS BECAUSE OF YOUR PARENTS...
OKAY, I'LL THROW AWAY THE BIAS I HAVE AGAINST YOU.
I'LL TREAT YOU LIKE EVERYONE ELSE.

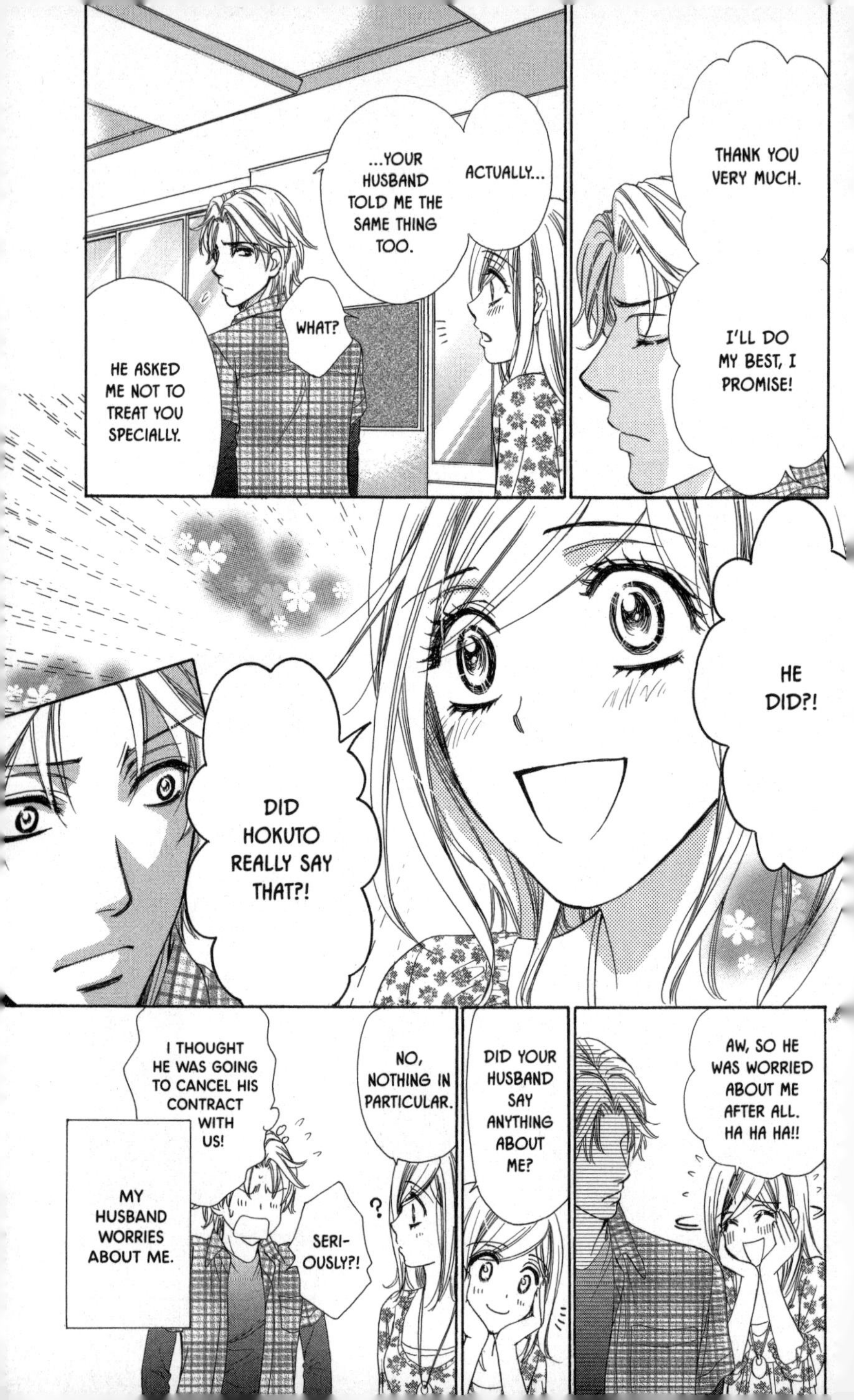
THANK YOU VERY MUCH.
I'LL DO MY BEST, I PROMISE!
ACTUALLY...
...YOUR HUSBAND TOLD ME THE SAME THING TOO.
WHAT?
HE ASKED ME NOT TO TREAT YOU SPECIALLY.
HE DID?!
DID HOKUTO REALLY SAY THAT?!
AW, SO HE WAS WORRIED ABOUT ME AFTER ALL. HA HA HA!!
DID YOUR HUSBAND SAY ANYTHING ABOUT ME?
NO, NOTHING IN PARTICULAR.
I THOUGHT HE WAS GOING TO CANCEL HIS CONTRACT WITH US!
SERI-OUSLY?!
MY HUSBAND WORRIES ABOUT ME.

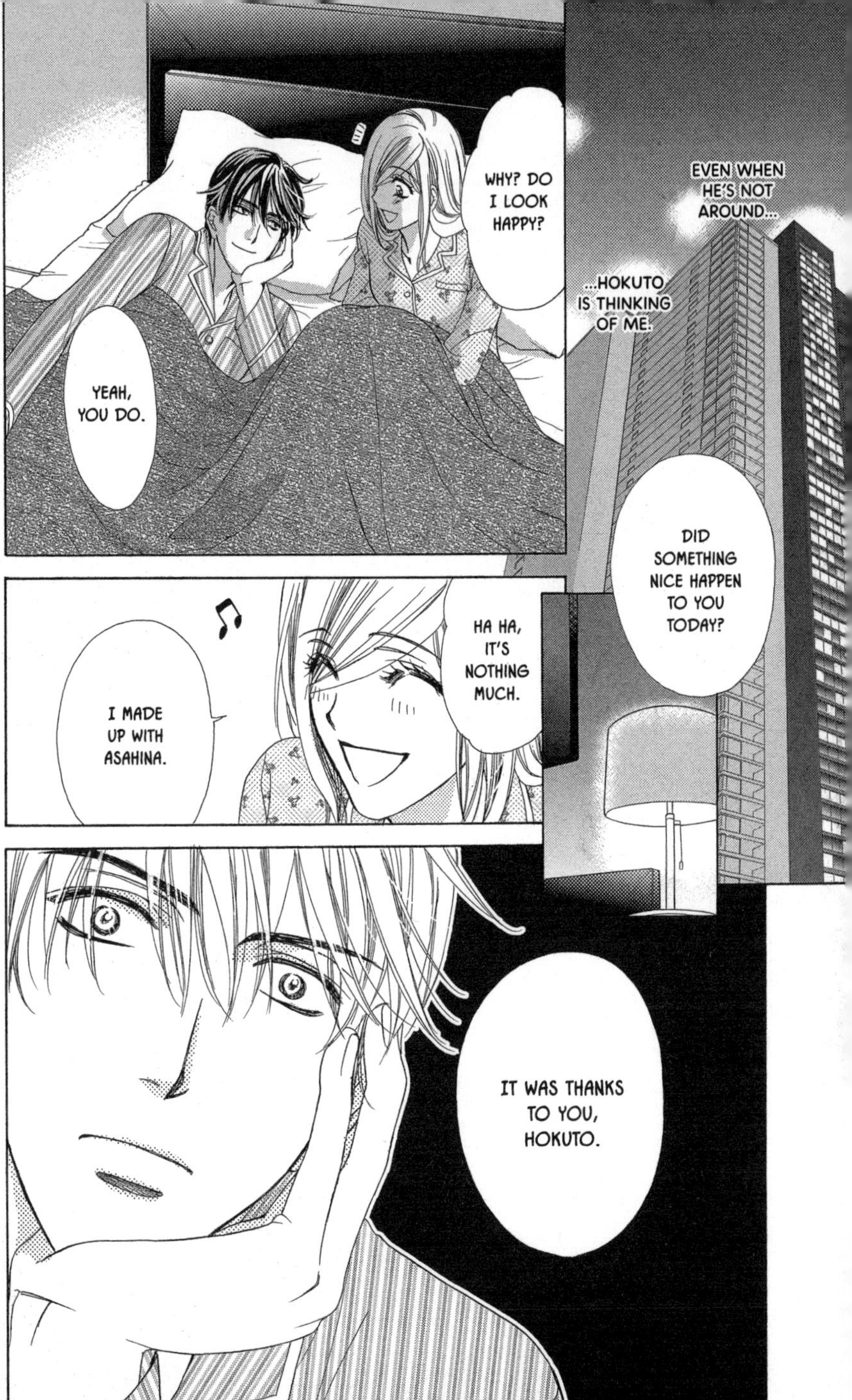
EVEN WHEN HE'S NOT AROUND...
...HOKUTO IS THINKING OF ME.
DID SOMETHING NICE HAPPEN TO YOU TODAY?
WHY? DO I LOOK HAPPY?
YEAH, YOU DO.
HA HA, IT'S NOTHING MUCH.
I MADE UP WITH ASAHINA.
IT WAS THANKS TO YOU, HOKUTO.

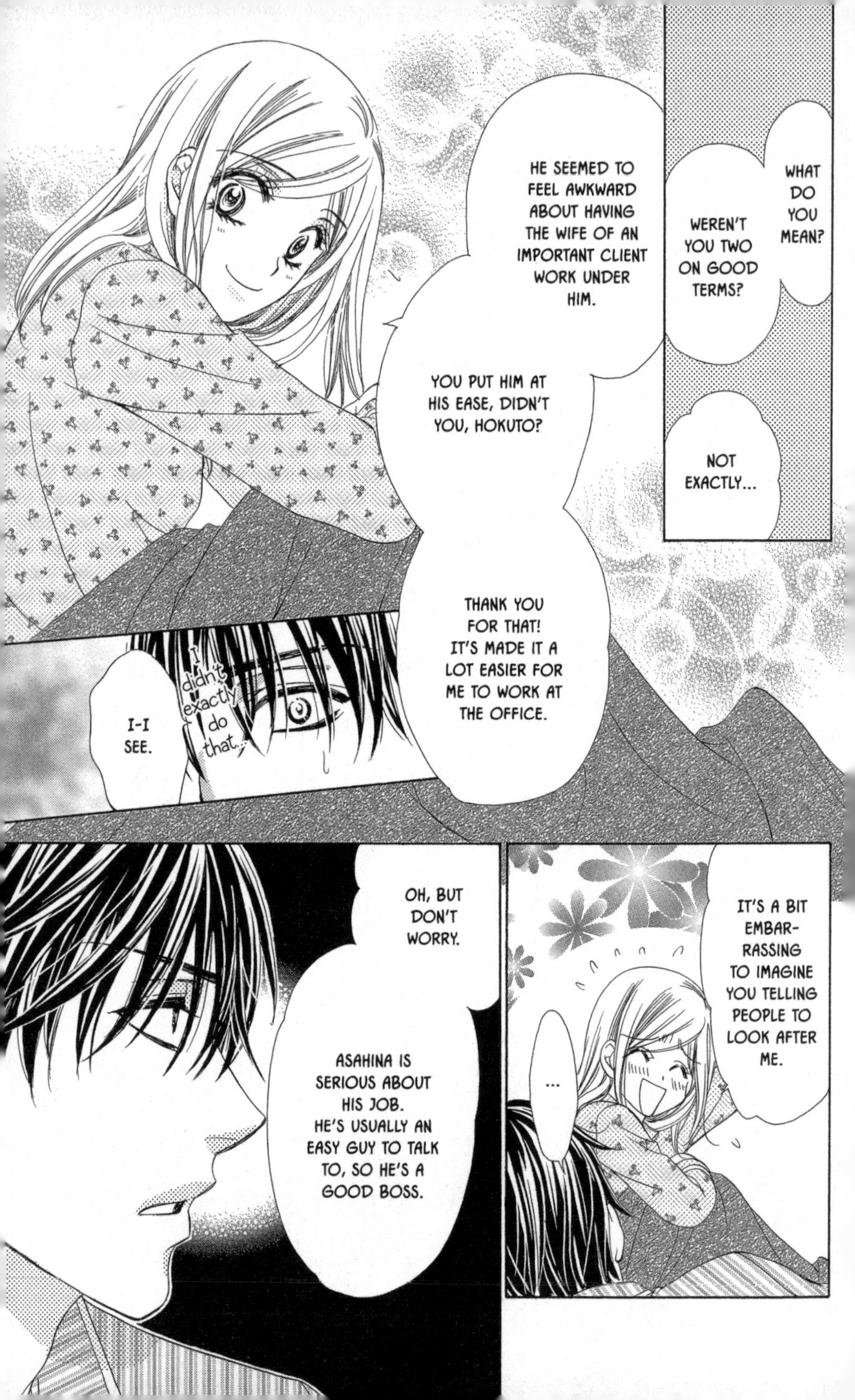
WHAT DO YOU MEAN?
WEREN'T YOU TWO ON GOOD TERMS?
NOT EXACTLY...
HE SEEMED TO FEEL AWKWARD ABOUT HAVING THE WIFE OF AN IMPORTANT CLIENT WORK UNDER HIM.
YOU PUT HIM AT HIS EASE, DIDN'T YOU, HOKUTO?
THANK YOU FOR THAT! IT'S MADE IT A LOT EASIER FOR ME TO WORK AT THE OFFICE.
I didn't exactly do that...
I-I SEE.
IT'S A BIT EMBAR-RASSING TO IMAGINE YOU TELLING PEOPLE TO LOOK AFTER ME.
...
OH, BUT DON'T WORRY.
ASAHINA IS SERIOUS ABOUT HIS JOB. HE'S USUALLY AN EASY GUY TO TALK TO, SO HE'S A GOOD BOSS.

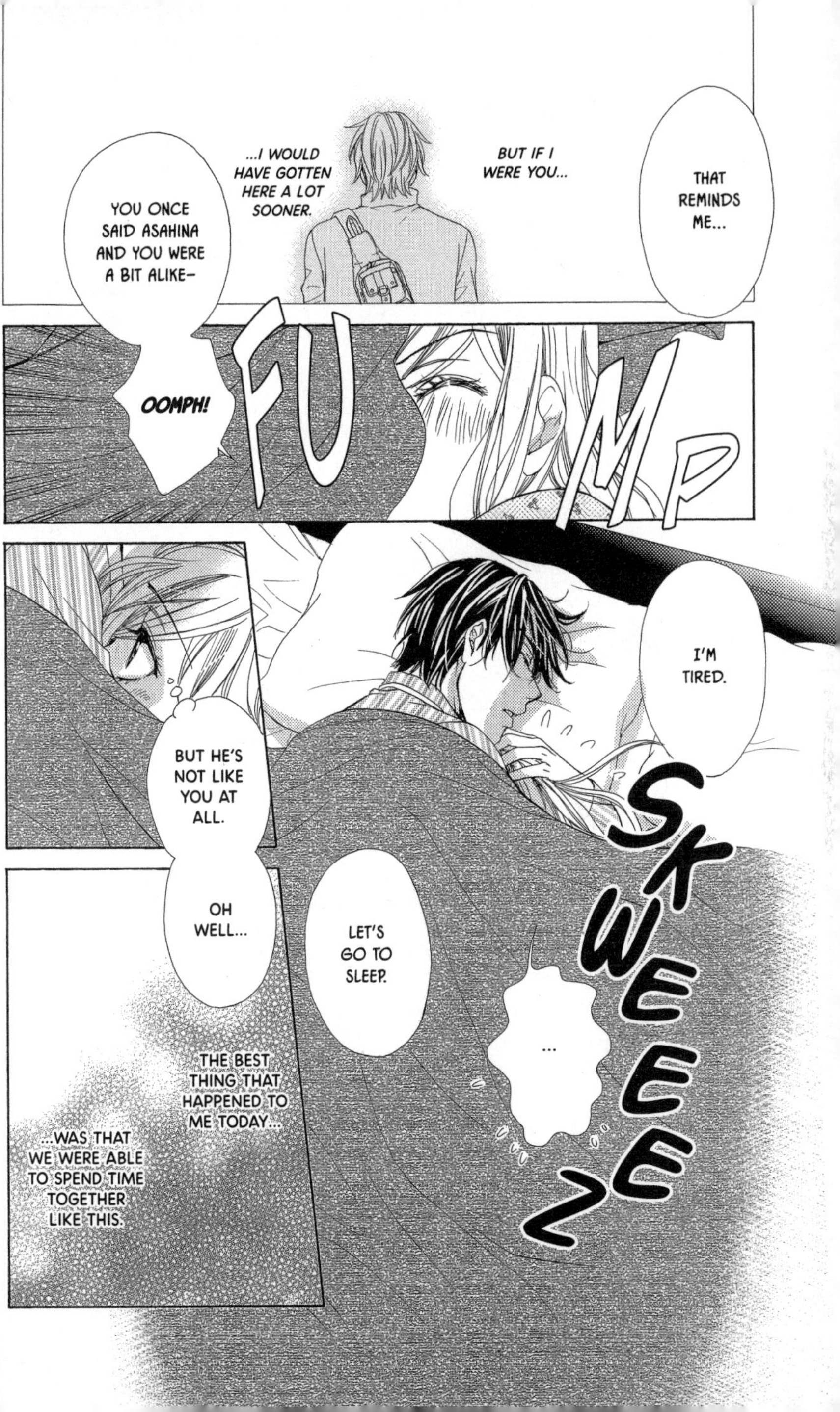
THAT REMINDS ME...
BUT IF I WERE YOU...
...I WOULD HAVE GOTTEN HERE A LOT SOONER.
YOU ONCE SAID ASAHINA AND YOU WERE A BIT ALIKE–
FUMP
OOMPH!
I'M TIRED.
SKWEEEZ
BUT HE'S NOT LIKE YOU AT ALL.
...
LET'S GO TO SLEEP.
OH WELL...
THE BEST THING THAT HAPPENED TO ME TODAY...
...WAS THAT WE WERE ABLE TO SPEND TIME TOGETHER LIKE THIS.

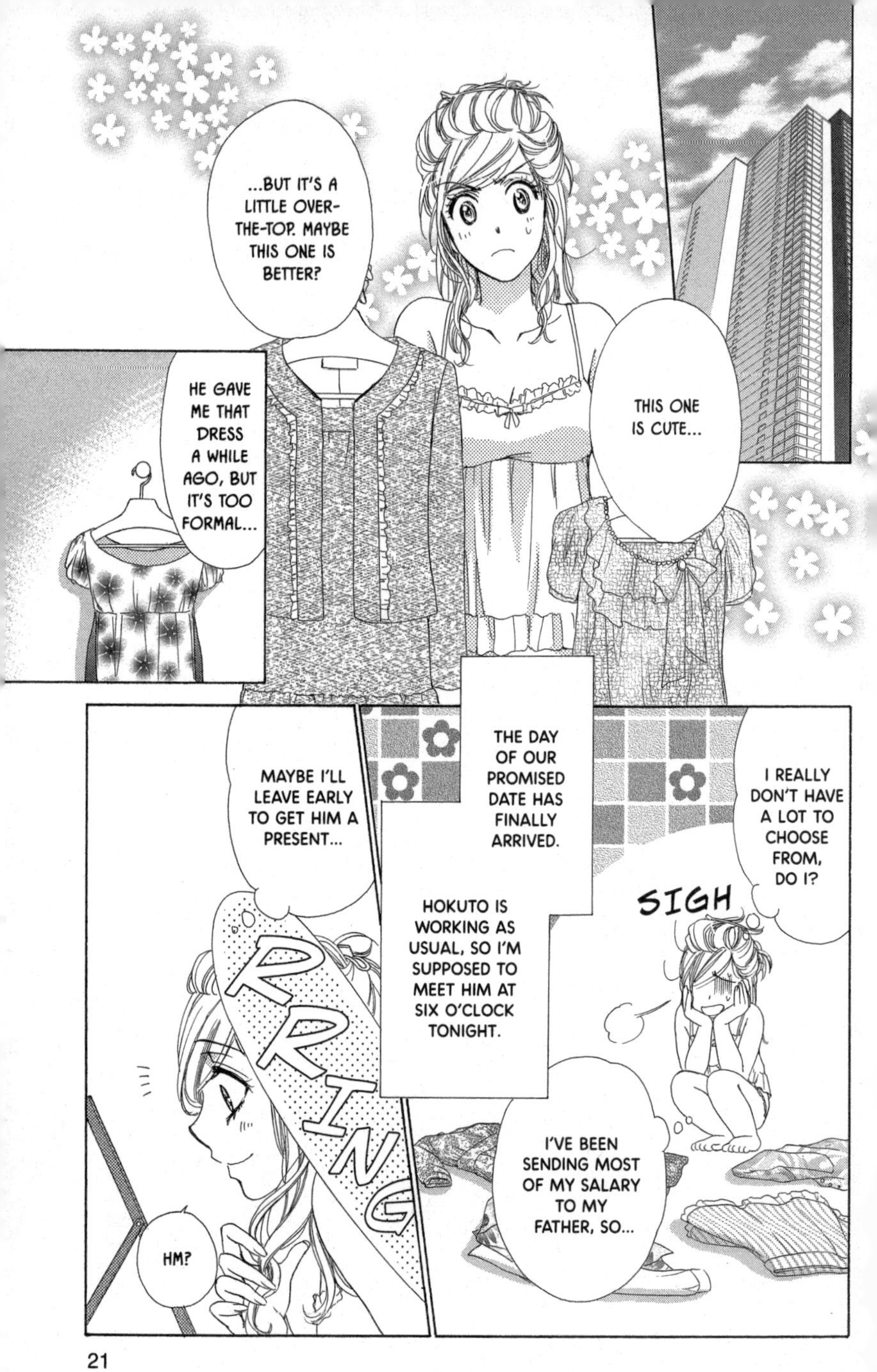
THIS ONE IS CUTE...
...BUT IT'S A LITTLE OVER-THE-TOP. MAYBE THIS ONE IS BETTER?
HE GAVE ME THAT DRESS A WHILE AGO, BUT IT'S TOO FORMAL...
I REALLY DON'T HAVE A LOT TO CHOOSE FROM, DO I?
SIGH
I'VE BEEN SENDING MOST OF MY SALARY TO MY FATHER, SO...
THE DAY OF OUR PROMISED DATE HAS FINALLY ARRIVED.
HOKUTO IS WORKING AS USUAL, SO I'M SUPPOSED TO MEET HIM AT SIX O'CLOCK TONIGHT.
MAYBE I'LL LEAVE EARLY TO GET HIM A PRESENT...
RRING
HM?

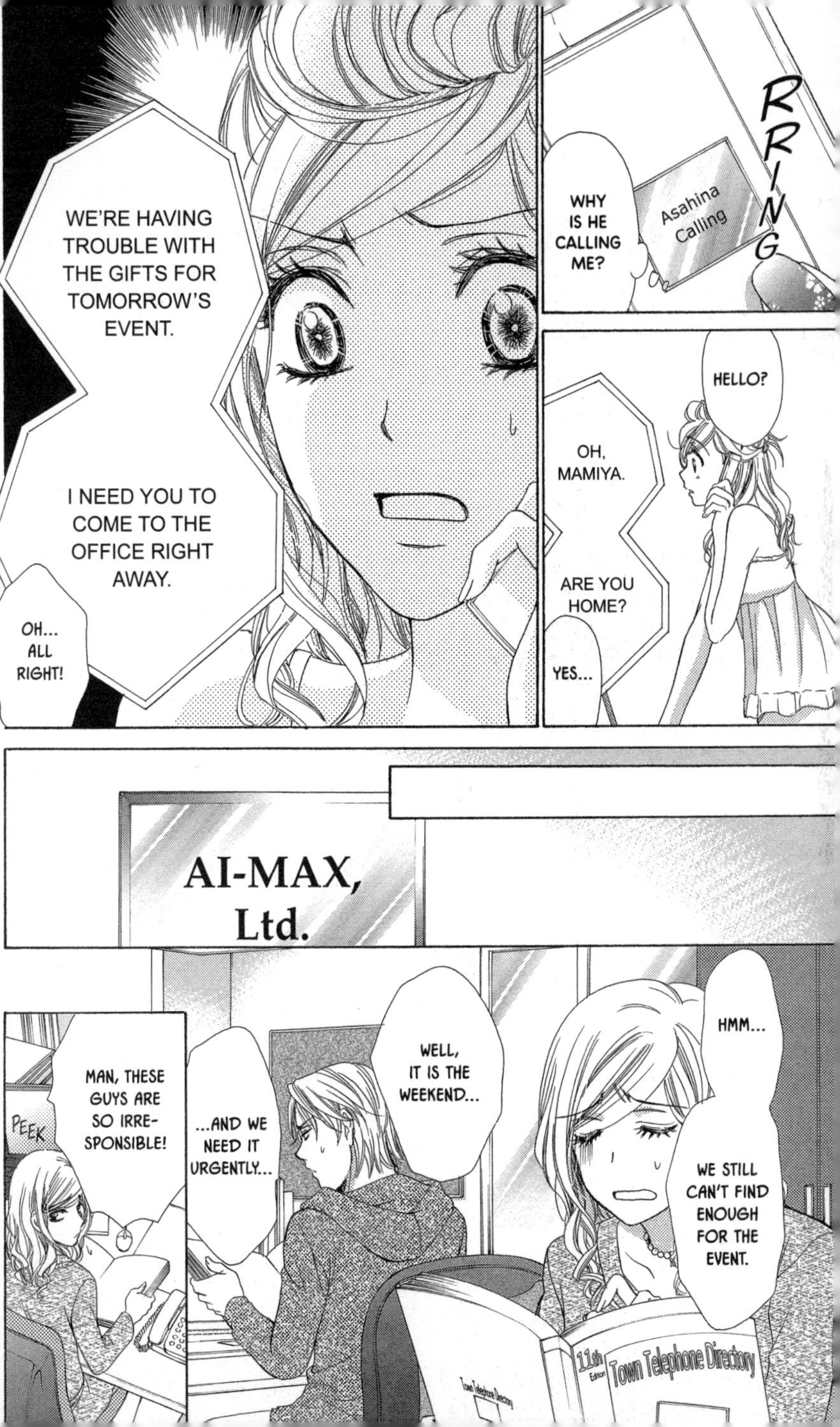
RRING
Asahina Calling
WHY IS HE CALLING ME?
HELLO?
OH, MAMIYA.
ARE YOU HOME?
YES...
WE'RE HAVING TROUBLE WITH THE GIFTS FOR TOMORROW'S EVENT.
I NEED YOU TO COME TO THE OFFICE RIGHT AWAY.
OH... ALL RIGHT!
AI-MAX, Ltd.
HMM...
WE STILL CAN'T FIND ENOUGH FOR THE EVENT.
11th Edition Town Telephone Directory
Town Telephone Directory
WELL, IT IS THE WEEKEND...
...AND WE NEED IT URGENTLY...
MAN, THESE GUYS ARE SO IRRE-SPONSIBLE!
PEEK

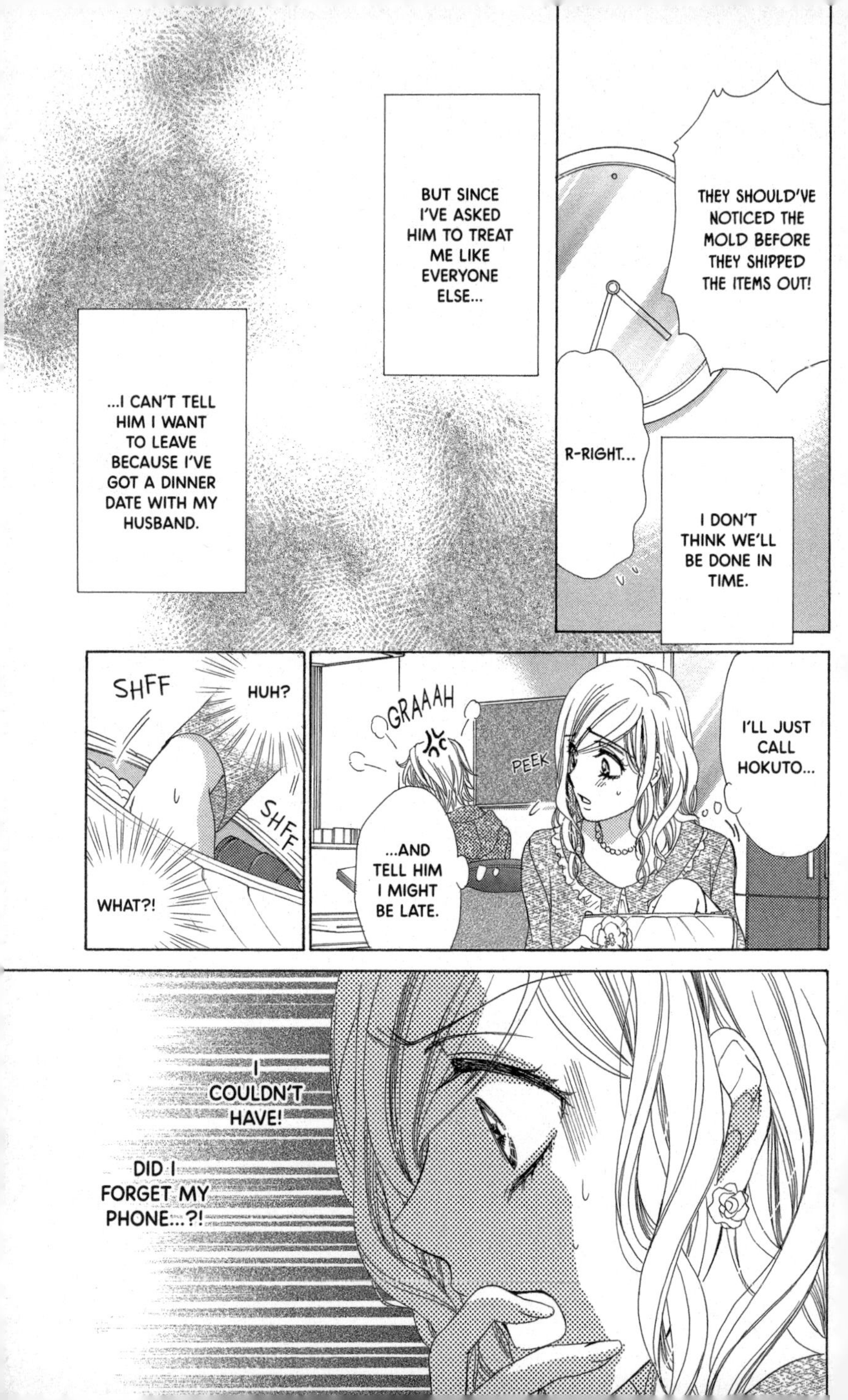
THEY SHOULD'VE NOTICED THE MOLD BEFORE THEY SHIPPED THE ITEMS OUT!
R-RIGHT...
I DON'T THINK WE'LL BE DONE IN TIME.
BUT SINCE I'VE ASKED HIM TO TREAT ME LIKE EVERYONE ELSE...
...I CAN'T TELL HIM I WANT TO LEAVE BECAUSE I'VE GOT A DINNER DATE WITH MY HUSBAND.
I'LL JUST CALL HOKUTO...
GRAAAH
PEEK
...AND TELL HIM I MIGHT BE LATE.
SHFF
HUH?
SHFF
WHAT?!
I COULDN'T HAVE!
DID I FORGET MY PHONE...?!

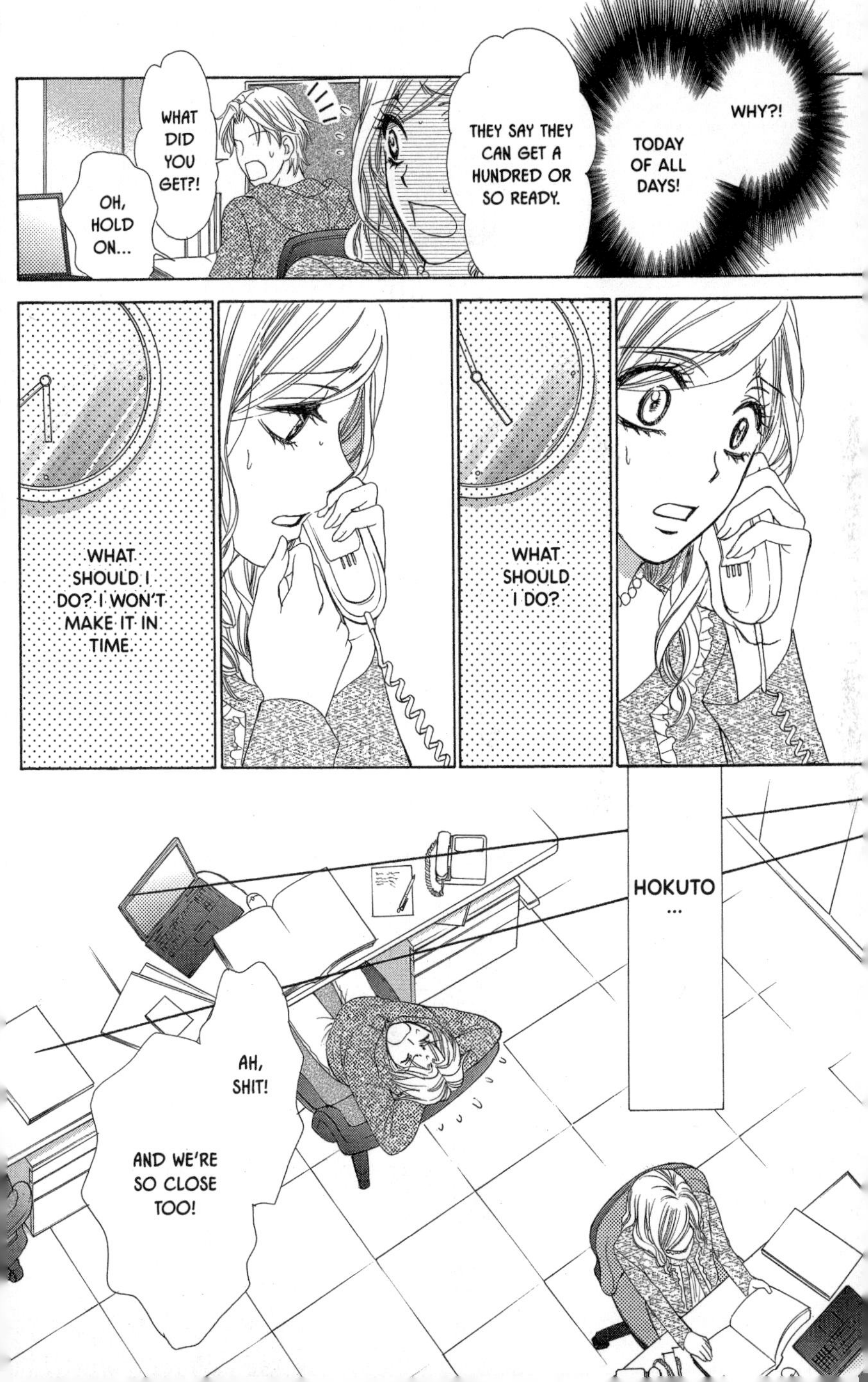
WHY?!
TODAY OF ALL DAYS!
THEY SAY THEY CAN GET A HUNDRED OR SO READY.
WHAT DID YOU GET?!
OH, HOLD ON...
WHAT SHOULD I DO?
WHAT SHOULD I DO? I WON'T MAKE IT IN TIME.
HOKUTO ...
AH, SHIT!
AND WE'RE SO CLOSE TOO!

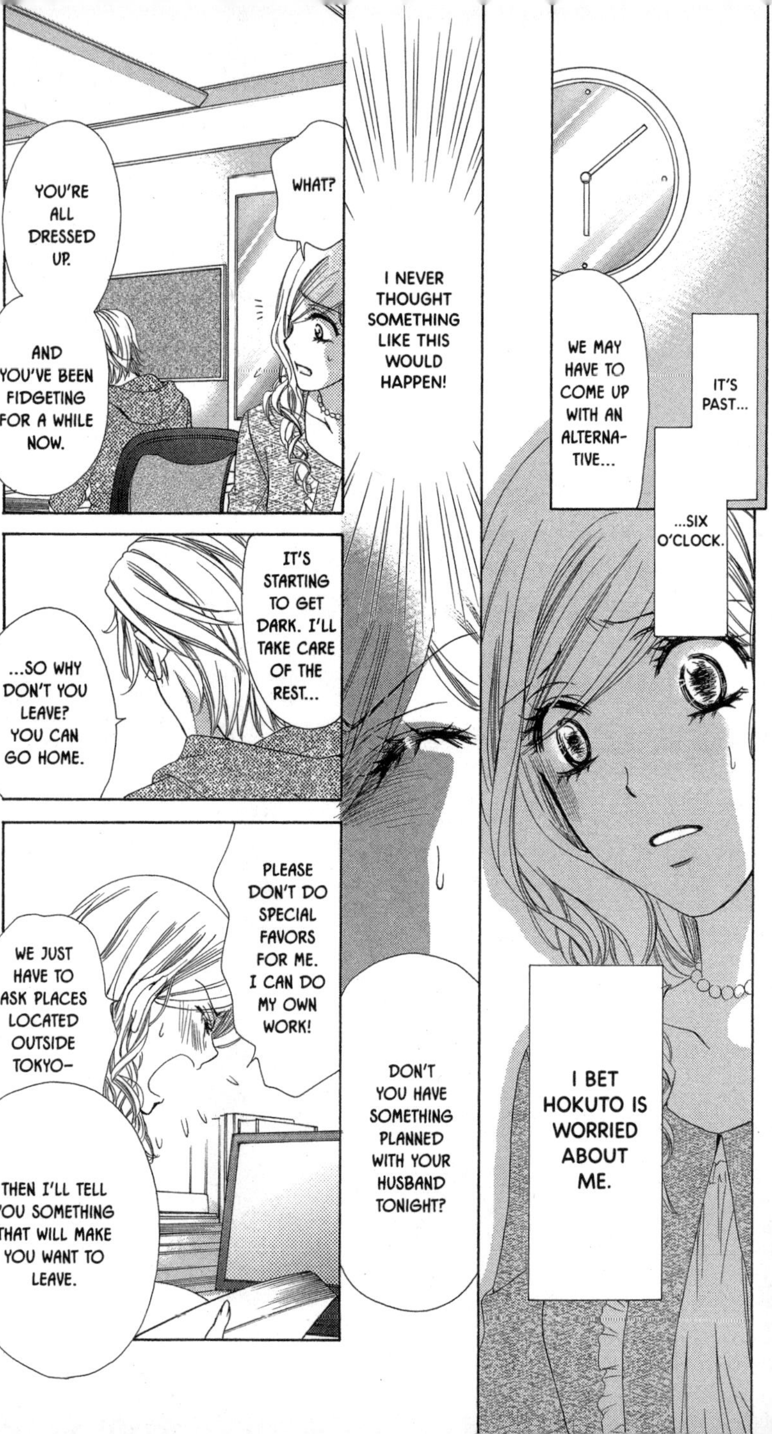
WE MAY HAVE TO COME UP WITH AN ALTERNATIVE...
IT'S PAST...
...SIX O'CLOCK.
I BET HOKUTO IS WORRIED ABOUT ME.
I NEVER THOUGHT SOMETHING LIKE THIS WOULD HAPPEN!
DON'T YOU HAVE SOMETHING PLANNED WITH YOUR HUSBAND TONIGHT?
WHAT?
YOU'RE ALL DRESSED UP.
AND YOU'VE BEEN FIDGETING FOR A WHILE NOW.
IT'S STARTING TO GET DARK. I'LL TAKE CARE OF THE REST...
...SO WHY DON'T YOU LEAVE? YOU CAN GO HOME.
PLEASE DON'T DO SPECIAL FAVORS FOR ME. I CAN DO MY OWN WORK!
WE JUST HAVE TO ASK PLACES LOCATED OUTSIDE TOKYO—
THEN I'LL TELL YOU SOMETHING THAT WILL MAKE YOU WANT TO LEAVE.

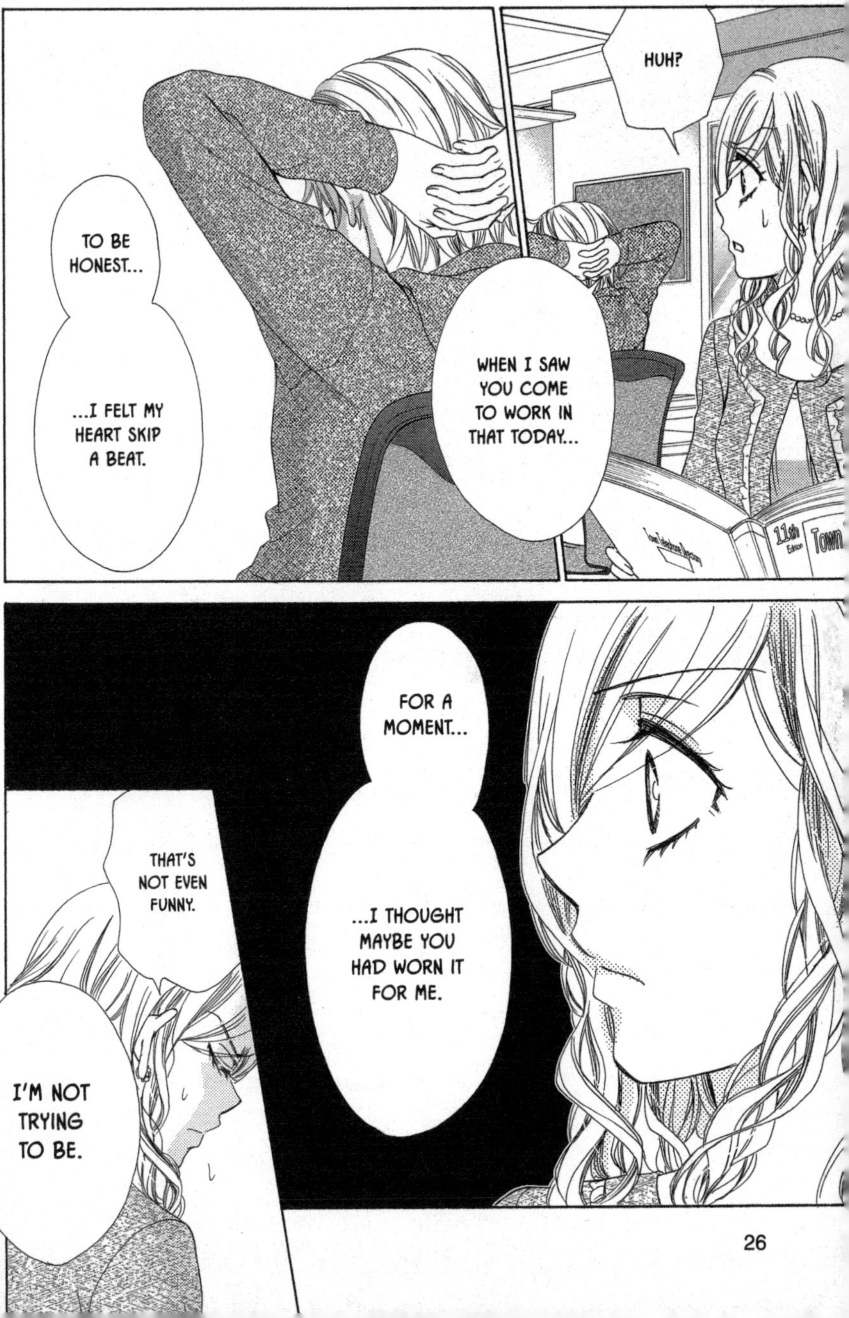
HUH?
WHEN I SAW YOU COME TO WORK IN THAT TODAY...
TO BE HONEST...
...I FELT MY HEART SKIP A BEAT.
FOR A MOMENT...
...I THOUGHT MAYBE YOU HAD WORN IT FOR ME.
THAT'S NOT EVEN FUNNY.
I'M NOT TRYING TO BE.

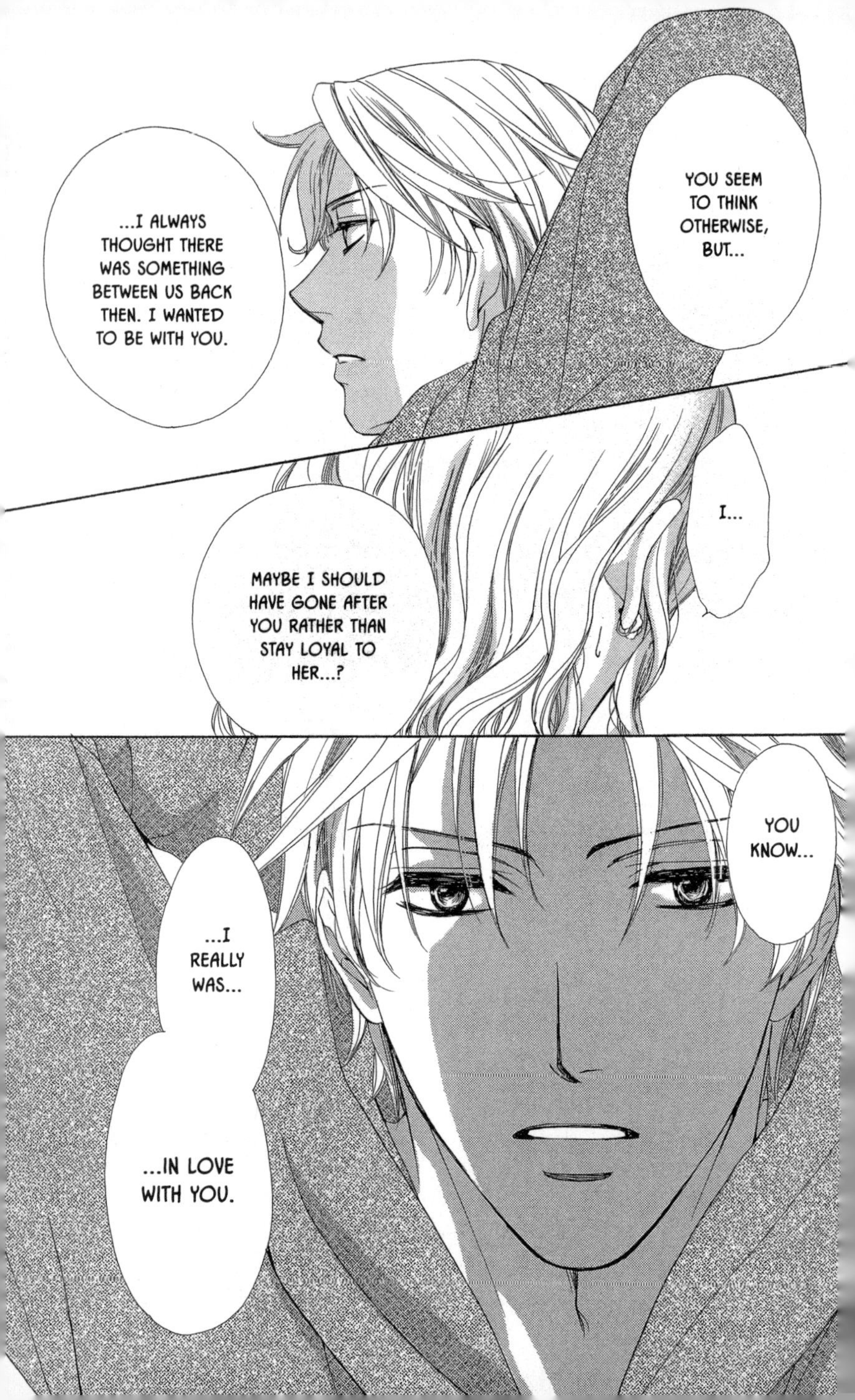
YOU SEEM TO THINK OTHERWISE, BUT...
...I ALWAYS THOUGHT THERE WAS SOMETHING BETWEEN US BACK THEN. I WANTED TO BE WITH YOU.
I...
MAYBE I SHOULD HAVE GONE AFTER YOU RATHER THAN STAY LOYAL TO HER...?
YOU KNOW...
...I REALLY WAS...
...IN LOVE WITH YOU.

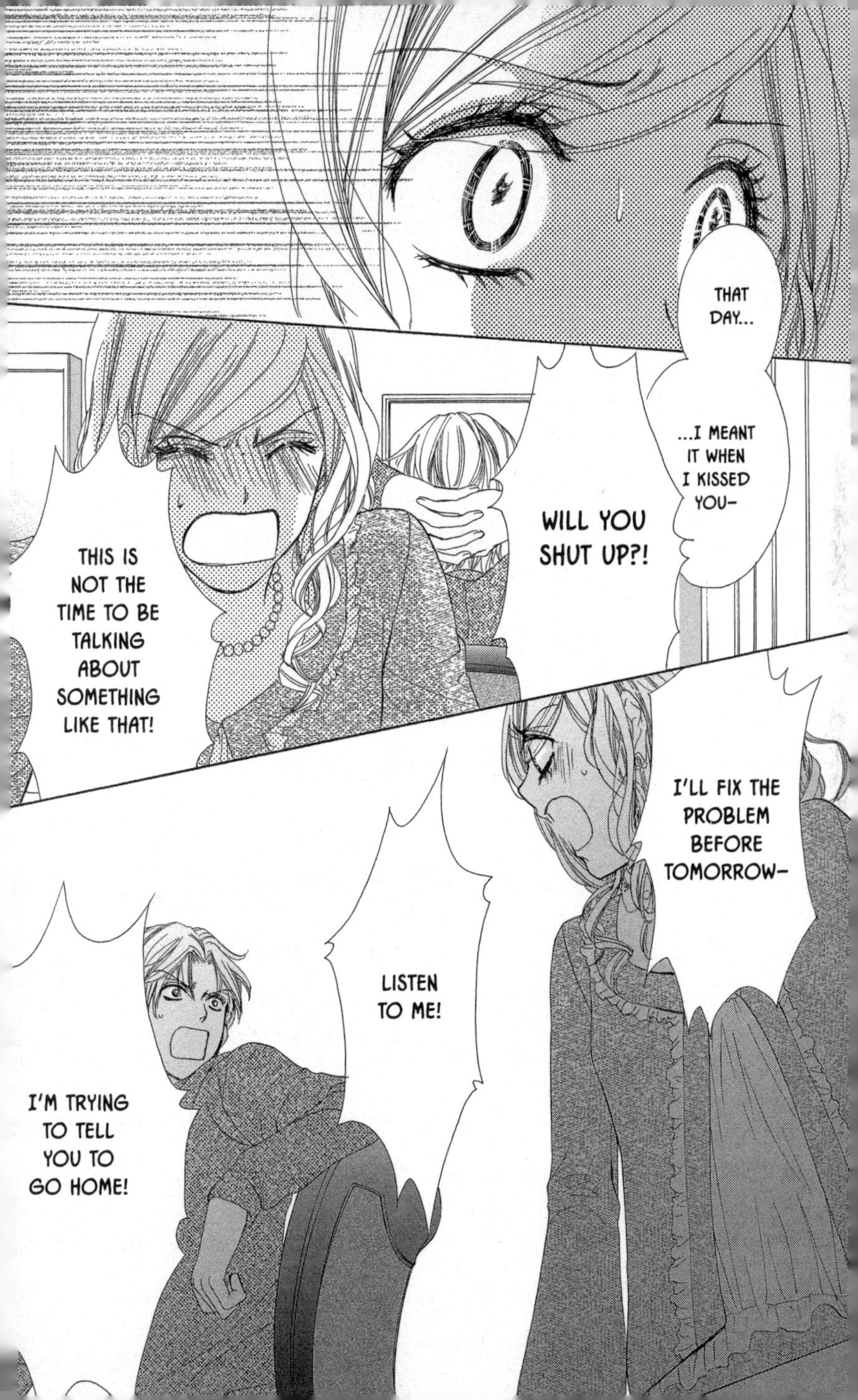
THAT DAY...
...I MEANT IT WHEN I KISSED YOU–
WILL YOU SHUT UP?!
THIS IS NOT THE TIME TO BE TALKING ABOUT SOMETHING LIKE THAT!
I'LL FIX THE PROBLEM BEFORE TOMORROW–
LISTEN TO ME!
I'M TRYING TO TELL YOU TO GO HOME!

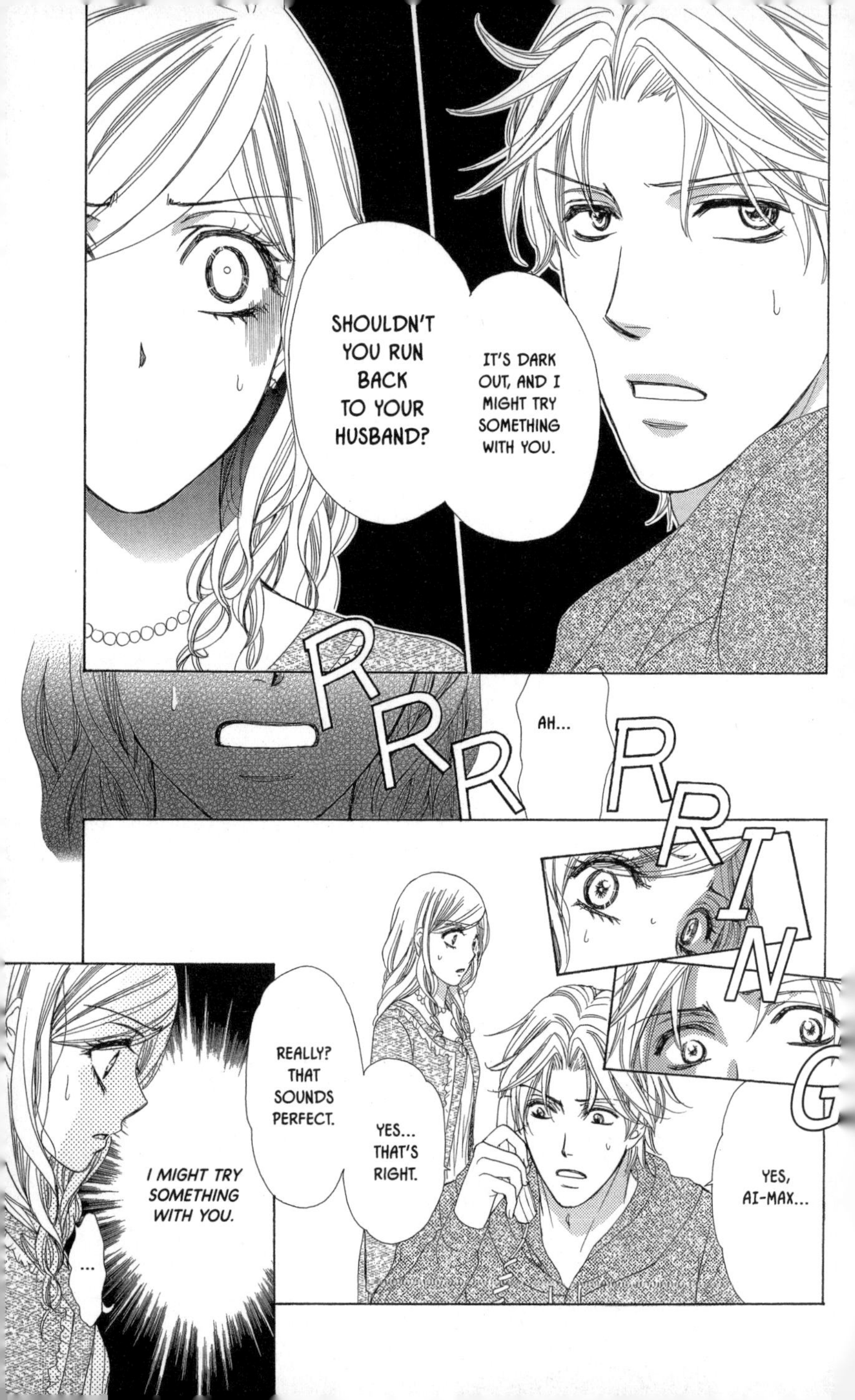
IT'S DARK OUT, AND I MIGHT TRY SOMETHING WITH YOU.
SHOULDN'T YOU RUN BACK TO YOUR HUSBAND?
AH...
RRRRRING
YES, AI-MAX...
YES... THAT'S RIGHT.
REALLY? THAT SOUNDS PERFECT.
I MIGHT TRY SOMETHING WITH YOU.
...

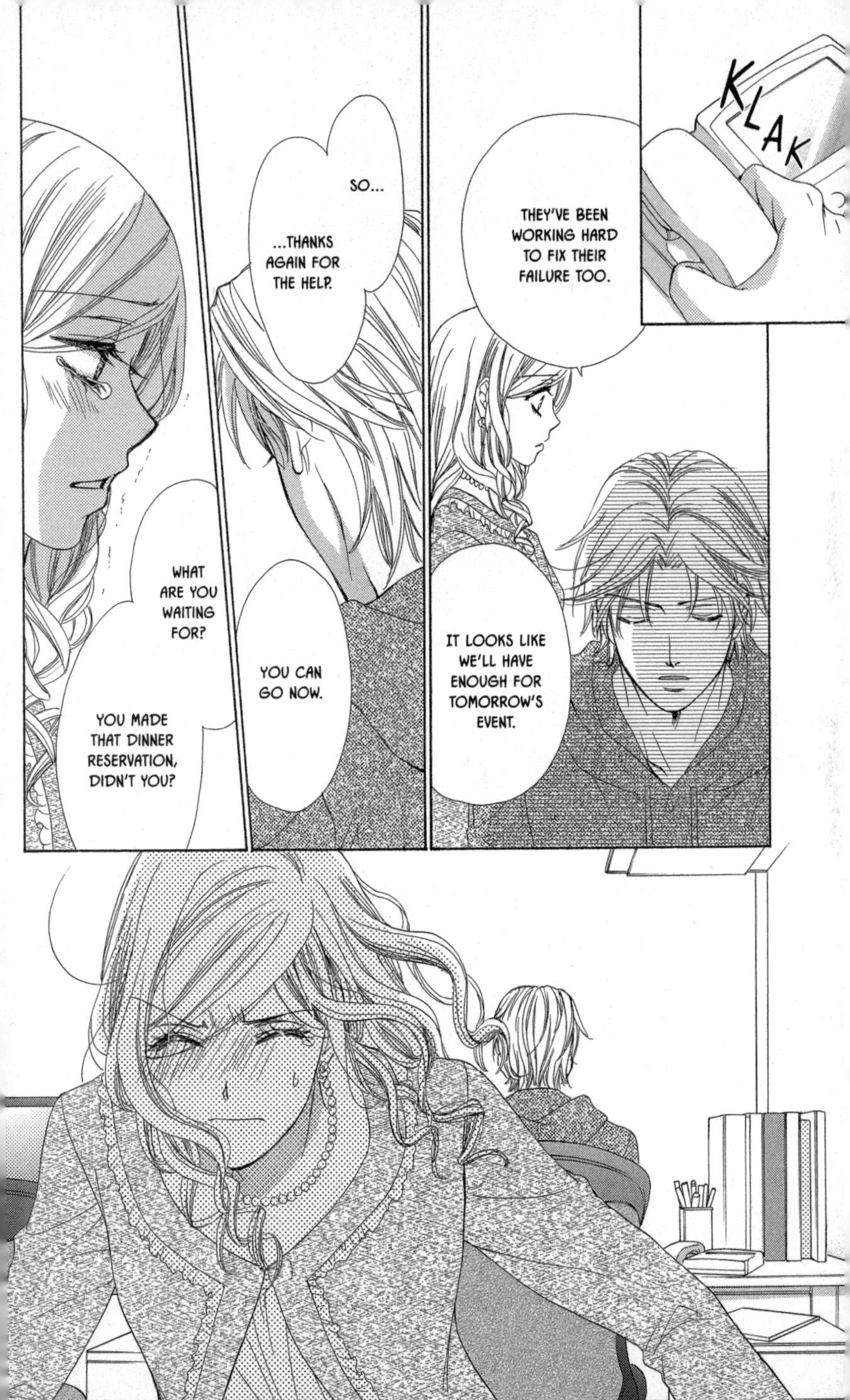
KLAK
THEY'VE BEEN WORKING HARD TO FIX THEIR FAILURE TOO.
IT LOOKS LIKE WE'LL HAVE ENOUGH FOR TOMORROW'S EVENT.
SO...
...THANKS AGAIN FOR THE HELP.
YOU CAN GO NOW.
WHAT ARE YOU WAITING FOR?
YOU MADE THAT DINNER RESERVATION, DIDN'T YOU?

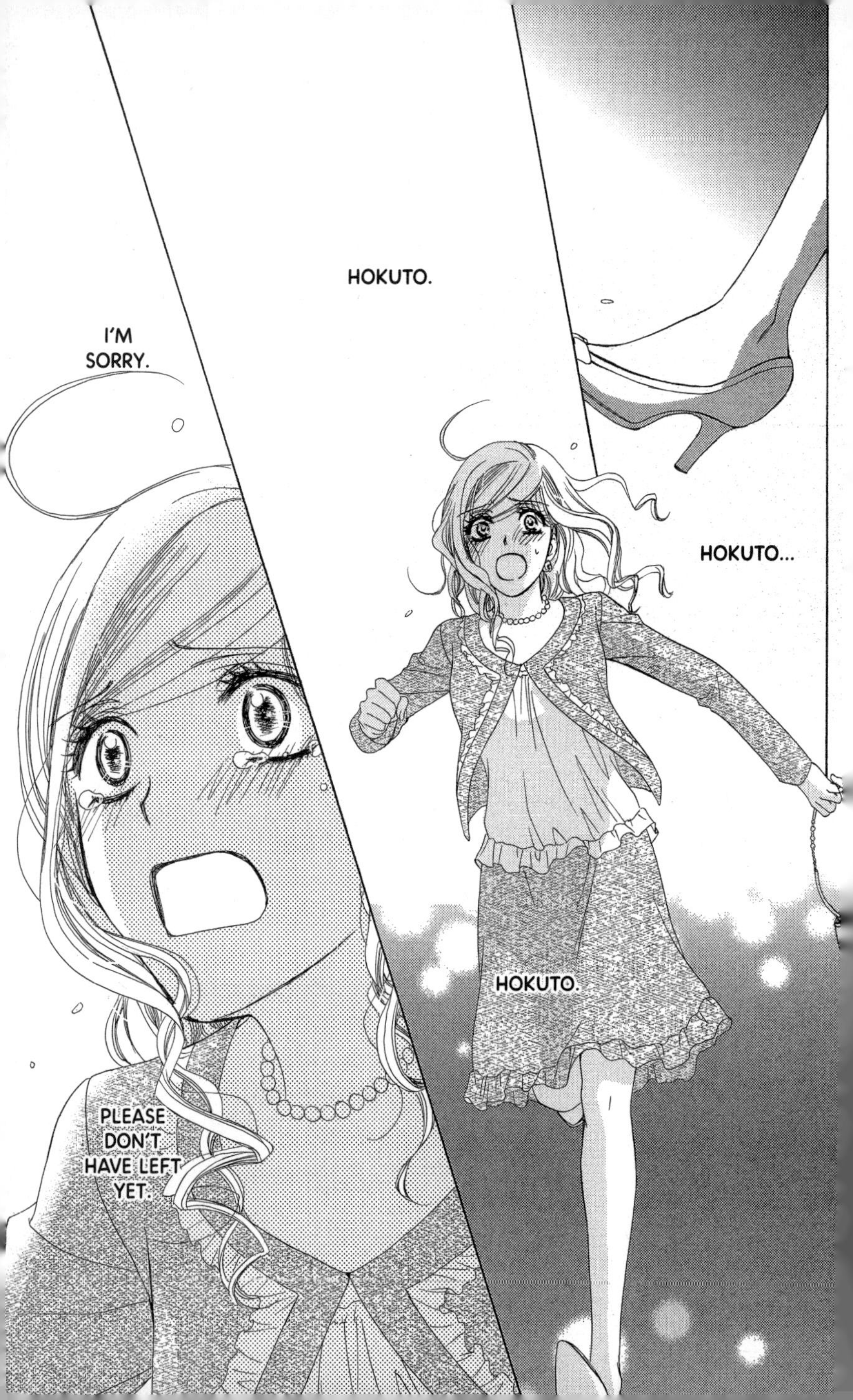
HOKUTO...
HOKUTO.
HOKUTO.
I'M SORRY.
PLEASE DON'T HAVE LEFT YET.

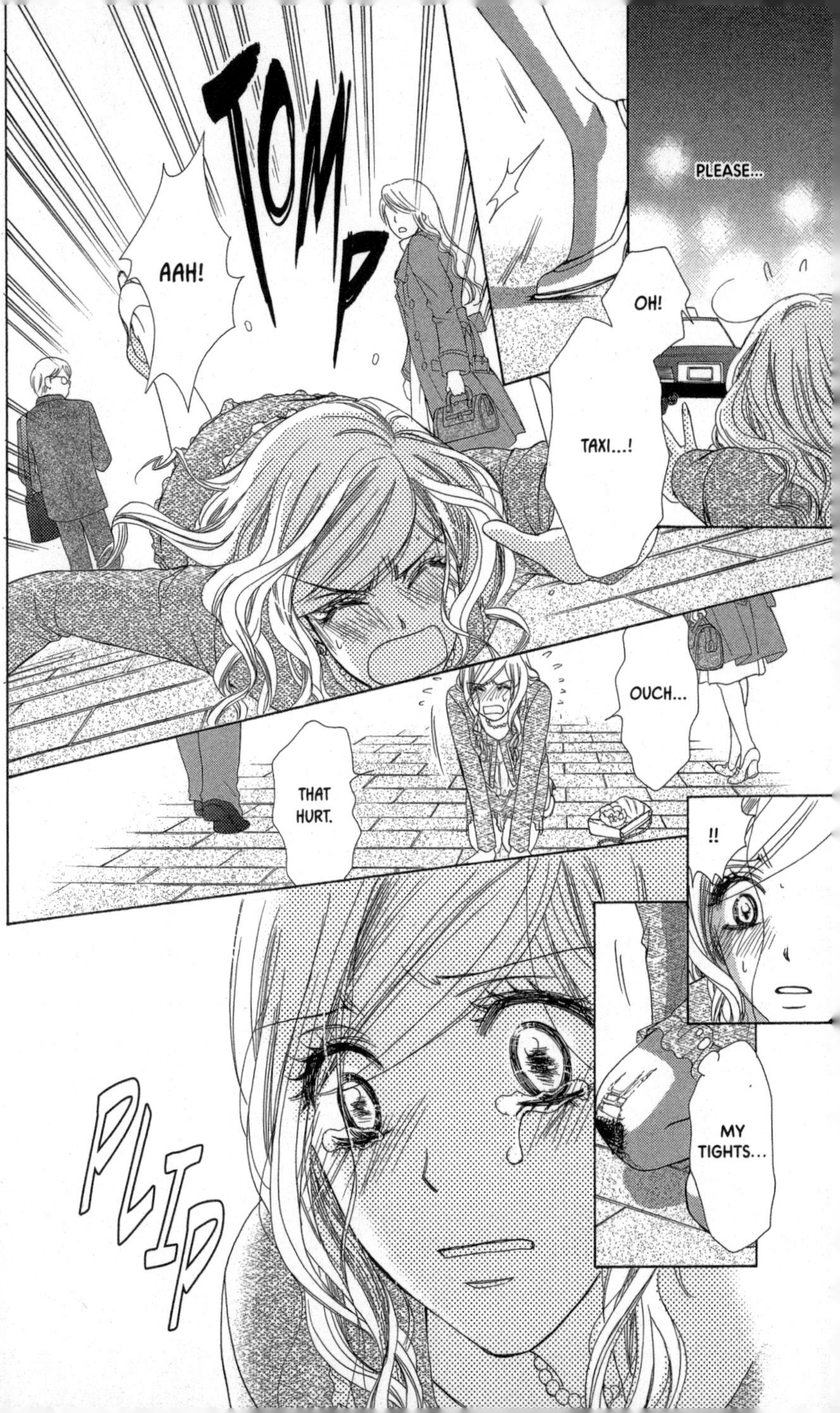
PLEASE...
OH!
TAXI...!
TOMP
AAH!
OUCH...
THAT HURT.
!!
MY TIGHTS...
PLIP

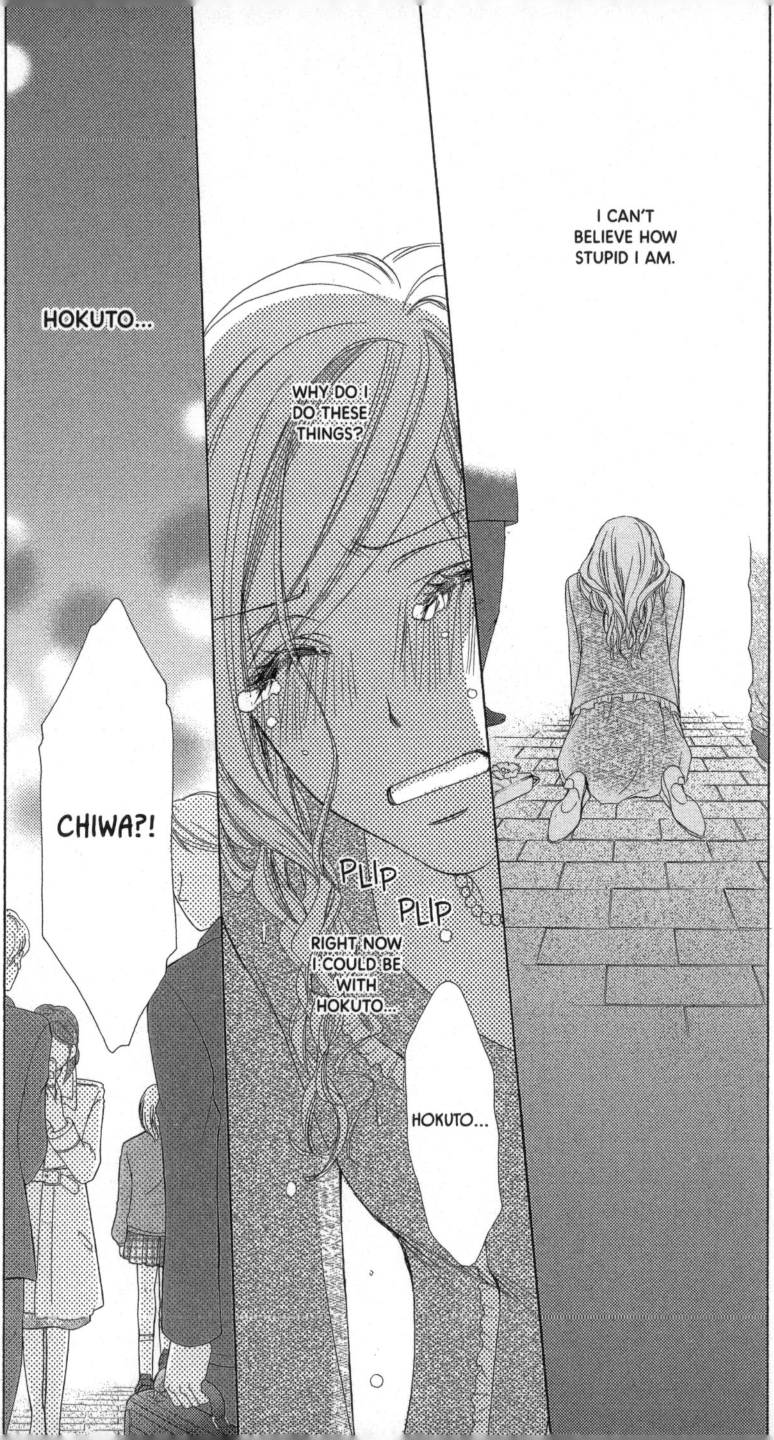
I CAN'T BELIEVE HOW STUPID I AM.
WHY DO I DO THESE THINGS?
PLIP
PLIP
RIGHT NOW I COULD BE WITH HOKUTO...
HOKUTO...
HOKUTO...
CHIWA?!

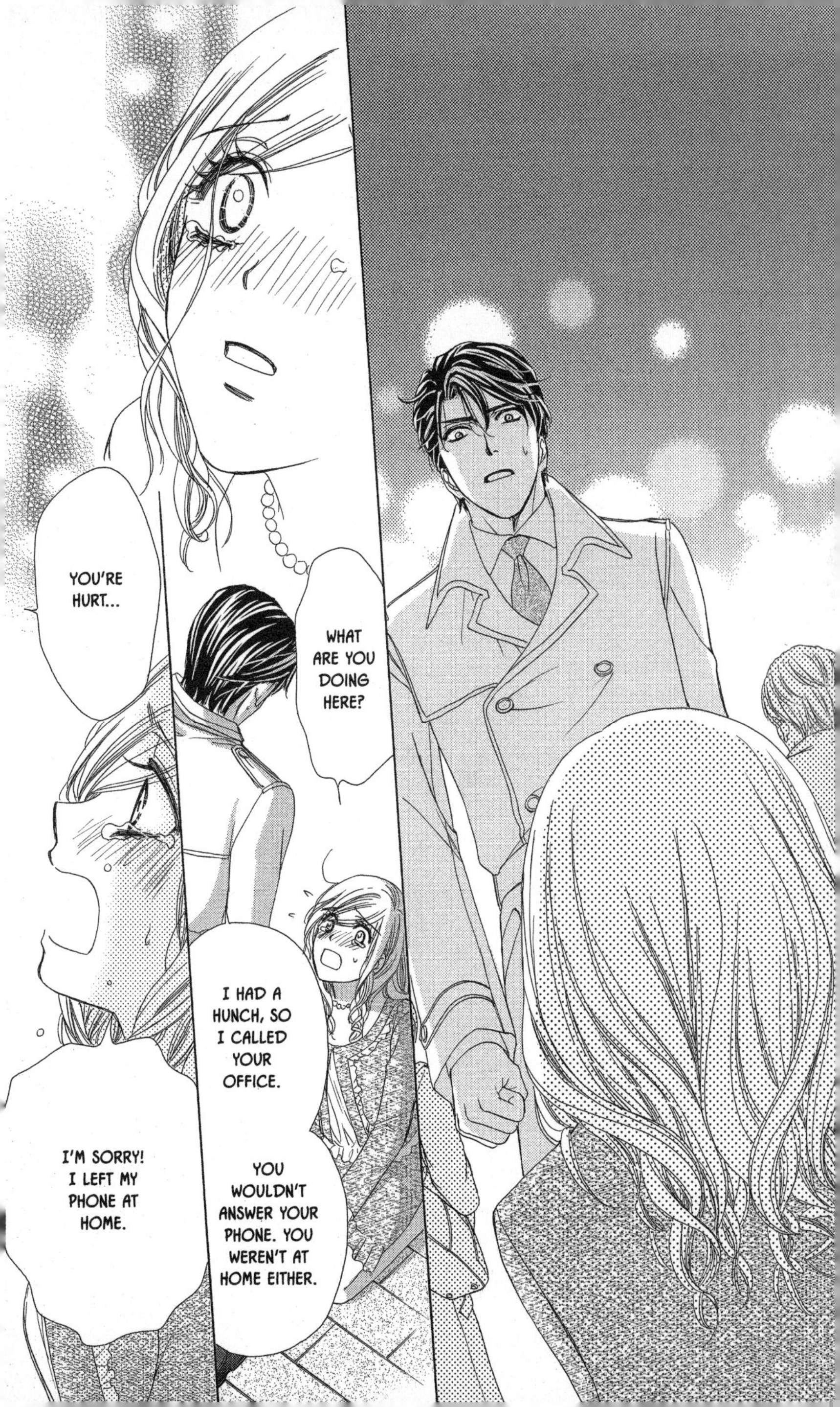
WHAT ARE YOU DOING HERE?
I HAD A HUNCH, SO I CALLED YOUR OFFICE.
YOU WOULDN'T ANSWER YOUR PHONE. YOU WEREN'T AT HOME EITHER.
YOU'RE HURT...
I'M SORRY! I LEFT MY PHONE AT HOME.

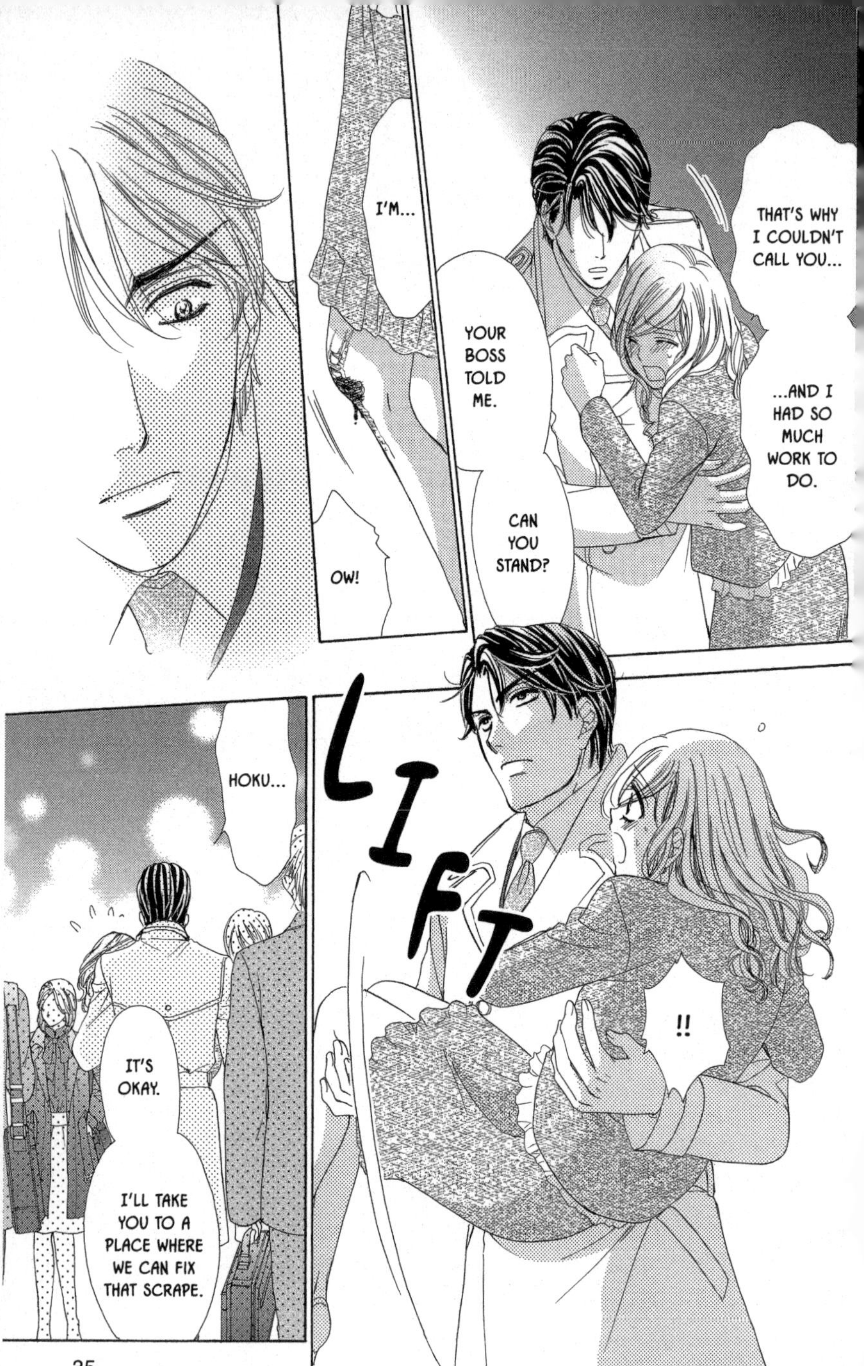
THAT'S WHY I COULDN'T CALL YOU...
...AND I HAD SO MUCH WORK TO DO.
YOUR BOSS TOLD ME.
CAN YOU STAND?
I'M...
OW!
LIFT
!!
HOKU...
IT'S OKAY.
I'LL TAKE YOU TO A PLACE WHERE WE CAN FIX THAT SCRAPE.

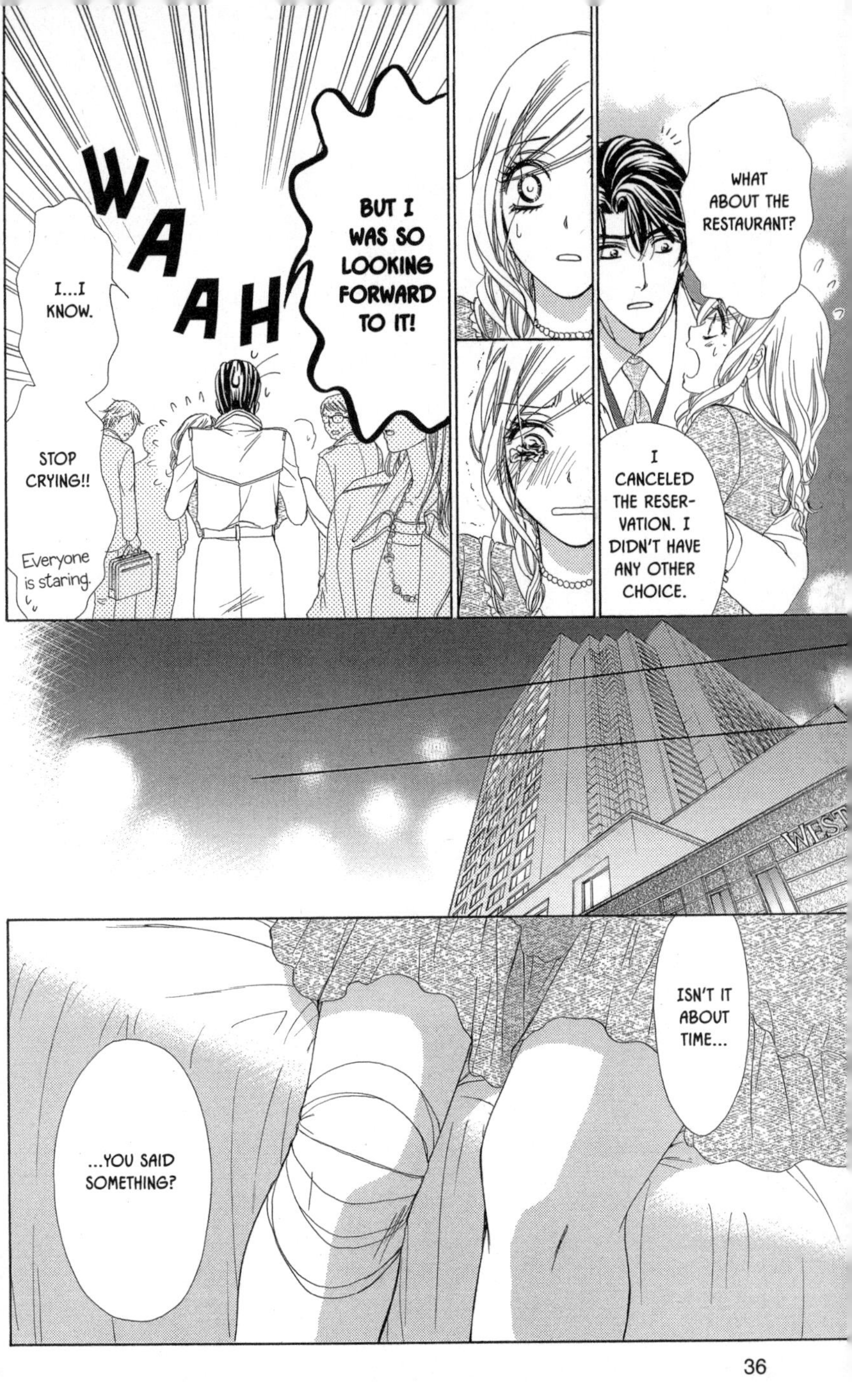
WHAT ABOUT THE RESTAURANT?
I CANCELED THE RESERVATION. I DIDN'T HAVE ANY OTHER CHOICE.
BUT I WAS SO LOOKING FORWARD TO IT!
WAAH
I...I KNOW.
STOP CRYING!!
Everyone is staring.
ISN'T IT ABOUT TIME...
...YOU SAID SOMETHING?

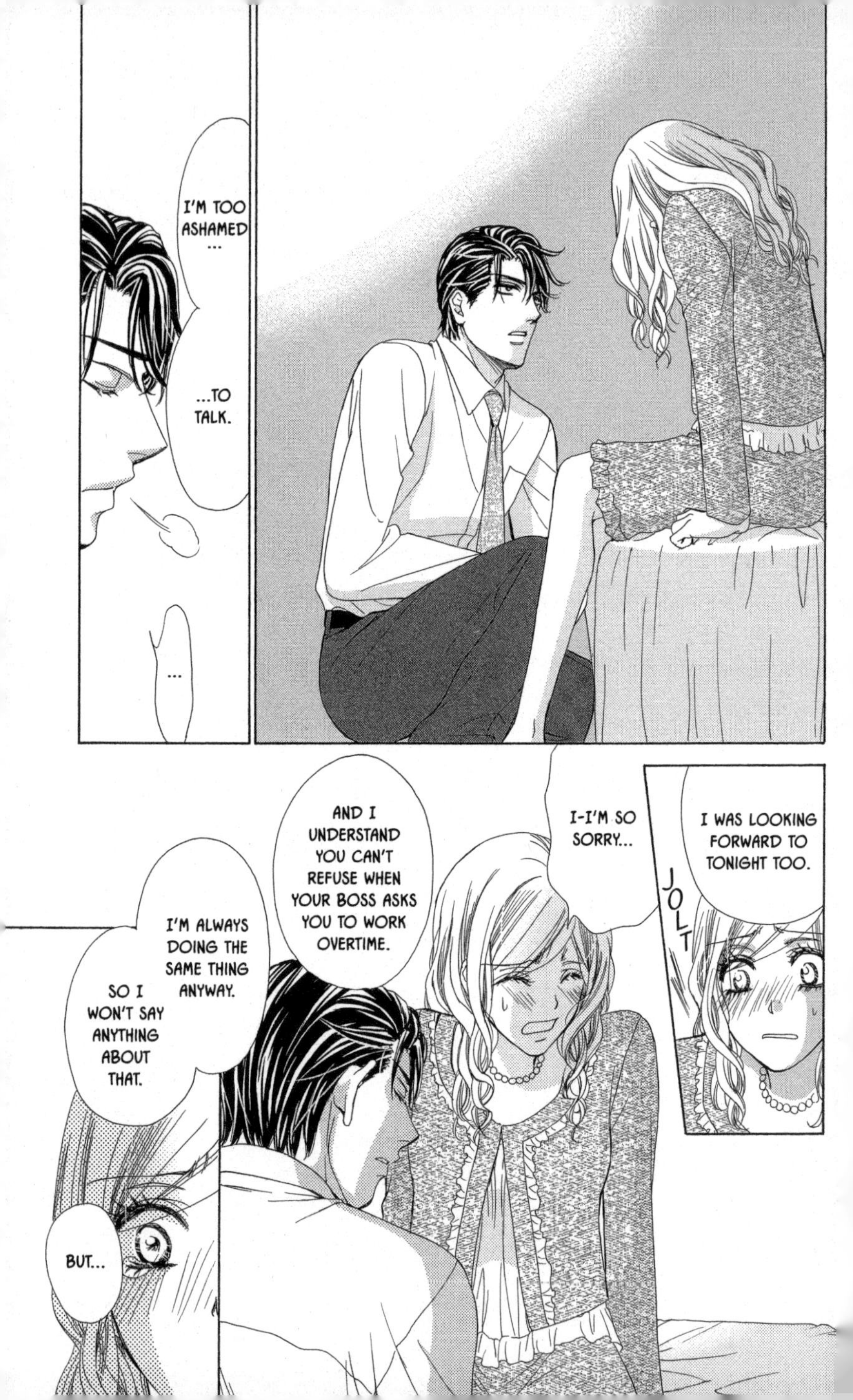
I'M TOO ASHAMED...
...TO TALK.
...
I WAS LOOKING FORWARD TO TONIGHT TOO.
JOLT
I-I'M SO SORRY...
AND I UNDERSTAND YOU CAN'T REFUSE WHEN YOUR BOSS ASKS YOU TO WORK OVERTIME.
I'M ALWAYS DOING THE SAME THING ANYWAY.
SO I WON'T SAY ANYTHING ABOUT THAT.
BUT...

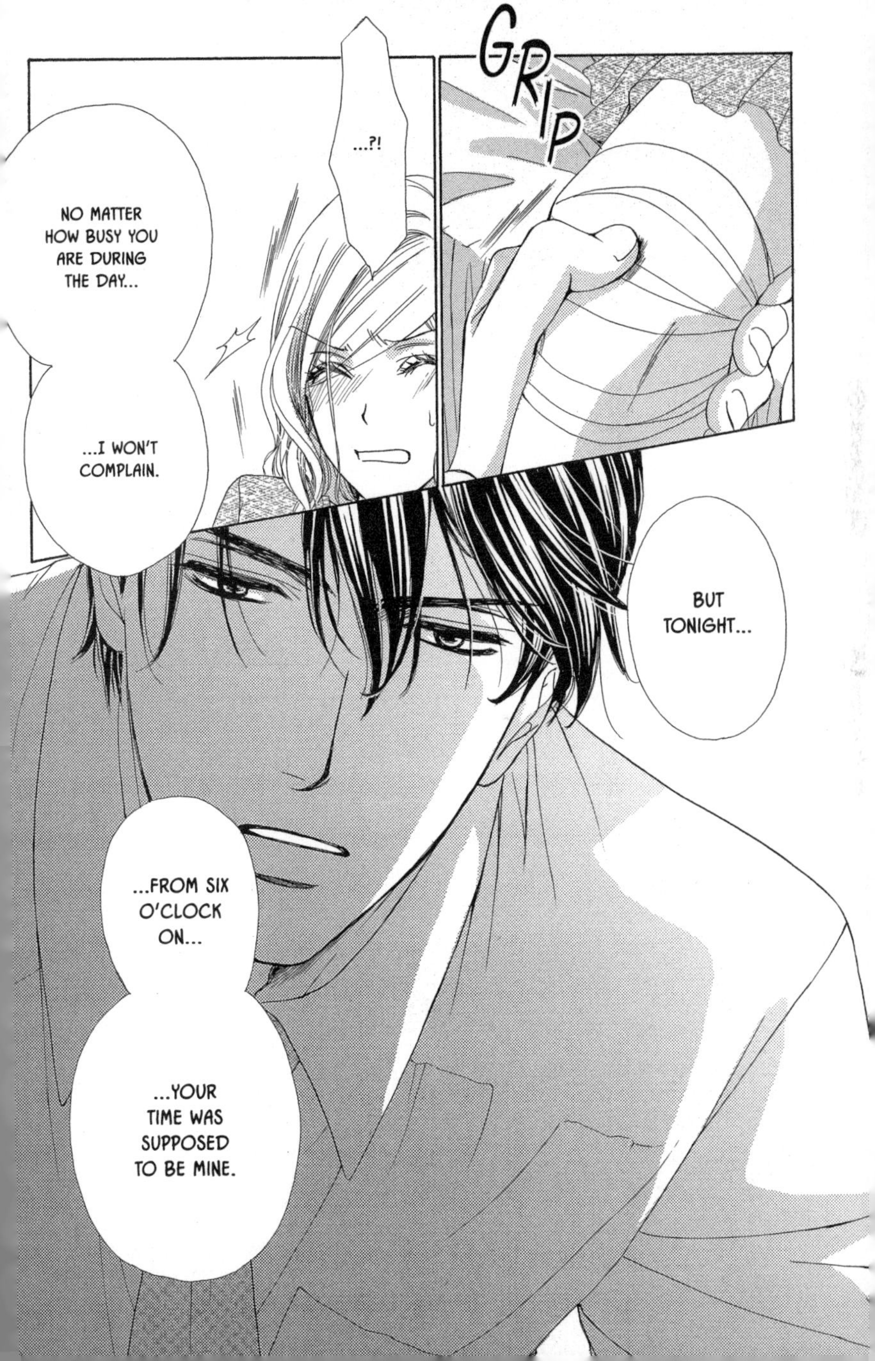
GRIP
...?!
NO MATTER HOW BUSY YOU ARE DURING THE DAY...
...I WON'T COMPLAIN.
BUT TONIGHT...
...FROM SIX O'CLOCK ON...
...YOUR TIME WAS SUPPOSED TO BE MINE.

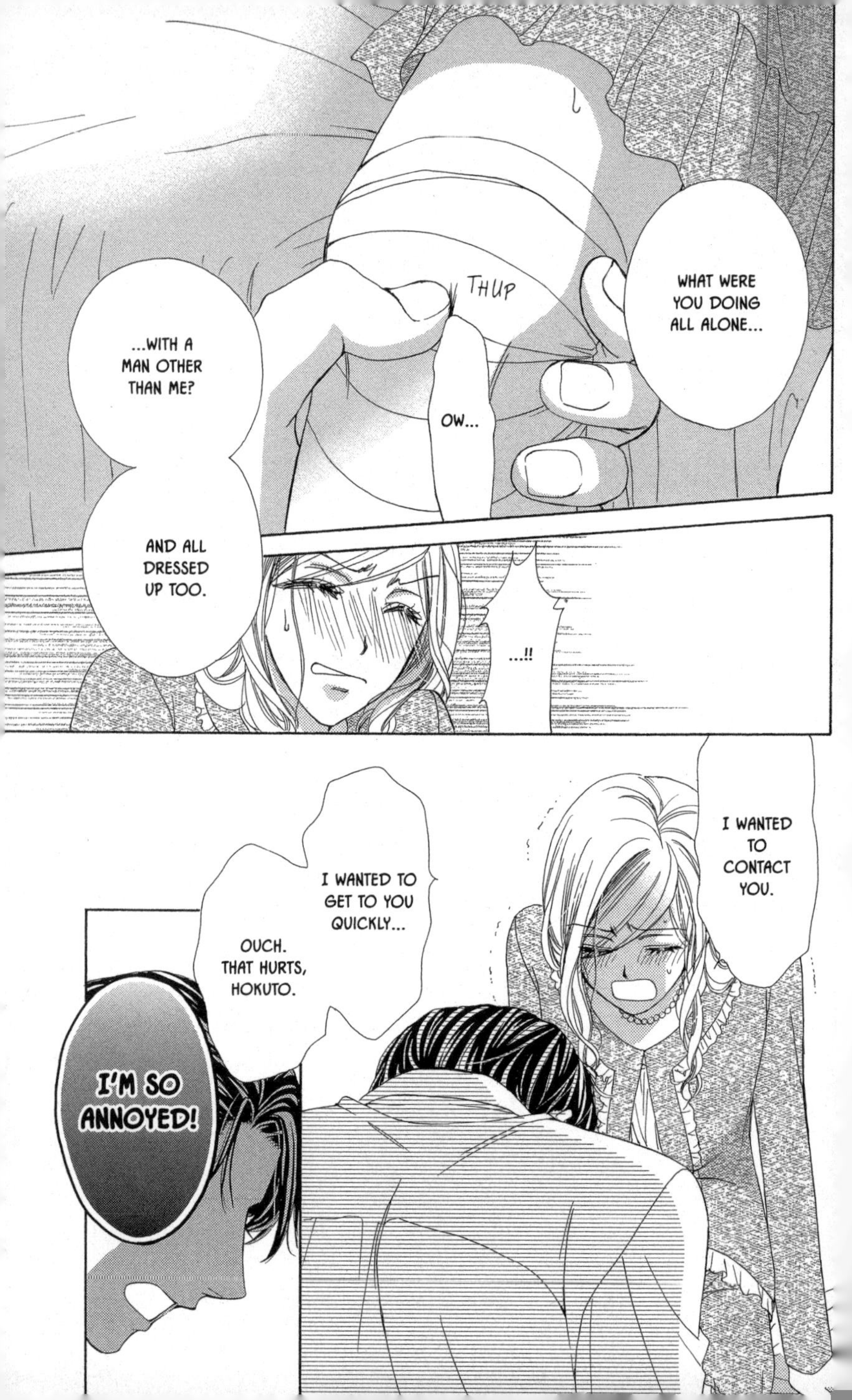
WHAT WERE YOU DOING ALL ALONE...
THUP
OW...
...WITH A MAN OTHER THAN ME?
AND ALL DRESSED UP TOO.
...!!
I WANTED TO CONTACT YOU.
I WANTED TO GET TO YOU QUICKLY...
OUCH. THAT HURTS, HOKUTO.
I'M SO ANNOYED!

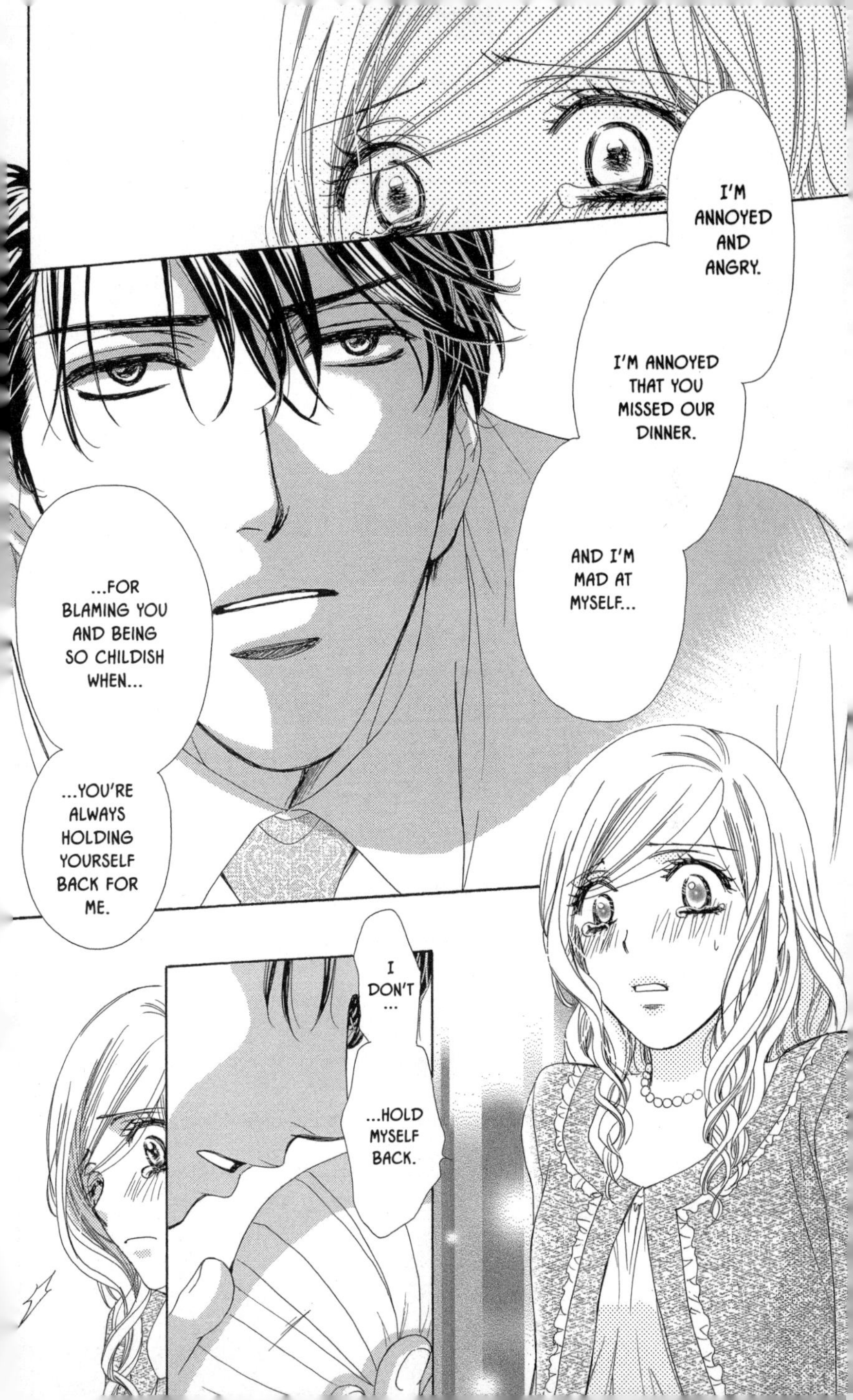
I'M ANNOYED AND ANGRY.
I'M ANNOYED THAT YOU MISSED OUR DINNER.
AND I'M MAD AT MYSELF...
...FOR BLAMING YOU AND BEING SO CHILDISH WHEN...
...YOU'RE ALWAYS HOLDING YOURSELF BACK FOR ME.
I DON'T ...
...HOLD MYSELF BACK.

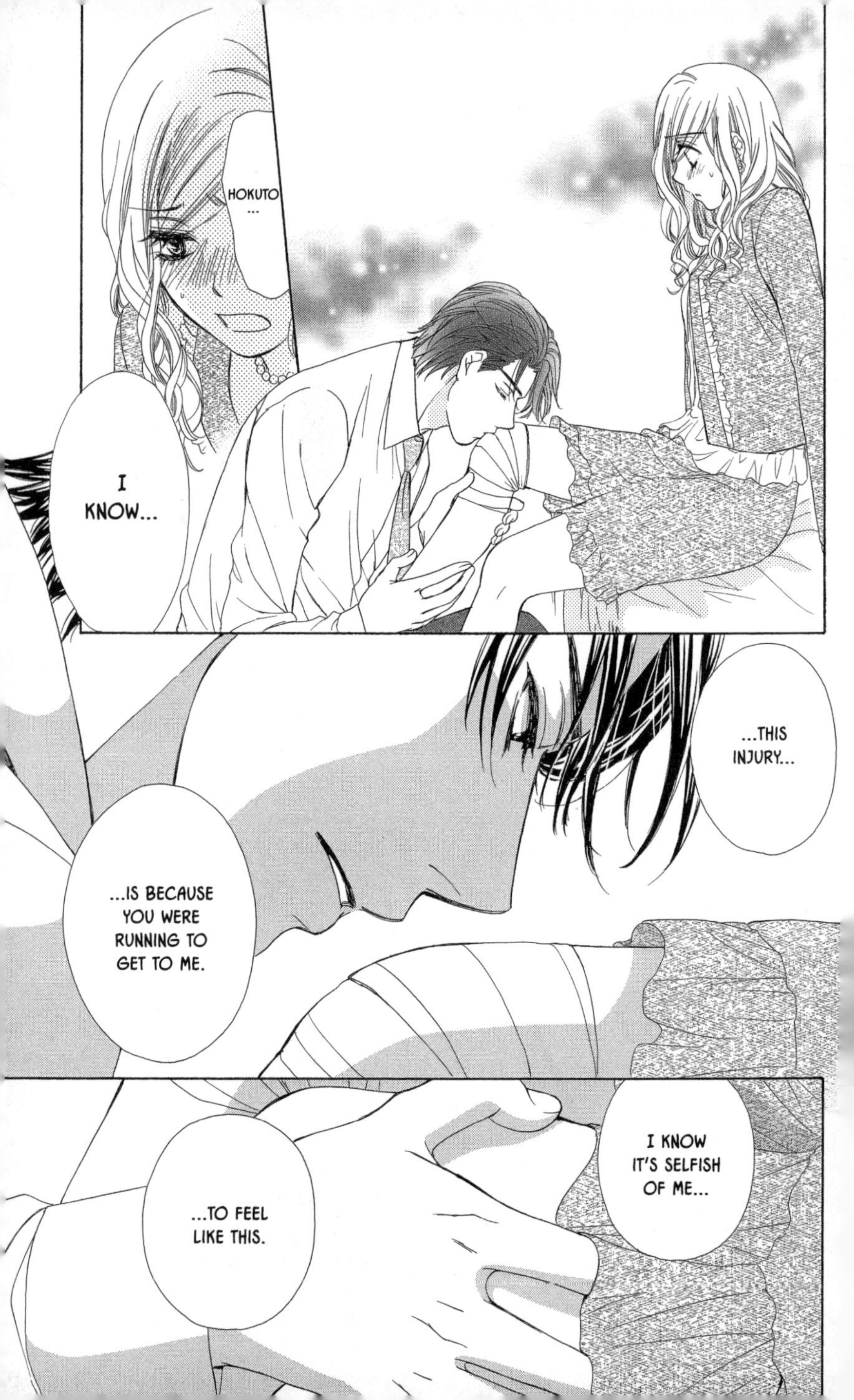
HOKUTO...
I KNOW...
...THIS INJURY...
...IS BECAUSE YOU WERE RUNNING TO GET TO ME.
I KNOW IT'S SELFISH OF ME...
...TO FEEL LIKE THIS.

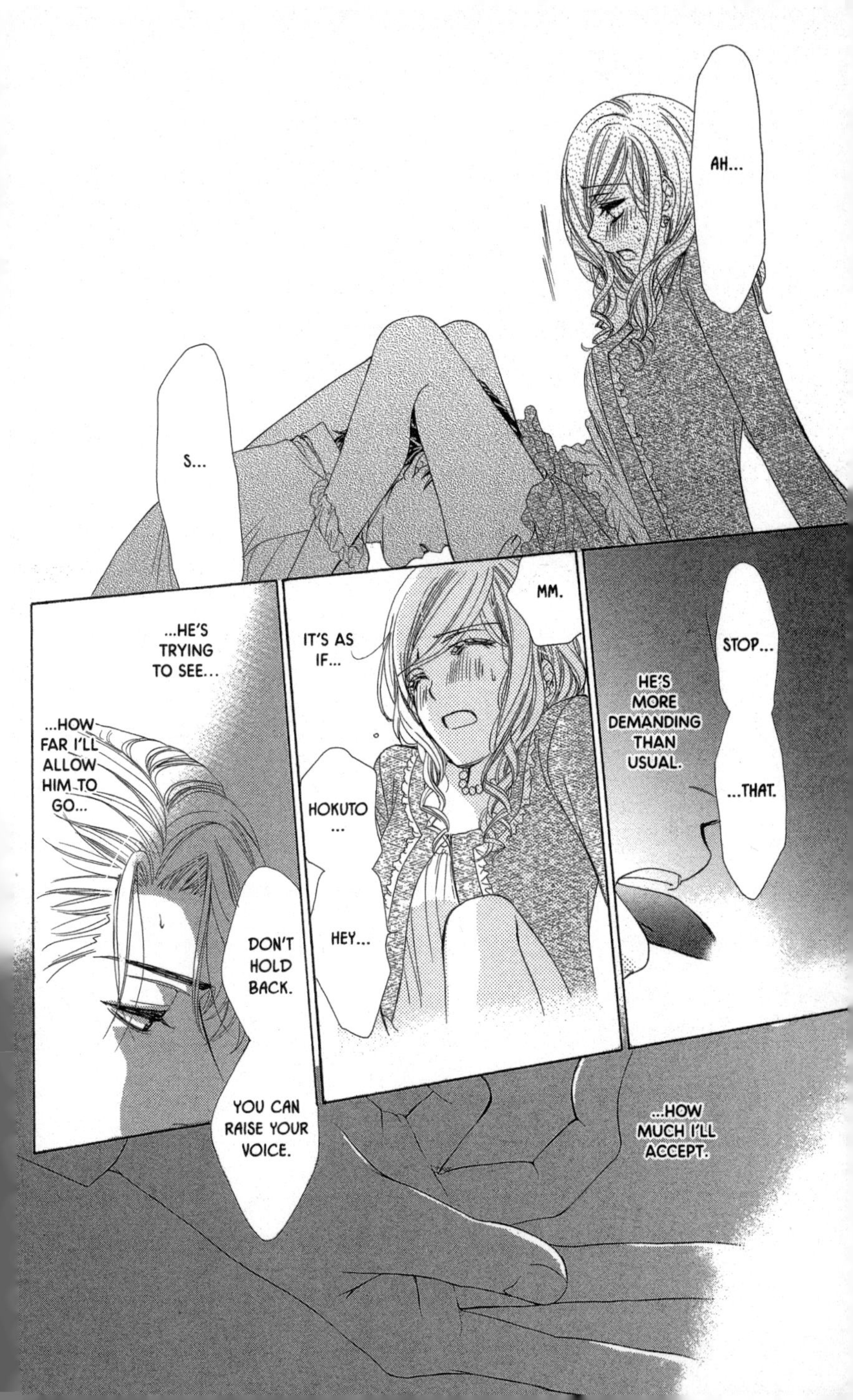
AH...
S...
STOP...
HE'S MORE DEMANDING THAN USUAL.
...THAT.
MM.
IT'S AS IF...
HOKUTO ...
HEY...
...HE'S TRYING TO SEE...
...HOW FAR I'LL ALLOW HIM TO GO...
DON'T HOLD BACK.
YOU CAN RAISE YOUR VOICE.
...HOW MUCH I'LL ACCEPT.

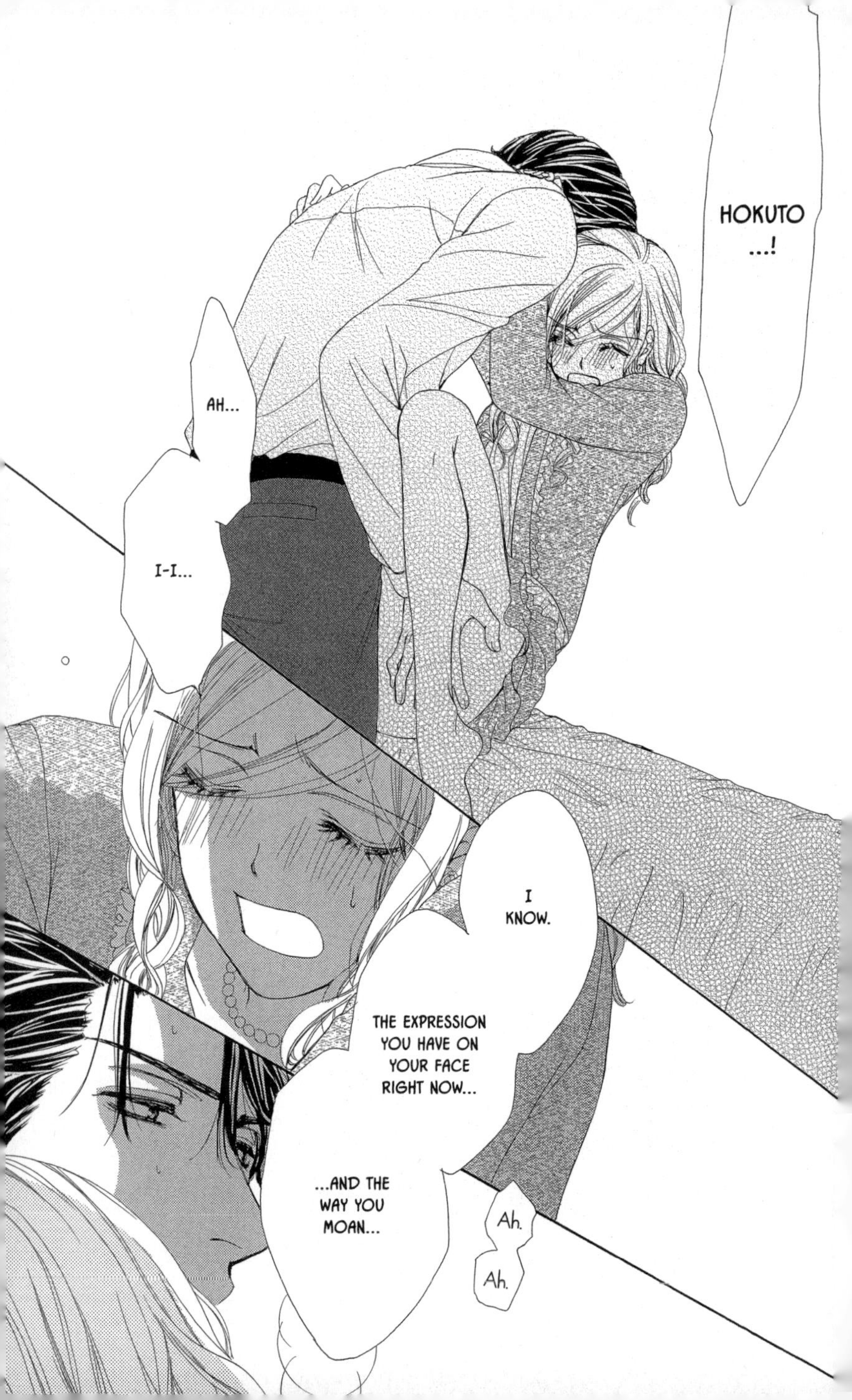
HOKUTO ...!
AH...
I-I...
I KNOW.
THE EXPRESSION YOU HAVE ON YOUR FACE RIGHT NOW...
...AND THE WAY YOU MOAN...
Ah.
Ah.

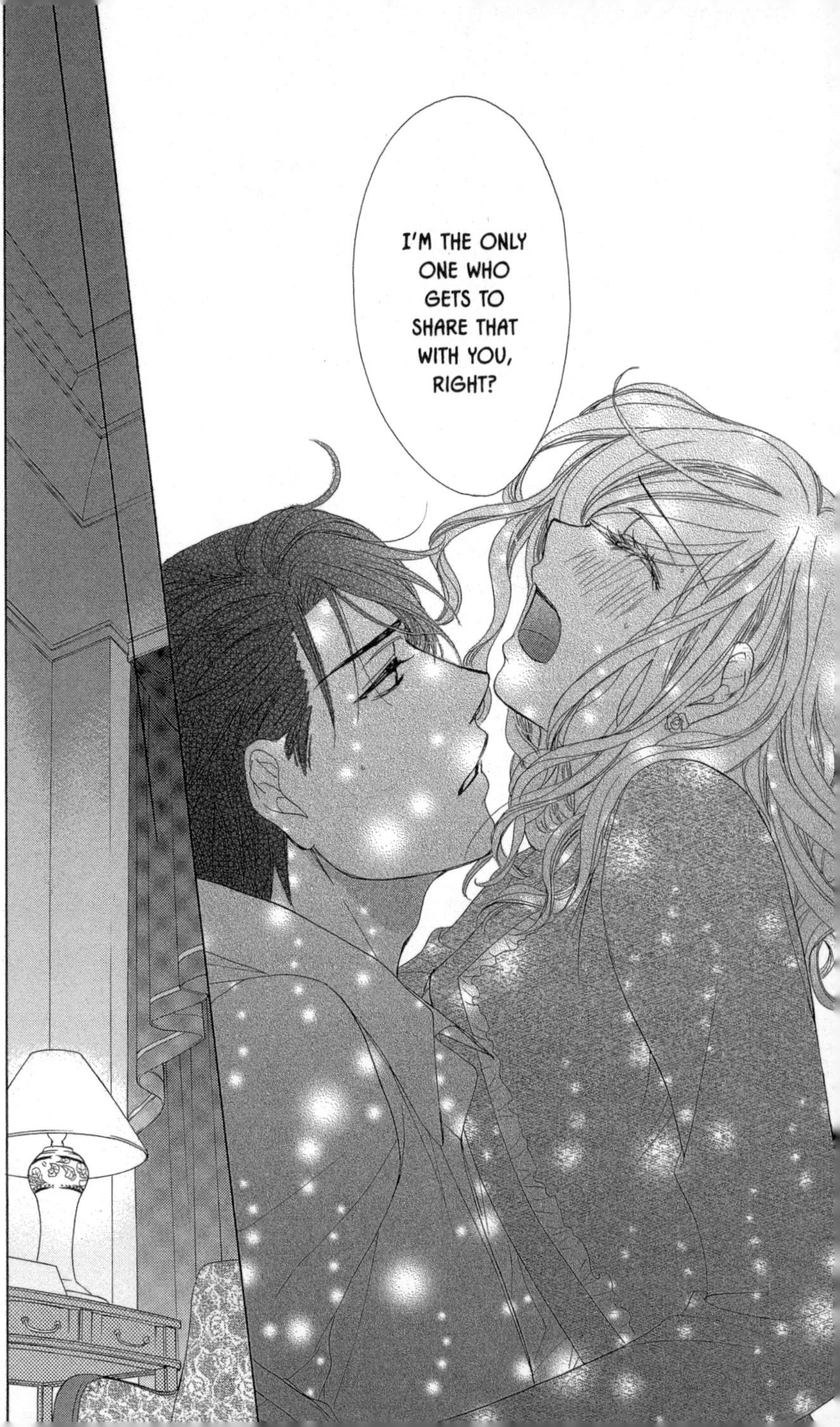
I'M THE ONLY ONE WHO GETS TO SHARE THAT WITH YOU, RIGHT?

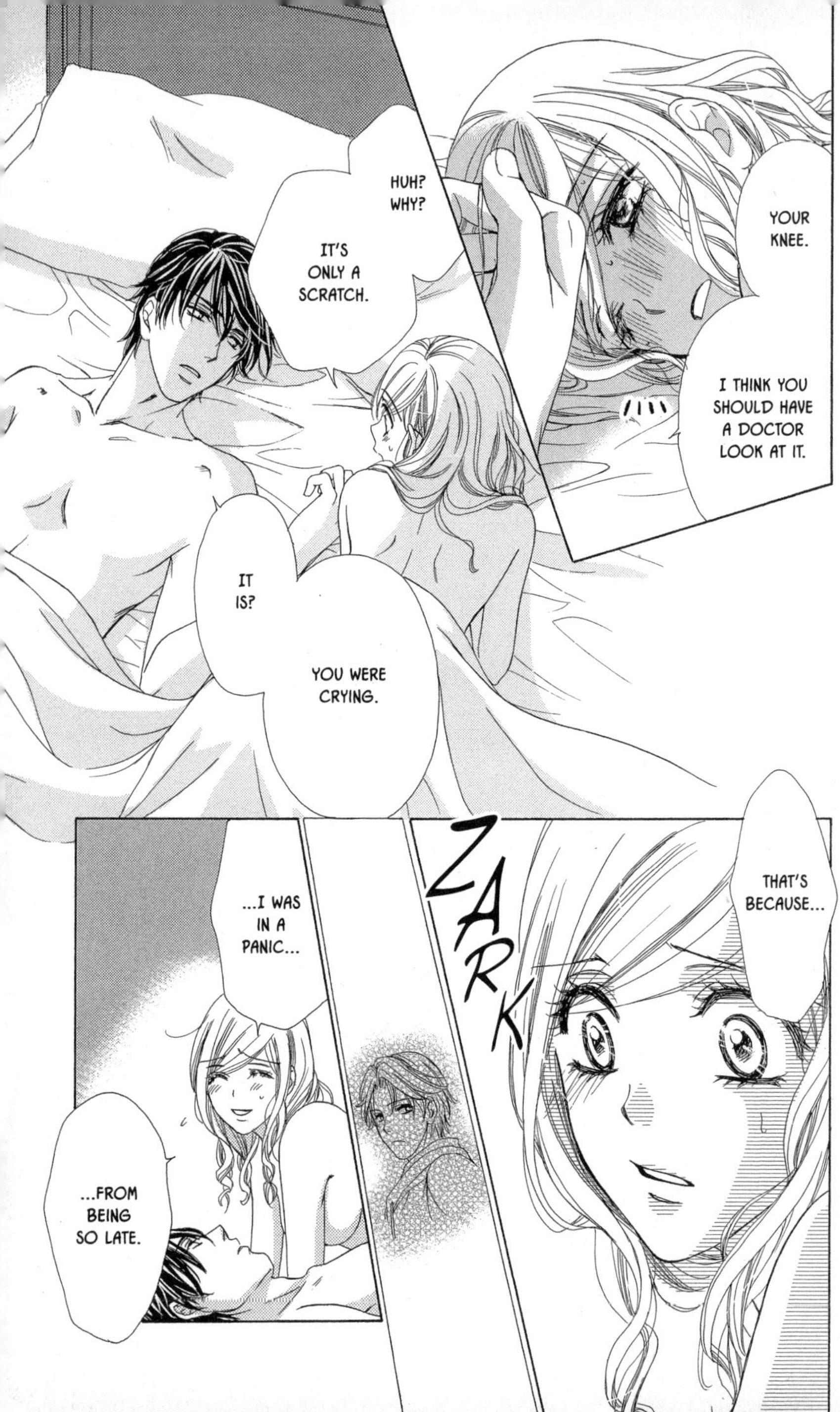
YOUR KNEE.
I THINK YOU SHOULD HAVE A DOCTOR LOOK AT IT.
HUH? WHY?
IT'S ONLY A SCRATCH.
IT IS?
YOU WERE CRYING.
THAT'S BECAUSE...
ZARK
...I WAS IN A PANIC...
...FROM BEING SO LATE.

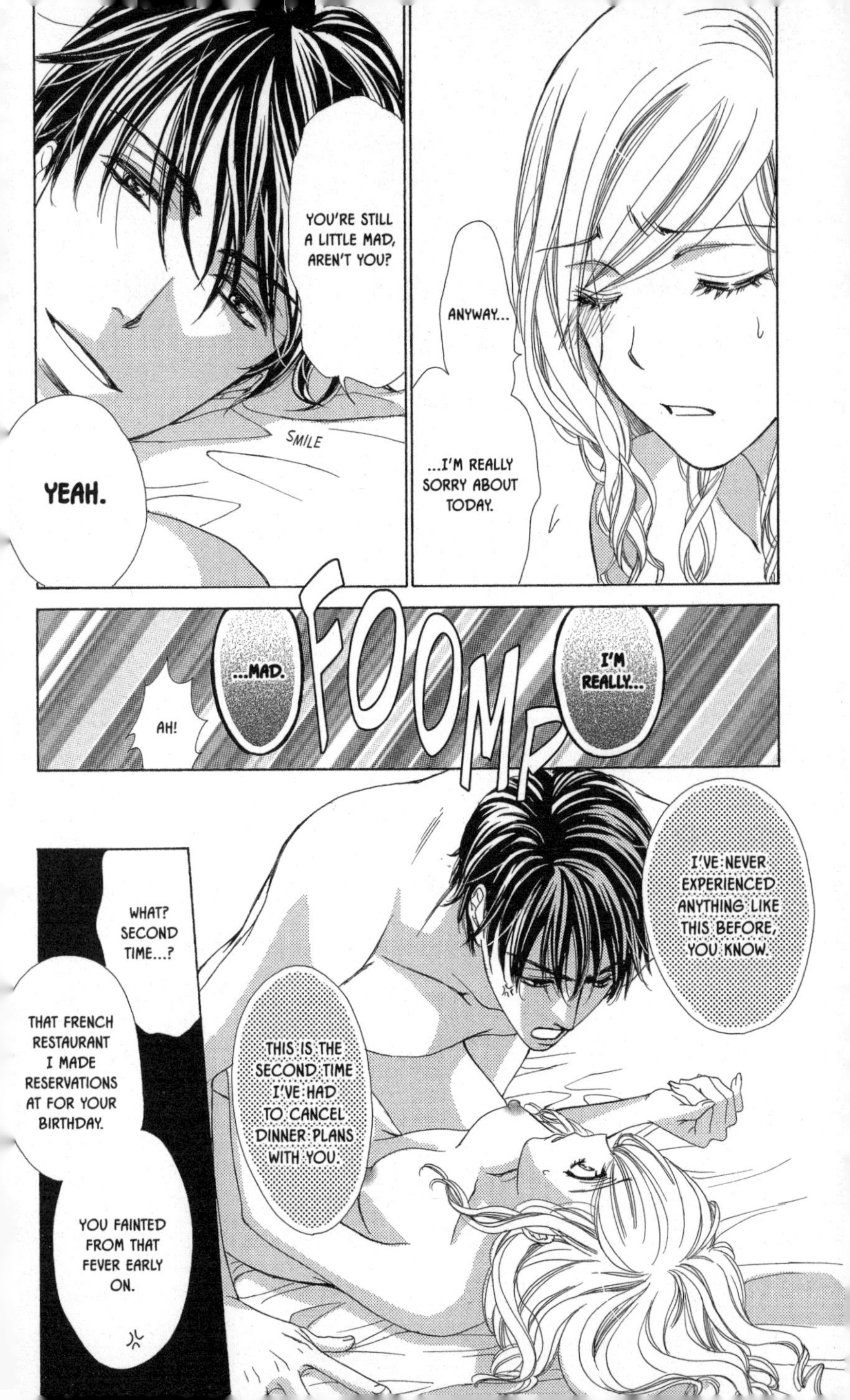
ANYWAY...
...I'M REALLY SORRY ABOUT TODAY.
YOU'RE STILL A LITTLE MAD, AREN'T YOU?
SMILE
YEAH.
I'M REALLY...
FOOMP
...MAD.
AH!
I'VE NEVER EXPERIENCED ANYTHING LIKE THIS BEFORE, YOU KNOW.
THIS IS THE SECOND TIME I'VE HAD TO CANCEL DINNER PLANS WITH YOU.
WHAT? SECOND TIME...?
THAT FRENCH RESTAURANT I MADE RESERVATIONS AT FOR YOUR BIRTHDAY.
YOU FAINTED FROM THAT FEVER EARLY ON.

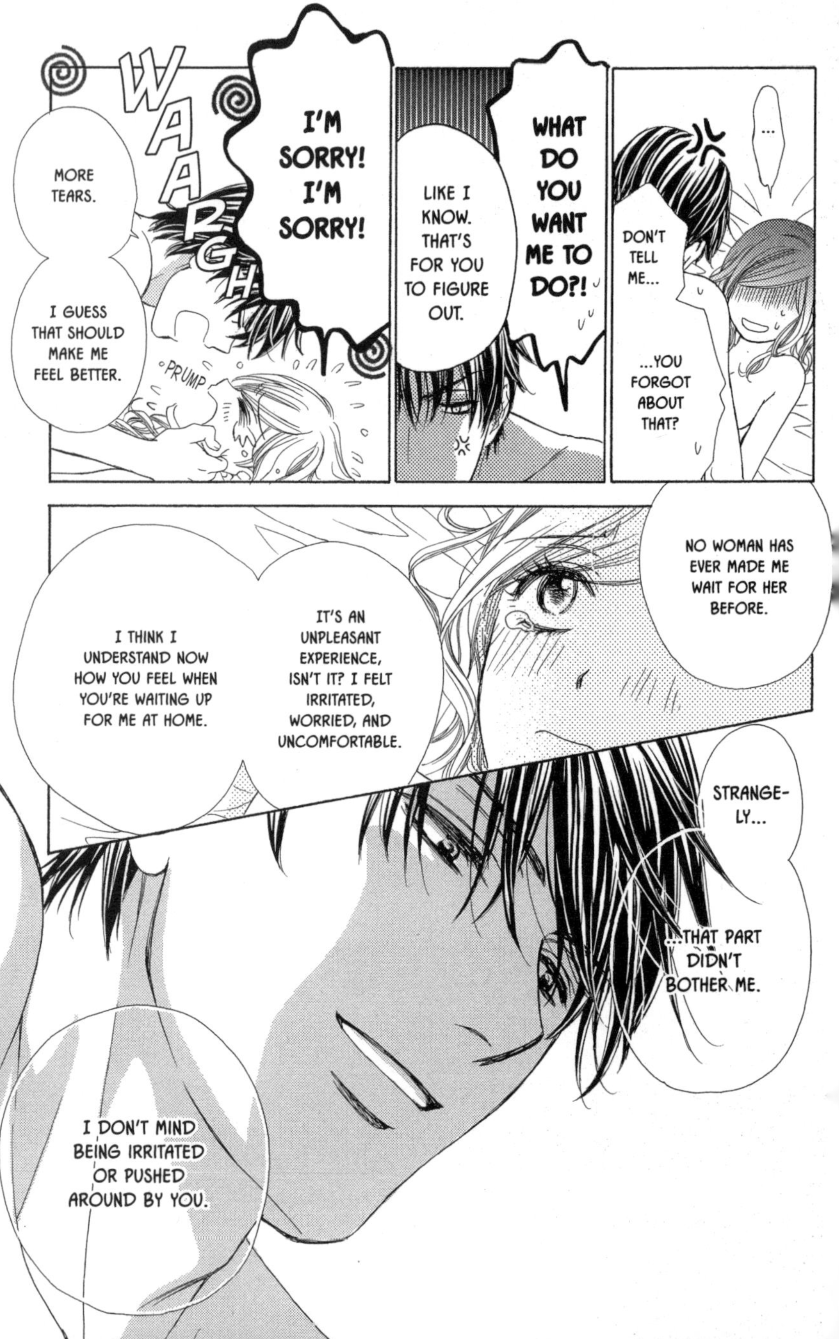
...
DON'T TELL ME...
...YOU FORGOT ABOUT THAT?
WHAT DO YOU WANT ME TO DO?!
LIKE I KNOW. THAT'S FOR YOU TO FIGURE OUT.
I'M SORRY! I'M SORRY!
WAARGH
MORE TEARS.
PRUMP
I GUESS THAT SHOULD MAKE ME FEEL BETTER.
NO WOMAN HAS EVER MADE ME WAIT FOR HER BEFORE.
IT'S AN UNPLEASANT EXPERIENCE, ISN'T IT? I FELT IRRITATED, WORRIED, AND UNCOMFORTABLE.
I THINK I UNDERSTAND NOW HOW YOU FEEL WHEN YOU'RE WAITING UP FOR ME AT HOME.
STRANGE-LY...
...THAT PART DIDN'T BOTHER ME.
I DON'T MIND BEING IRRITATED OR PUSHED AROUND BY YOU.

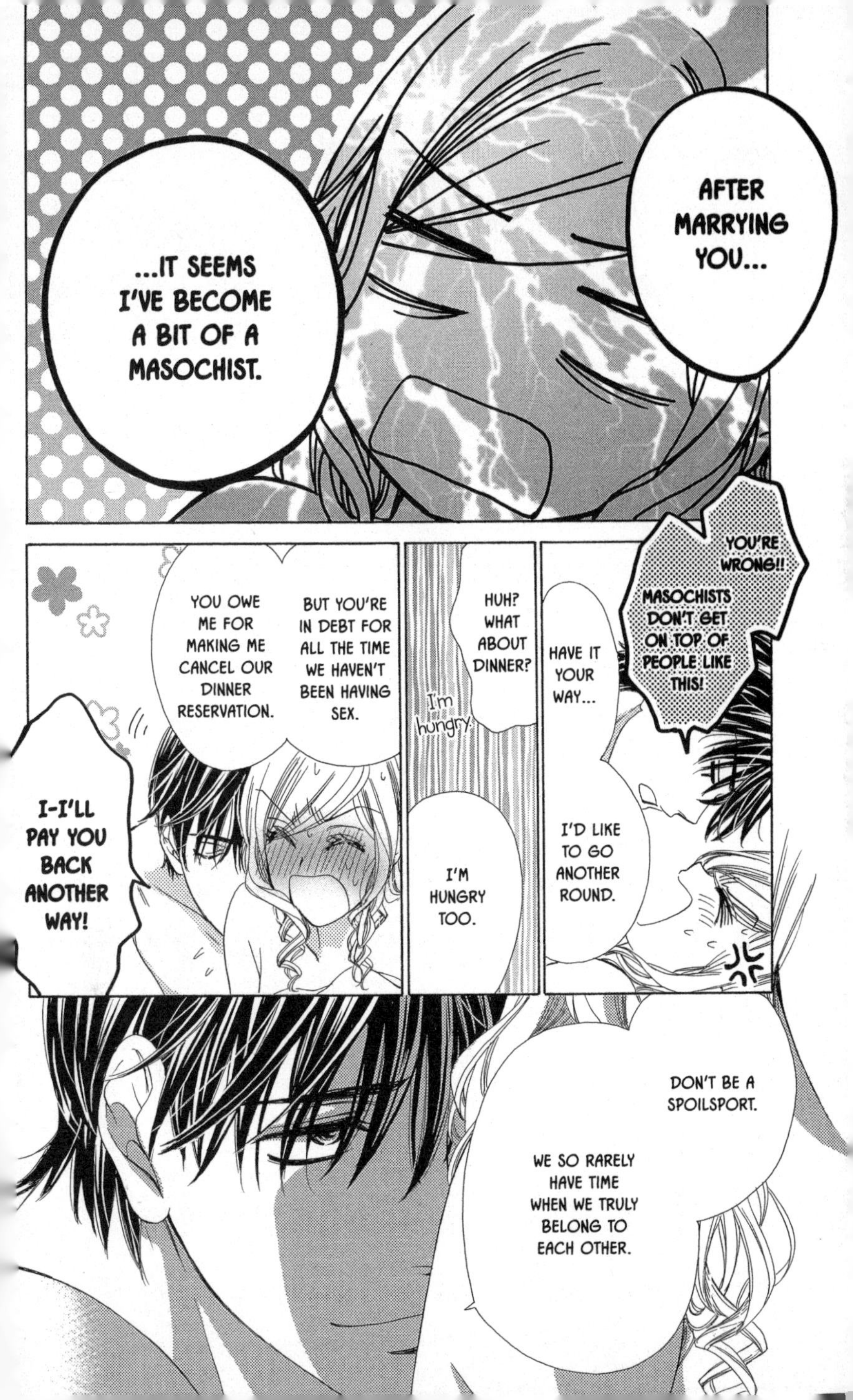
AFTER MARRYING YOU...
...IT SEEMS I'VE BECOME A BIT OF A MASOCHIST.
YOU'RE WRONG!! MASOCHISTS DON'T GET ON TOP OF PEOPLE LIKE THIS!
HAVE IT YOUR WAY...
I'D LIKE TO GO ANOTHER ROUND.
HUH? WHAT ABOUT DINNER?
I'm hungry.
I'M HUNGRY TOO.
BUT YOU'RE IN DEBT FOR ALL THE TIME WE HAVEN'T BEEN HAVING SEX.
YOU OWE ME FOR MAKING ME CANCEL OUR DINNER RESERVATION.
I-I'LL PAY YOU BACK ANOTHER WAY!
DON'T BE A SPOILSPORT.
WE SO RARELY HAVE TIME WHEN WE TRULY BELONG TO EACH OTHER.

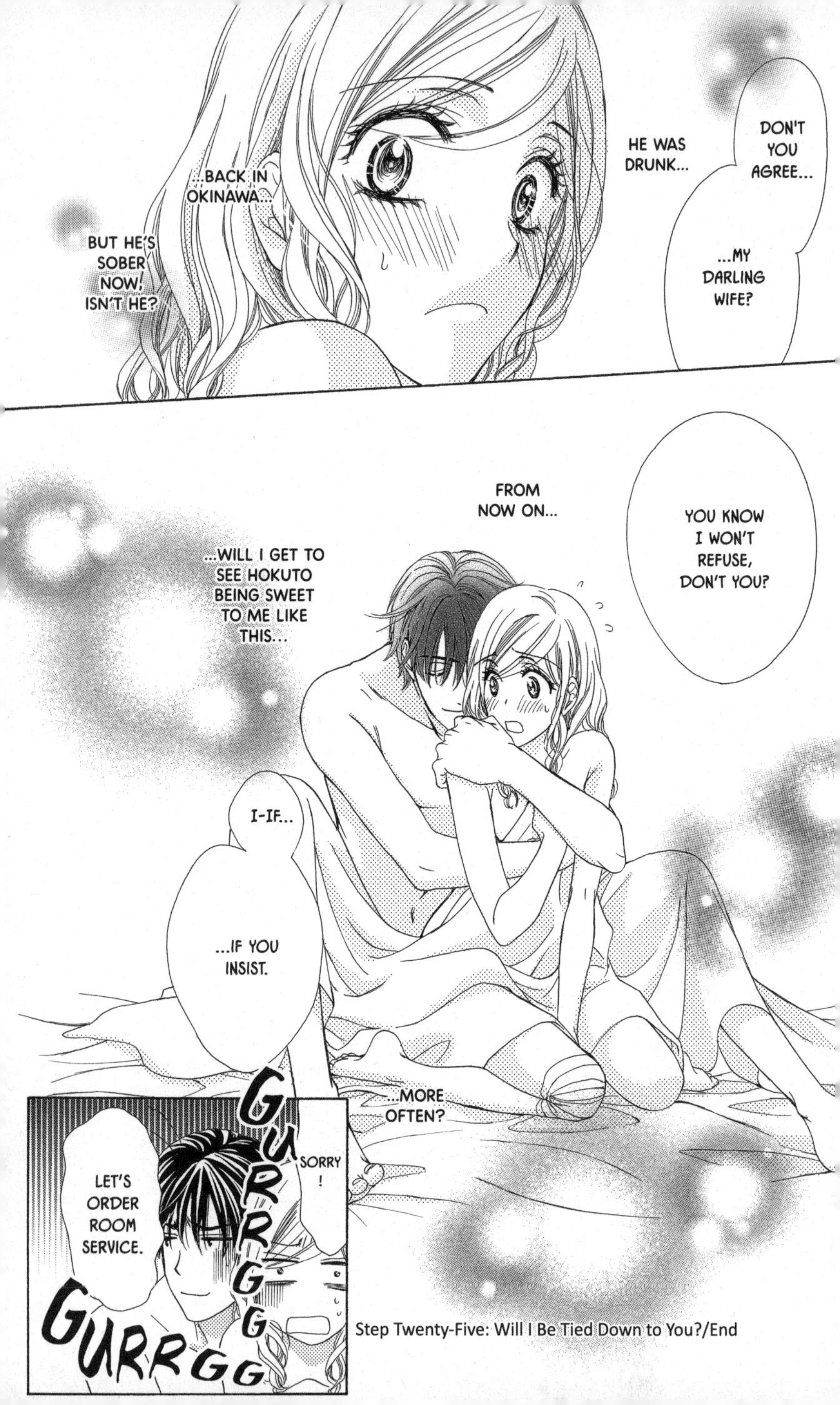
DON'T YOU AGREE...
...MY DARLING WIFE?
HE WAS DRUNK...
...BACK IN OKINAWA...
BUT HE'S SOBER NOW! ISN'T HE?
YOU KNOW I WON'T REFUSE, DON'T YOU?
FROM NOW ON...
...WILL I GET TO SEE HOKUTO BEING SWEET TO ME LIKE THIS...
...MORE OFTEN?
I-IF...
...IF YOU INSIST.
GURRRGG
SORRY!
GURRRGG
LET'S ORDER ROOM SERVICE.

Step Twenty-Five: Will I Be Tied Down to You?/End

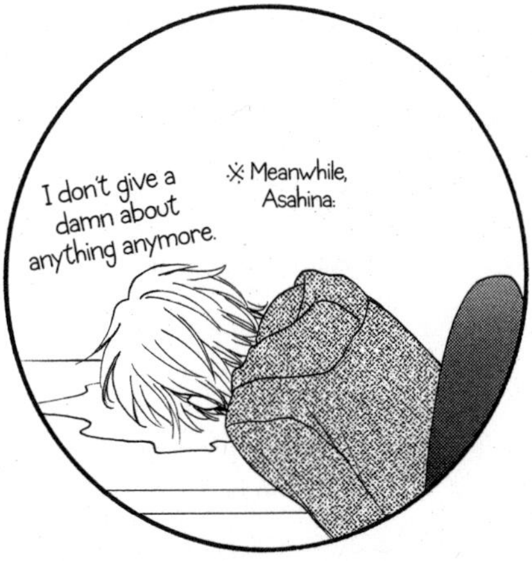
※ Meanwhile, Asahina:
I don't give a damn about anything anymore.

Step Twenty-Six: What Must I Do to Reach You?

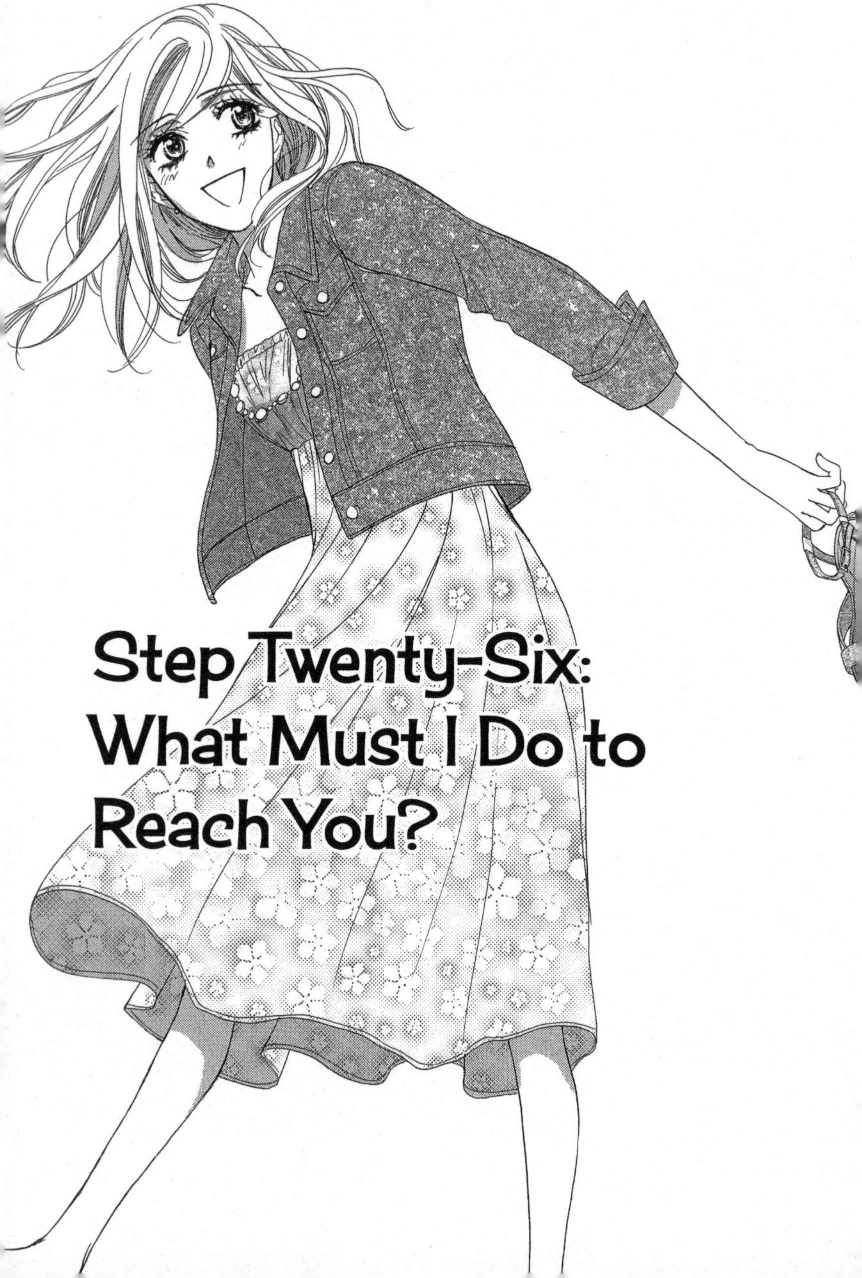

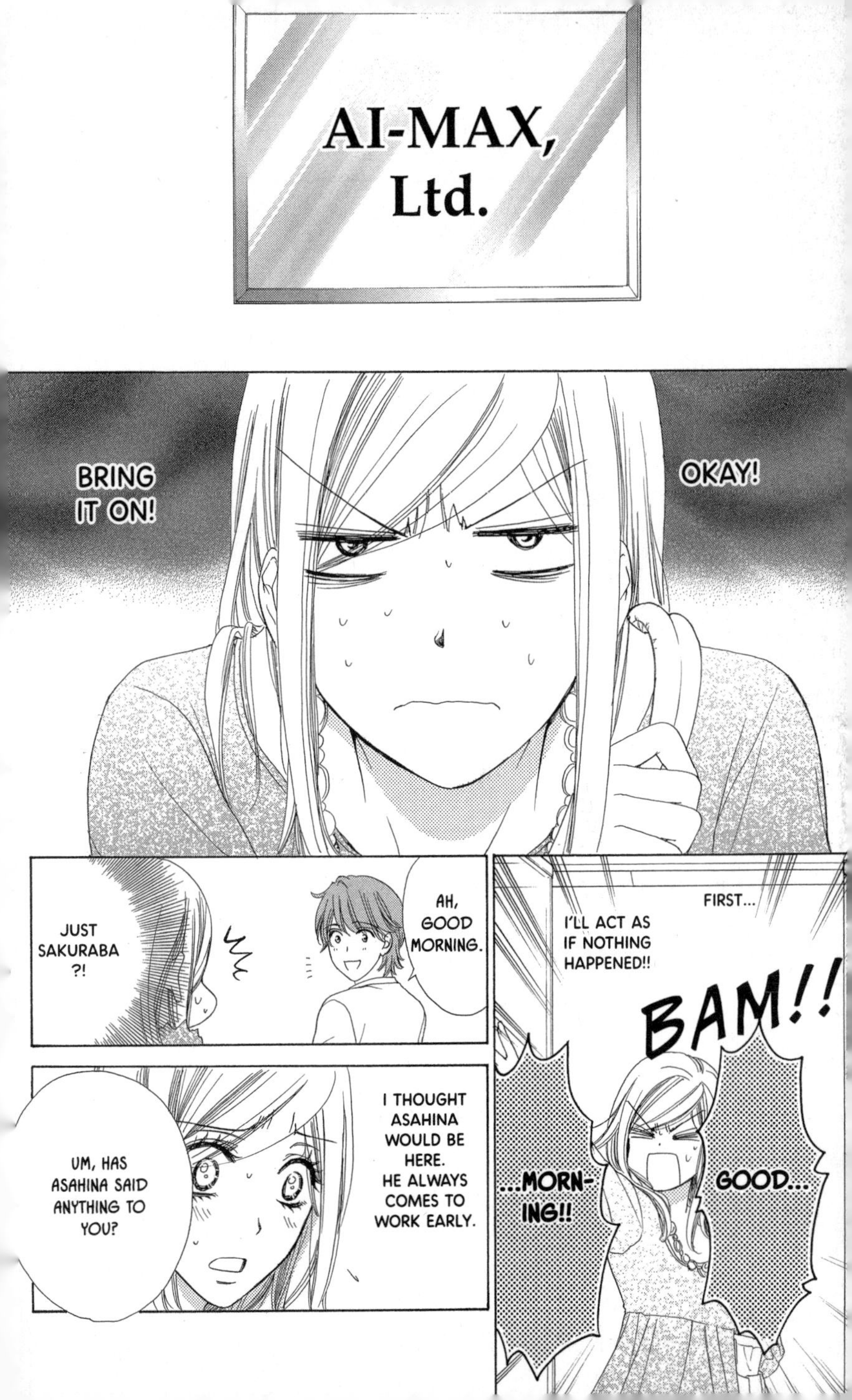
AI-MAX, Ltd.
OKAY!
BRING IT ON!
FIRST...
I'LL ACT AS IF NOTHING HAPPENED!!
BAM!!
GOOD...
...MORNING!!
AH, GOOD MORNING.
JUST SAKURABA?!
I THOUGHT ASAHINA WOULD BE HERE. HE ALWAYS COMES TO WORK EARLY.
UM, HAS ASAHINA SAID ANYTHING TO YOU?

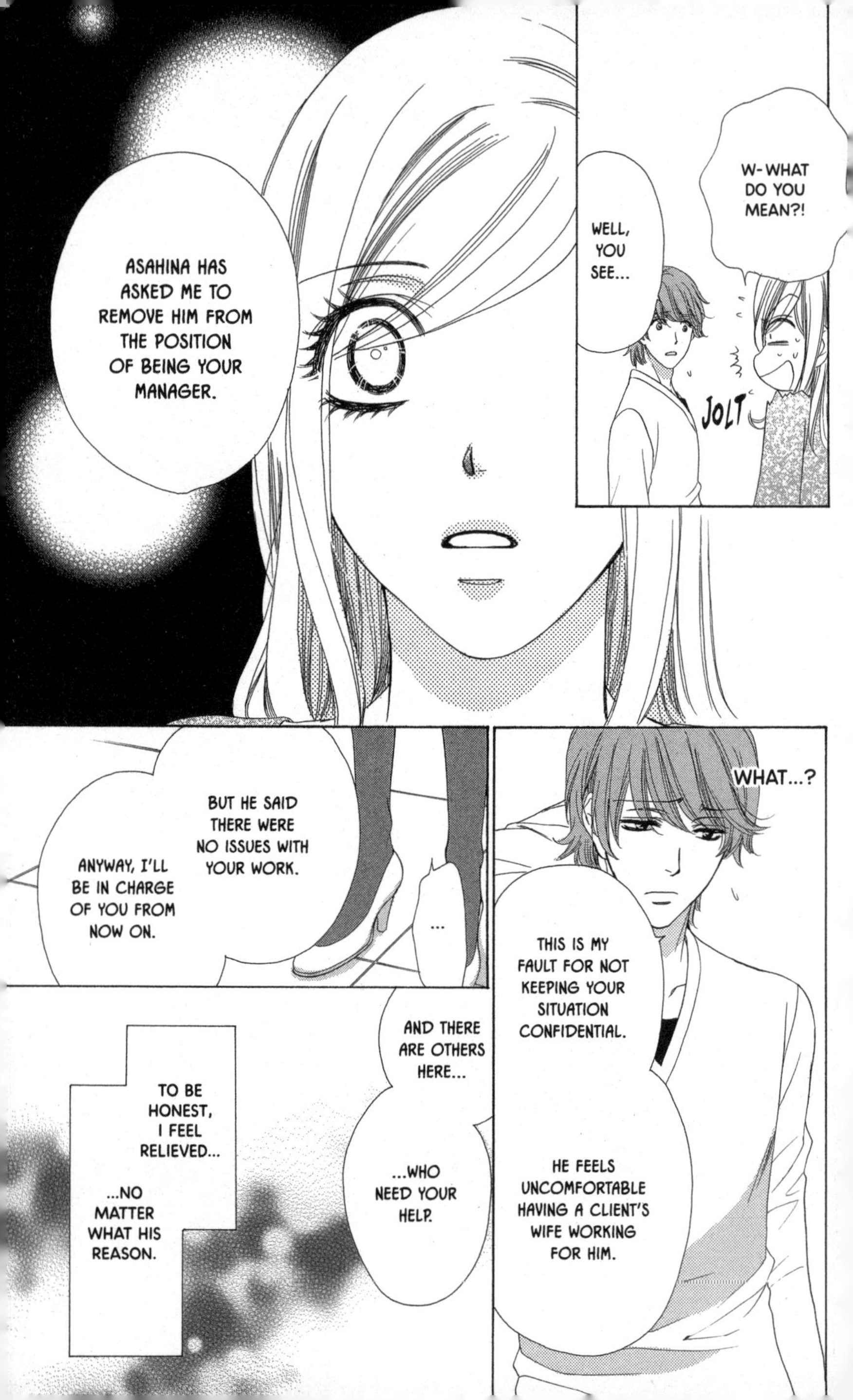
W-WHAT DO YOU MEAN?!
WELL, YOU SEE...
JOLT
ASAHINA HAS ASKED ME TO REMOVE HIM FROM THE POSITION OF BEING YOUR MANAGER.
WHAT...?
THIS IS MY FAULT FOR NOT KEEPING YOUR SITUATION CONFIDENTIAL.
HE FEELS UNCOMFORTABLE HAVING A CLIENT'S WIFE WORKING FOR HIM.
BUT HE SAID THERE WERE NO ISSUES WITH YOUR WORK.
...
ANYWAY, I'LL BE IN CHARGE OF YOU FROM NOW ON.
AND THERE ARE OTHERS HERE...
...WHO NEED YOUR HELP.
TO BE HONEST, I FEEL RELIEVED...
...NO MATTER WHAT HIS REASON.

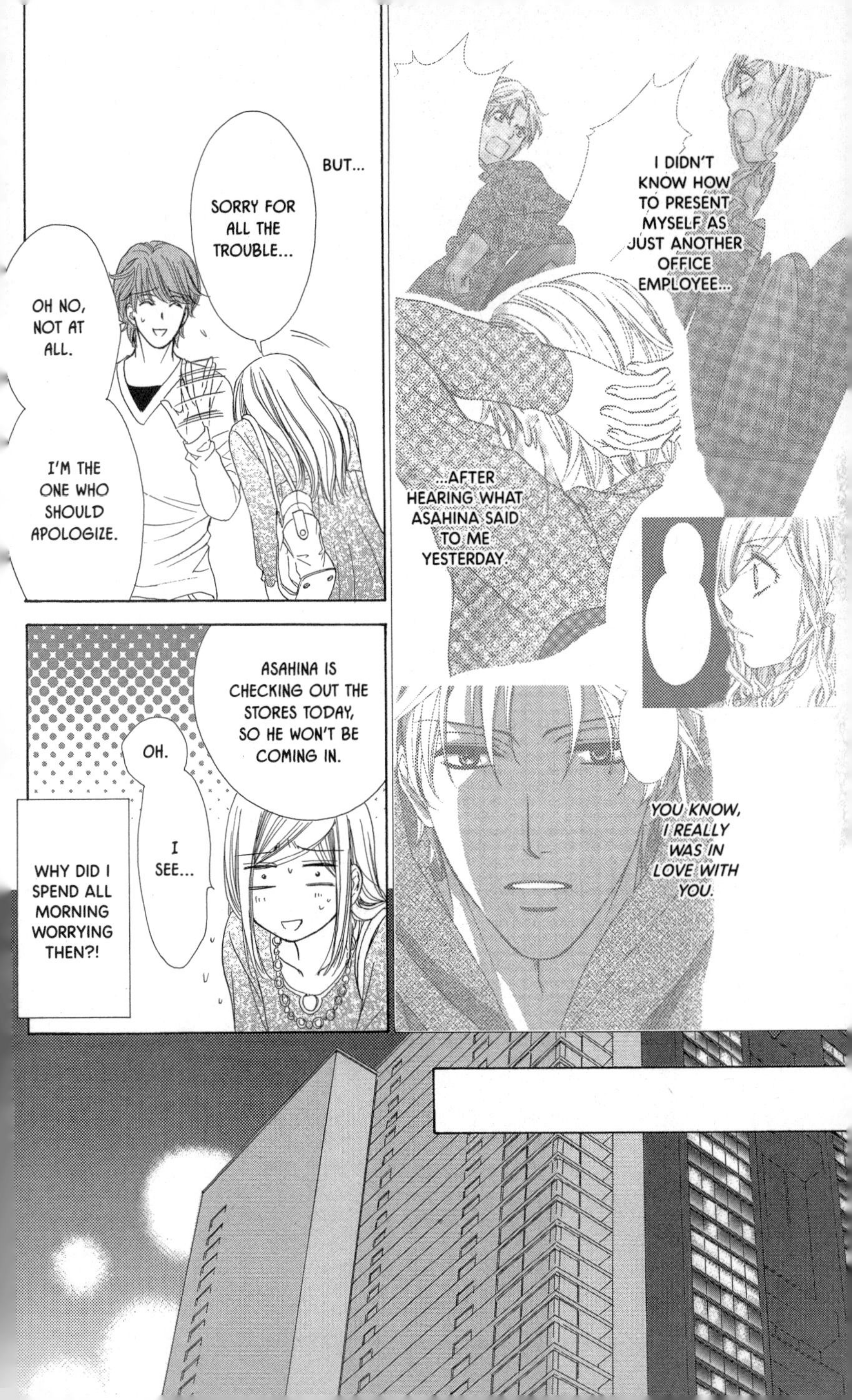
I DIDN'T KNOW HOW TO PRESENT MYSELF AS JUST ANOTHER OFFICE EMPLOYEE...
...AFTER HEARING WHAT ASAHINA SAID TO ME YESTERDAY.
YOU KNOW, I REALLY WAS IN LOVE WITH YOU.
BUT...
SORRY FOR ALL THE TROUBLE...
OH NO, NOT AT ALL.
I'M THE ONE WHO SHOULD APOLOGIZE.
ASAHINA IS CHECKING OUT THE STORES TODAY, SO HE WON'T BE COMING IN.
OH.
I SEE...
WHY DID I SPEND ALL MORNING WORRYING THEN?!

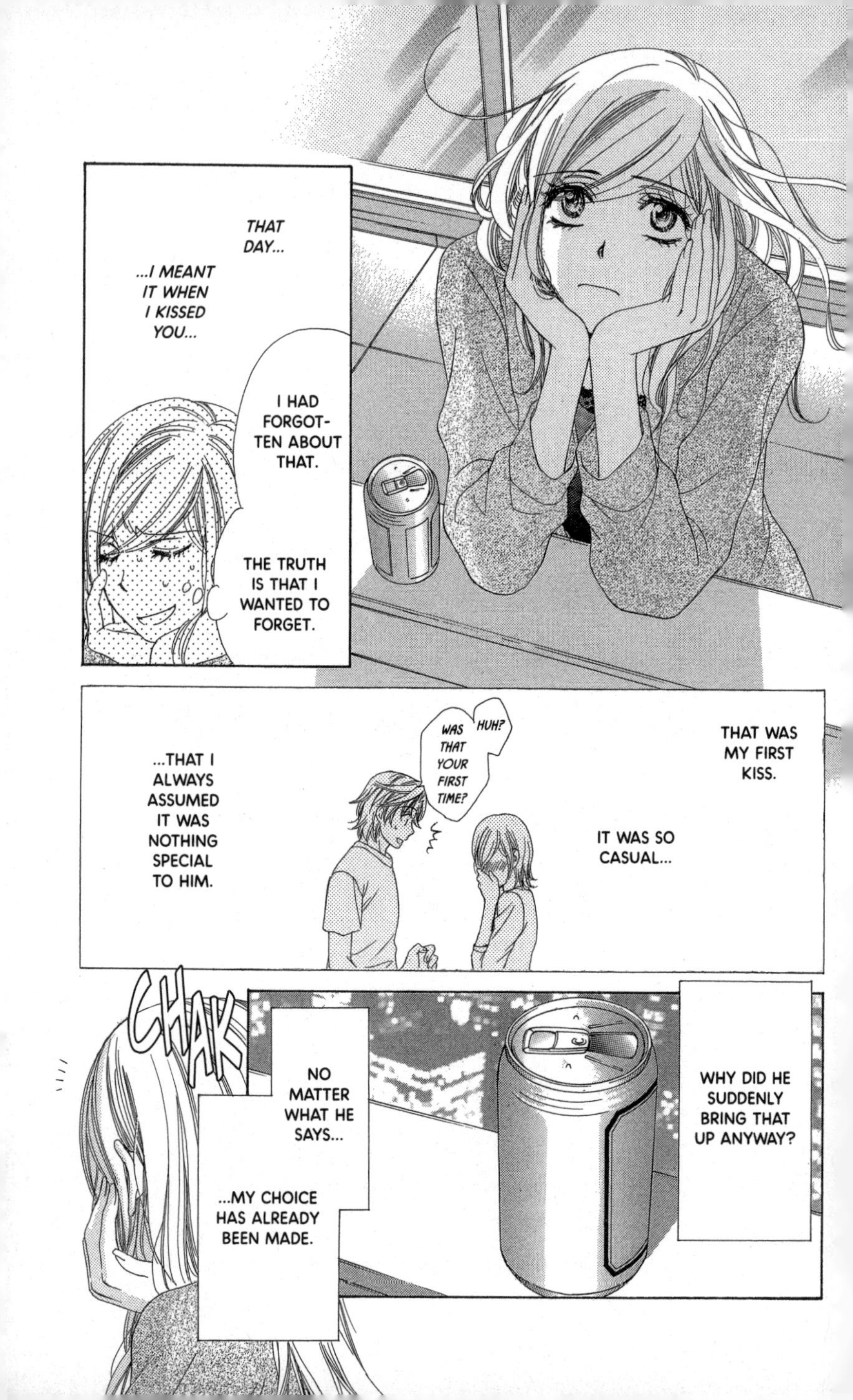
THAT DAY...
...I MEANT IT WHEN I KISSED YOU...
I HAD FORGOT-TEN ABOUT THAT.
THE TRUTH IS THAT I WANTED TO FORGET.
THAT WAS MY FIRST KISS.
IT WAS SO CASUAL...
HUH?
WAS THAT YOUR FIRST TIME?
...THAT I ALWAYS ASSUMED IT WAS NOTHING SPECIAL TO HIM.
WHY DID HE SUDDENLY BRING THAT UP ANYWAY?
CHAK
NO MATTER WHAT HE SAYS...
...MY CHOICE HAS ALREADY BEEN MADE.

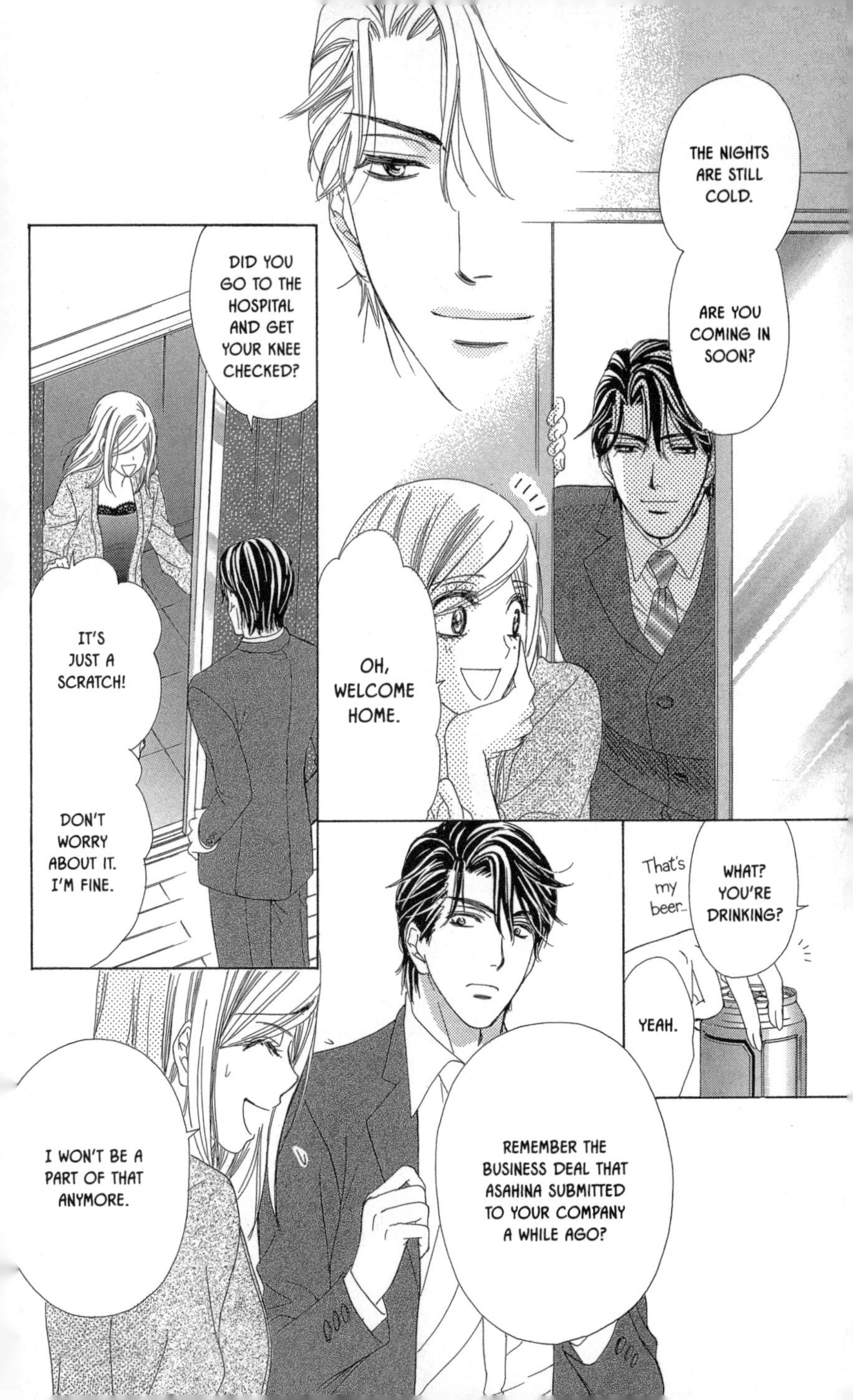
THE NIGHTS ARE STILL COLD.
ARE YOU COMING IN SOON?
OH, WELCOME HOME.
DID YOU GO TO THE HOSPITAL AND GET YOUR KNEE CHECKED?
IT'S JUST A SCRATCH!
DON'T WORRY ABOUT IT. I'M FINE.
WHAT? YOU'RE DRINKING?
That's my beer...
YEAH.
REMEMBER THE BUSINESS DEAL THAT ASAHINA SUBMITTED TO YOUR COMPANY A WHILE AGO?
I WON'T BE A PART OF THAT ANYMORE.

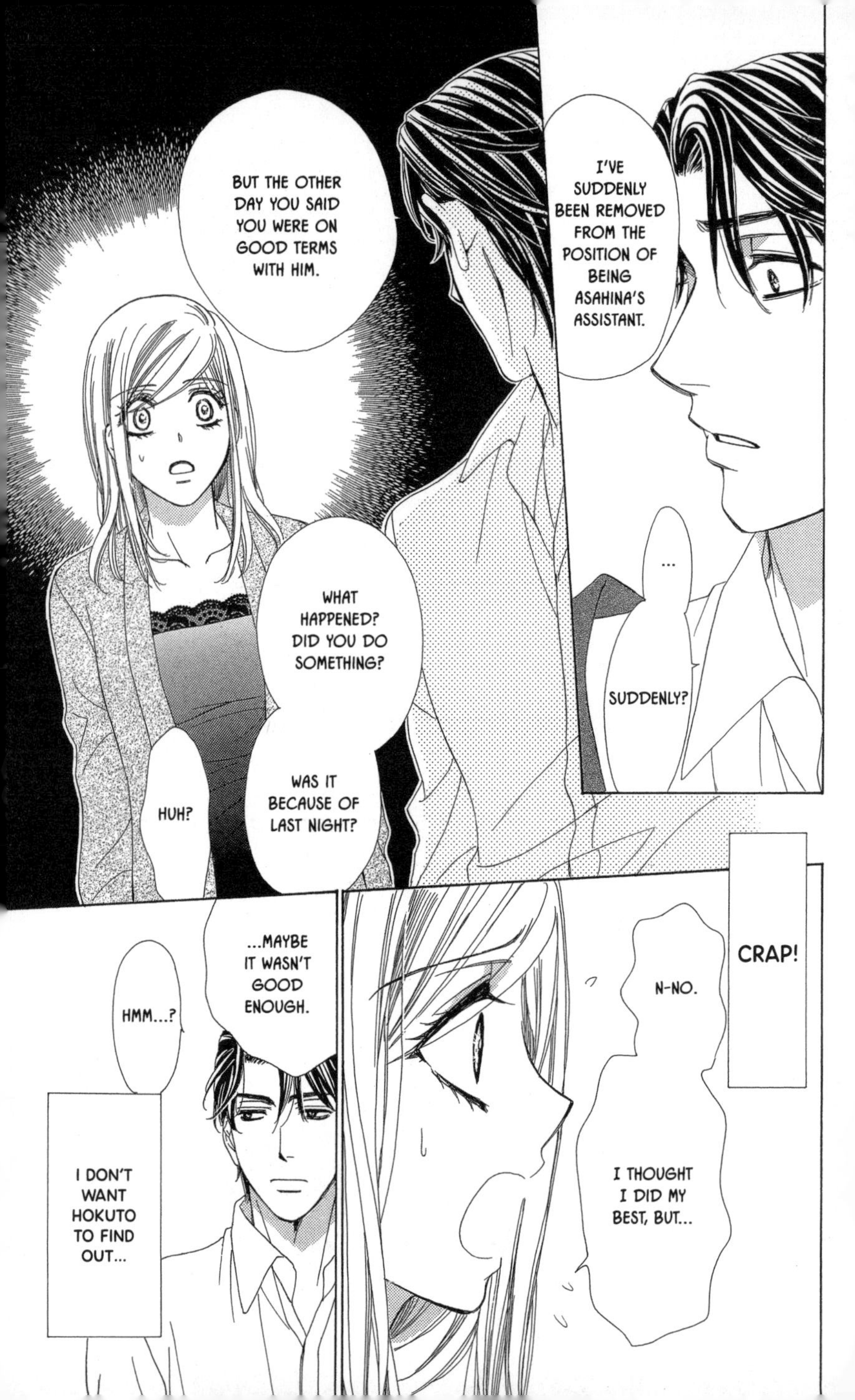
I'VE SUDDENLY BEEN REMOVED FROM THE POSITION OF BEING ASAHINA'S ASSISTANT.
...
SUDDENLY?
BUT THE OTHER DAY YOU SAID YOU WERE ON GOOD TERMS WITH HIM.
WHAT HAPPENED? DID YOU DO SOMETHING?
WAS IT BECAUSE OF LAST NIGHT?
HUH?
CRAP!
N-NO.
I THOUGHT I DID MY BEST, BUT...
...MAYBE IT WASN'T GOOD ENOUGH.
HMM...?
I DON'T WANT HOKUTO TO FIND OUT...

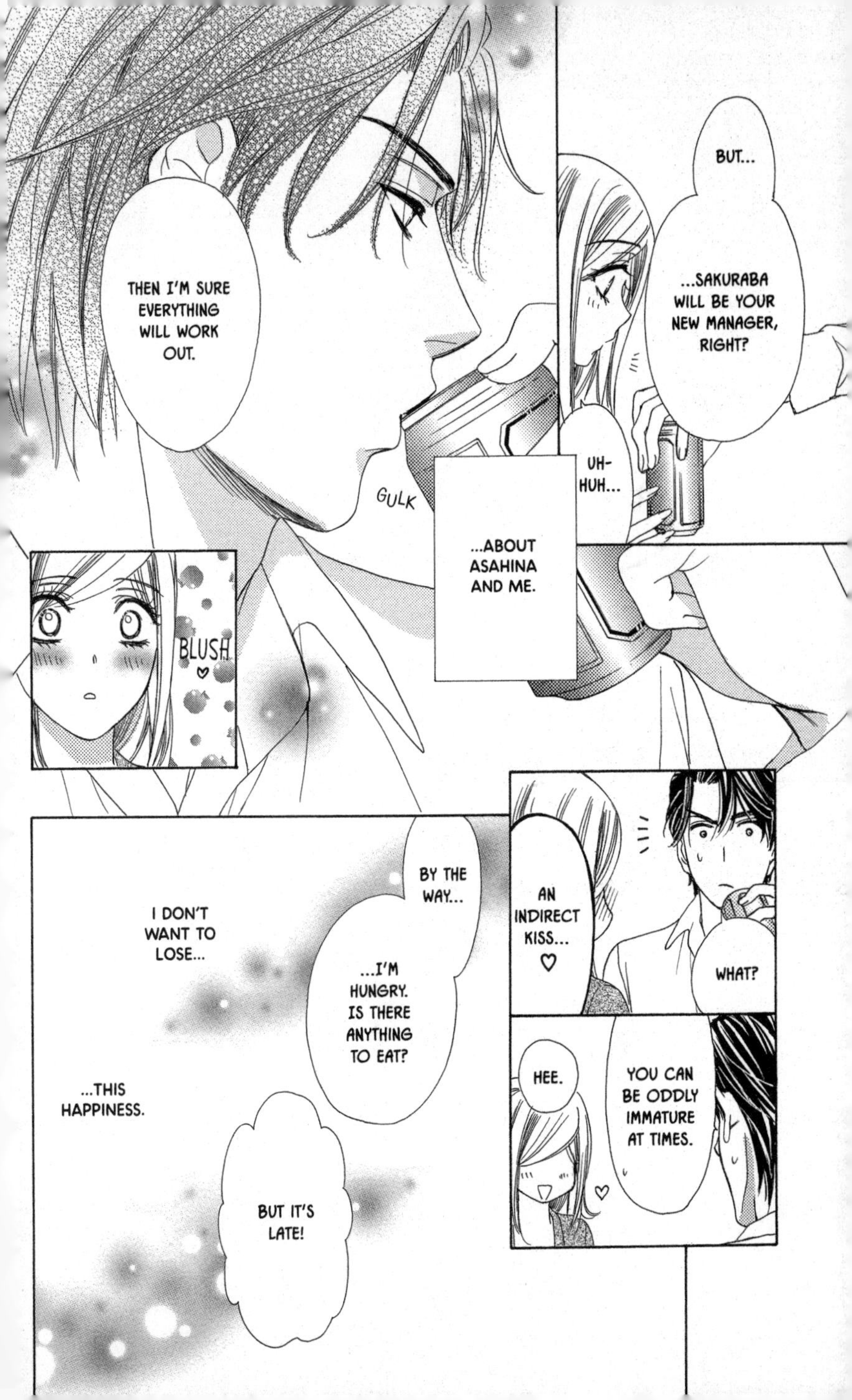
BUT...
...SAKURABA WILL BE YOUR NEW MANAGER, RIGHT?
UH-HUH...
THEN I'M SURE EVERYTHING WILL WORK OUT.
GULK
...ABOUT ASAHINA AND ME.
BLUSH ♡
AN INDIRECT KISS... ♡
WHAT?
YOU CAN BE ODDLY IMMATURE AT TIMES.
HEE.
BY THE WAY...
...I'M HUNGRY. IS THERE ANYTHING TO EAT?
I DON'T WANT TO LOSE...
...THIS HAPPINESS.
BUT IT'S LATE!

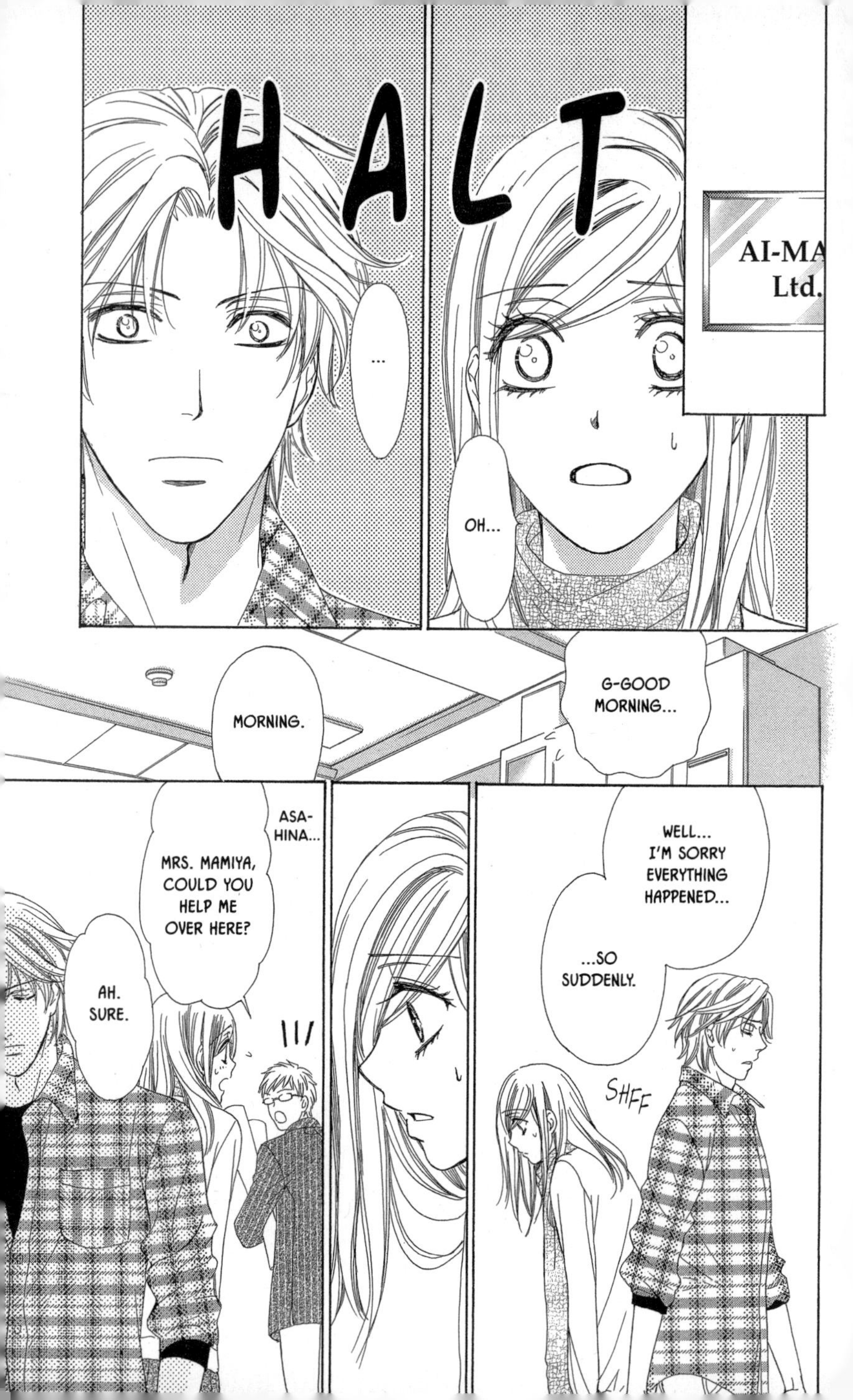
HALT
AI-MA
Ltd.
OH...
...
G-GOOD MORNING...
MORNING.
WELL... I'M SORRY EVERYTHING HAPPENED...
...SO SUDDENLY.
SHFF
ASA-HINA...
MRS. MAMIYA, COULD YOU HELP ME OVER HERE?
AH. SURE.

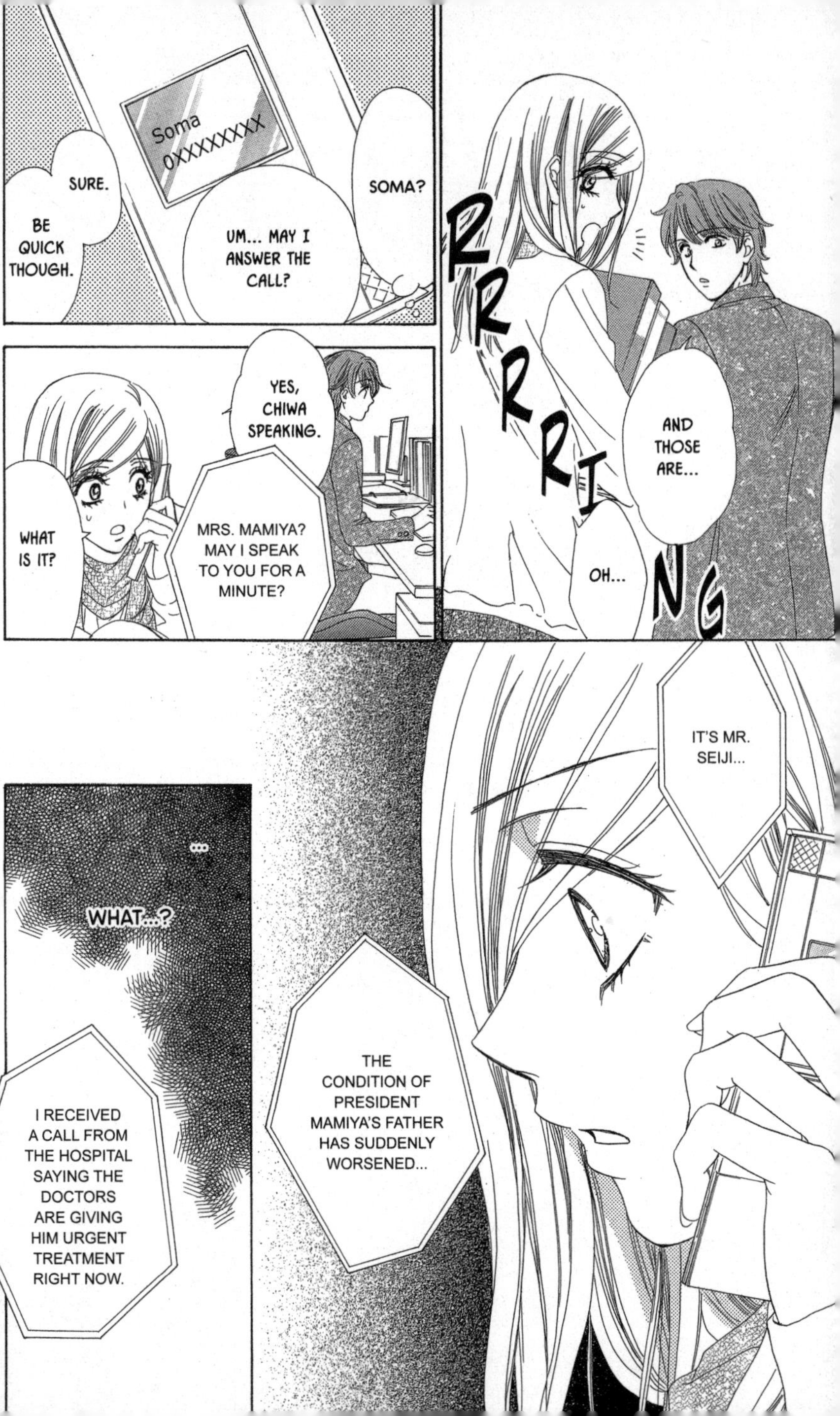
AND THOSE ARE...
RRRRING
OH...
SOMA?
Soma
0XXXXXXX
UM... MAY I ANSWER THE CALL?
SURE.
BE QUICK THOUGH.
YES, CHIWA SPEAKING.
MRS. MAMIYA? MAY I SPEAK TO YOU FOR A MINUTE?
WHAT IS IT?
IT'S MR. SEIJI...
THE CONDITION OF PRESIDENT MAMIYA'S FATHER HAS SUDDENLY WORSENED...
...
WHAT...?
I RECEIVED A CALL FROM THE HOSPITAL SAYING THE DOCTORS ARE GIVING HIM URGENT TREATMENT RIGHT NOW.

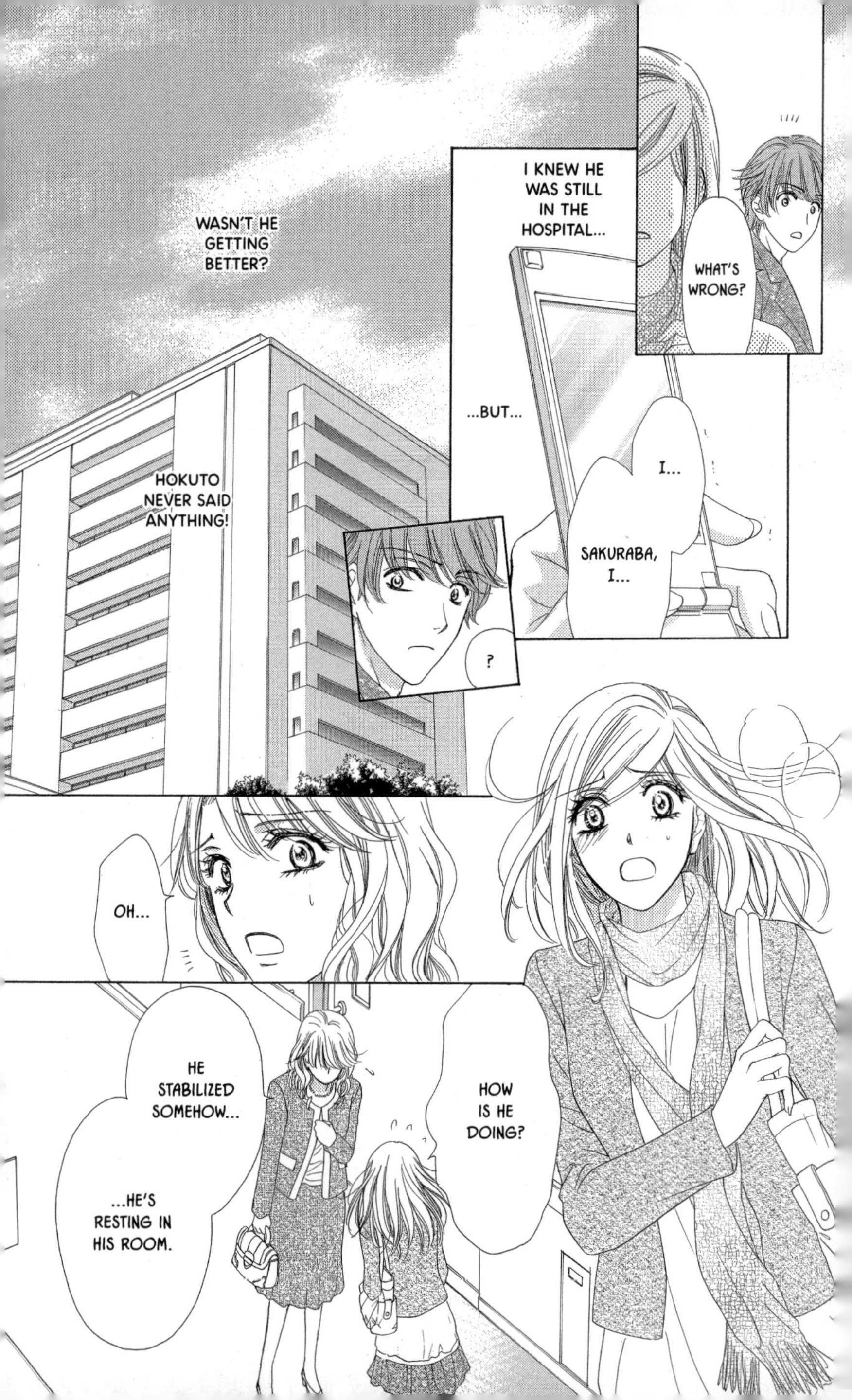
WHAT'S WRONG?
I KNEW HE WAS STILL IN THE HOSPITAL...
...BUT...
I...
SAKURABA, I...
?
WASN'T HE GETTING BETTER?
HOKUTO NEVER SAID ANYTHING!
OH...
HOW IS HE DOING?
HE STABILIZED SOMEHOW...
...HE'S RESTING IN HIS ROOM.

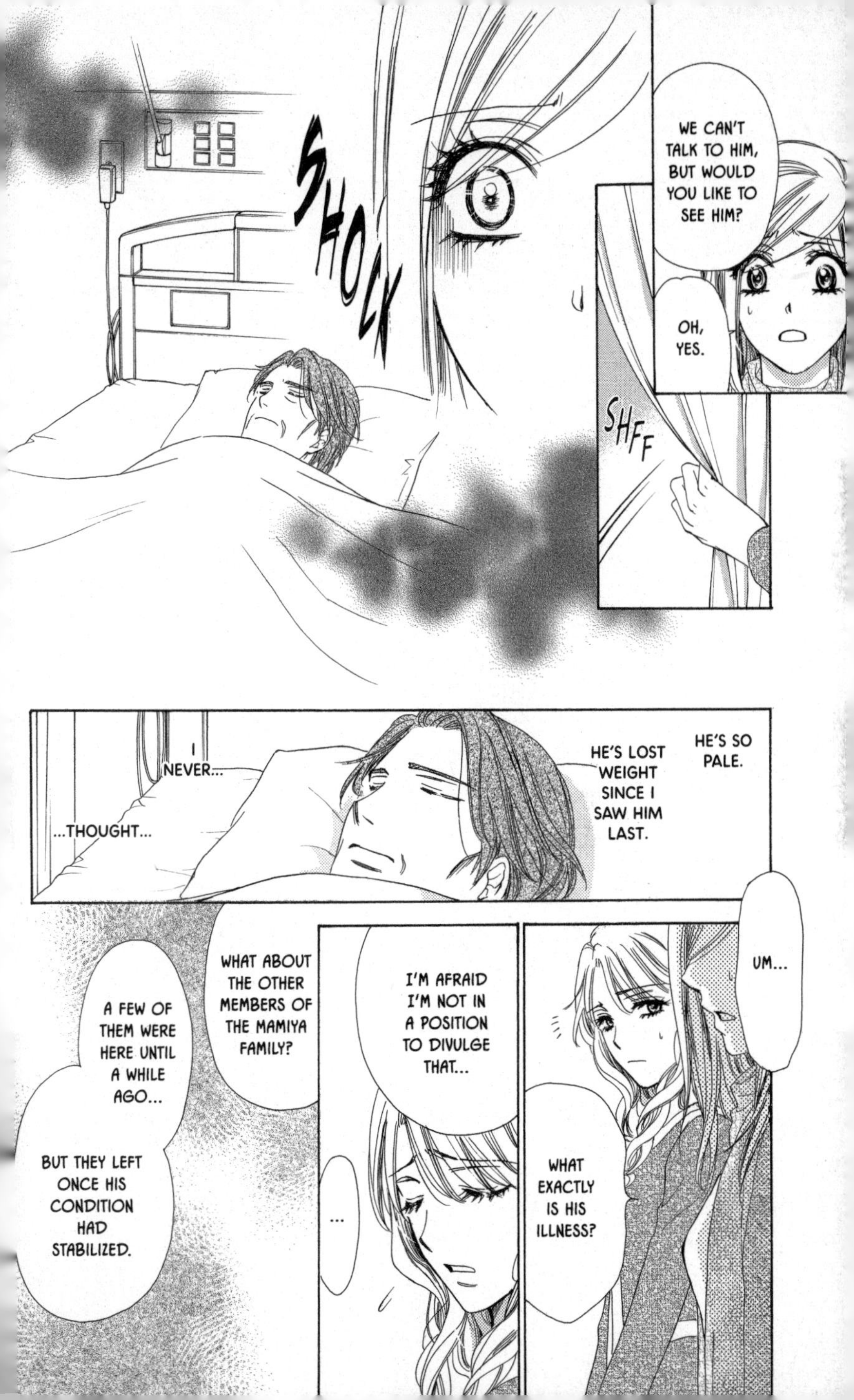
WE CAN'T TALK TO HIM, BUT WOULD YOU LIKE TO SEE HIM?
OH, YES.
SHFF
SHOCK
HE'S SO PALE.
HE'S LOST WEIGHT SINCE I SAW HIM LAST.
I NEVER...
...THOUGHT...
UM...
WHAT EXACTLY IS HIS ILLNESS?
I'M AFRAID I'M NOT IN A POSITION TO DIVULGE THAT...
...
WHAT ABOUT THE OTHER MEMBERS OF THE MAMIYA FAMILY?
A FEW OF THEM WERE HERE UNTIL A WHILE AGO...
BUT THEY LEFT ONCE HIS CONDITION HAD STABILIZED.

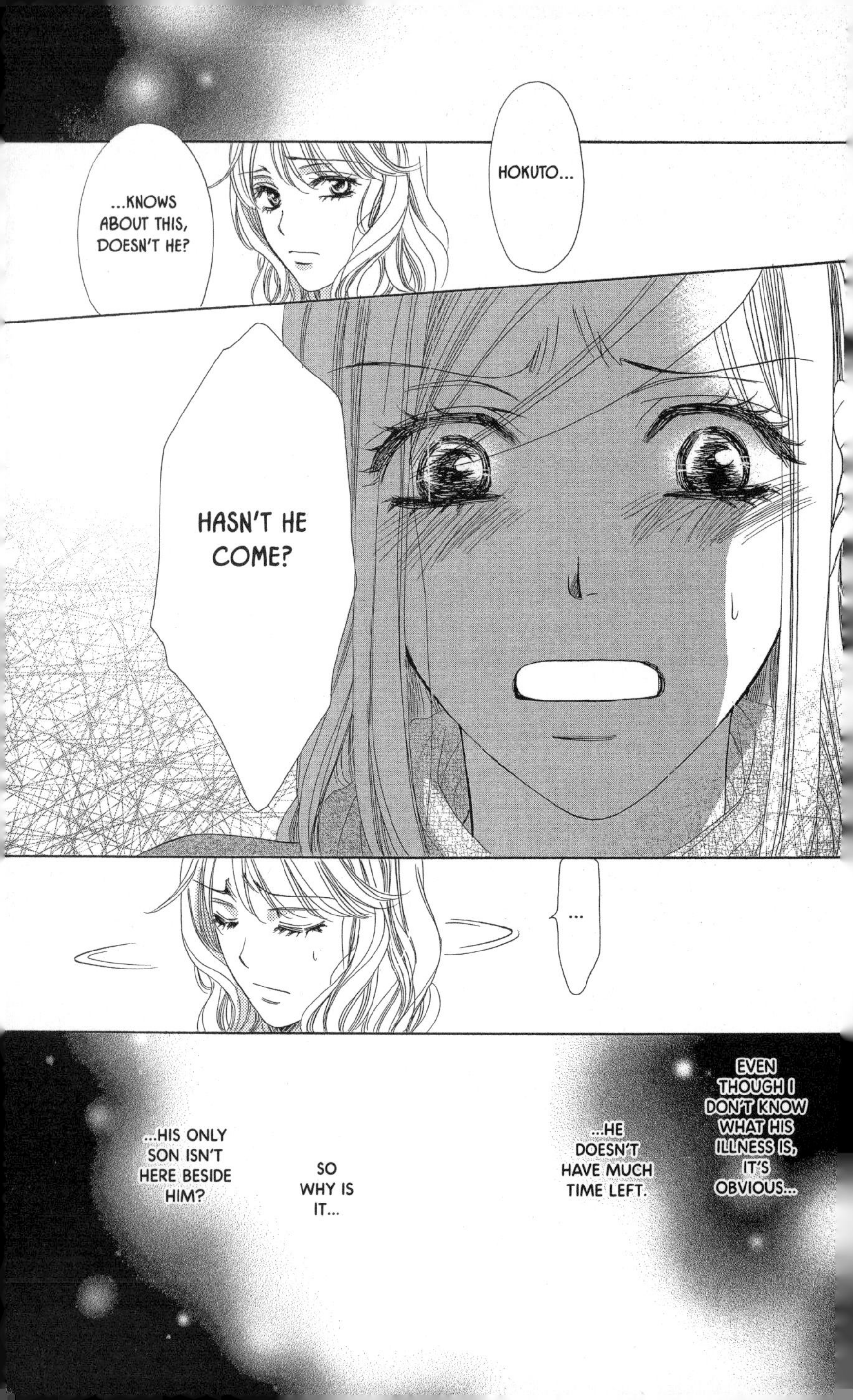
HOKUTO...
...KNOWS ABOUT THIS, DOESN'T HE?
HASN'T HE COME?
...
EVEN THOUGH I DON'T KNOW WHAT HIS ILLNESS IS, IT'S OBVIOUS...
...HE DOESN'T HAVE MUCH TIME LEFT.
SO WHY IS IT...
...HIS ONLY SON ISN'T HERE BESIDE HIM?

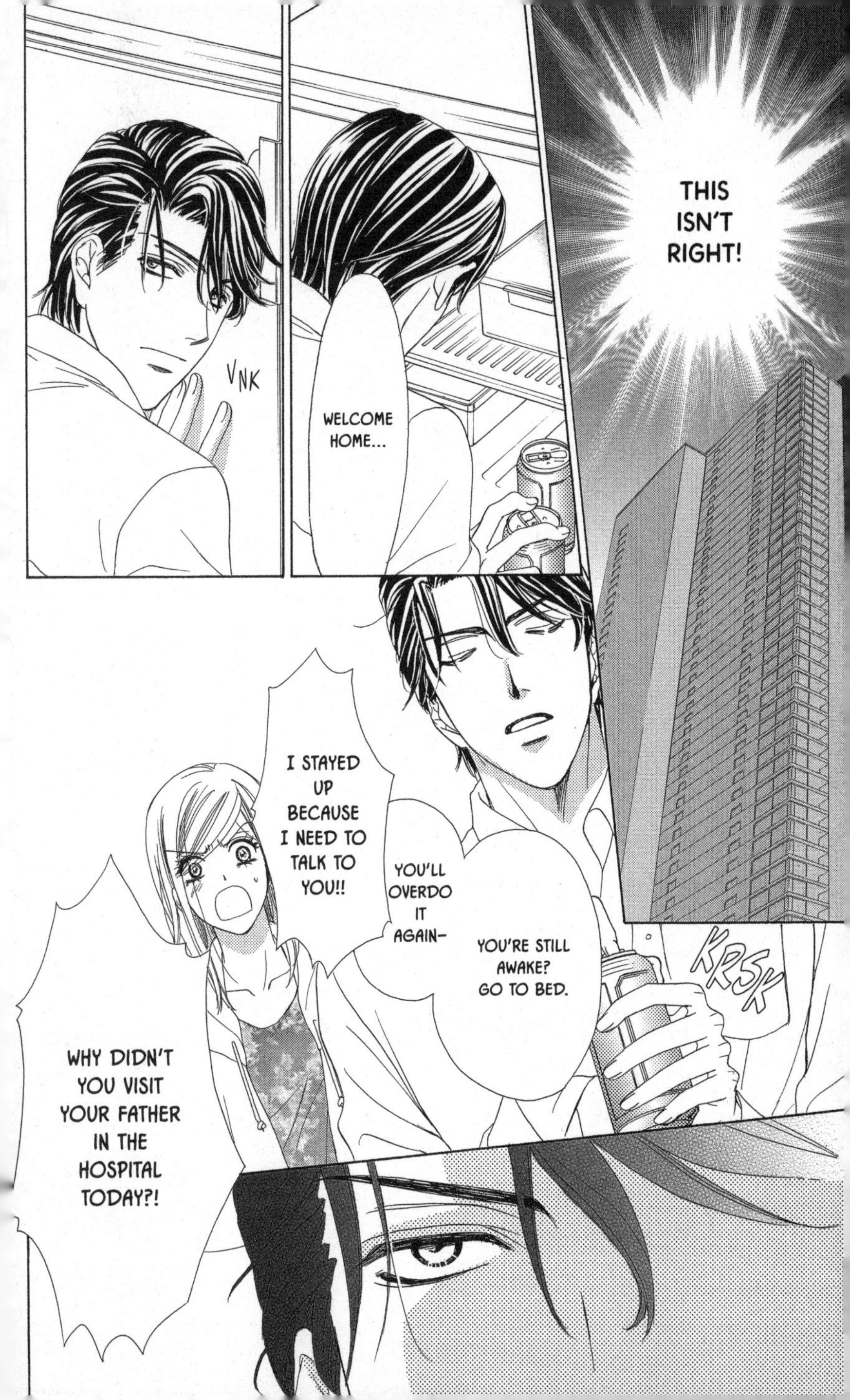
THIS ISN'T RIGHT!
WELCOME HOME...
VNK
KRSK
YOU'RE STILL AWAKE? GO TO BED.
YOU'LL OVERDO IT AGAIN-
I STAYED UP BECAUSE I NEED TO TALK TO YOU!!
WHY DIDN'T YOU VISIT YOUR FATHER IN THE HOSPITAL TODAY?!

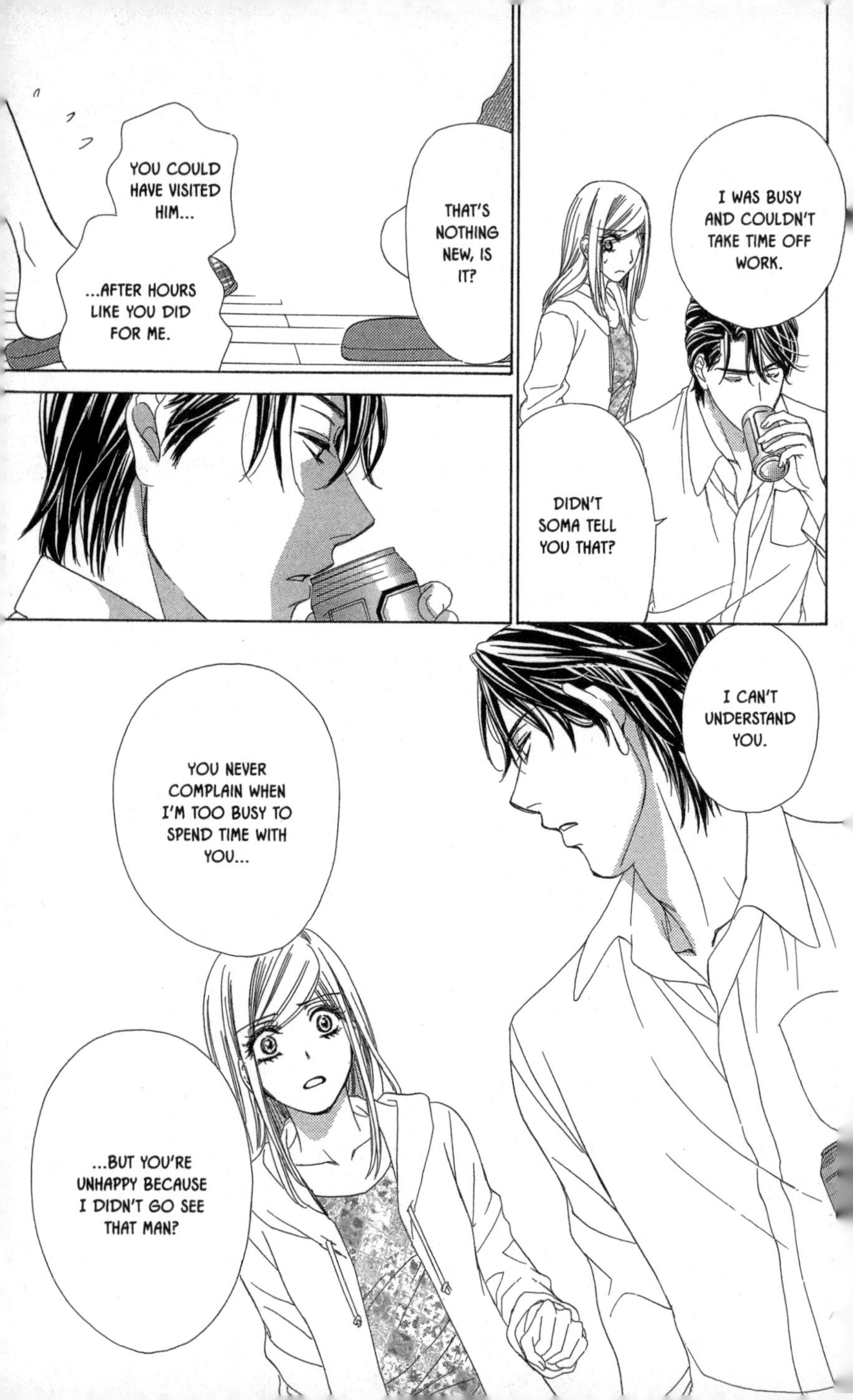
I WAS BUSY AND COULDN'T TAKE TIME OFF WORK.
DIDN'T SOMA TELL YOU THAT?
THAT'S NOTHING NEW, IS IT?
YOU COULD HAVE VISITED HIM...
...AFTER HOURS LIKE YOU DID FOR ME.
I CAN'T UNDERSTAND YOU.
YOU NEVER COMPLAIN WHEN I'M TOO BUSY TO SPEND TIME WITH YOU...
...BUT YOU'RE UNHAPPY BECAUSE I DIDN'T GO SEE THAT MAN?

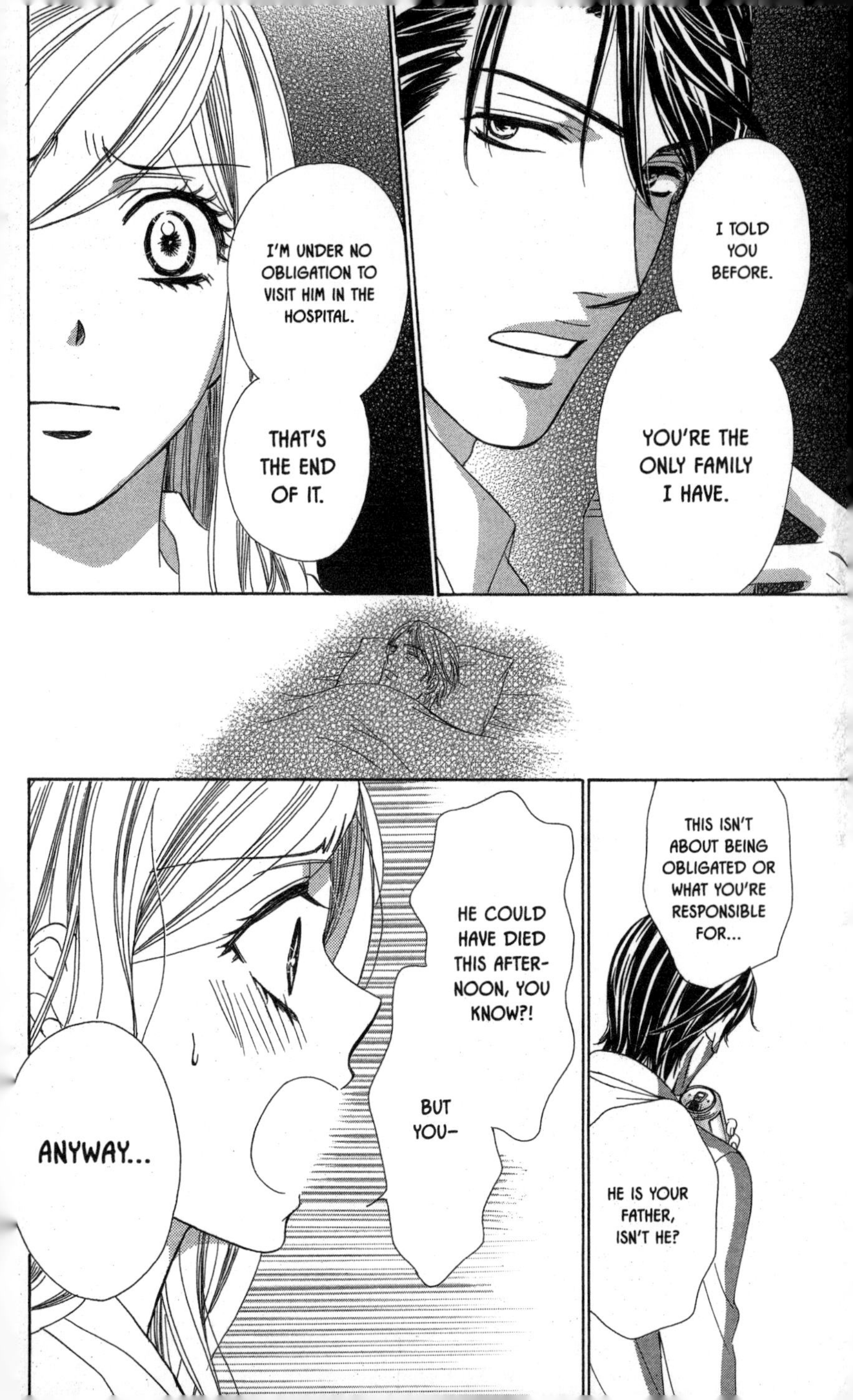
I TOLD YOU BEFORE.
YOU'RE THE ONLY FAMILY I HAVE.
I'M UNDER NO OBLIGATION TO VISIT HIM IN THE HOSPITAL.
THAT'S THE END OF IT.
THIS ISN'T ABOUT BEING OBLIGATED OR WHAT YOU'RE RESPONSIBLE FOR...
HE IS YOUR FATHER, ISN'T HE?
HE COULD HAVE DIED THIS AFTER-NOON, YOU KNOW?!
BUT YOU-
ANYWAY...

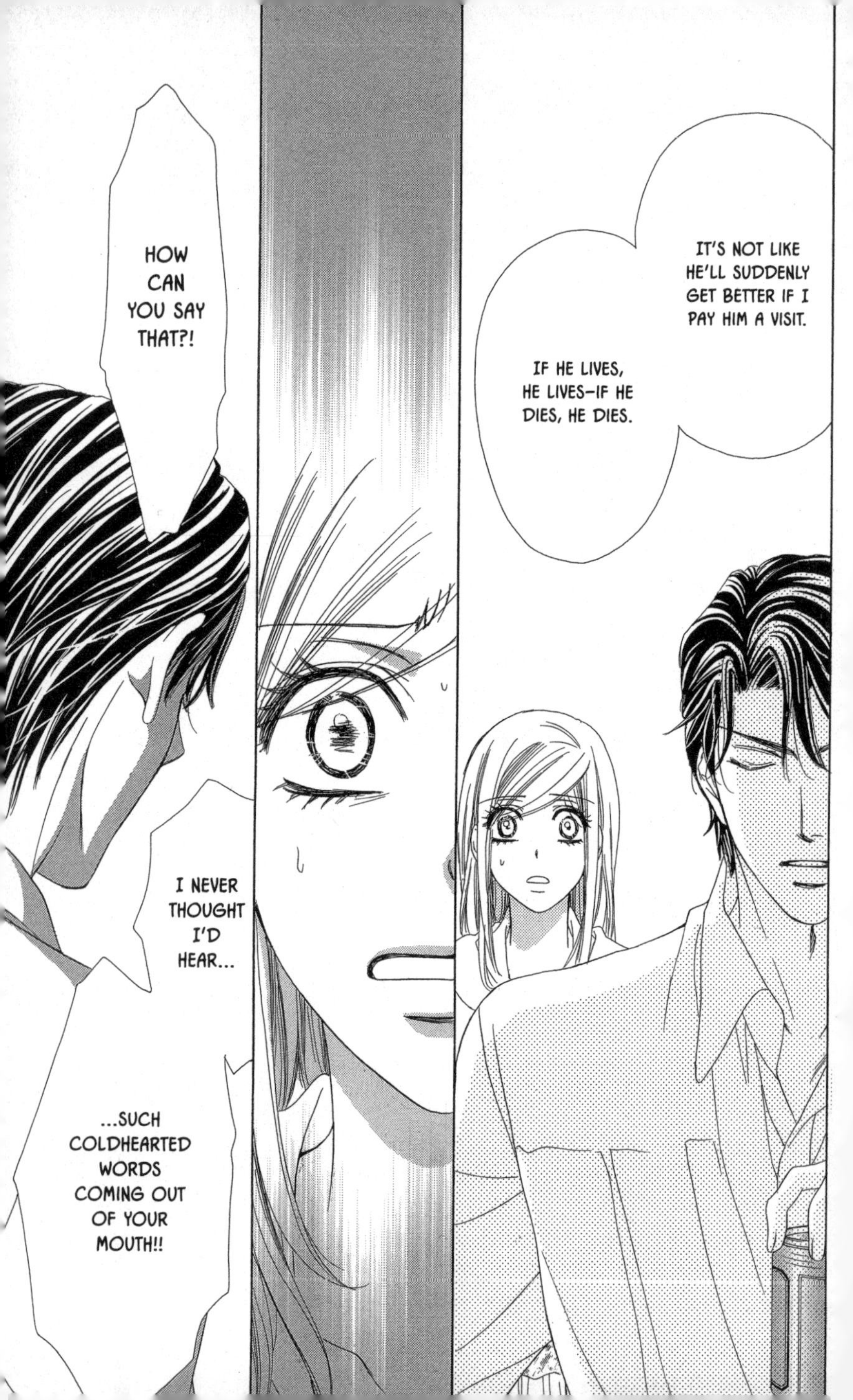
IT'S NOT LIKE HE'LL SUDDENLY GET BETTER IF I PAY HIM A VISIT.
IF HE LIVES, HE LIVES—IF HE DIES, HE DIES.
HOW CAN YOU SAY THAT?!
I NEVER THOUGHT I'D HEAR...
...SUCH COLDHEARTED WORDS COMING OUT OF YOUR MOUTH!!

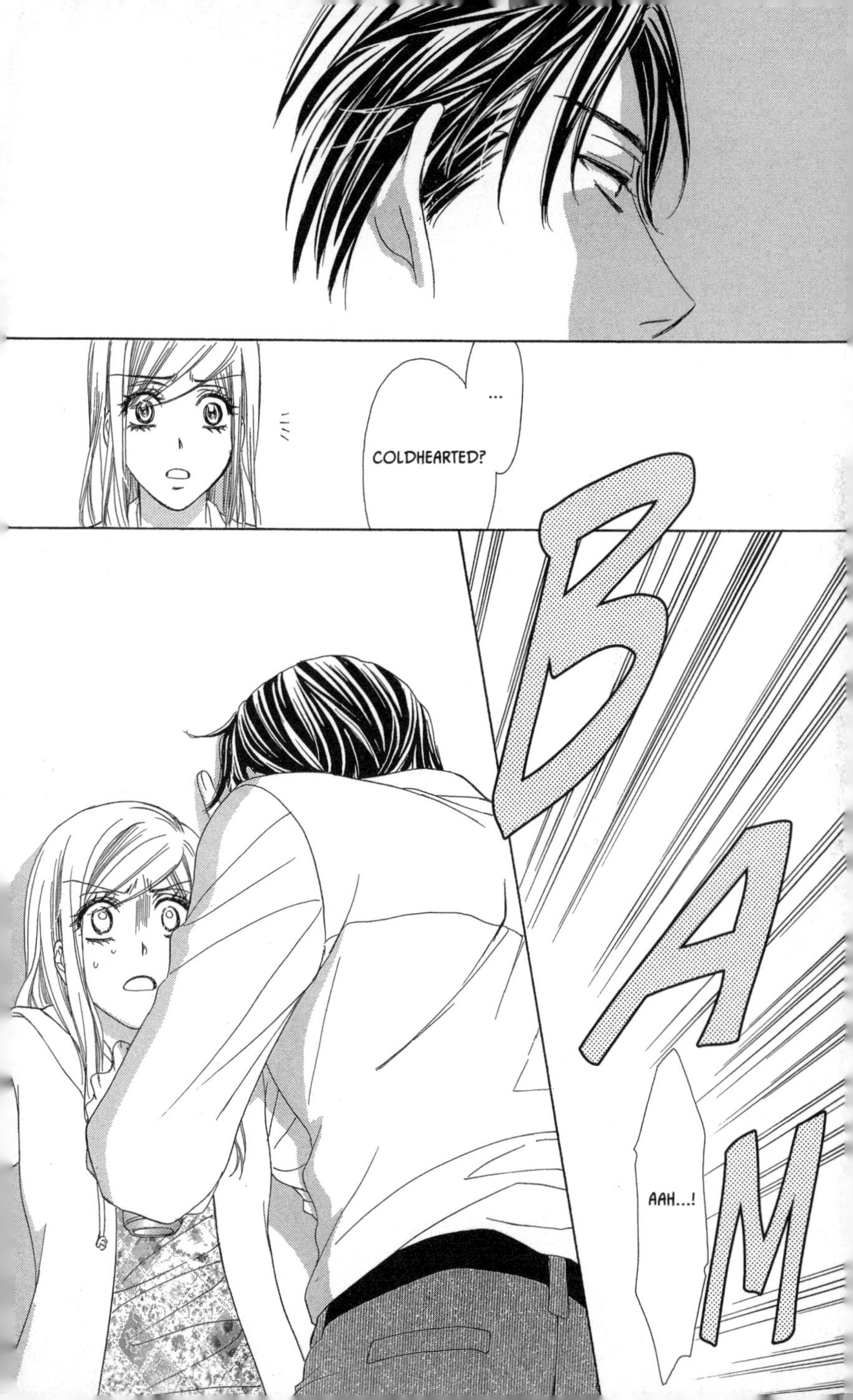
...
COLDHEARTED?
BAM
AAH...!

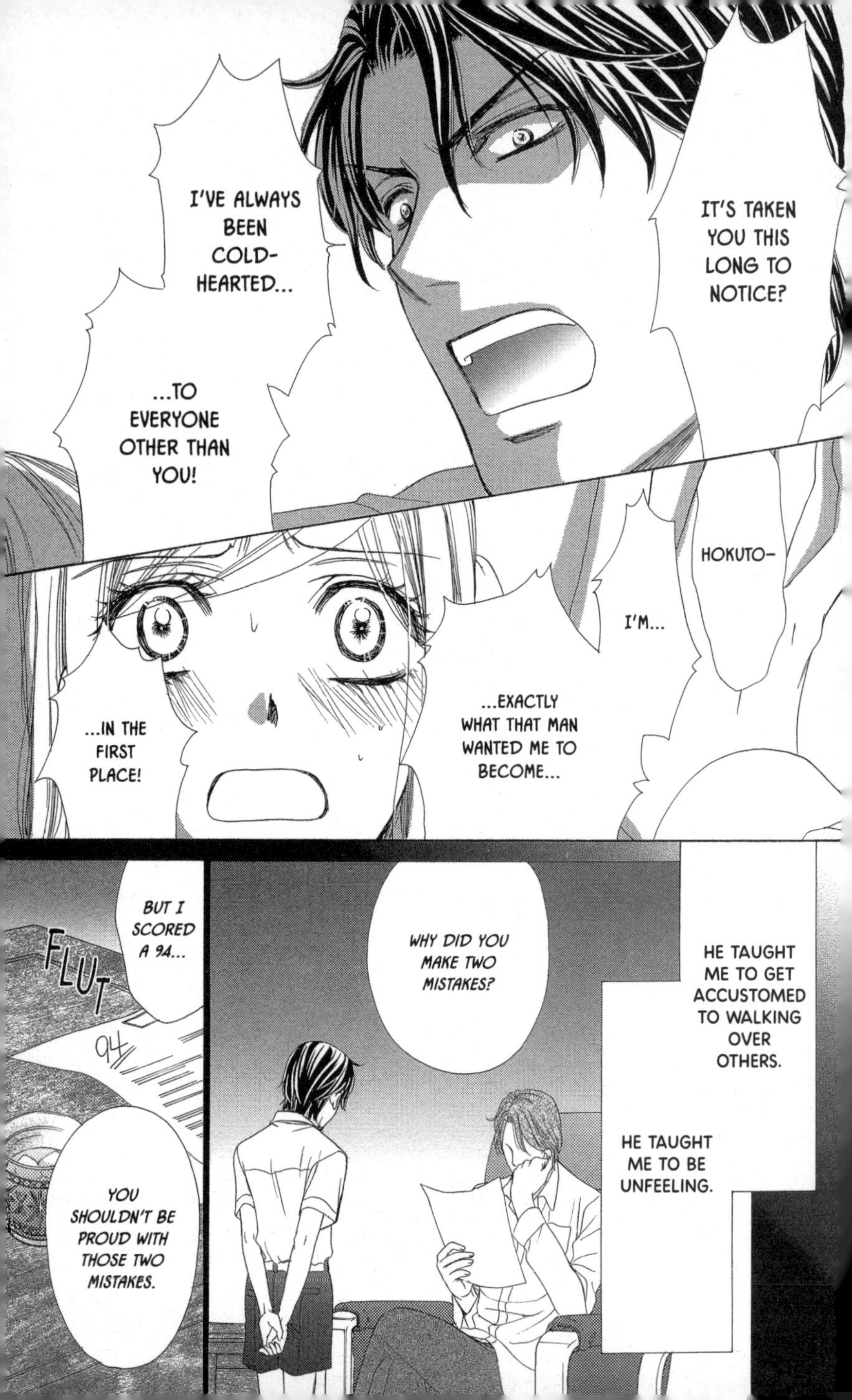
IT'S TAKEN YOU THIS LONG TO NOTICE?
I'VE ALWAYS BEEN COLD-HEARTED...
...TO EVERYONE OTHER THAN YOU!
HOKUTO–
I'M...
...EXACTLY WHAT THAT MAN WANTED ME TO BECOME...
...IN THE FIRST PLACE!
HE TAUGHT ME TO GET ACCUSTOMED TO WALKING OVER OTHERS.
HE TAUGHT ME TO BE UNFEELING.
WHY DID YOU MAKE TWO MISTAKES?
BUT I SCORED A 94...
FLUT
94
YOU SHOULDN'T BE PROUD WITH THOSE TWO MISTAKES.

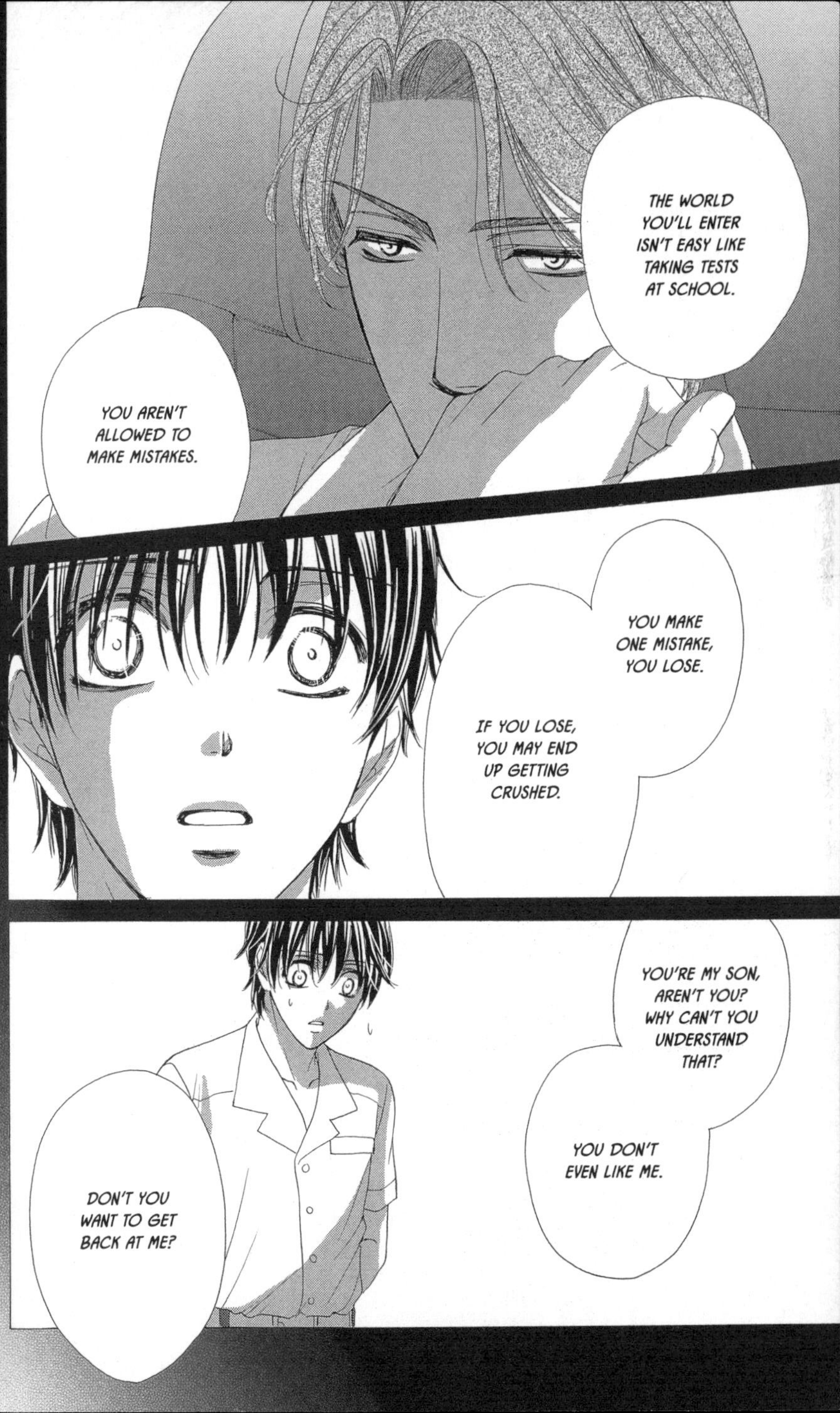
THE WORLD YOU'LL ENTER ISN'T EASY LIKE TAKING TESTS AT SCHOOL.
YOU AREN'T ALLOWED TO MAKE MISTAKES.
YOU MAKE ONE MISTAKE, YOU LOSE.
IF YOU LOSE, YOU MAY END UP GETTING CRUSHED.
YOU'RE MY SON, AREN'T YOU? WHY CAN'T YOU UNDERSTAND THAT?
YOU DON'T EVEN LIKE ME.
DON'T YOU WANT TO GET BACK AT ME?

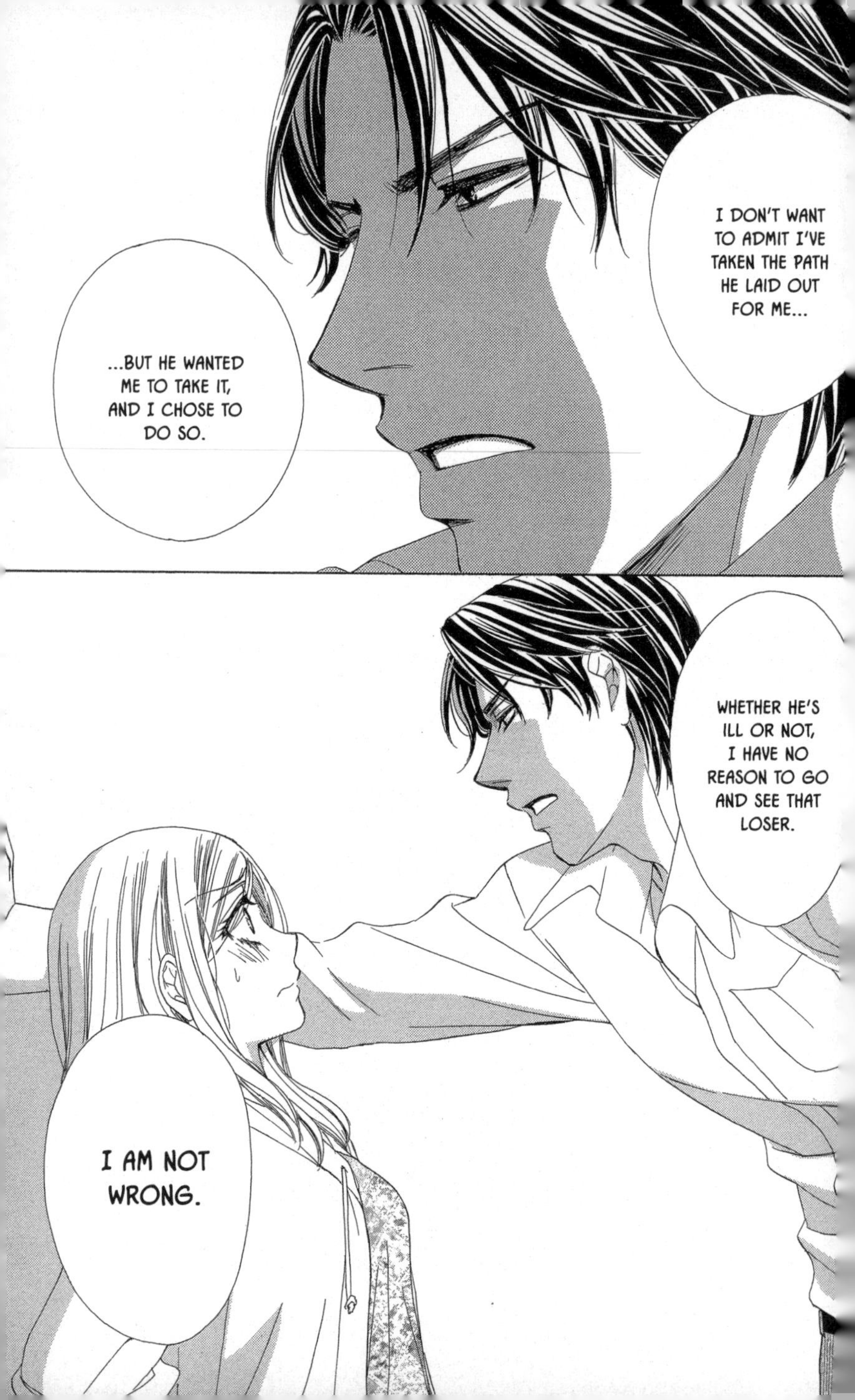
I DON'T WANT TO ADMIT I'VE TAKEN THE PATH HE LAID OUT FOR ME...
...BUT HE WANTED ME TO TAKE IT, AND I CHOSE TO DO SO.
WHETHER HE'S ILL OR NOT, I HAVE NO REASON TO GO AND SEE THAT LOSER.
I AM NOT WRONG.

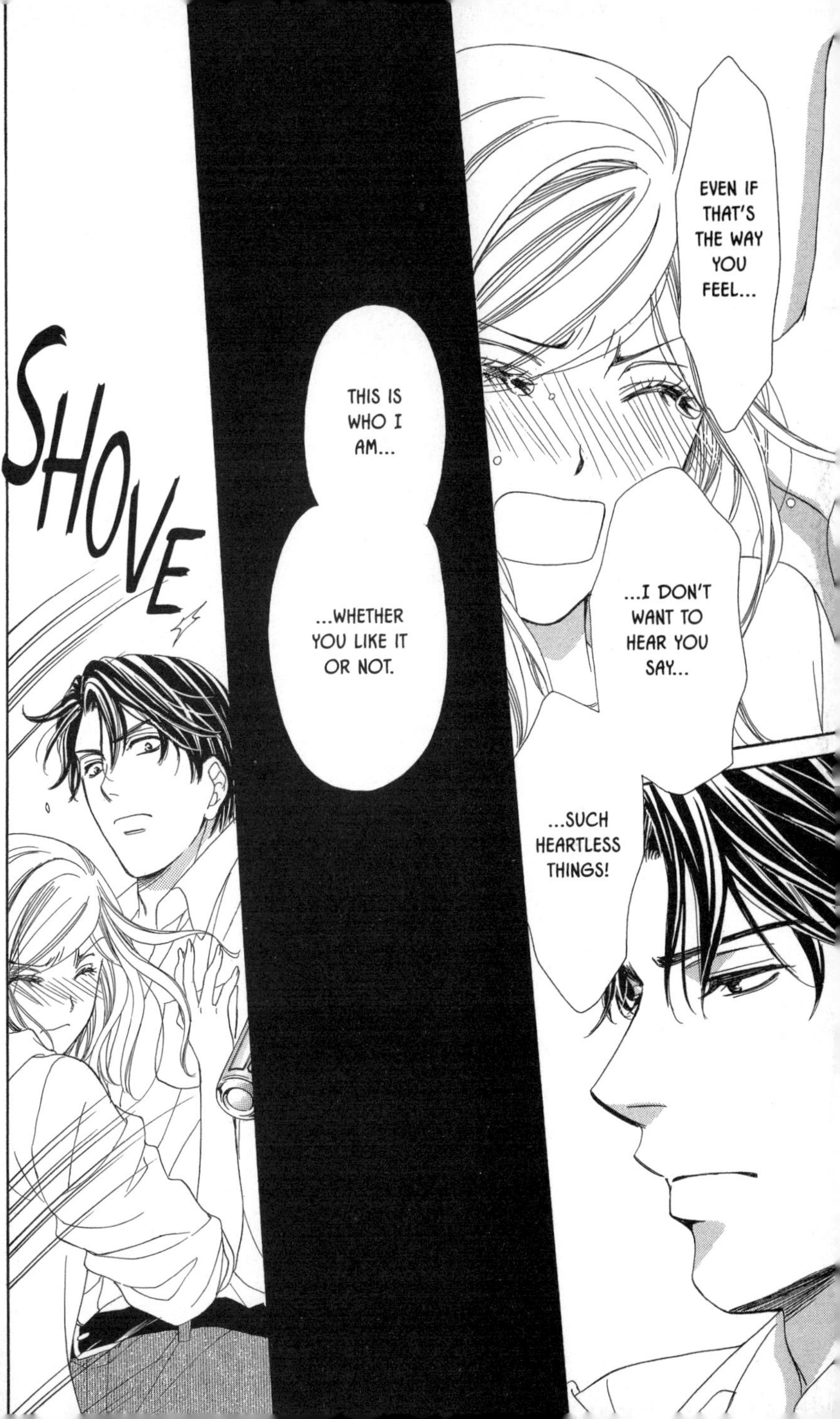
EVEN IF THAT'S THE WAY YOU FEEL...
...I DON'T WANT TO HEAR YOU SAY...
...SUCH HEARTLESS THINGS!
THIS IS WHO I AM...
...WHETHER YOU LIKE IT OR NOT.
SHOVE

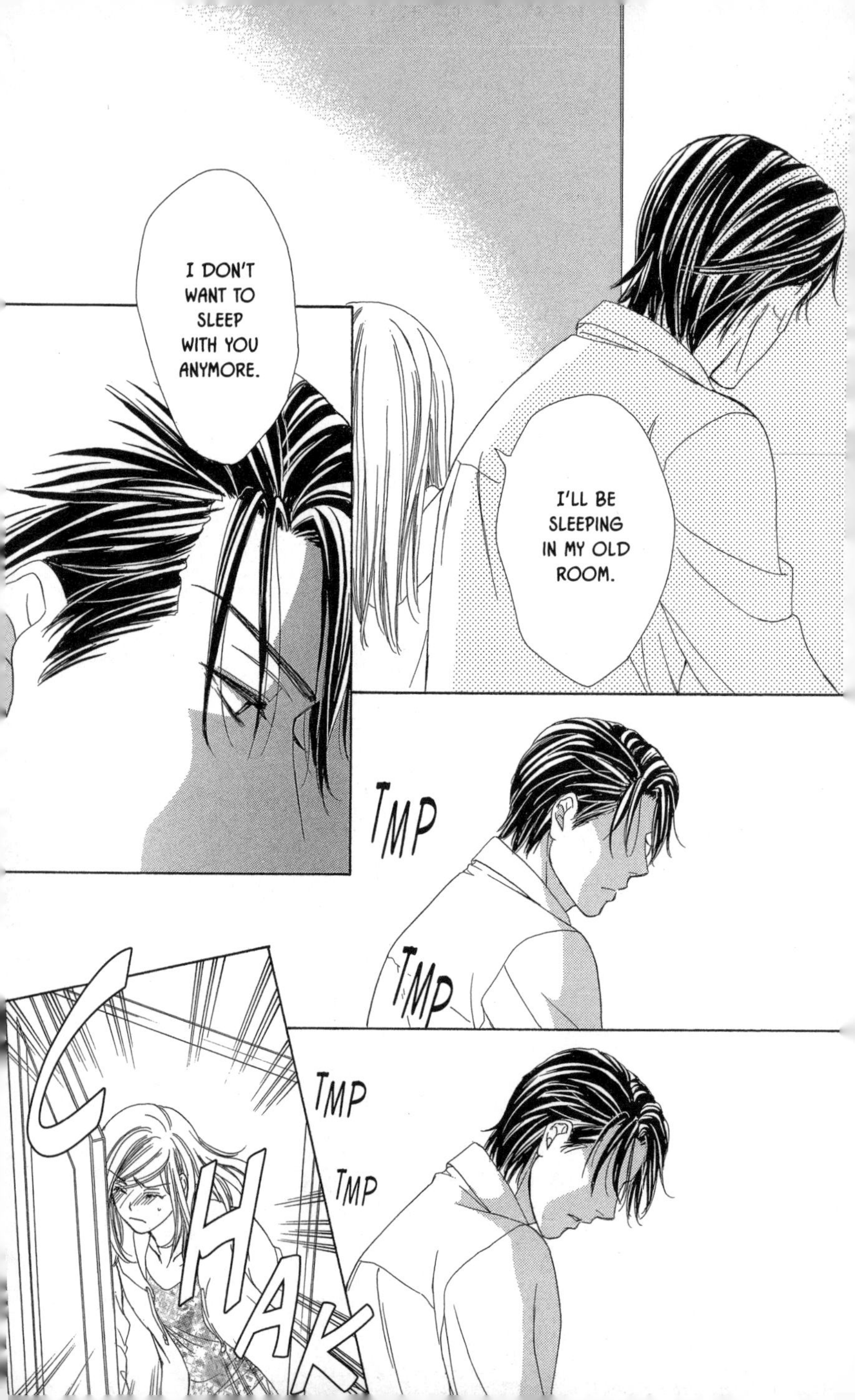
I'LL BE SLEEPING IN MY OLD ROOM.
I DON'T WANT TO SLEEP WITH YOU ANYMORE.
TMP
TMP
TMP
TMP
CHAK

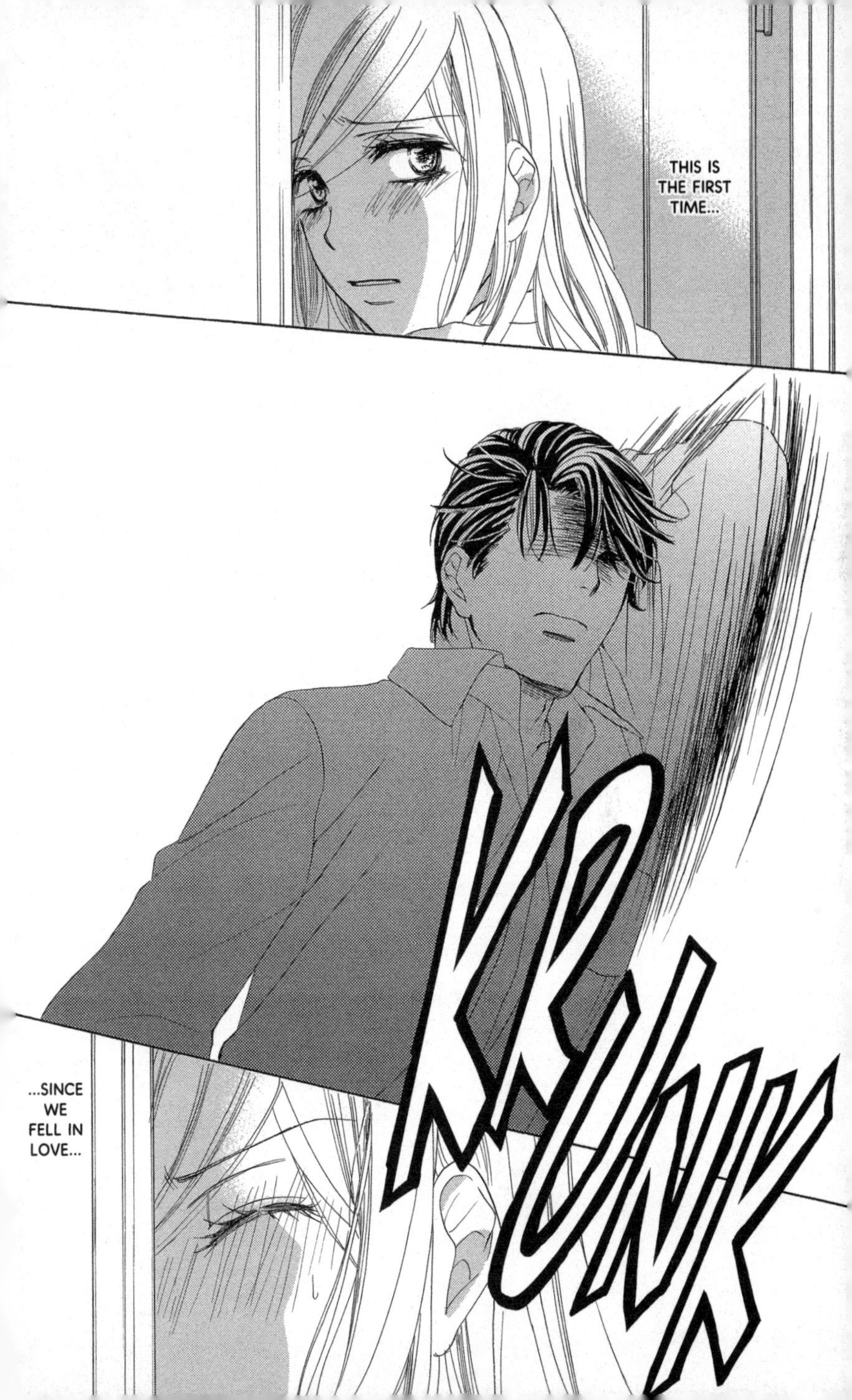
THIS IS THE FIRST TIME...
KLUNK
...SINCE WE FELL IN LOVE...

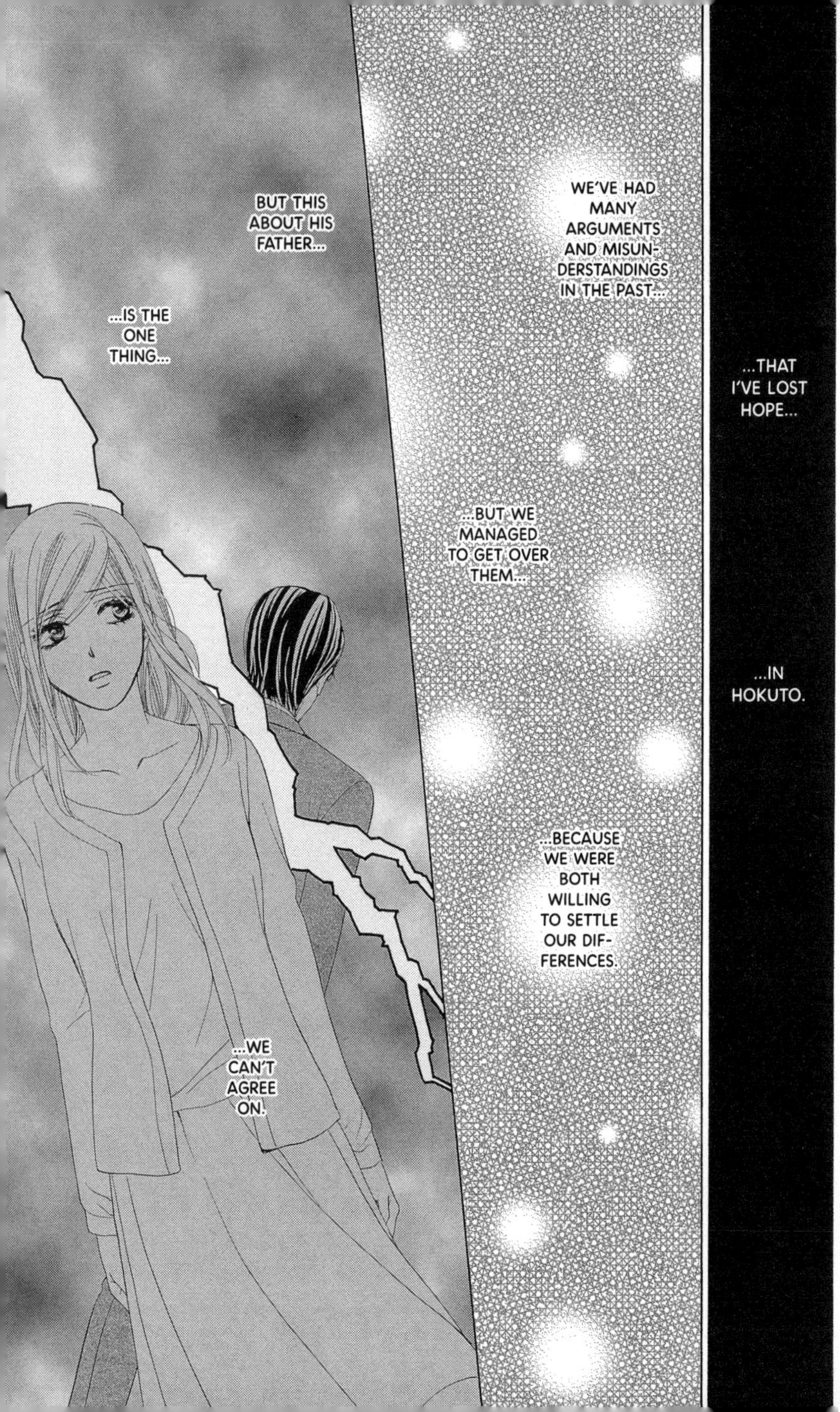
...THAT I'VE LOST HOPE...
...IN HOKUTO.
WE'VE HAD MANY ARGUMENTS AND MISUN- DERSTANDINGS IN THE PAST...
...BUT WE MANAGED TO GET OVER THEM...
...BECAUSE WE WERE BOTH WILLING TO SETTLE OUR DIF- FERENCES.
BUT THIS ABOUT HIS FATHER...
...IS THE ONE THING...
...WE CAN'T AGREE ON.

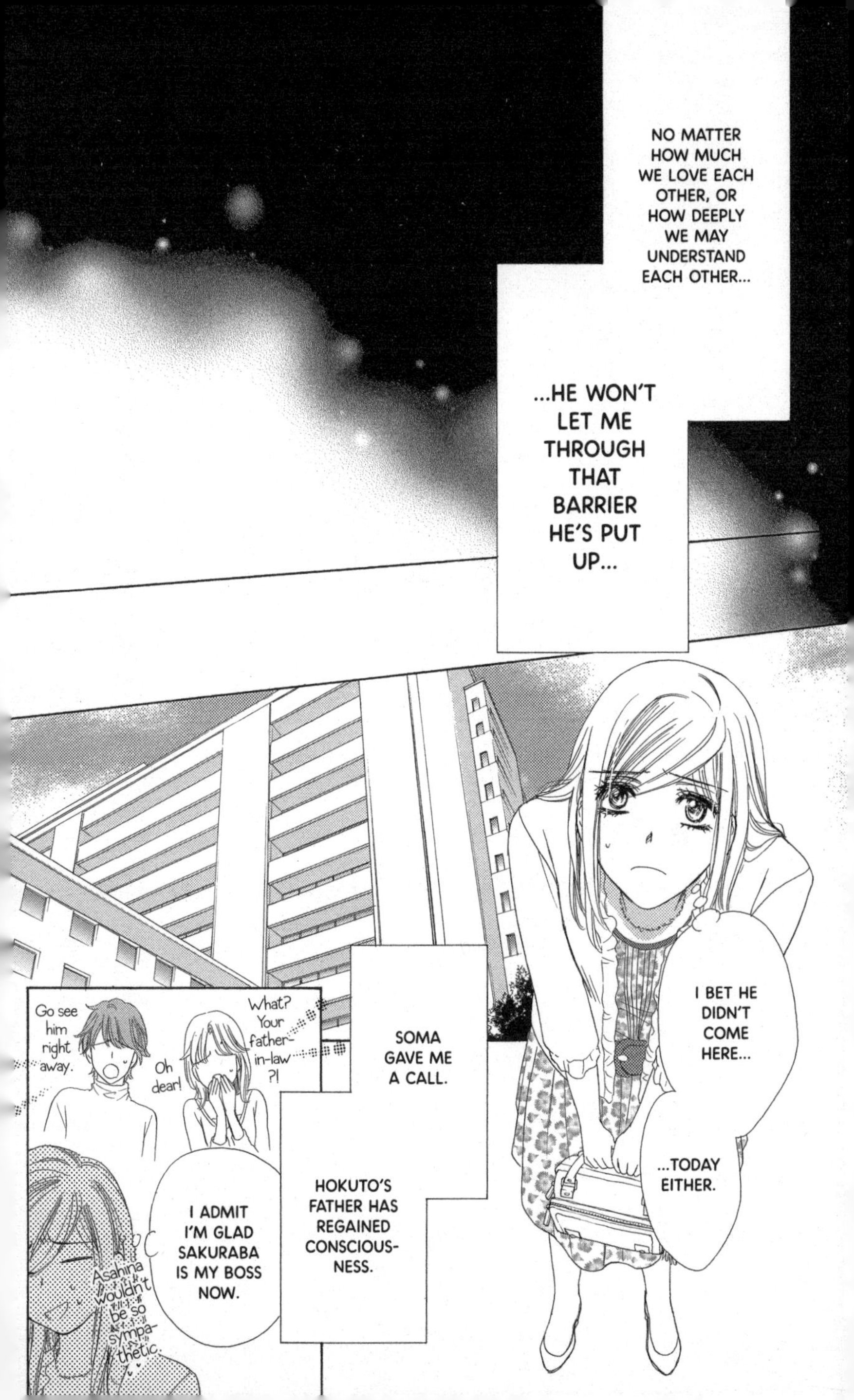
NO MATTER HOW MUCH WE LOVE EACH OTHER, OR HOW DEEPLY WE MAY UNDERSTAND EACH OTHER...
...HE WON'T LET ME THROUGH THAT BARRIER HE'S PUT UP...
I BET HE DIDN'T COME HERE...
...TODAY EITHER.
SOMA GAVE ME A CALL.
HOKUTO'S FATHER HAS REGAINED CONSCIOUS-NESS.
What? Your father-in-law?!
Oh dear!
Go see him right away.
I ADMIT I'M GLAD SAKURABA IS MY BOSS NOW.
Asahina wouldn't be so sympa-thetic.

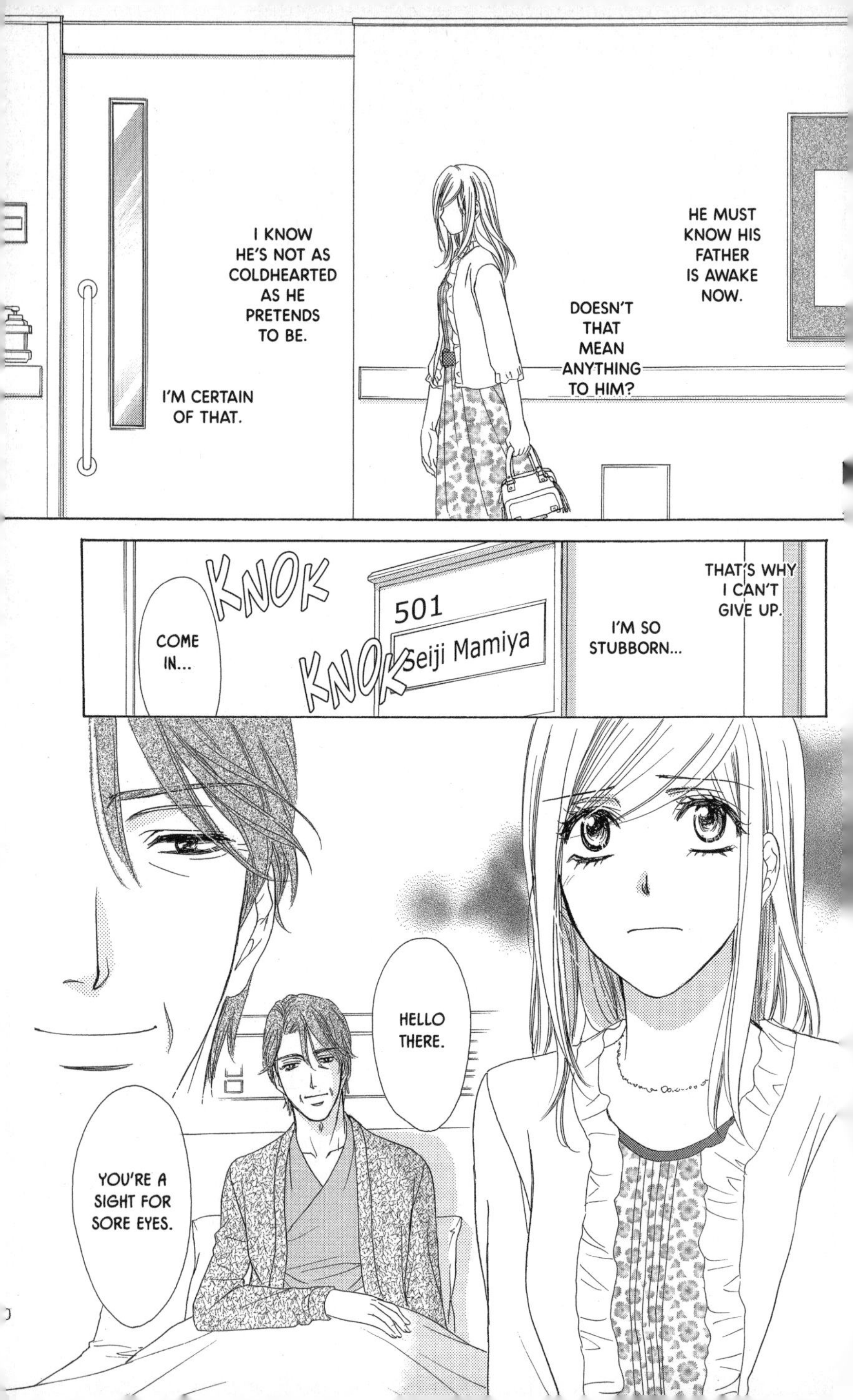
HE MUST KNOW HIS FATHER IS AWAKE NOW.
DOESN'T THAT MEAN ANYTHING TO HIM?
I KNOW HE'S NOT AS COLDHEARTED AS HE PRETENDS TO BE.
I'M CERTAIN OF THAT.
THAT'S WHY I CAN'T GIVE UP.
I'M SO STUBBORN...
501
Seiji Mamiya
KNOK
KNOK
COME IN...
HELLO THERE.
YOU'RE A SIGHT FOR SORE EYES.

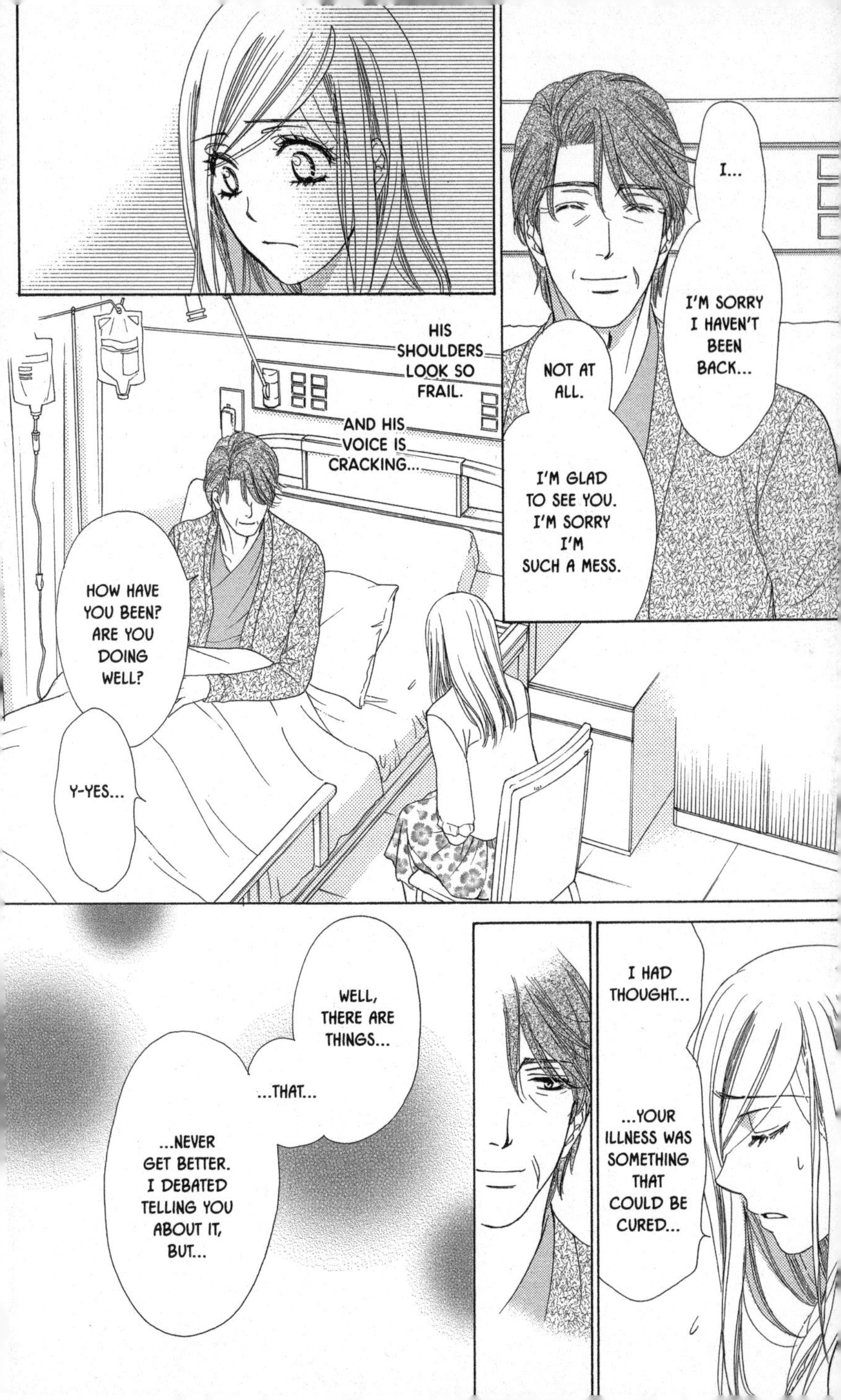
I...
I'M SORRY I HAVEN'T BEEN BACK...
NOT AT ALL.
I'M GLAD TO SEE YOU. I'M SORRY I'M SUCH A MESS.
HIS SHOULDERS LOOK SO FRAIL.
AND HIS VOICE IS CRACKING...
HOW HAVE YOU BEEN? ARE YOU DOING WELL?
Y-YES...
I HAD THOUGHT...
...YOUR ILLNESS WAS SOMETHING THAT COULD BE CURED...
WELL, THERE ARE THINGS...
...THAT...
...NEVER GET BETTER. I DEBATED TELLING YOU ABOUT IT, BUT...

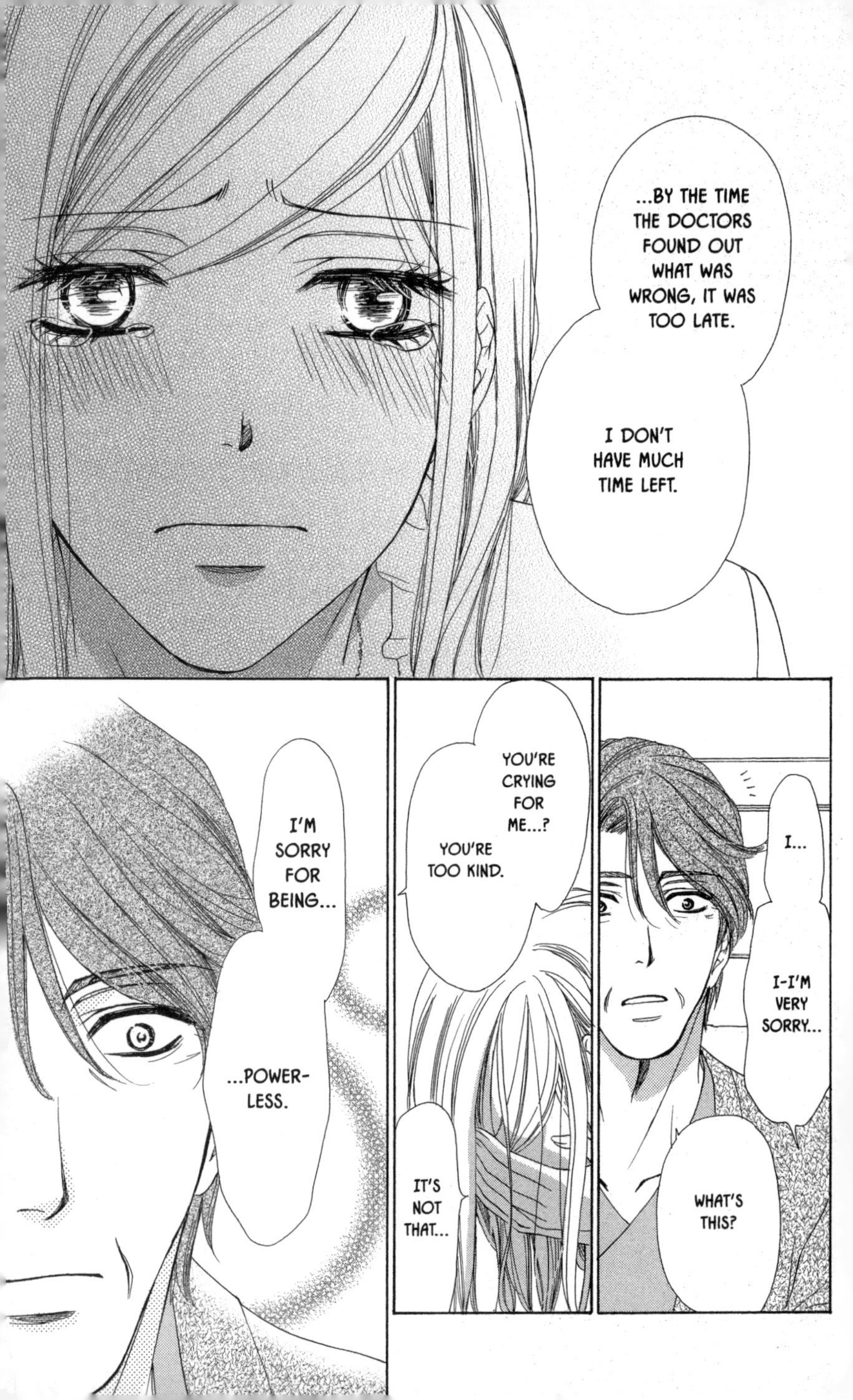
...BY THE TIME THE DOCTORS FOUND OUT WHAT WAS WRONG, IT WAS TOO LATE.
I DON'T HAVE MUCH TIME LEFT.
I...
I-I'M VERY SORRY...
WHAT'S THIS?
YOU'RE CRYING FOR ME...?
YOU'RE TOO KIND.
IT'S NOT THAT...
I'M SORRY FOR BEING...
...POWER-LESS.

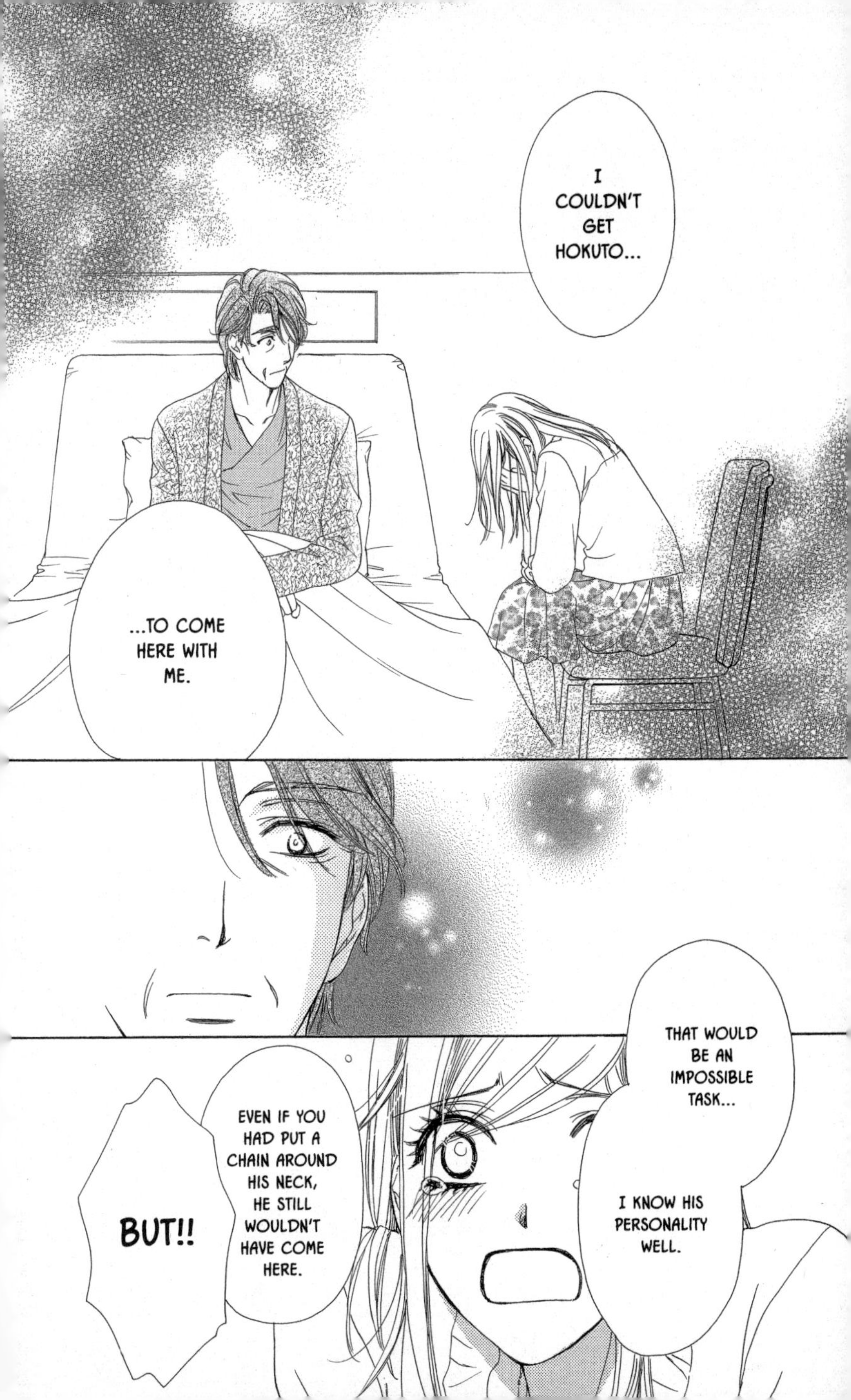
I COULDN'T GET HOKUTO...
...TO COME HERE WITH ME.
THAT WOULD BE AN IMPOSSIBLE TASK...
I KNOW HIS PERSONALITY WELL.
EVEN IF YOU HAD PUT A CHAIN AROUND HIS NECK, HE STILL WOULDN'T HAVE COME HERE.
BUT!!

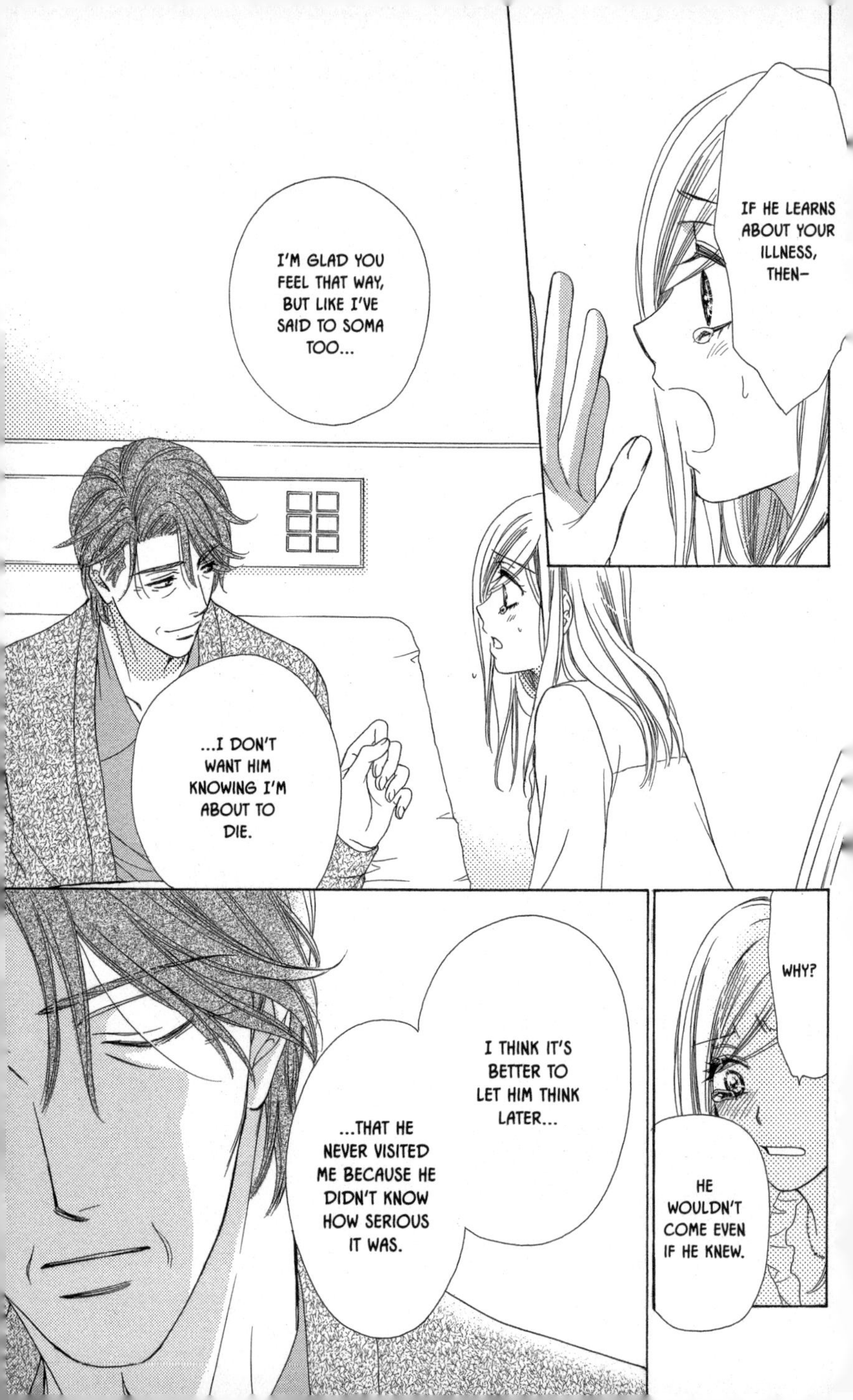
IF HE LEARNS ABOUT YOUR ILLNESS, THEN–
I'M GLAD YOU FEEL THAT WAY, BUT LIKE I'VE SAID TO SOMA TOO...
...I DON'T WANT HIM KNOWING I'M ABOUT TO DIE.
WHY?
HE WOULDN'T COME EVEN IF HE KNEW.
I THINK IT'S BETTER TO LET HIM THINK LATER...
...THAT HE NEVER VISITED ME BECAUSE HE DIDN'T KNOW HOW SERIOUS IT WAS.

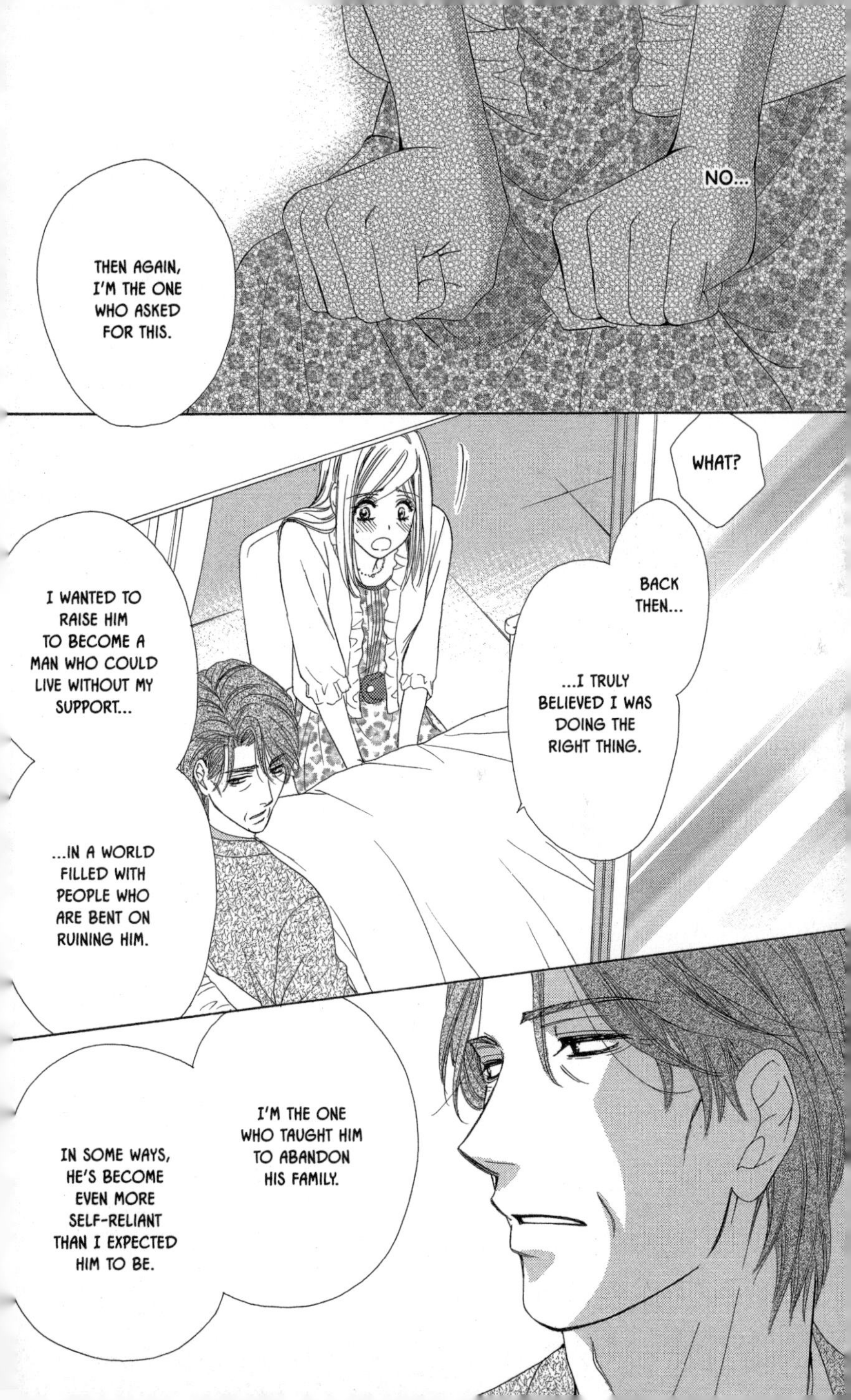
NO...
THEN AGAIN, I'M THE ONE WHO ASKED FOR THIS.
WHAT?
BACK THEN...
...I TRULY BELIEVED I WAS DOING THE RIGHT THING.
I WANTED TO RAISE HIM TO BECOME A MAN WHO COULD LIVE WITHOUT MY SUPPORT...
...IN A WORLD FILLED WITH PEOPLE WHO ARE BENT ON RUINING HIM.
I'M THE ONE WHO TAUGHT HIM TO ABANDON HIS FAMILY.
IN SOME WAYS, HE'S BECOME EVEN MORE SELF-RELIANT THAN I EXPECTED HIM TO BE.

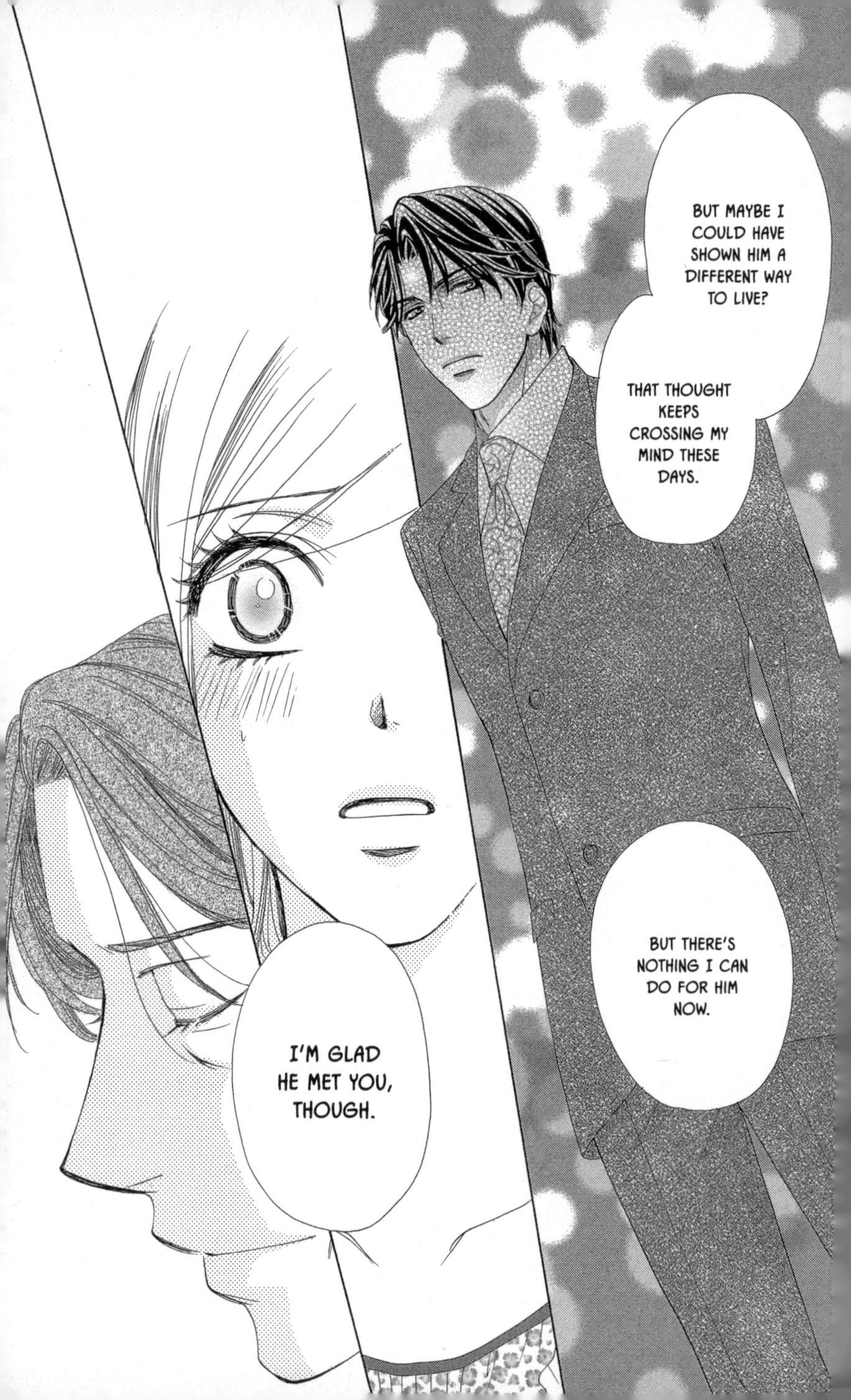
BUT MAYBE I COULD HAVE SHOWN HIM A DIFFERENT WAY TO LIVE?
THAT THOUGHT KEEPS CROSSING MY MIND THESE DAYS.
BUT THERE'S NOTHING I CAN DO FOR HIM NOW.
I'M GLAD HE MET YOU, THOUGH.

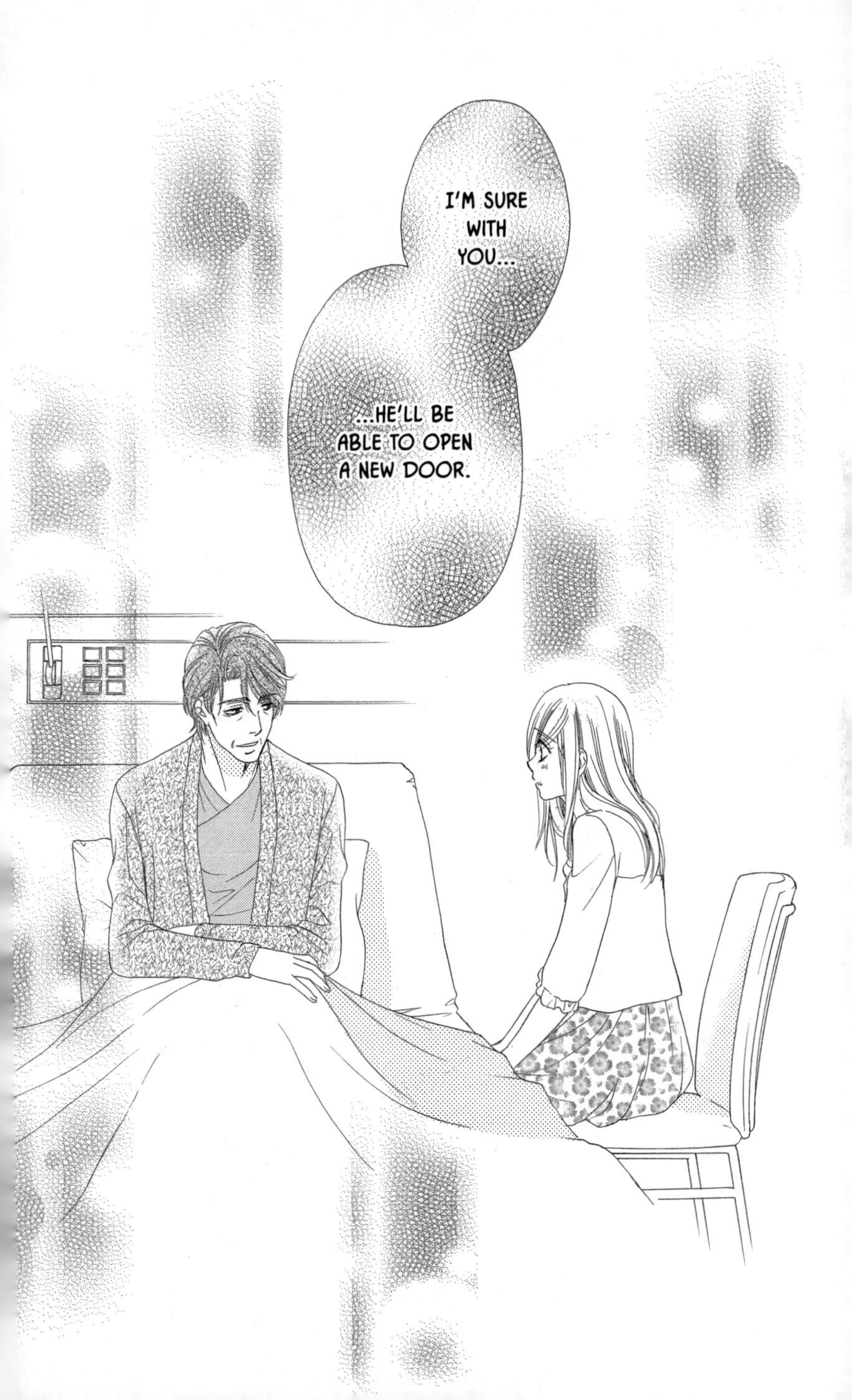
I'M SURE WITH YOU...
...HE'LL BE ABLE TO OPEN A NEW DOOR.

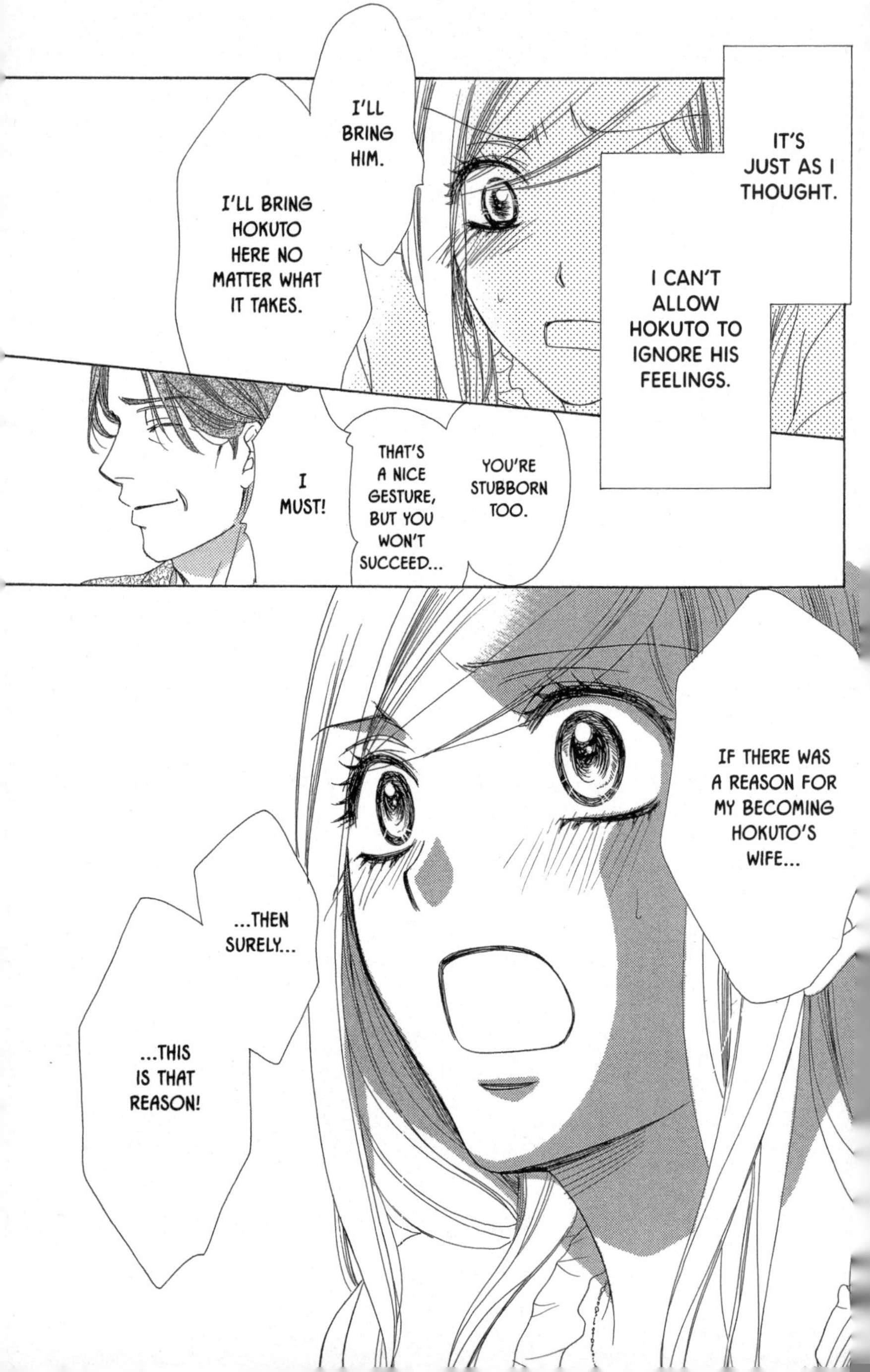
IT'S JUST AS I THOUGHT.
I CAN'T ALLOW HOKUTO TO IGNORE HIS FEELINGS.
I'LL BRING HIM.
I'LL BRING HOKUTO HERE NO MATTER WHAT IT TAKES.
YOU'RE STUBBORN TOO.
THAT'S A NICE GESTURE, BUT YOU WON'T SUCCEED...
I MUST!
IF THERE WAS A REASON FOR MY BECOMING HOKUTO'S WIFE...
...THEN SURELY...
...THIS IS THAT REASON!

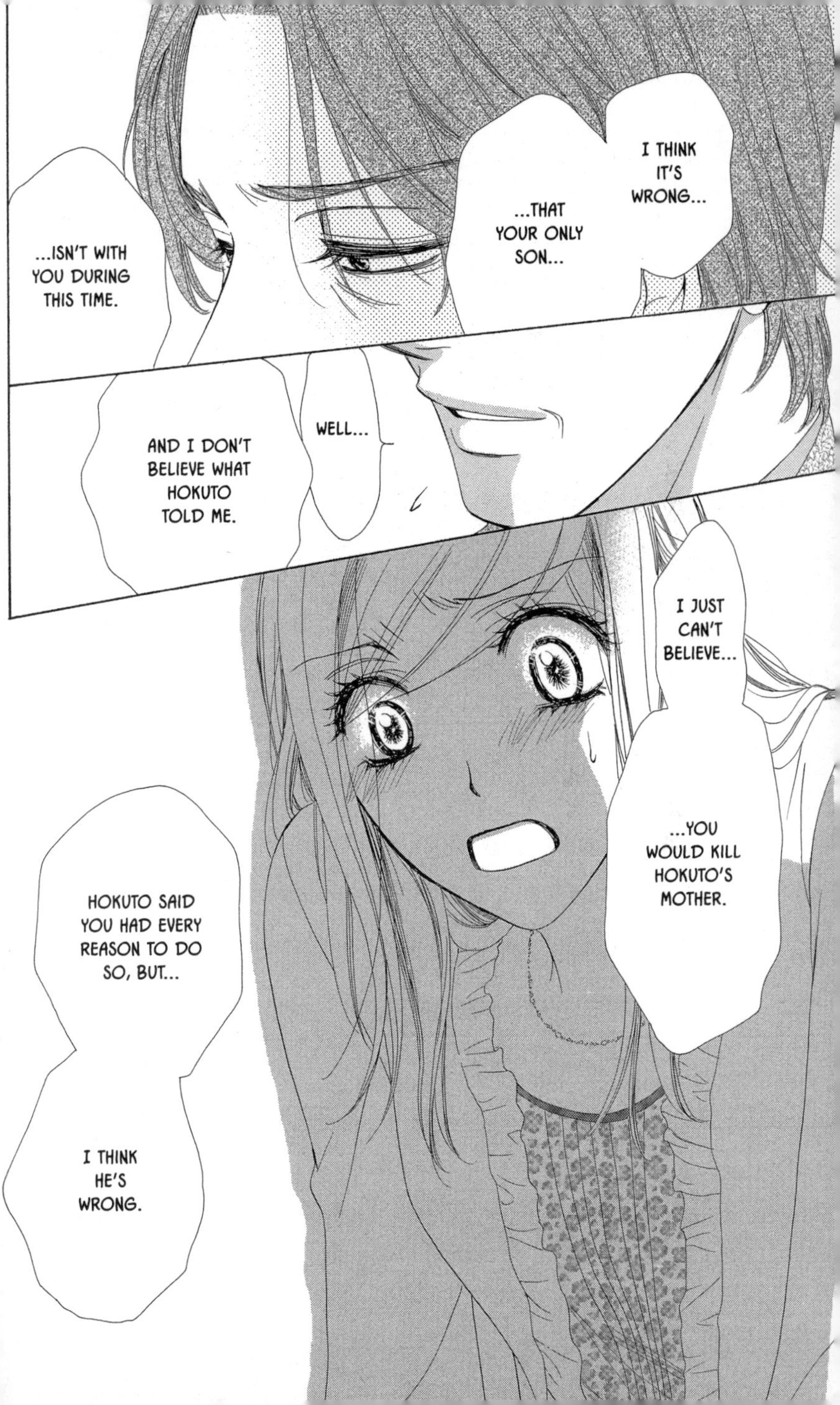
I THINK IT'S WRONG...
...THAT YOUR ONLY SON...
...ISN'T WITH YOU DURING THIS TIME.
WELL...
AND I DON'T BELIEVE WHAT HOKUTO TOLD ME.
I JUST CAN'T BELIEVE...
...YOU WOULD KILL HOKUTO'S MOTHER.
HOKUTO SAID YOU HAD EVERY REASON TO DO SO, BUT...
I THINK HE'S WRONG.

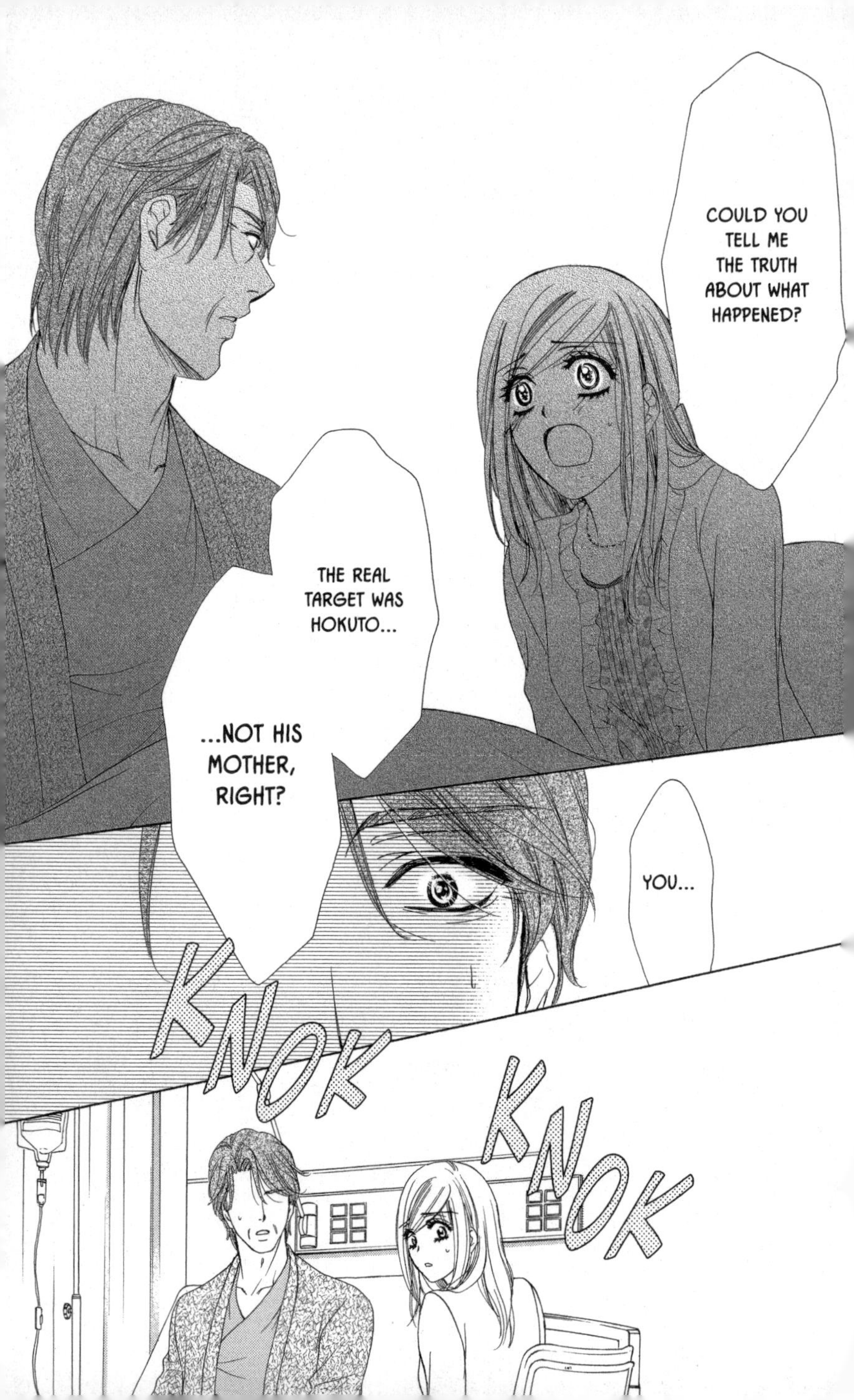
COULD YOU TELL ME THE TRUTH ABOUT WHAT HAPPENED?
THE REAL TARGET WAS HOKUTO...
...NOT HIS MOTHER, RIGHT?
YOU...
KNOK
KNOK

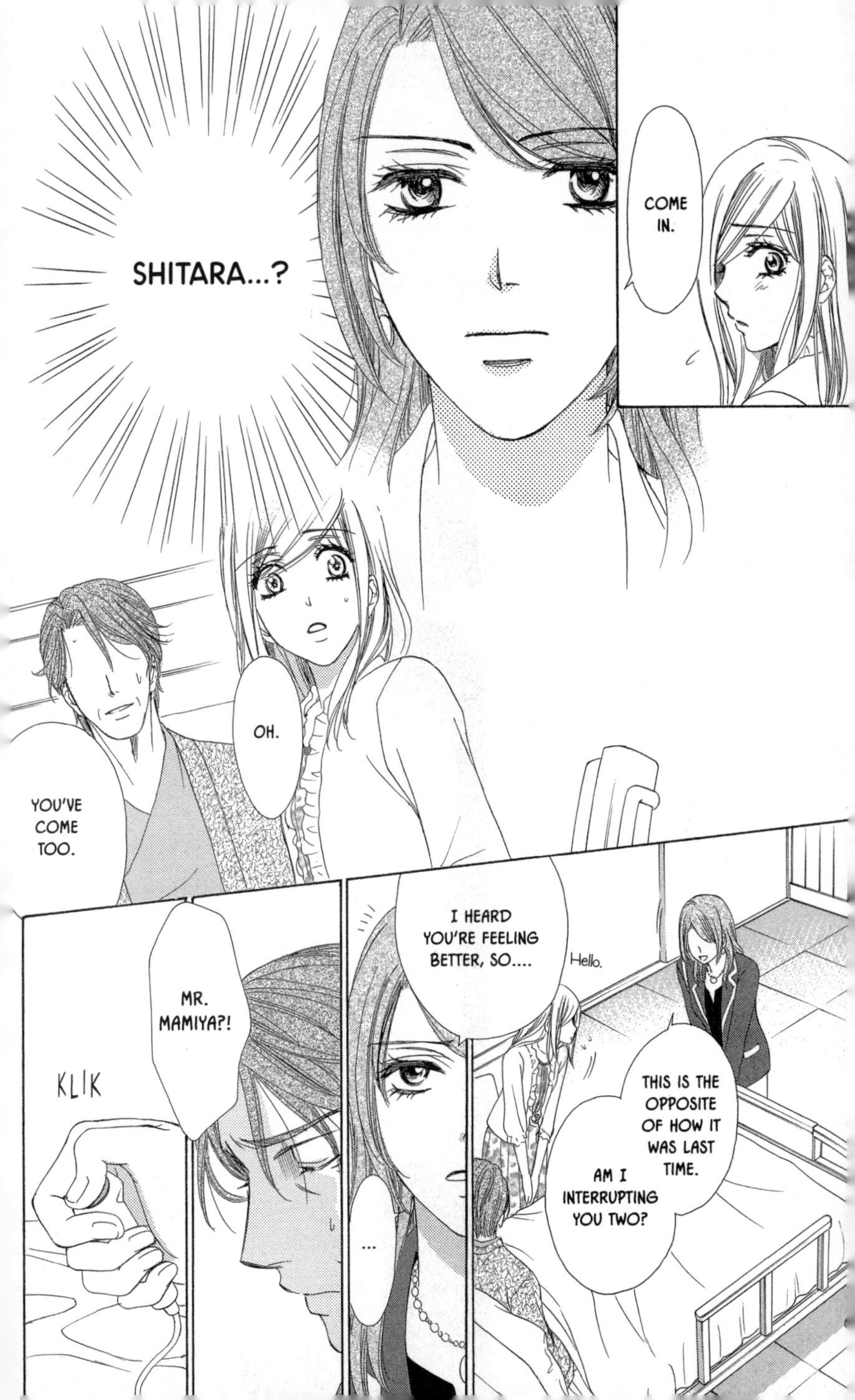
COME IN.
SHITARA...?
OH.
YOU'VE COME TOO.
Hello.
I HEARD YOU'RE FEELING BETTER, SO....
THIS IS THE OPPOSITE OF HOW IT WAS LAST TIME.
AM I INTERRUPTING YOU TWO?
...
MR. MAMIYA?!
KLIK

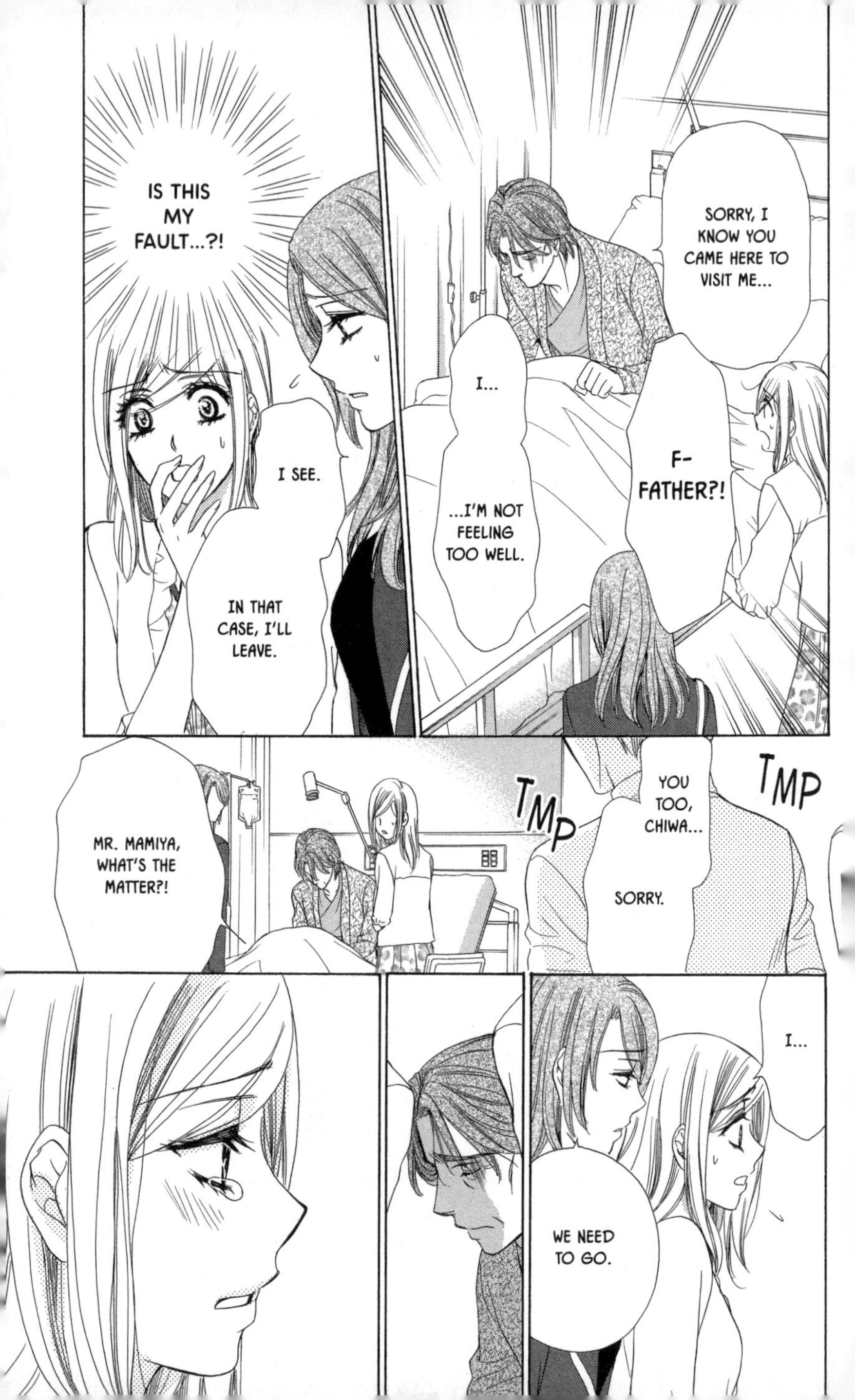
SORRY, I KNOW YOU CAME HERE TO VISIT ME...
F-FATHER?!
I...
...I'M NOT FEELING TOO WELL.
I SEE.
IN THAT CASE, I'LL LEAVE.
IS THIS MY FAULT...?!
TMP
YOU TOO, CHIWA...
SORRY.
TMP
MR. MAMIYA, WHAT'S THE MATTER?!
I...
WE NEED TO GO.

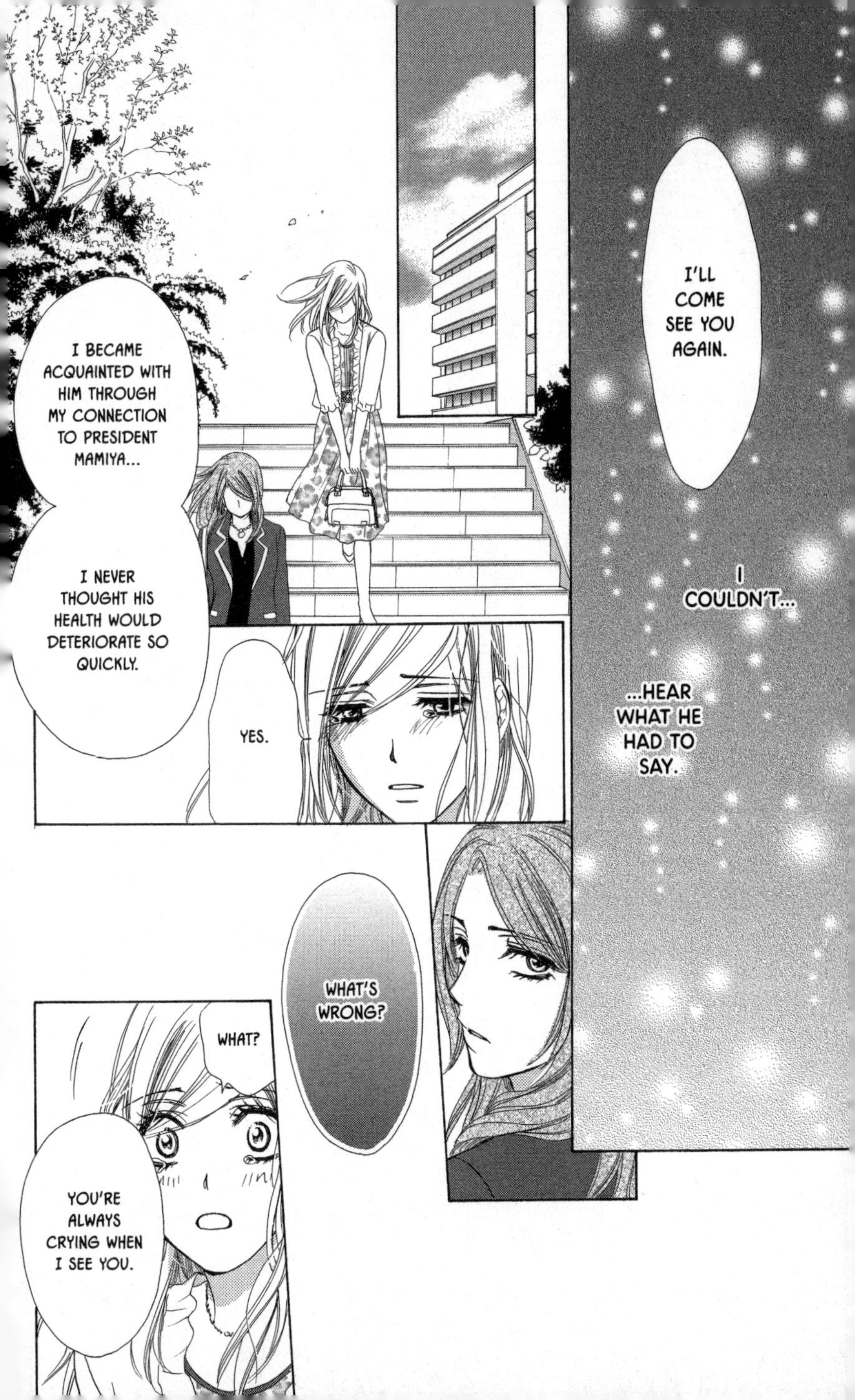
I'LL COME SEE YOU AGAIN.
I COULDN'T...
...HEAR WHAT HE HAD TO SAY.
I BECAME ACQUAINTED WITH HIM THROUGH MY CONNECTION TO PRESIDENT MAMIYA...
I NEVER THOUGHT HIS HEALTH WOULD DETERIORATE SO QUICKLY.
YES.
WHAT'S WRONG?
WHAT?
YOU'RE ALWAYS CRYING WHEN I SEE YOU.

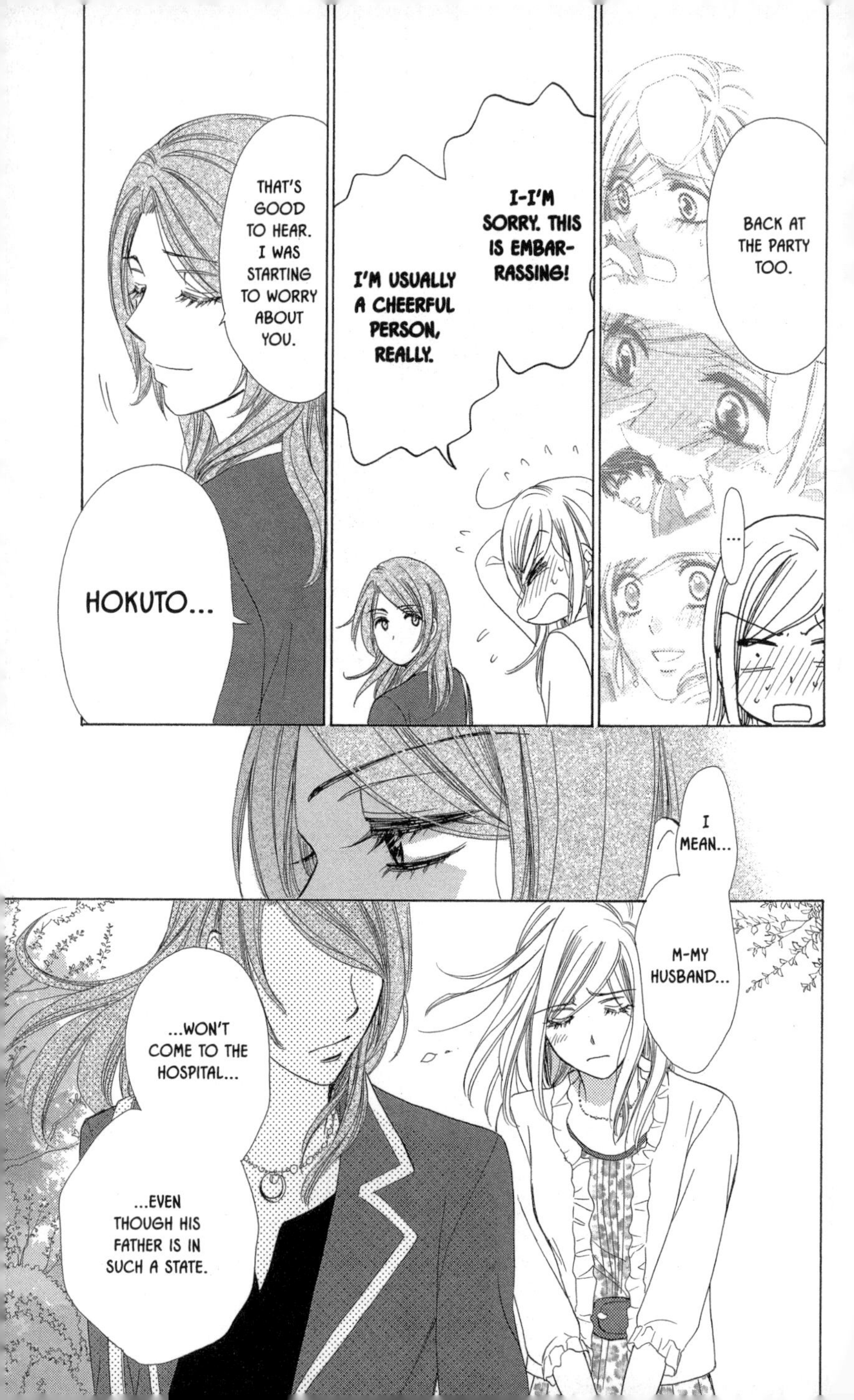
BACK AT THE PARTY TOO.
...
I-I'M SORRY. THIS IS EMBARRASSING!
I'M USUALLY A CHEERFUL PERSON, REALLY.
THAT'S GOOD TO HEAR. I WAS STARTING TO WORRY ABOUT YOU.
HOKUTO...
I MEAN...
M-MY HUSBAND...
...WON'T COME TO THE HOSPITAL...
...EVEN THOUGH HIS FATHER IS IN SUCH A STATE.

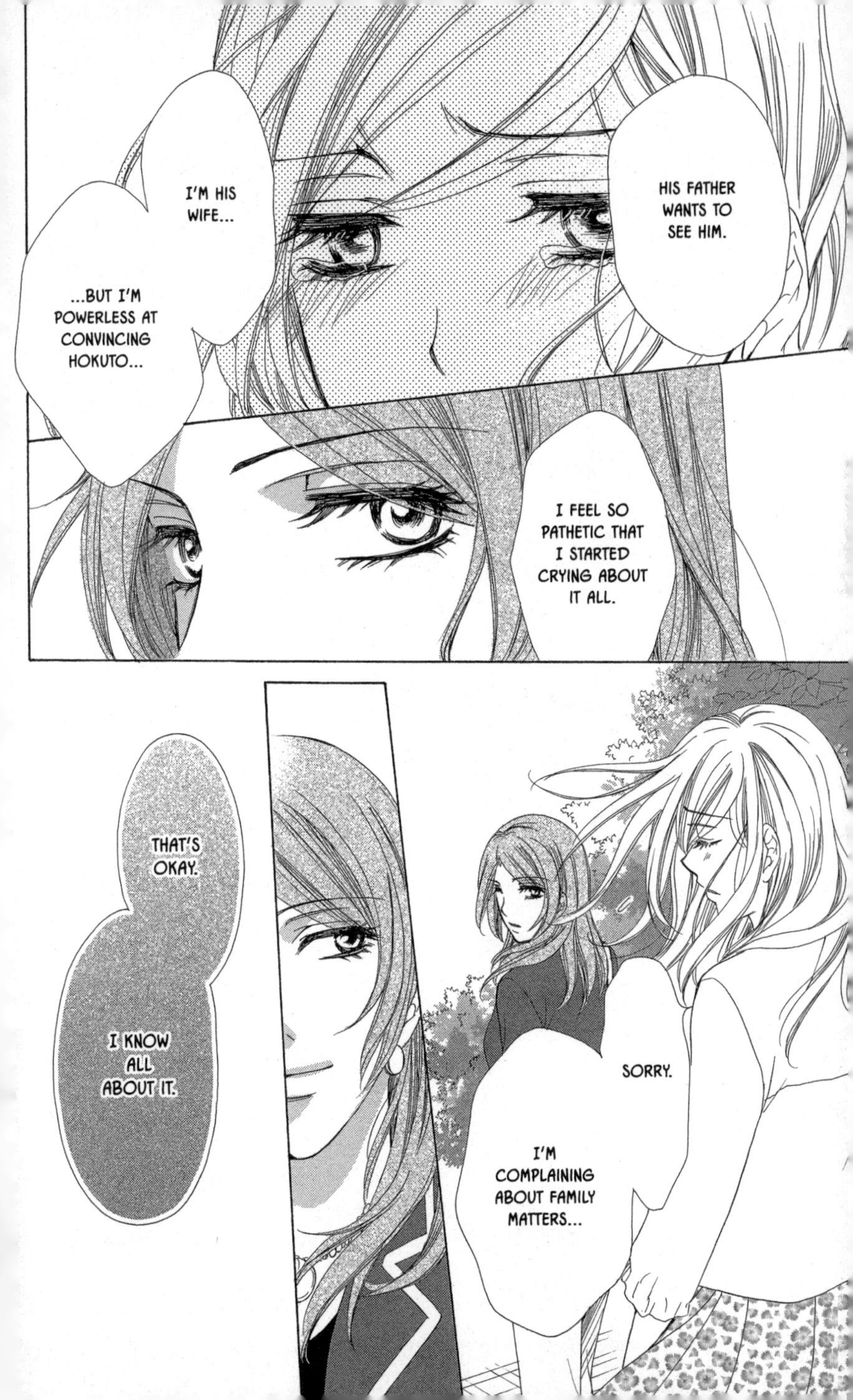
HIS FATHER WANTS TO SEE HIM.
I'M HIS WIFE...
...BUT I'M POWERLESS AT CONVINCING HOKUTO...
I FEEL SO PATHETIC THAT I STARTED CRYING ABOUT IT ALL.
SORRY.
I'M COMPLAINING ABOUT FAMILY MATTERS...
THAT'S OKAY.
I KNOW ALL ABOUT IT.

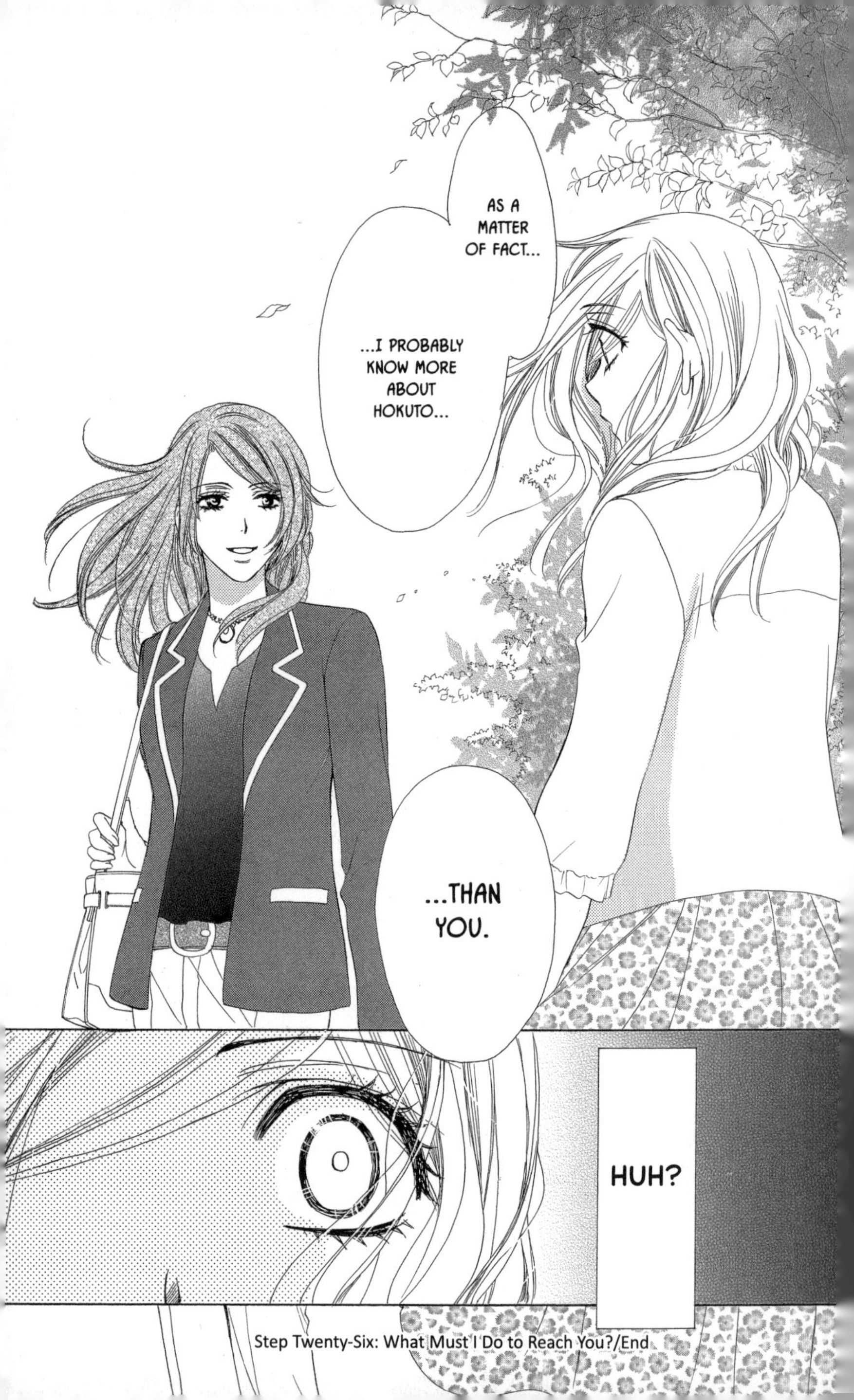
AS A MATTER OF FACT...
...I PROBABLY KNOW MORE ABOUT HOKUTO...
...THAN YOU.
HUH?

Step Twenty-Six: What Must I Do to Reach You?/End

Step Twenty-Seven: Can We Make Up?

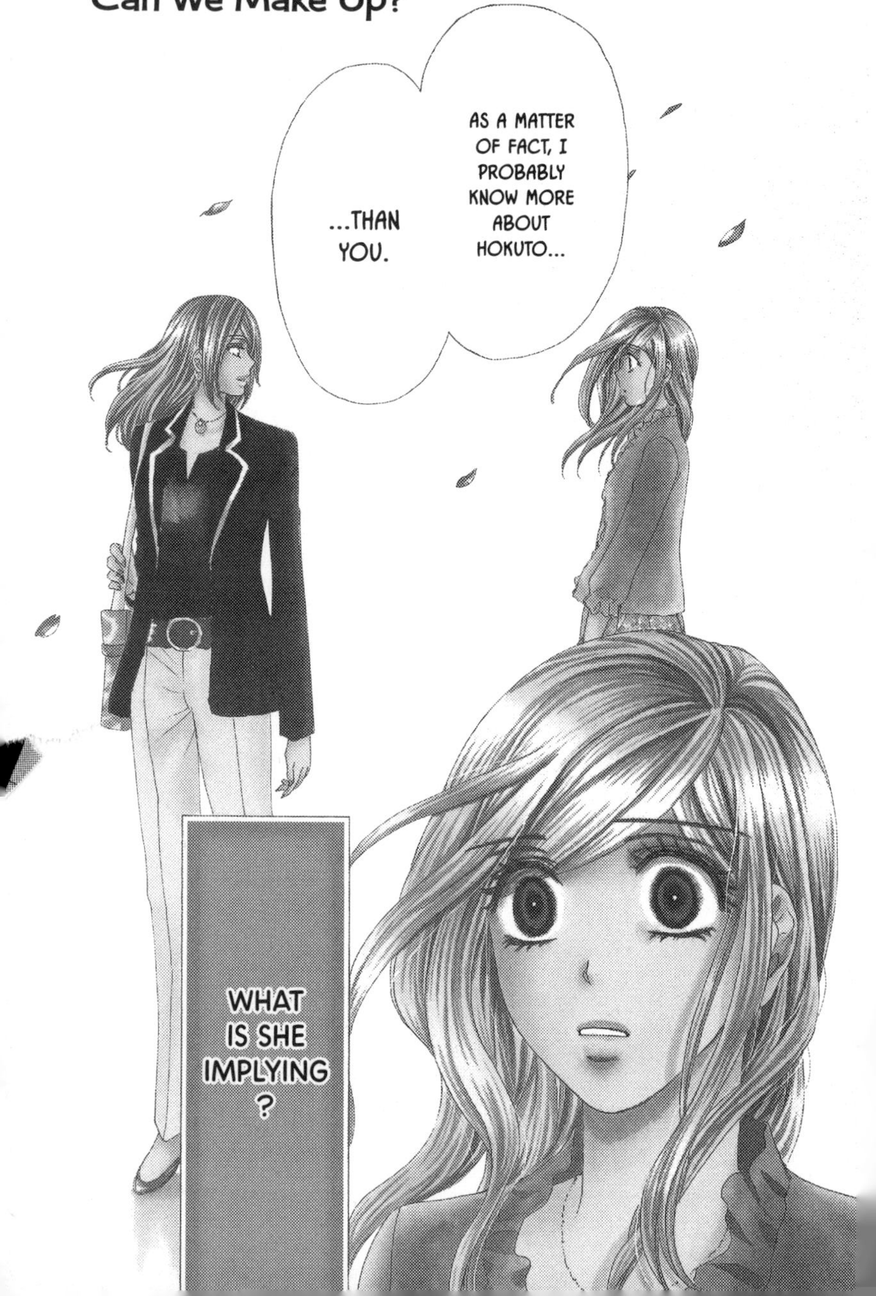
AS A MATTER OF FACT, I PROBABLY KNOW MORE ABOUT HOKUTO...
...THAN YOU.
WHAT IS SHE IMPLYING?

Step Twenty-Seven: Can We Make Up?

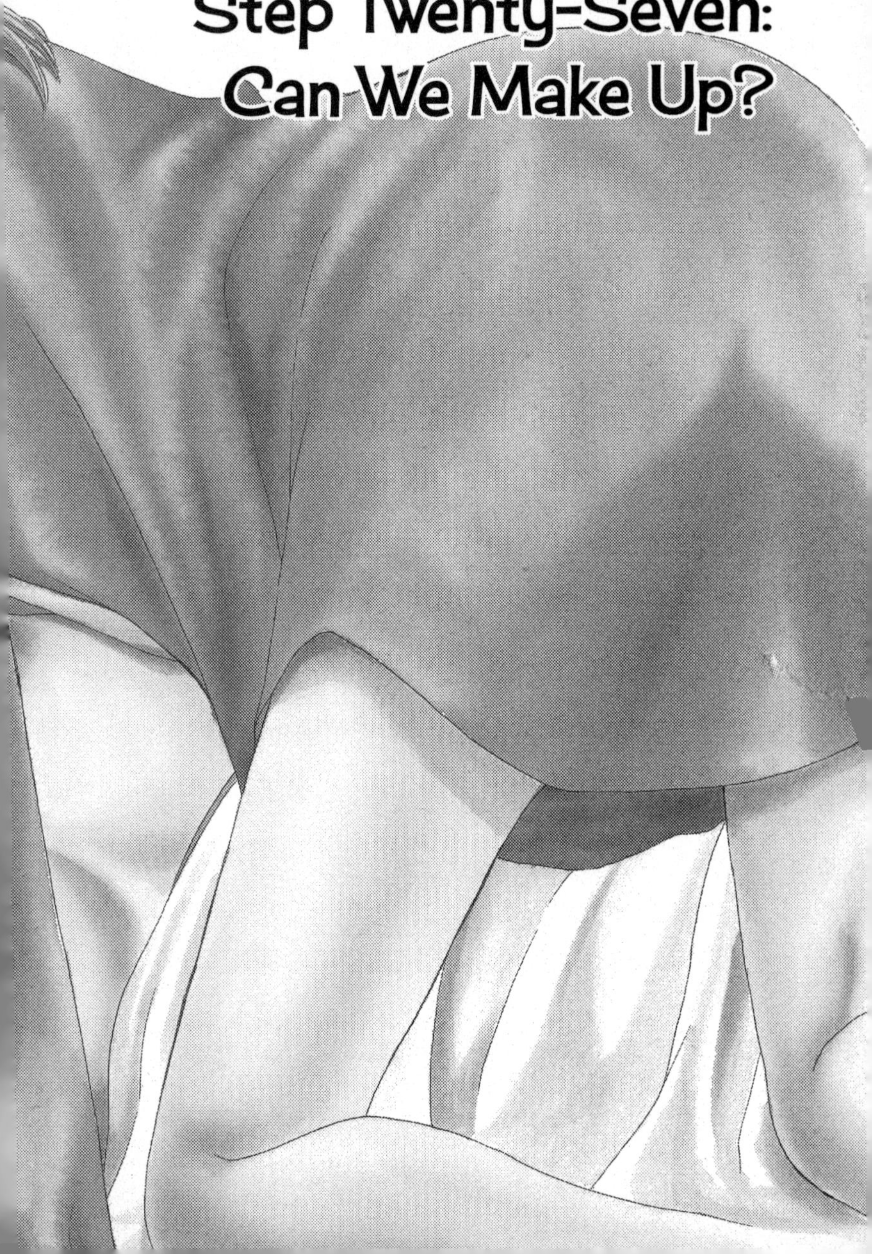

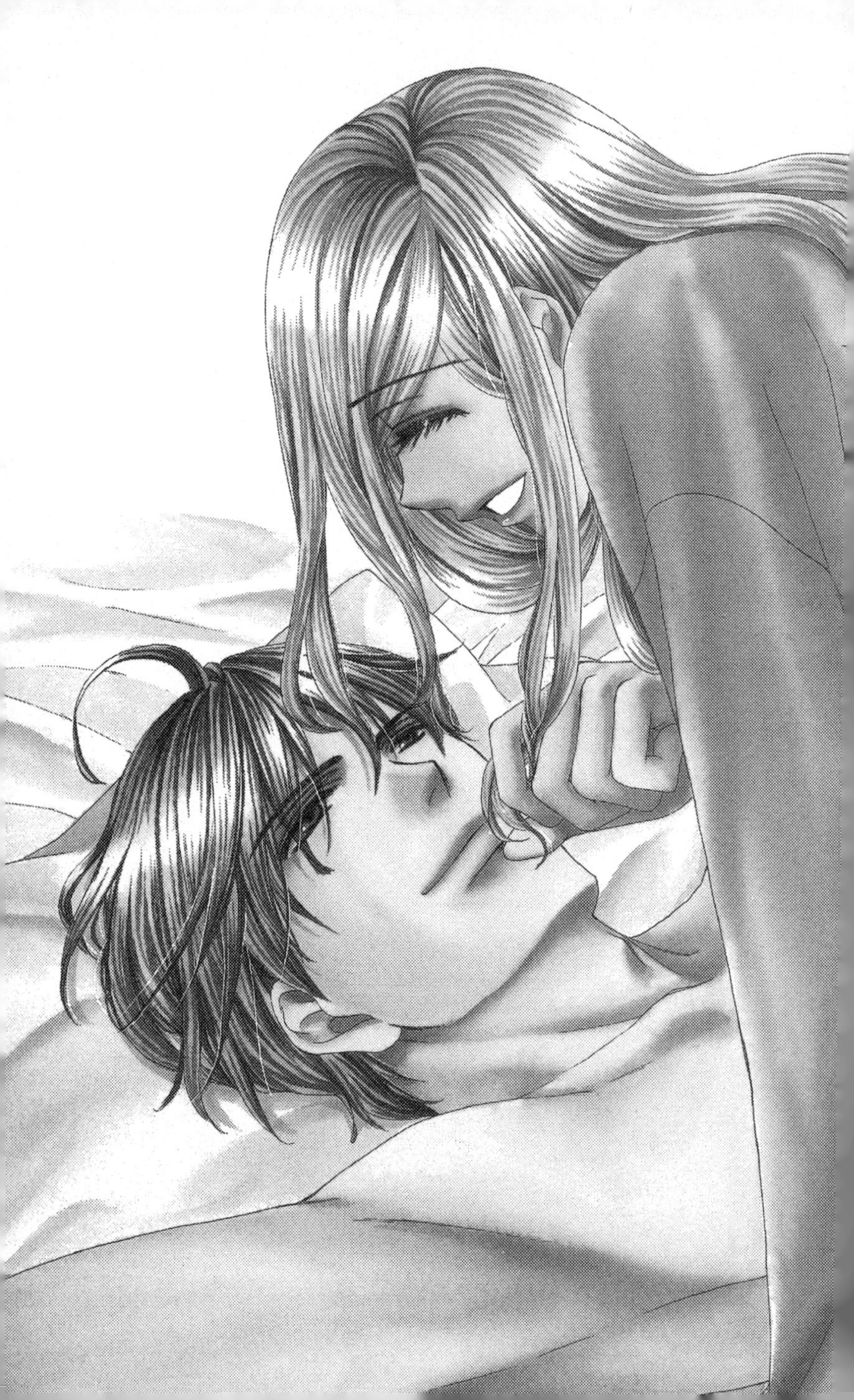

Special Thanks

Assistants

K. Sano
E. Shimojo
Y. Michishita
N. Hori

Editor

M. Okada

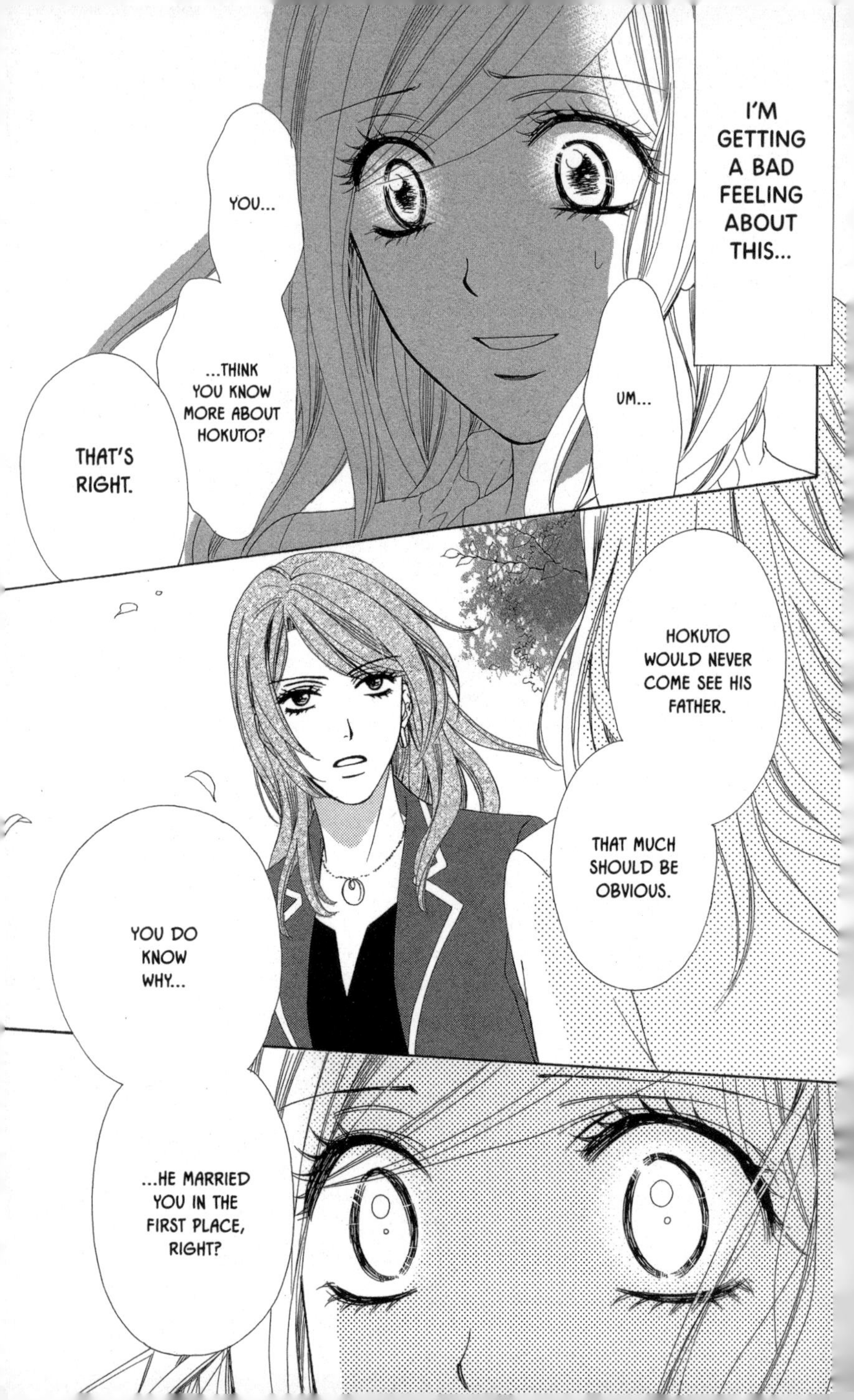
I'M GETTING A BAD FEELING ABOUT THIS...
YOU...
...THINK YOU KNOW MORE ABOUT HOKUTO?
UM...
THAT'S RIGHT.
HOKUTO WOULD NEVER COME SEE HIS FATHER.
THAT MUCH SHOULD BE OBVIOUS.
YOU DO KNOW WHY...
...HE MARRIED YOU IN THE FIRST PLACE, RIGHT?

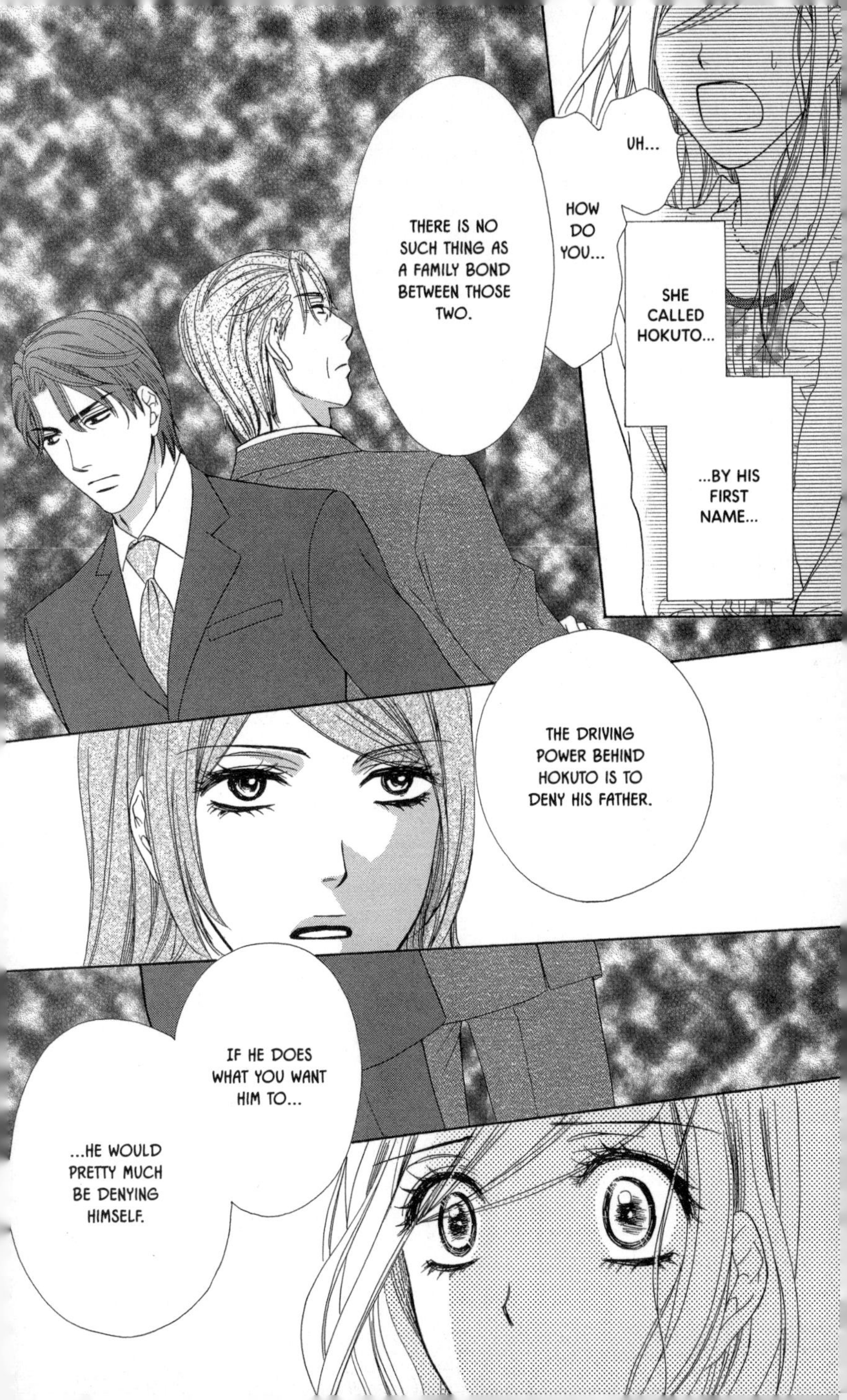
UH...
HOW DO YOU...
SHE CALLED HOKUTO...
...BY HIS FIRST NAME...
THERE IS NO SUCH THING AS A FAMILY BOND BETWEEN THOSE TWO.
THE DRIVING POWER BEHIND HOKUTO IS TO DENY HIS FATHER.
IF HE DOES WHAT YOU WANT HIM TO...
...HE WOULD PRETTY MUCH BE DENYING HIMSELF.

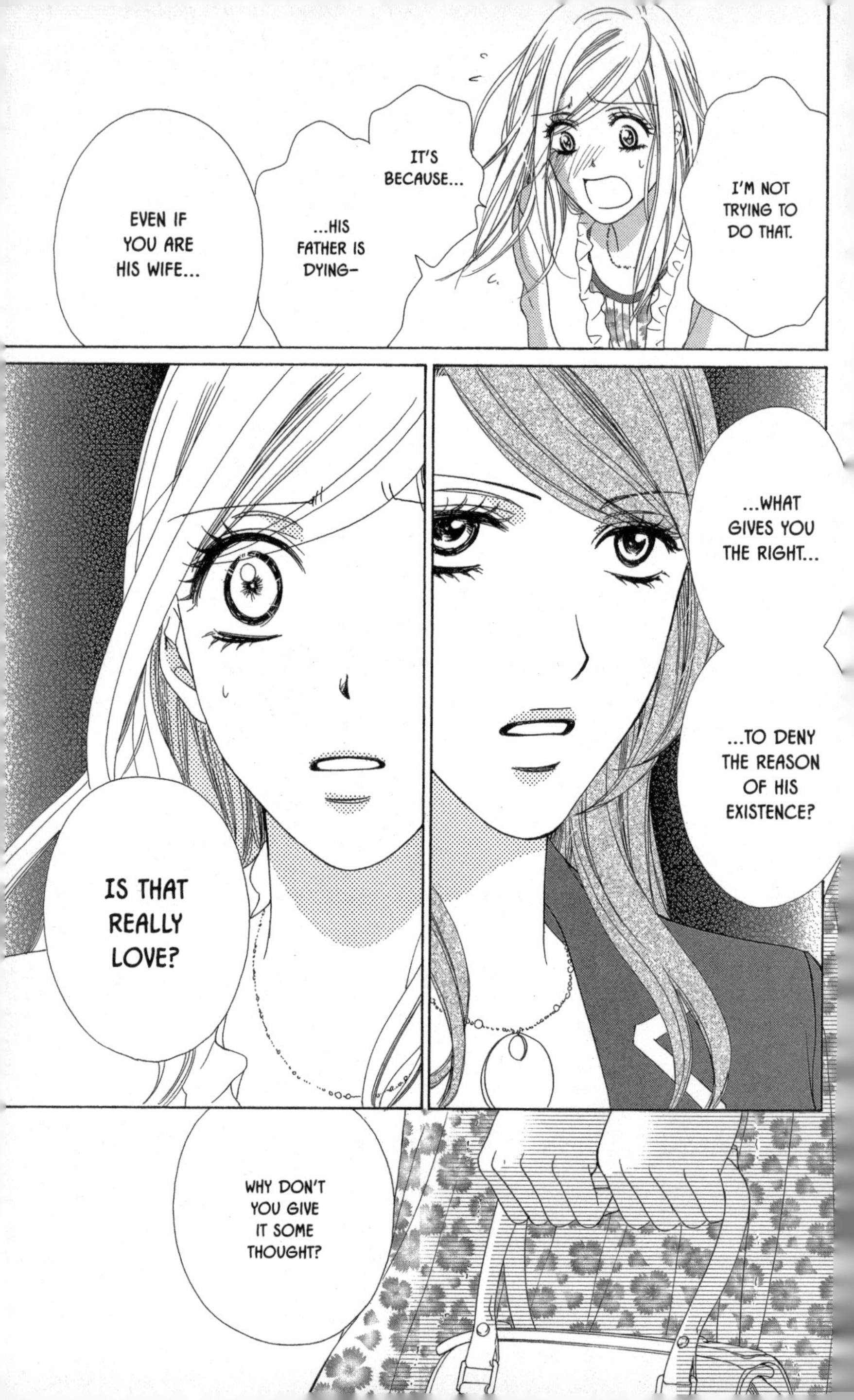
I'M NOT TRYING TO DO THAT.
IT'S BECAUSE...
...HIS FATHER IS DYING—
EVEN IF YOU ARE HIS WIFE...
...WHAT GIVES YOU THE RIGHT...
...TO DENY THE REASON OF HIS EXISTENCE?
IS THAT REALLY LOVE?
WHY DON'T YOU GIVE IT SOME THOUGHT?

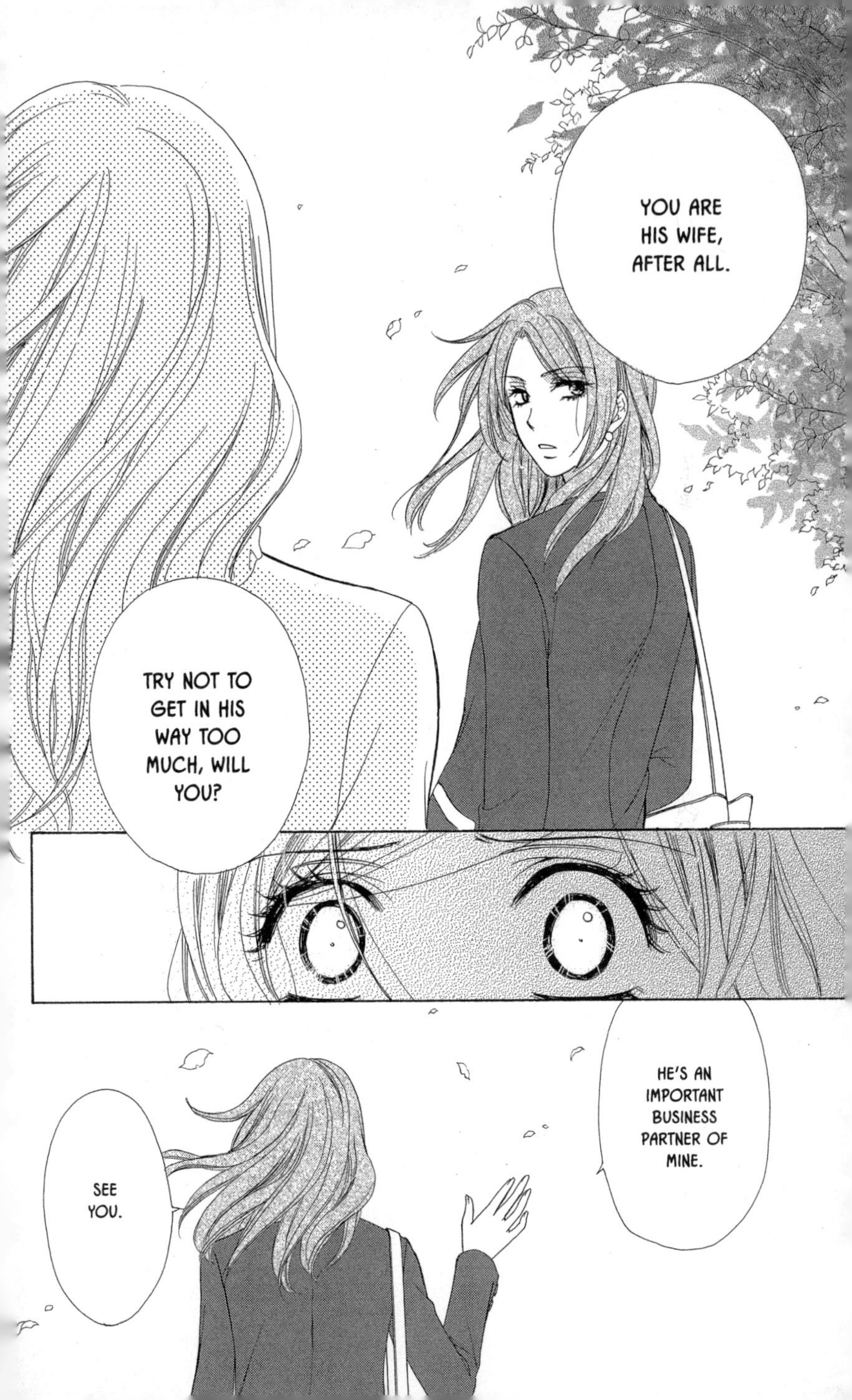
YOU ARE HIS WIFE, AFTER ALL.
TRY NOT TO GET IN HIS WAY TOO MUCH, WILL YOU?
HE'S AN IMPORTANT BUSINESS PARTNER OF MINE.
SEE YOU.

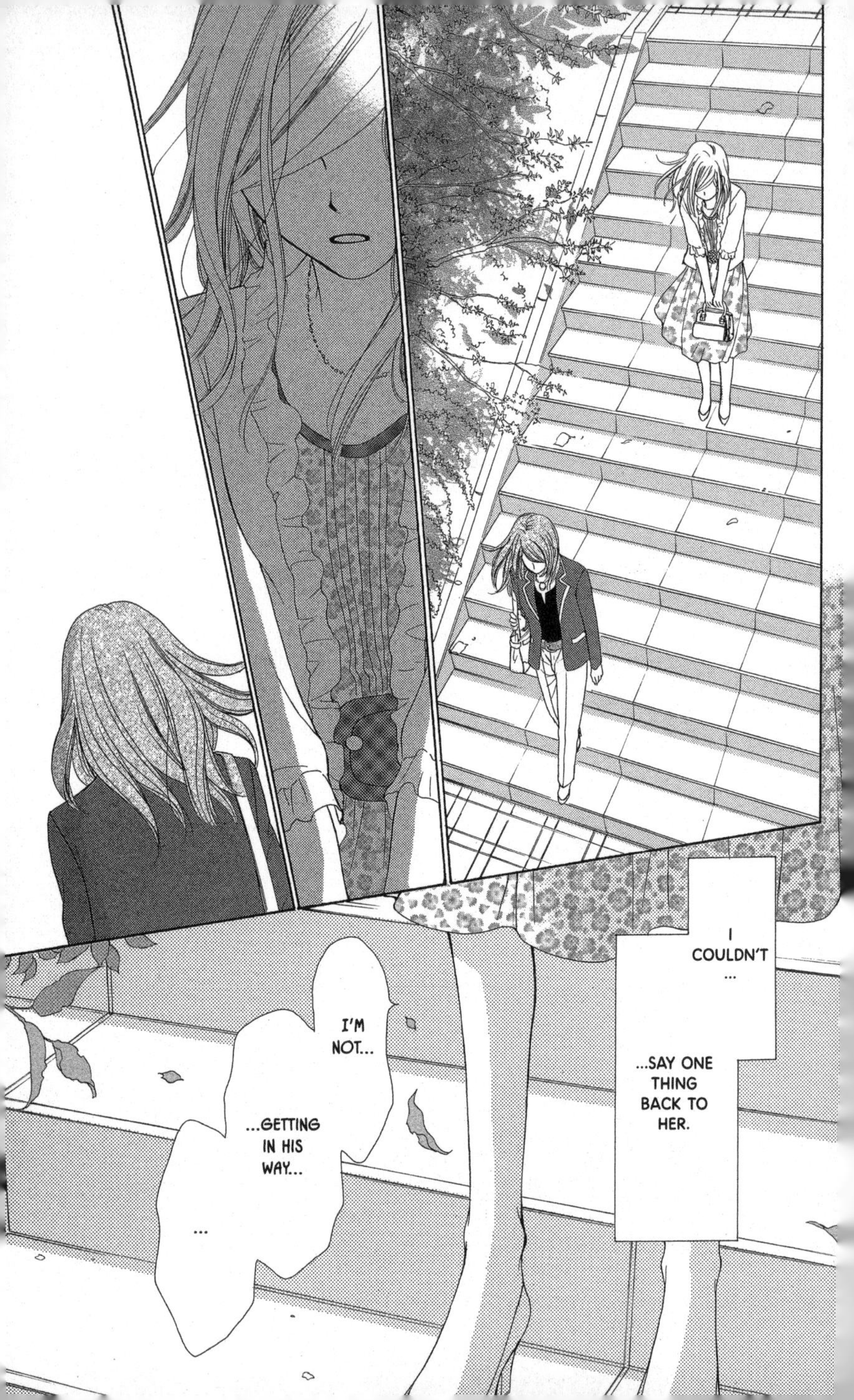
I COULDN'T ...
...SAY ONE THING BACK TO HER.
I'M NOT...
...GETTING IN HIS WAY...
...

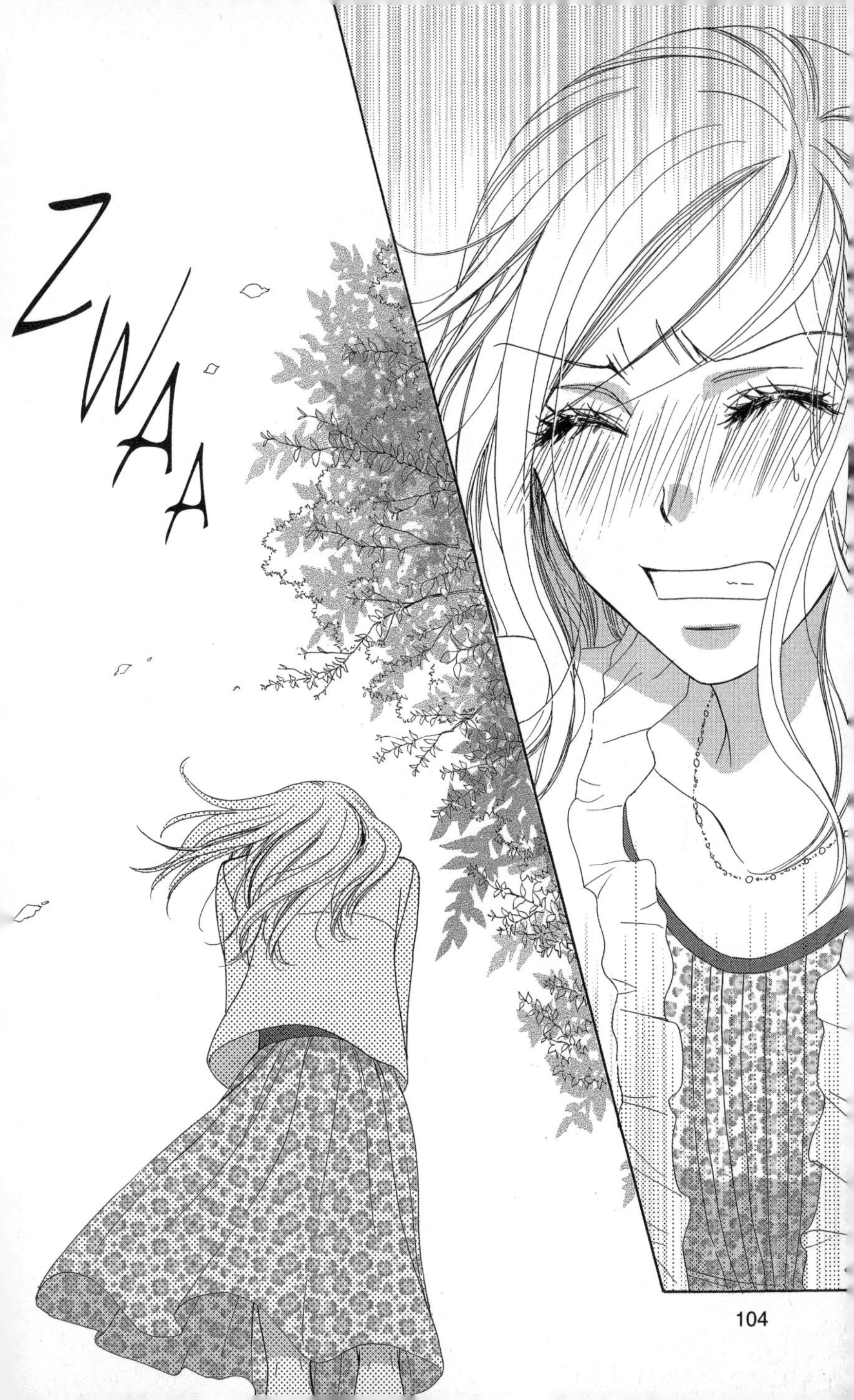
ZWAA

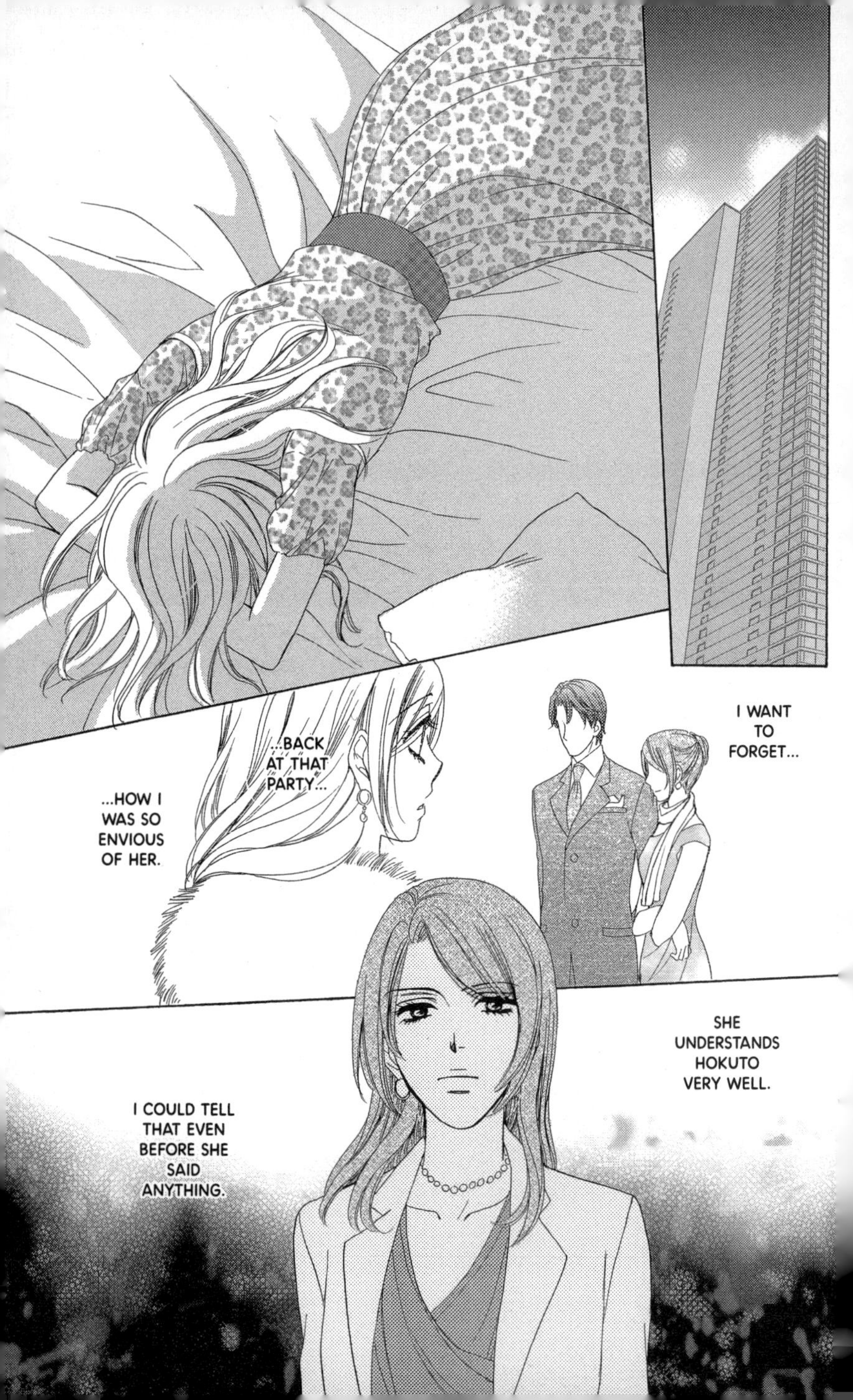
I WANT TO FORGET...
...BACK AT THAT PARTY...
...HOW I WAS SO ENVIOUS OF HER.
SHE UNDERSTANDS HOKUTO VERY WELL.
I COULD TELL THAT EVEN BEFORE SHE SAID ANYTHING.

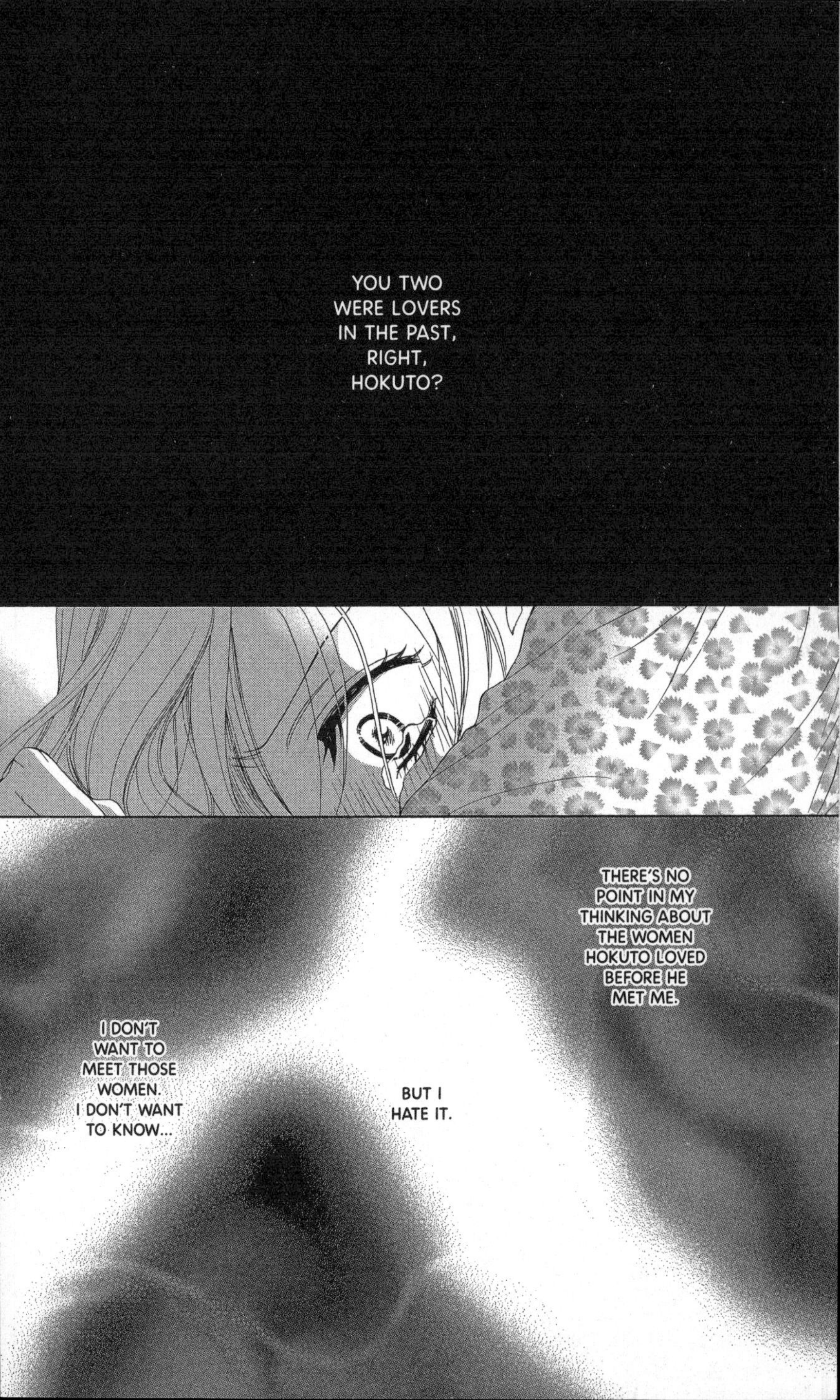
YOU TWO WERE LOVERS IN THE PAST, RIGHT, HOKUTO?
THERE'S NO POINT IN MY THINKING ABOUT THE WOMEN HOKUTO LOVED BEFORE HE MET ME.
BUT I HATE IT.
I DON'T WANT TO MEET THOSE WOMEN. I DON'T WANT TO KNOW...

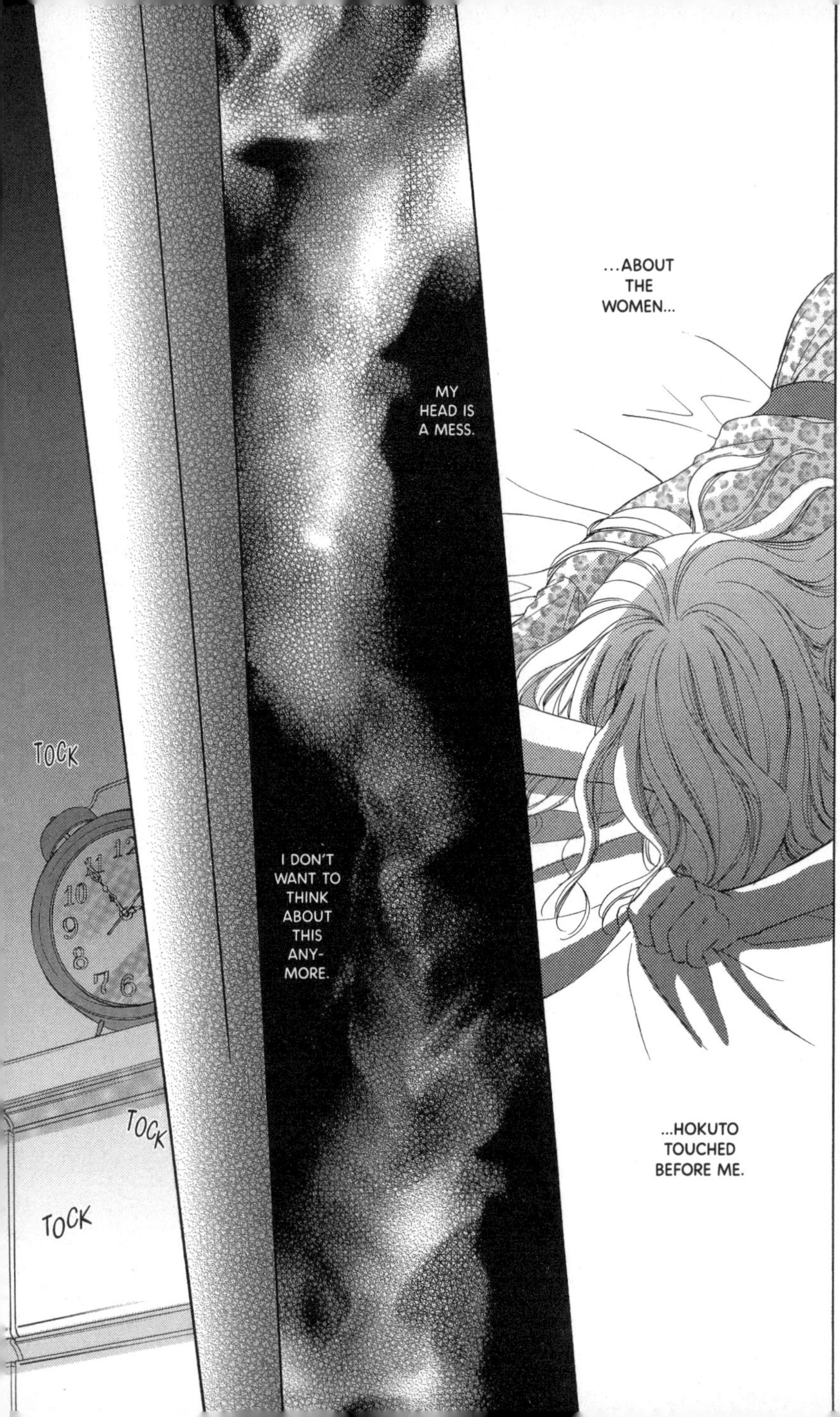
...ABOUT THE WOMEN...
...HOKUTO TOUCHED BEFORE ME.
MY HEAD IS A MESS.
I DON'T WANT TO THINK ABOUT THIS ANY-MORE.
TOCK
TOCK
TOCK

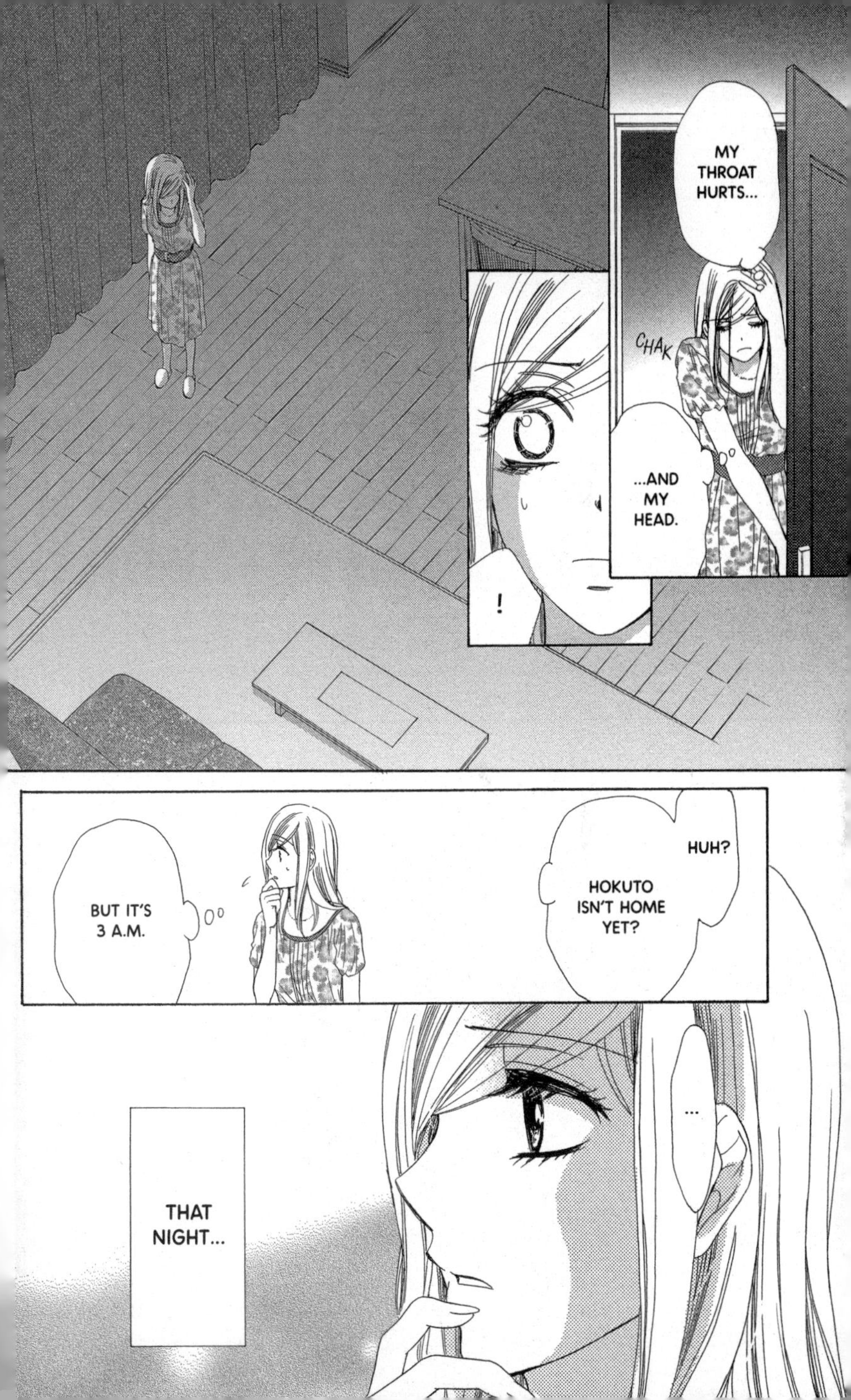
MY THROAT HURTS...
CHAK
...AND MY HEAD.
!
HUH?
HOKUTO ISN'T HOME YET?
BUT IT'S 3 A.M.
...
THAT NIGHT...

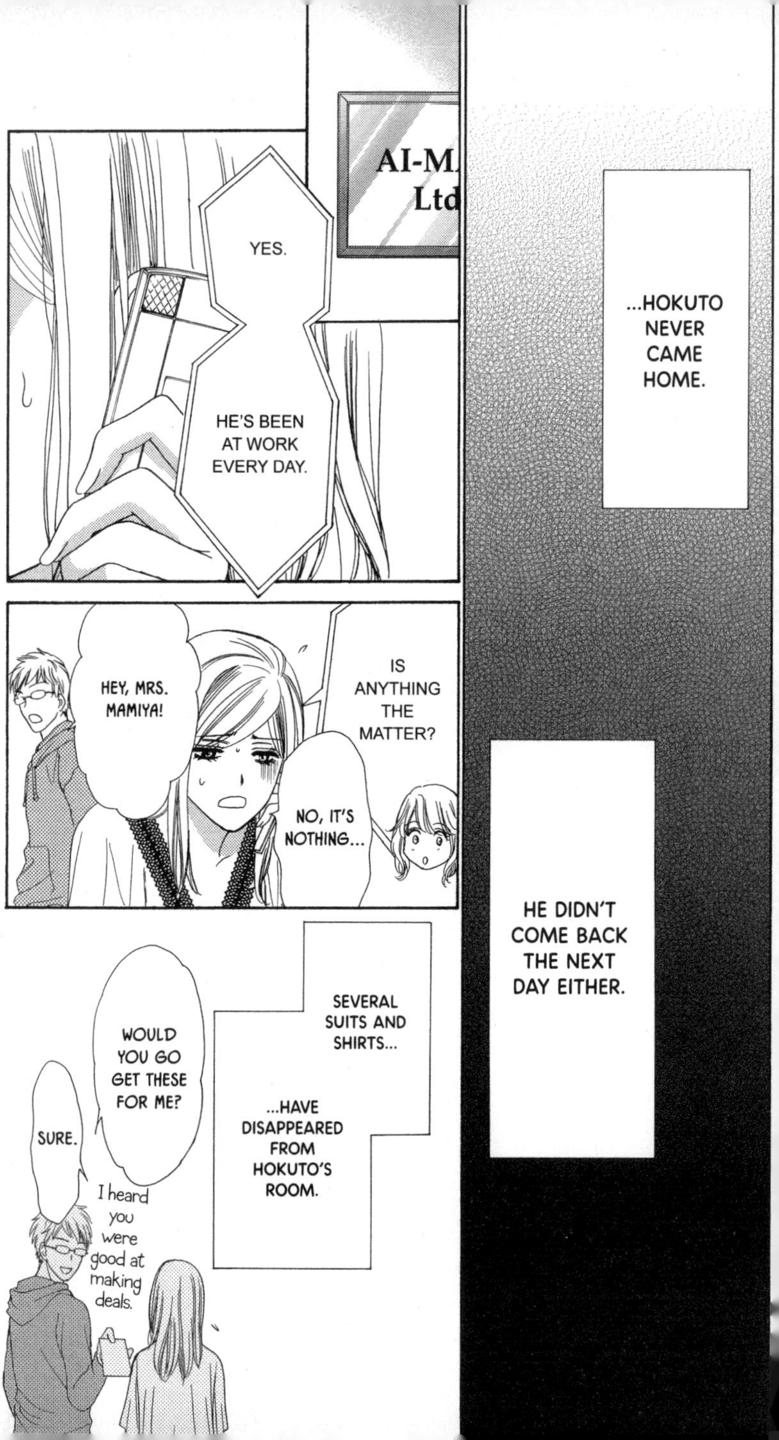
...HOKUTO NEVER CAME HOME.
HE DIDN'T COME BACK THE NEXT DAY EITHER.
AI-M
Ltd
YES.
HE'S BEEN AT WORK EVERY DAY.
IS ANYTHING THE MATTER?
NO, IT'S NOTHING...
HEY, MRS. MAMIYA!
SEVERAL SUITS AND SHIRTS...
...HAVE DISAPPEARED FROM HOKUTO'S ROOM.
WOULD YOU GO GET THESE FOR ME?
SURE.
I heard you were good at making deals.

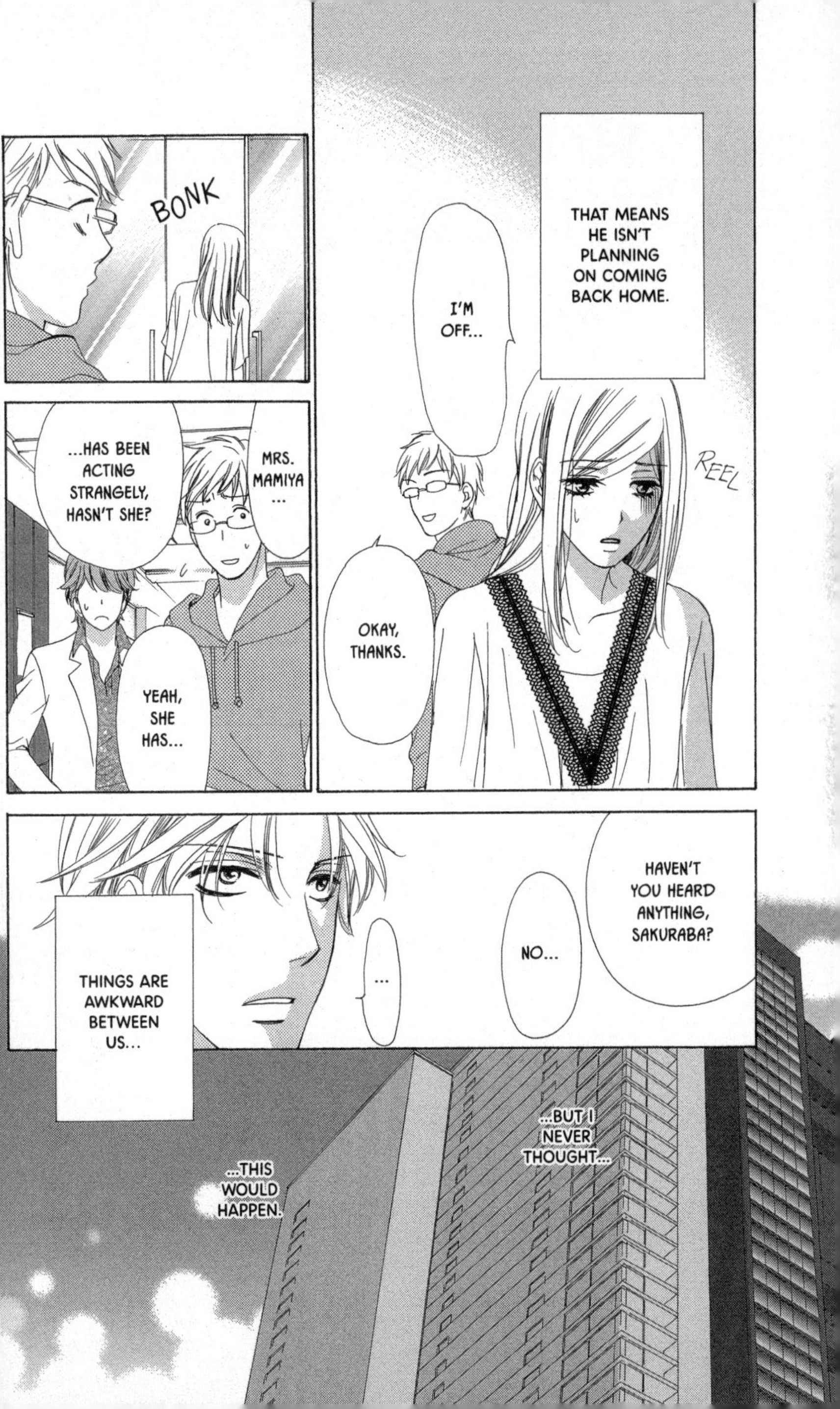
THAT MEANS HE ISN'T PLANNING ON COMING BACK HOME.
I'M OFF...
REEL
OKAY, THANKS.
BONK
MRS. MAMIYA...
...HAS BEEN ACTING STRANGELY, HASN'T SHE?
YEAH, SHE HAS...
HAVEN'T YOU HEARD ANYTHING, SAKURABA?
NO...
...
THINGS ARE AWKWARD BETWEEN US...
...BUT I NEVER THOUGHT...
...THIS WOULD HAPPEN.

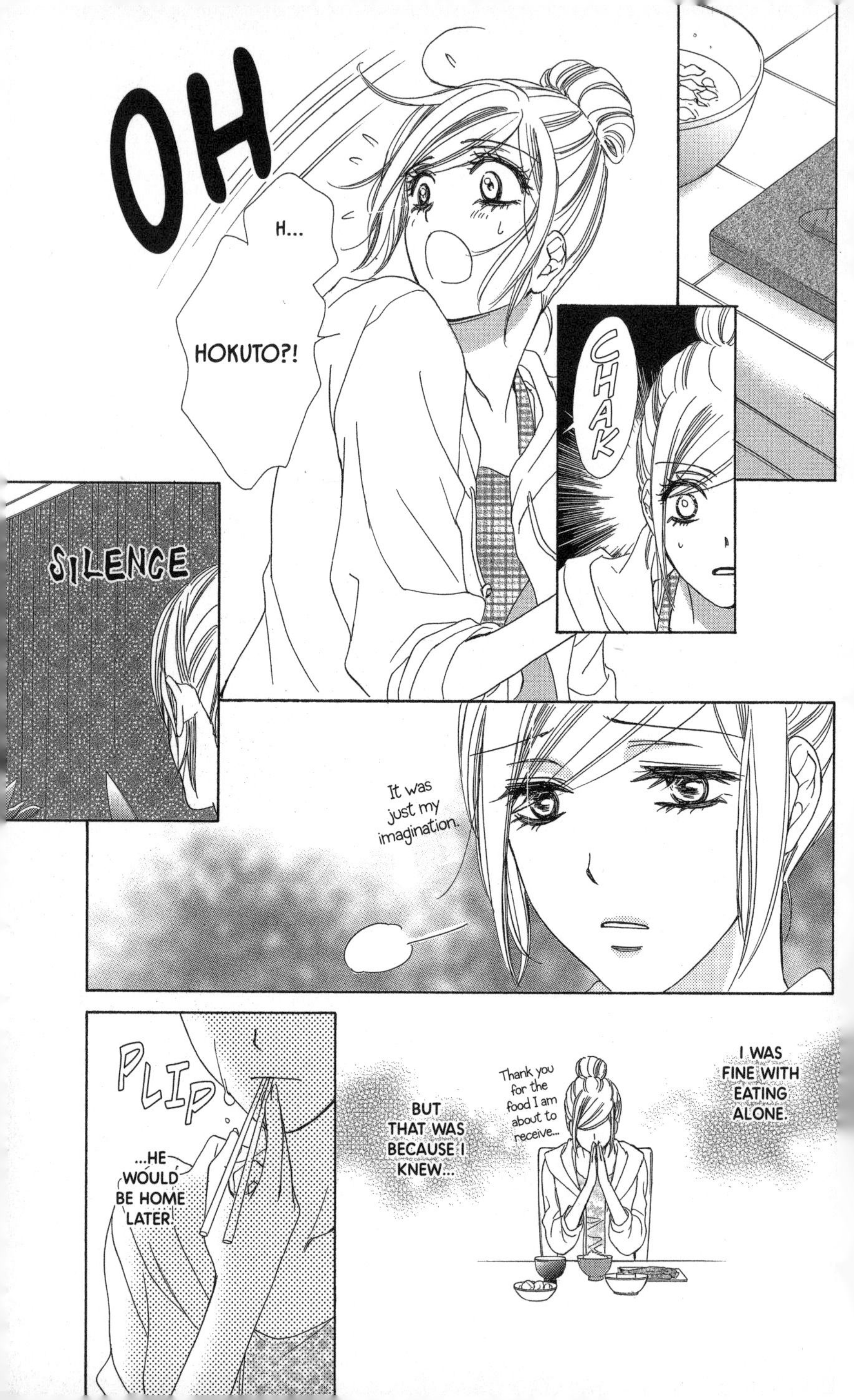
OH
H...
HOKUTO?!
CHAK
SILENCE
It was just my imagination.
I WAS FINE WITH EATING ALONE.
Thank you for the food I am about to receive...
BUT THAT WAS BECAUSE I KNEW...
PLIP
...HE WOULD BE HOME LATER.

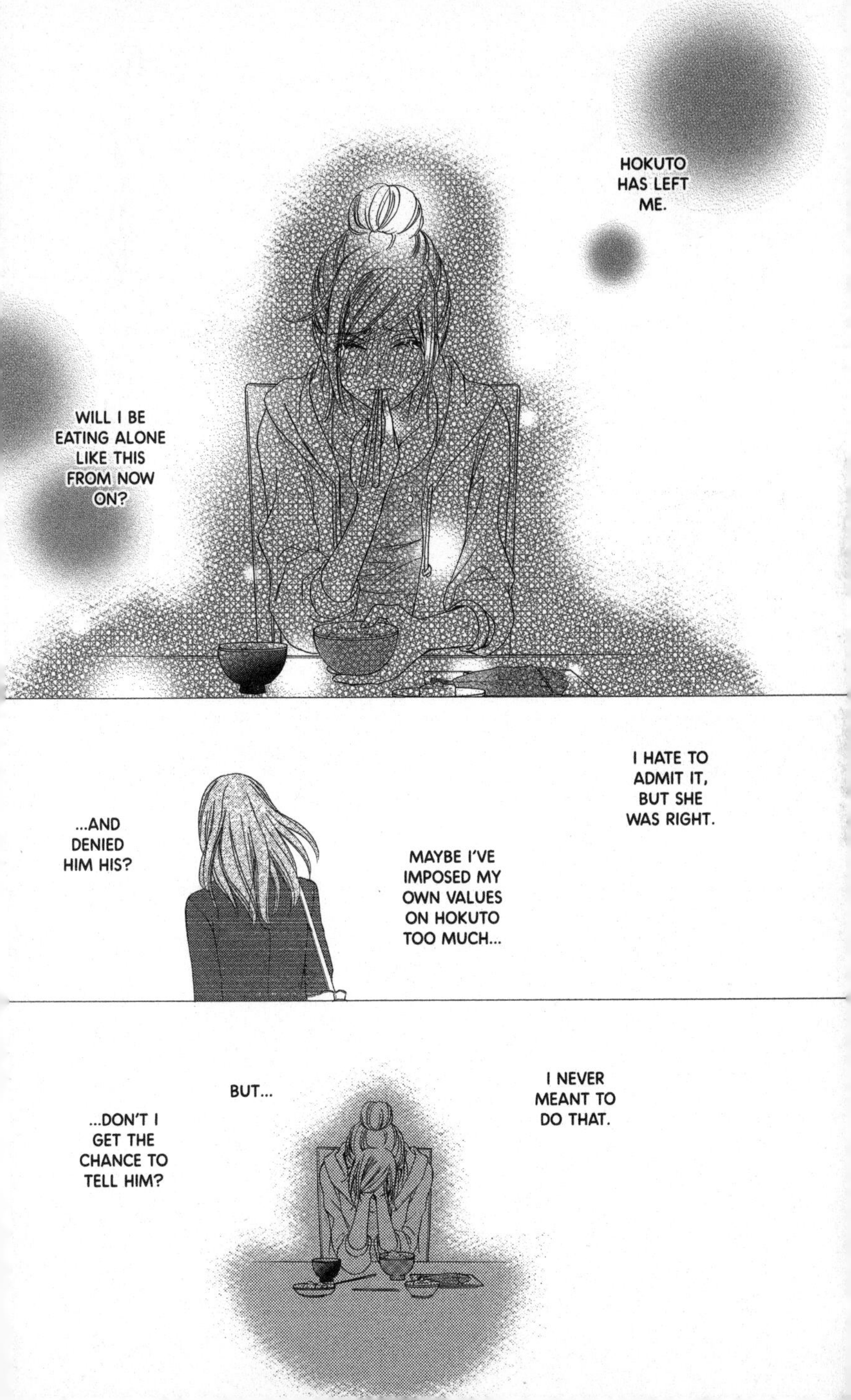
HOKUTO HAS LEFT ME.
WILL I BE EATING ALONE LIKE THIS FROM NOW ON?
I HATE TO ADMIT IT, BUT SHE WAS RIGHT.
MAYBE I'VE IMPOSED MY OWN VALUES ON HOKUTO TOO MUCH...
...AND DENIED HIM HIS?
I NEVER MEANT TO DO THAT.
BUT...
...DON'T I GET THE CHANCE TO TELL HIM?

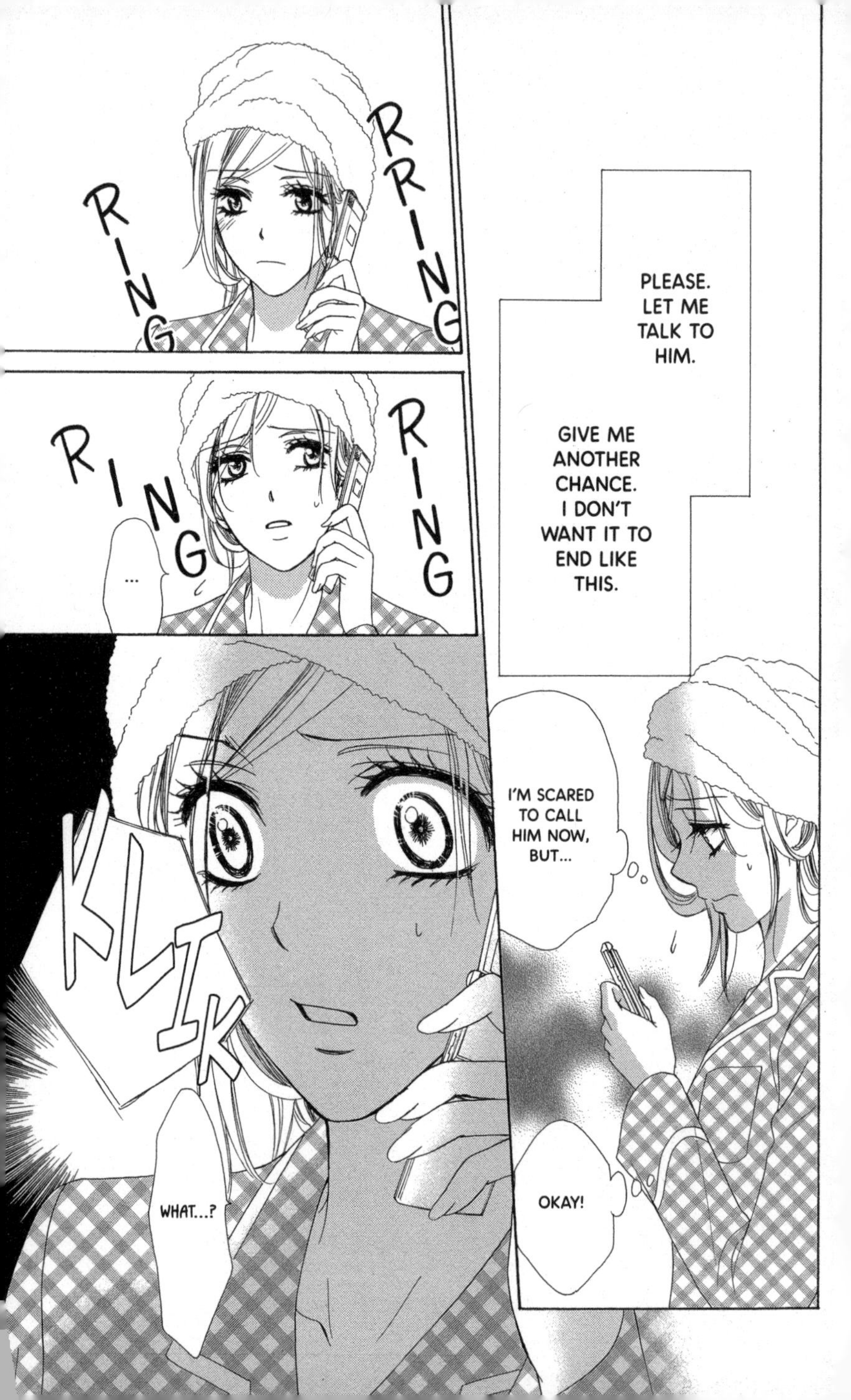
PLEASE. LET ME TALK TO HIM.
GIVE ME ANOTHER CHANCE. I DON'T WANT IT TO END LIKE THIS.
I'M SCARED TO CALL HIM NOW, BUT...
OKAY!
RRING
RING
RING
RING
...
KLIK
WHAT...?

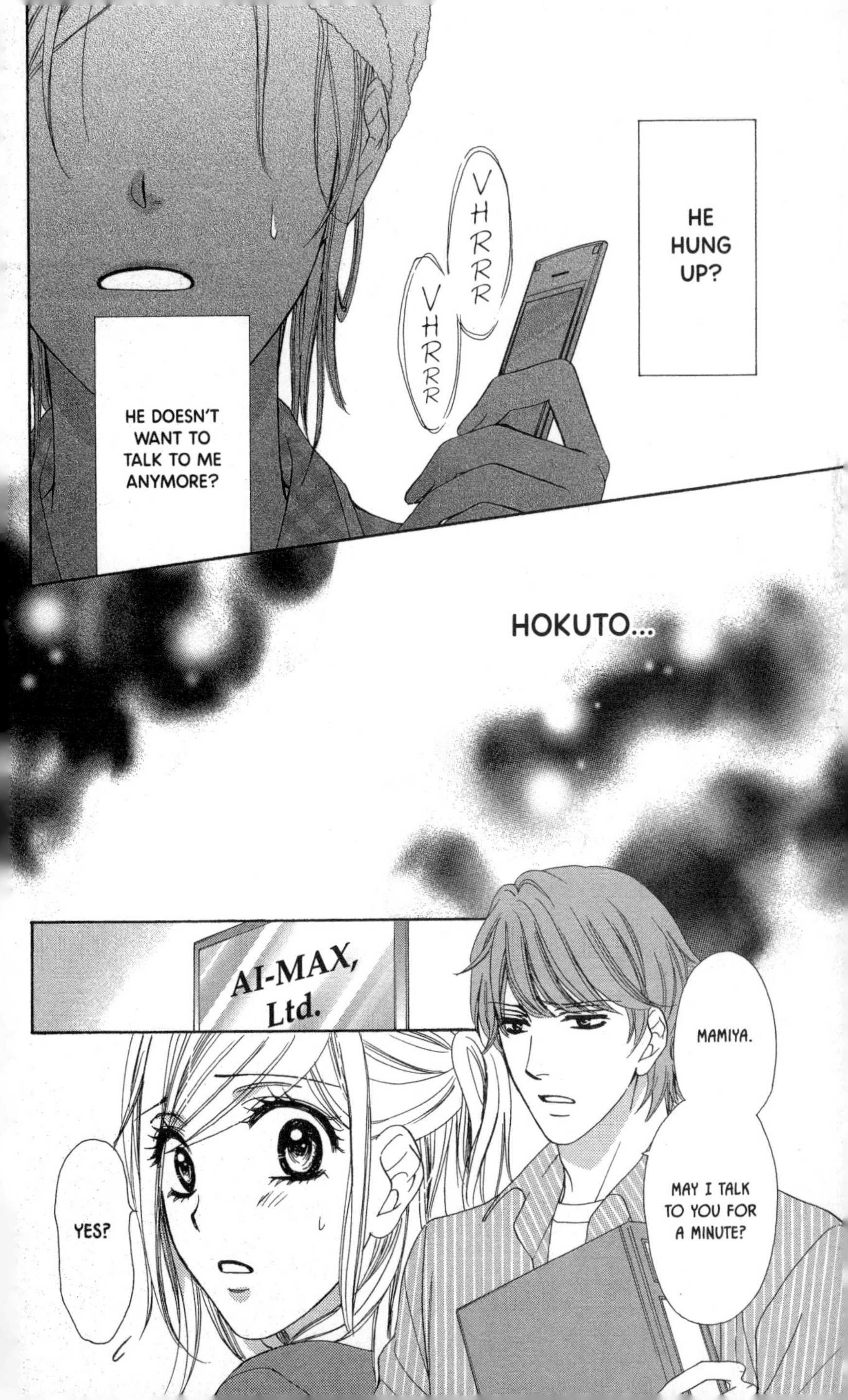
HE HUNG UP?
VHRRR
VHRRR
HE DOESN'T WANT TO TALK TO ME ANYMORE?
HOKUTO...
AI-MAX, Ltd.
MAMIYA.
MAY I TALK TO YOU FOR A MINUTE?
YES?

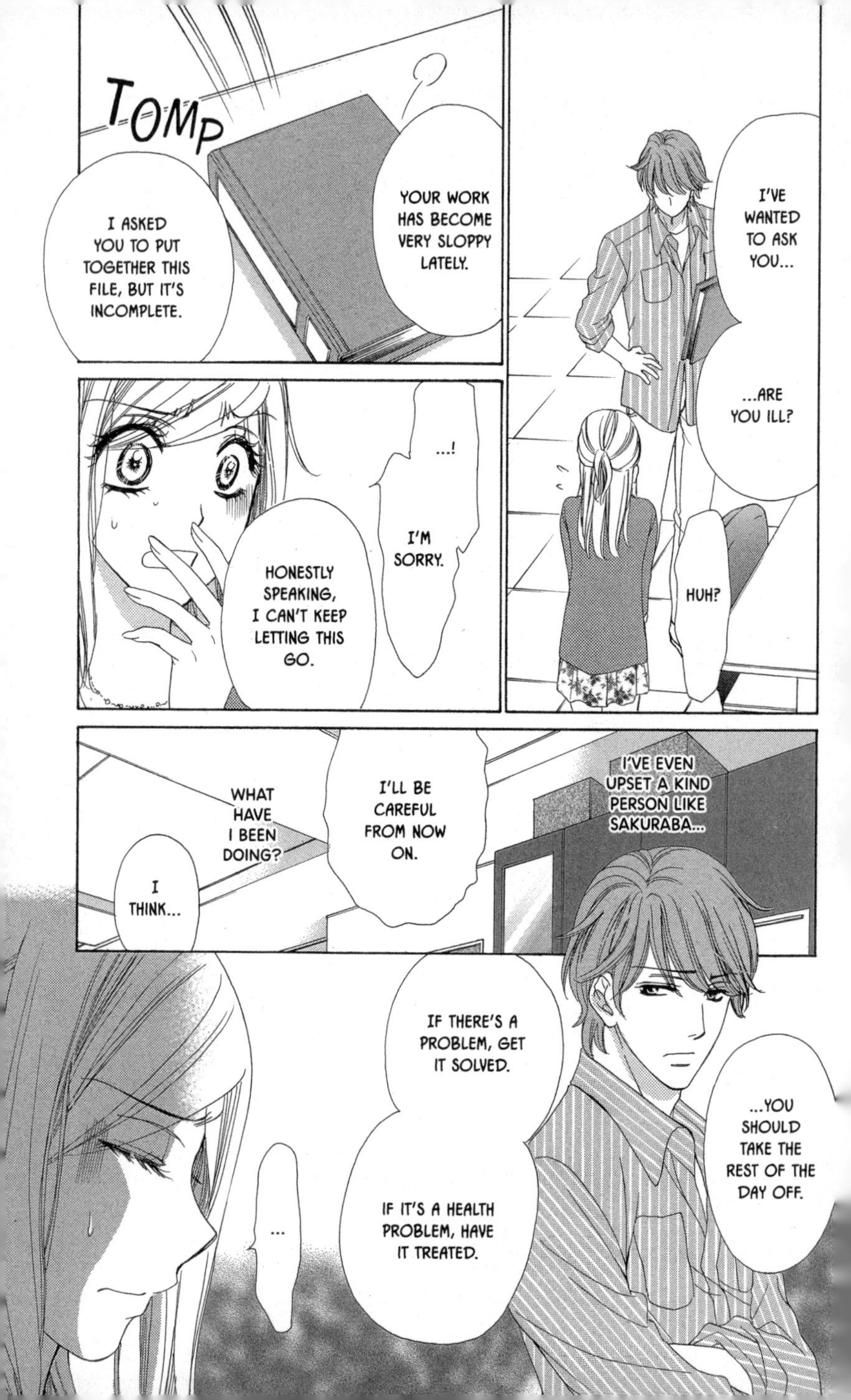
I'VE WANTED TO ASK YOU...
...ARE YOU ILL?
HUH?
TOMP
YOUR WORK HAS BECOME VERY SLOPPY LATELY.
I ASKED YOU TO PUT TOGETHER THIS FILE, BUT IT'S INCOMPLETE.
...!
I'M SORRY.
HONESTLY SPEAKING, I CAN'T KEEP LETTING THIS GO.
I'VE EVEN UPSET A KIND PERSON LIKE SAKURABA...
I'LL BE CAREFUL FROM NOW ON.
WHAT HAVE I BEEN DOING?
I THINK...
...YOU SHOULD TAKE THE REST OF THE DAY OFF.
IF THERE'S A PROBLEM, GET IT SOLVED.
IF IT'S A HEALTH PROBLEM, HAVE IT TREATED.
...

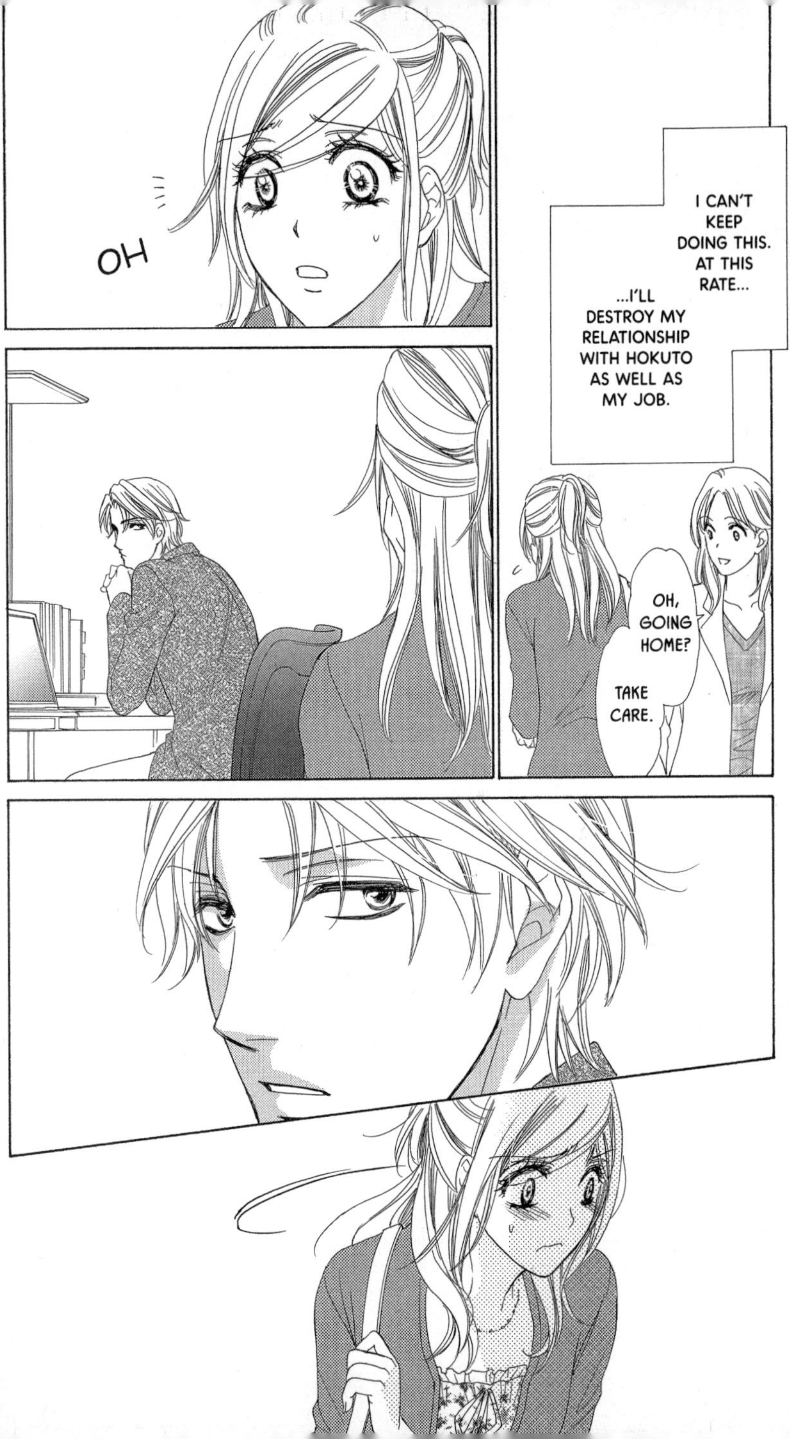
I CAN'T KEEP DOING THIS. AT THIS RATE...
...I'LL DESTROY MY RELATIONSHIP WITH HOKUTO AS WELL AS MY JOB.
OH, GOING HOME?
TAKE CARE.
OH

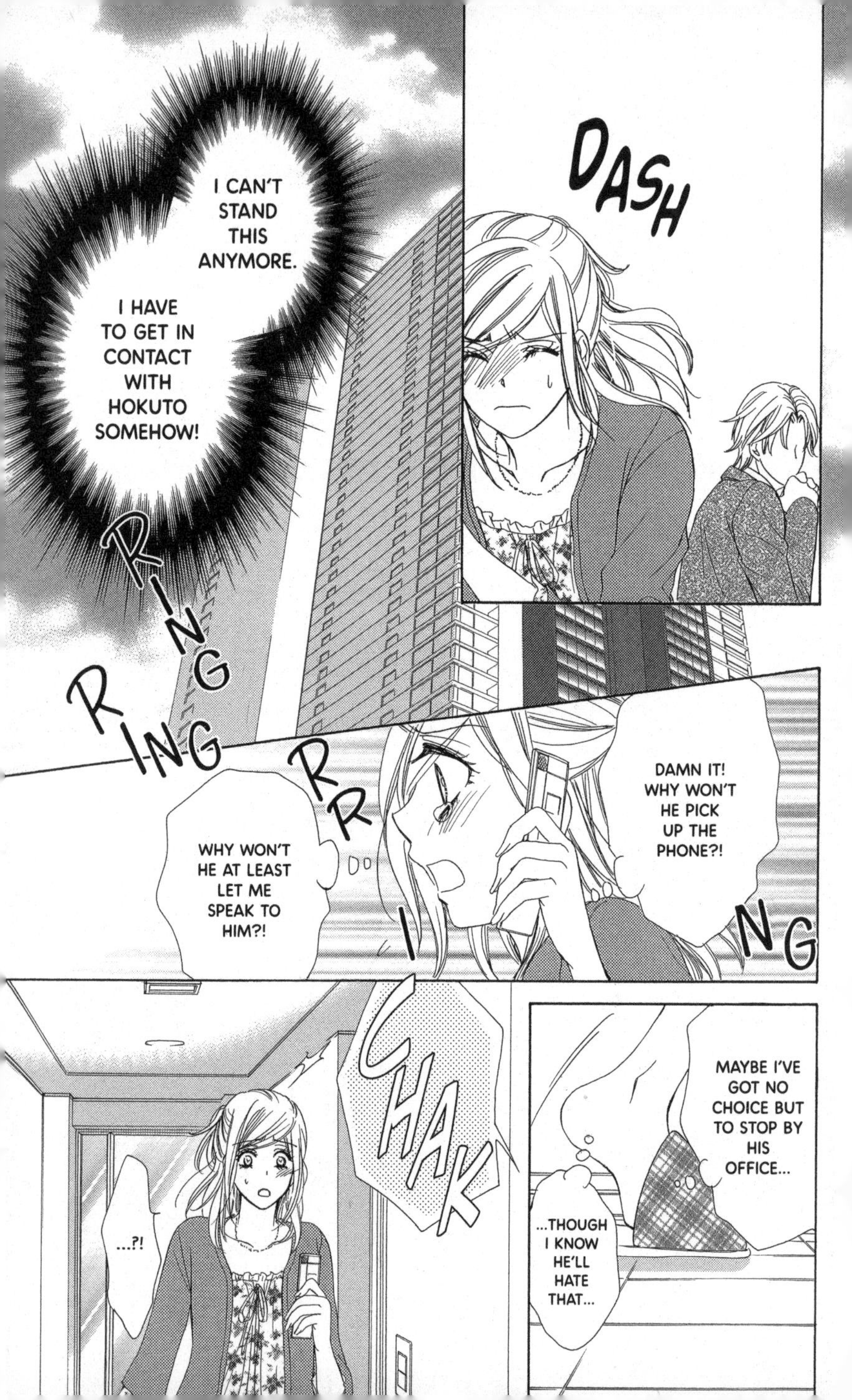
DASH
I CAN'T STAND THIS ANYMORE.
I HAVE TO GET IN CONTACT WITH HOKUTO SOMEHOW!
RING RING
DAMN IT! WHY WON'T HE PICK UP THE PHONE?!
RRRING
WHY WON'T HE AT LEAST LET ME SPEAK TO HIM?!
MAYBE I'VE GOT NO CHOICE BUT TO STOP BY HIS OFFICE...
...THOUGH I KNOW HE'LL HATE THAT...
CHAK
...?!

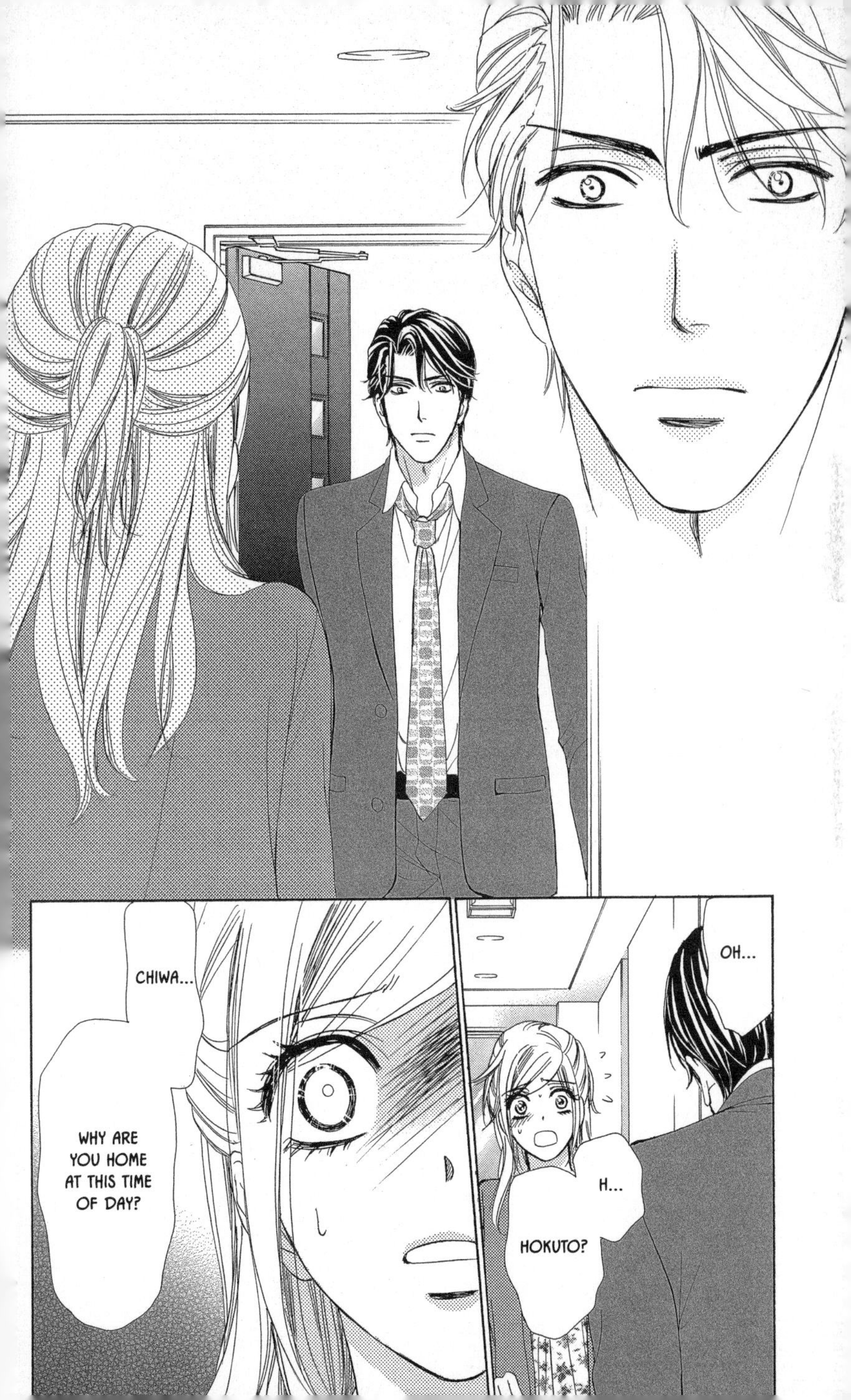
OH...
H...
HOKUTO?
CHIWA...
WHY ARE YOU HOME AT THIS TIME OF DAY?

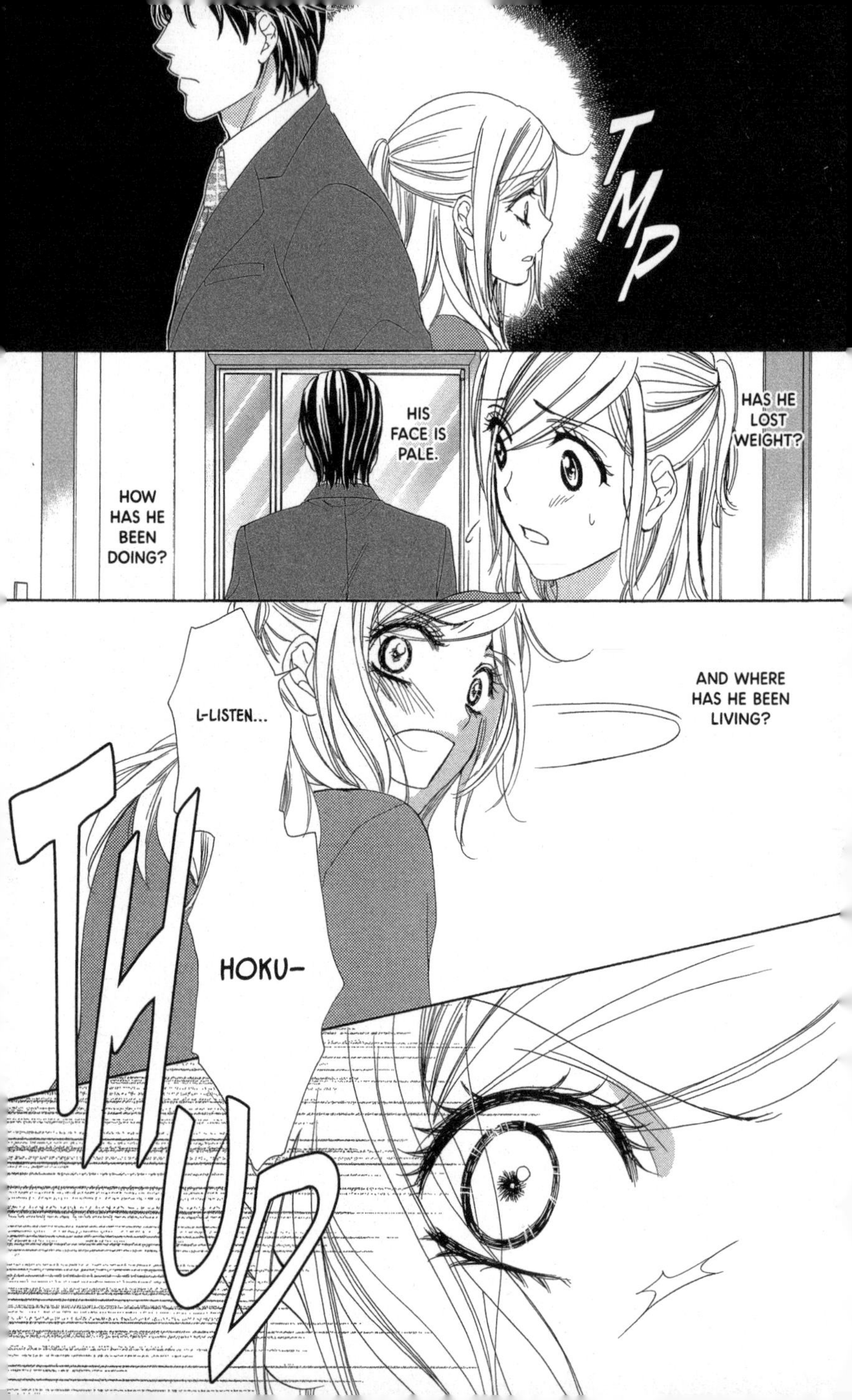
TMP
HAS HE LOST WEIGHT?
HIS FACE IS PALE.
HOW HAS HE BEEN DOING?
AND WHERE HAS HE BEEN LIVING?
L-LISTEN...
HOKU-
THUD

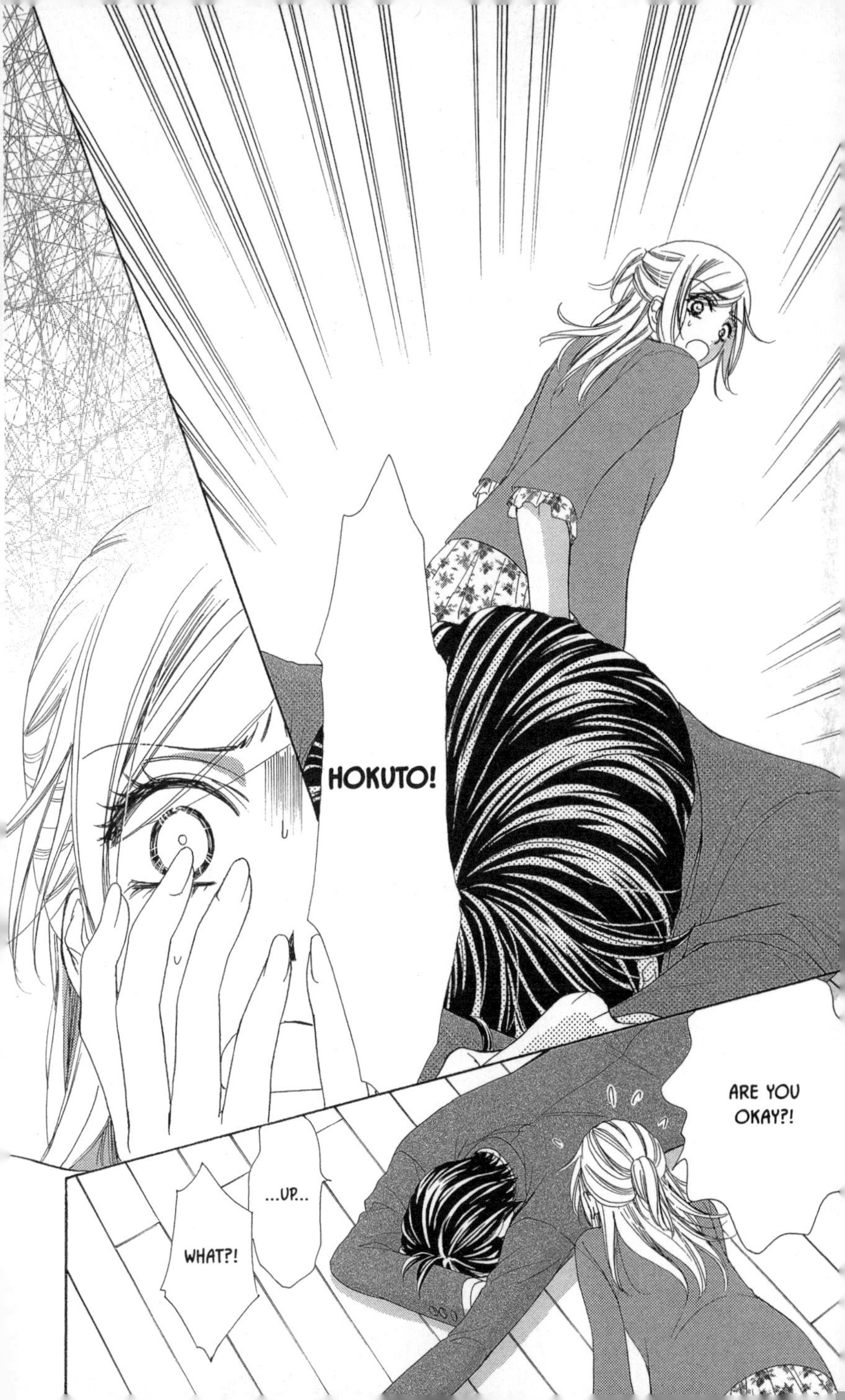
HOKUTO!
ARE YOU OKAY?!
...UP...
WHAT?!

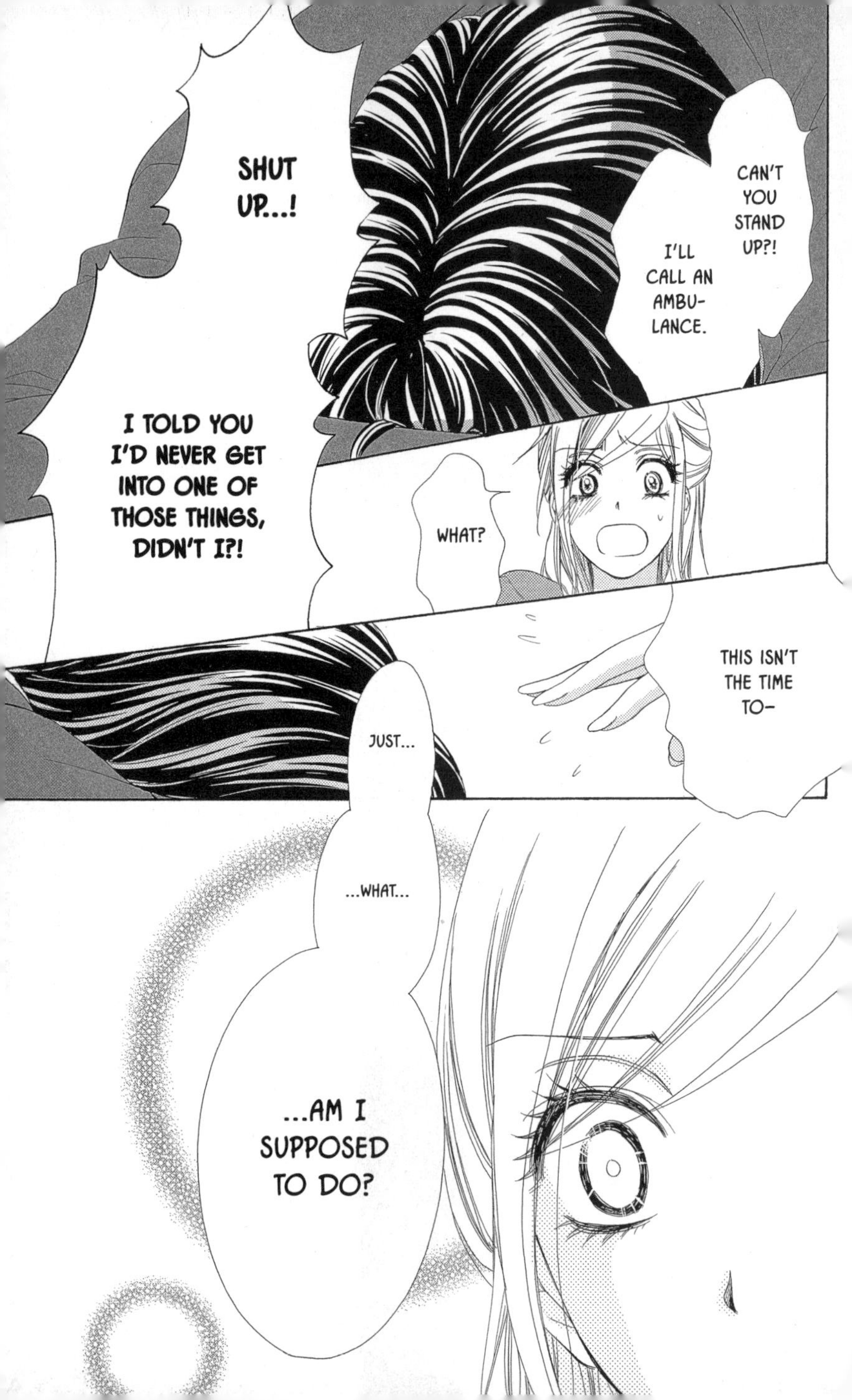
CAN'T YOU STAND UP?!
I'LL CALL AN AMBULANCE.
SHUT UP...!
I TOLD YOU I'D NEVER GET INTO ONE OF THOSE THINGS, DIDN'T I?!
WHAT?
THIS ISN'T THE TIME TO–
JUST...
...WHAT...
...AM I SUPPOSED TO DO?

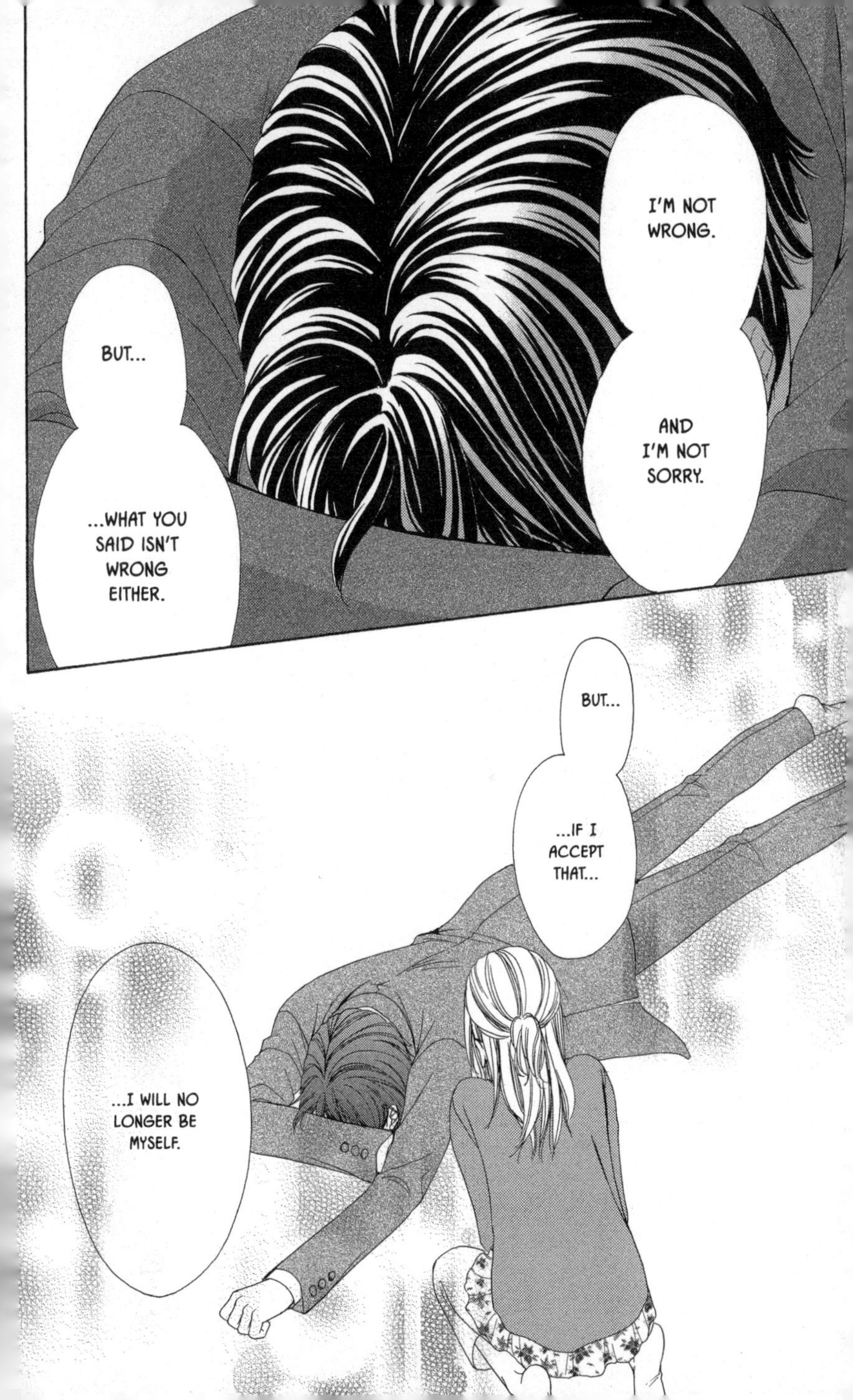
I'M NOT WRONG.
AND I'M NOT SORRY.
BUT...
...WHAT YOU SAID ISN'T WRONG EITHER.
BUT...
...IF I ACCEPT THAT...
...I WILL NO LONGER BE MYSELF.

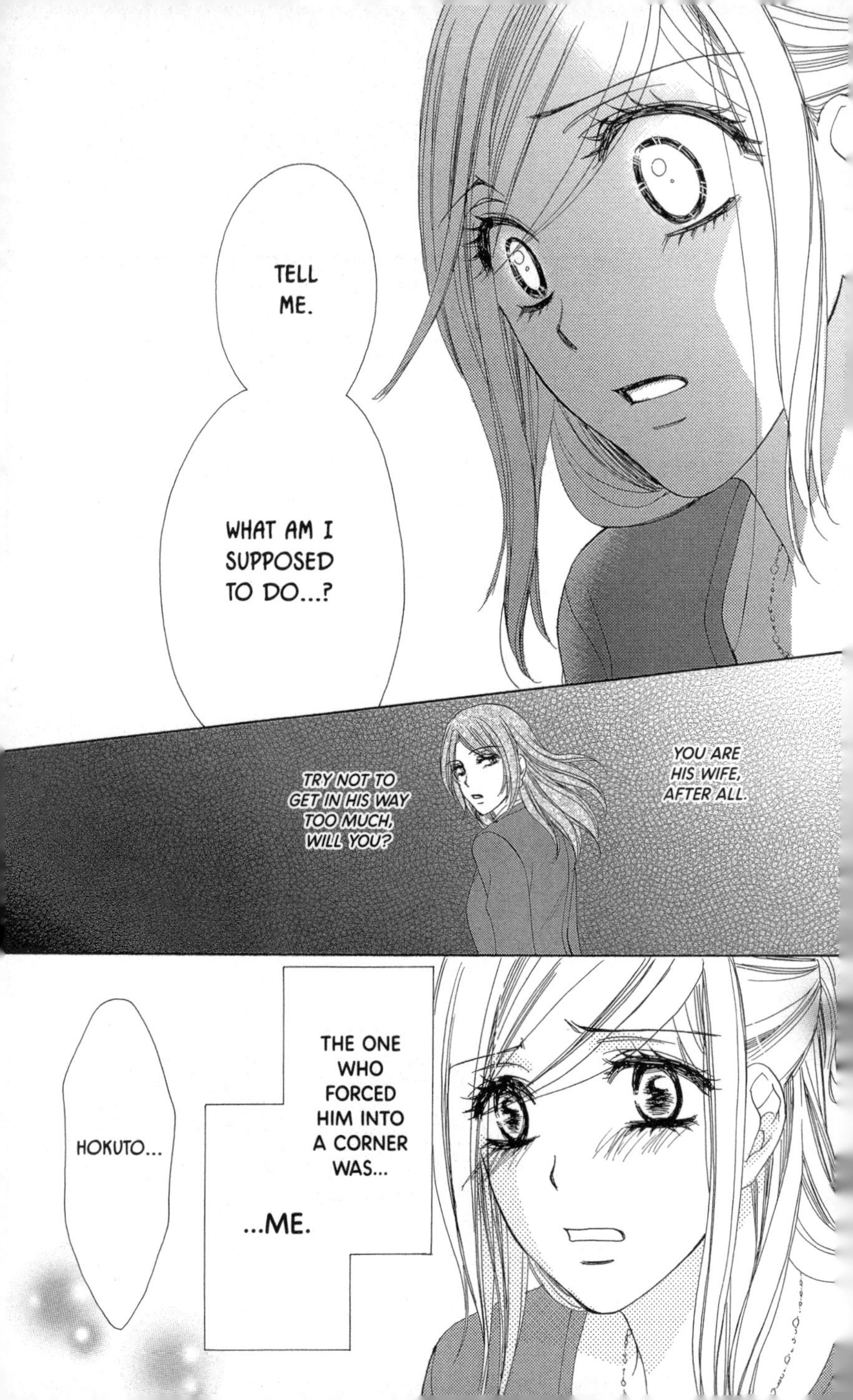
TELL ME.
WHAT AM I SUPPOSED TO DO...?
YOU ARE HIS WIFE, AFTER ALL.
TRY NOT TO GET IN HIS WAY TOO MUCH, WILL YOU?
THE ONE WHO FORCED HIM INTO A CORNER WAS...
...ME.
HOKUTO...

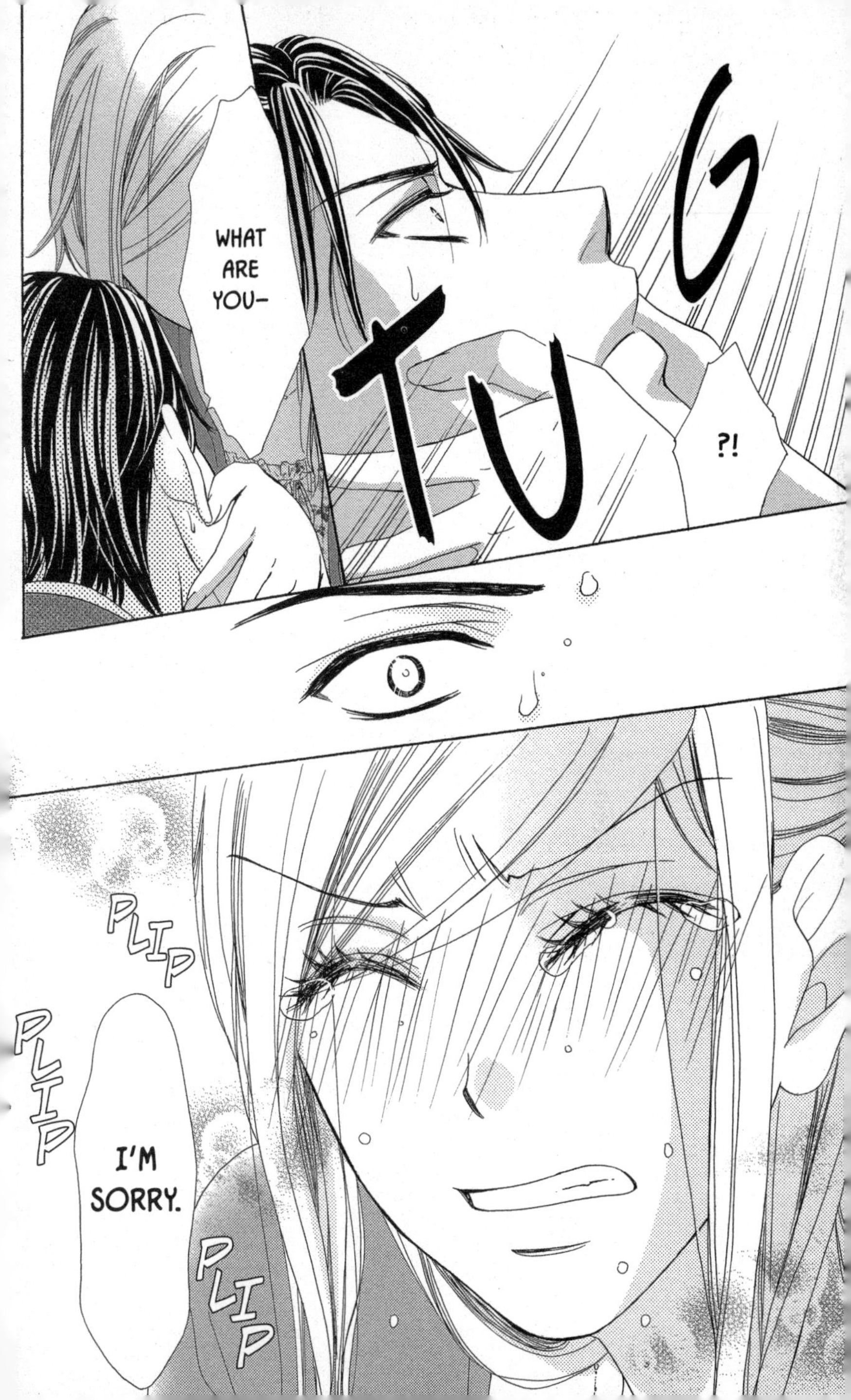
?!
TUG
WHAT ARE YOU–
PLIP PLIP
I'M SORRY.
PLIP PLIP

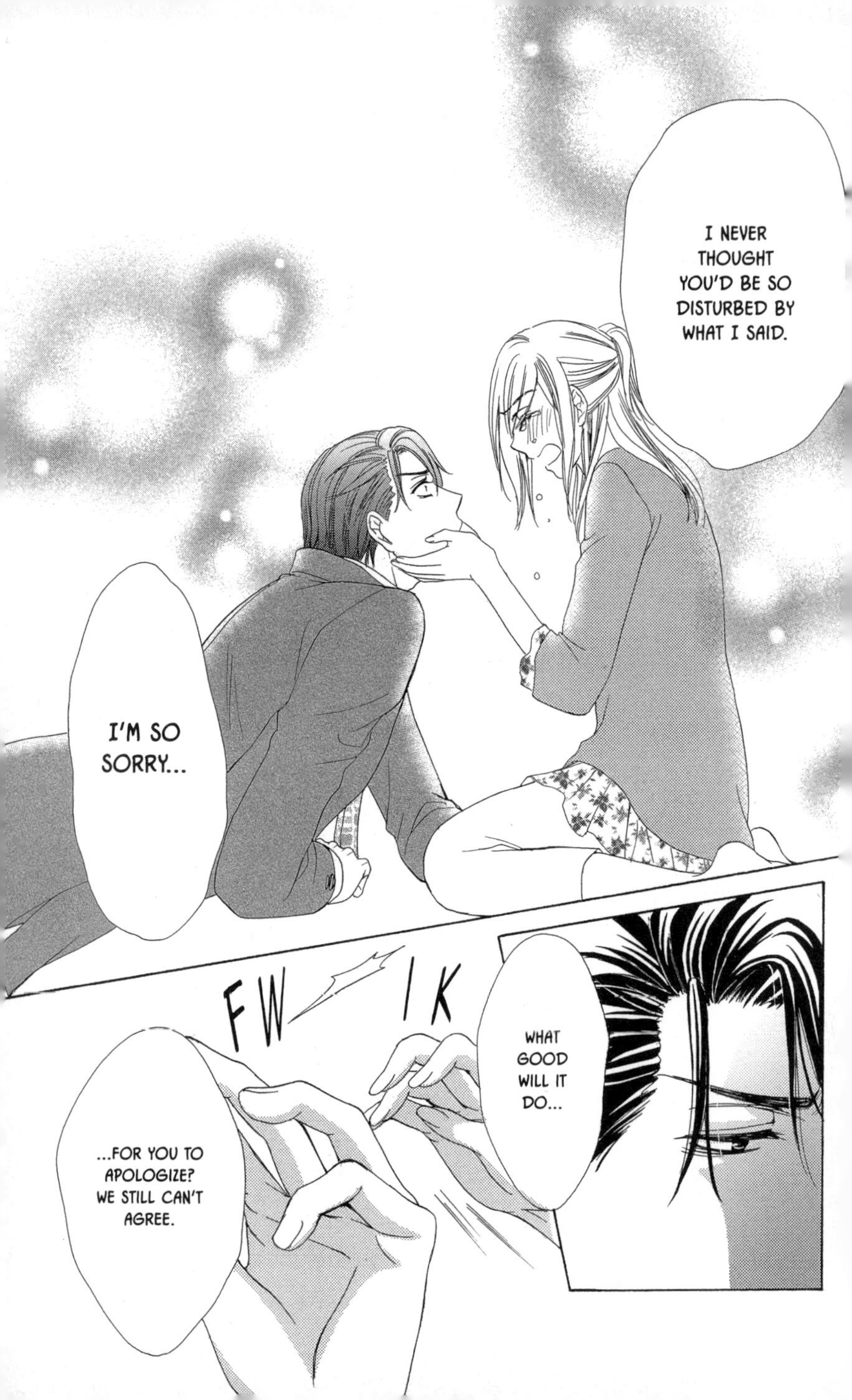
I NEVER THOUGHT YOU'D BE SO DISTURBED BY WHAT I SAID.
I'M SO SORRY...
WHAT GOOD WILL IT DO...
FW IK
...FOR YOU TO APOLOGIZE? WE STILL CAN'T AGREE.

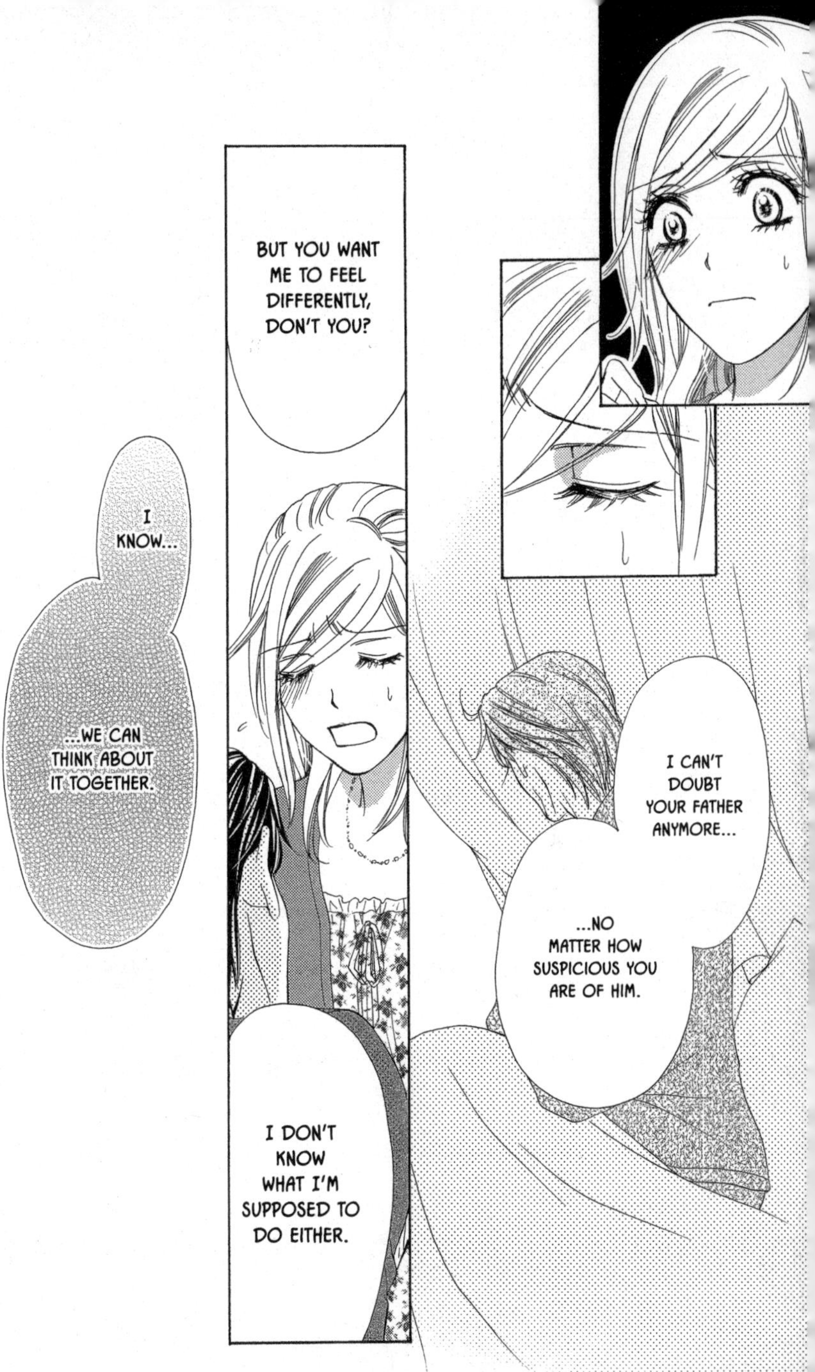
I CAN'T DOUBT YOUR FATHER ANYMORE...
...NO MATTER HOW SUSPICIOUS YOU ARE OF HIM.
BUT YOU WANT ME TO FEEL DIFFERENTLY, DON'T YOU?
I DON'T KNOW WHAT I'M SUPPOSED TO DO EITHER.
I KNOW...
...WE CAN THINK ABOUT IT TOGETHER.

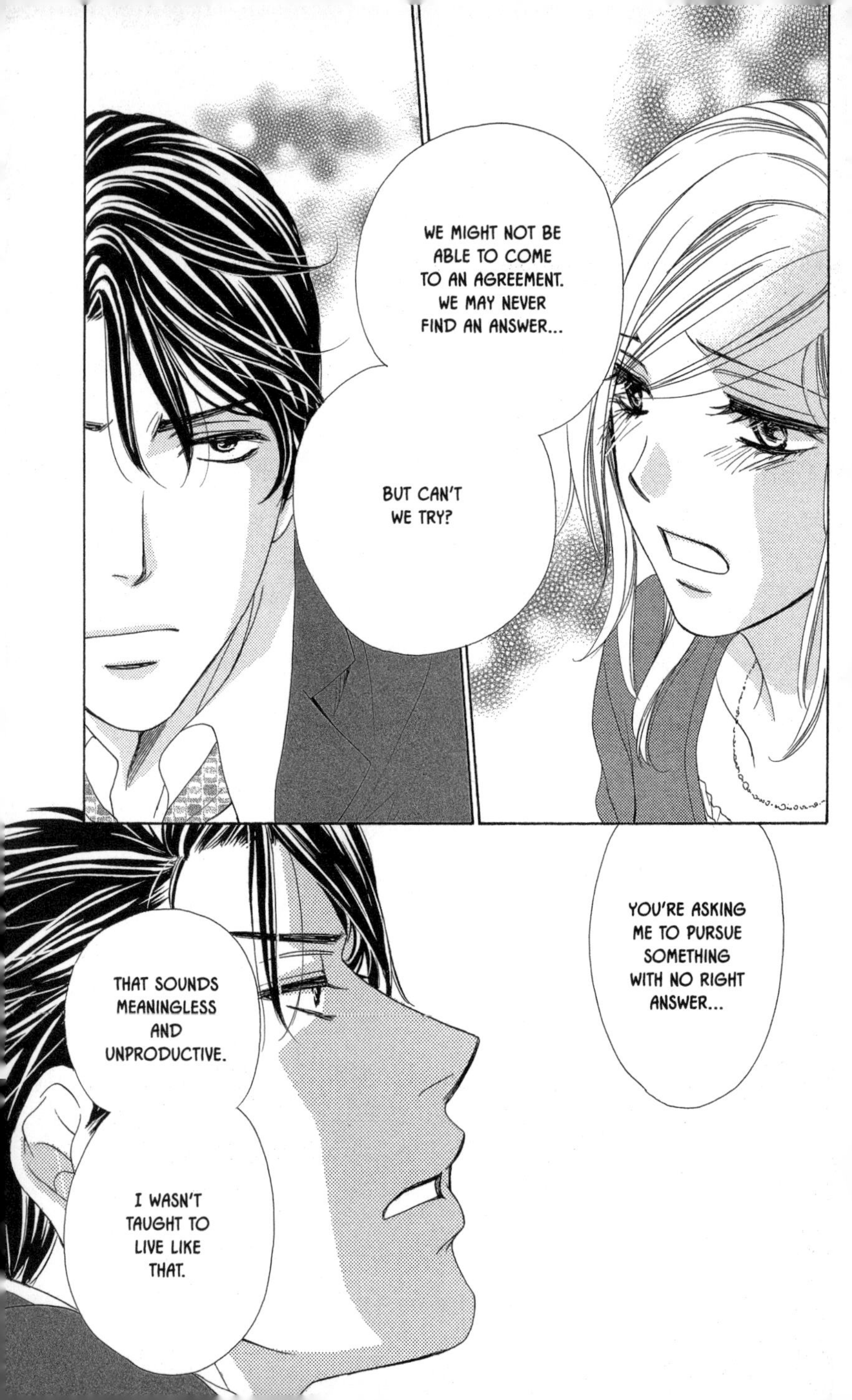
WE MIGHT NOT BE ABLE TO COME TO AN AGREEMENT. WE MAY NEVER FIND AN ANSWER...
BUT CAN'T WE TRY?
YOU'RE ASKING ME TO PURSUE SOMETHING WITH NO RIGHT ANSWER...
THAT SOUNDS MEANINGLESS AND UNPRODUCTIVE.
I WASN'T TAUGHT TO LIVE LIKE THAT.

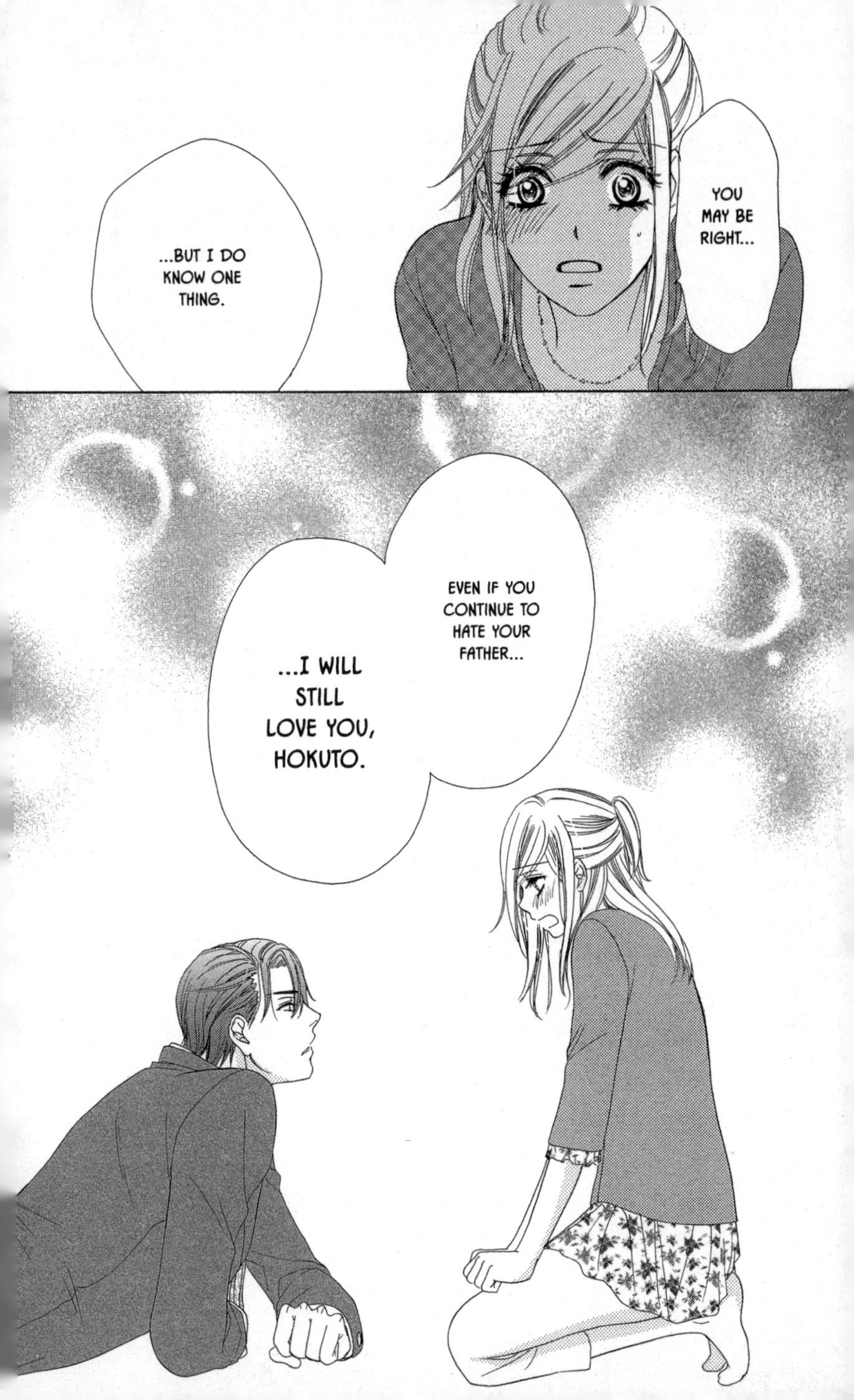
YOU MAY BE RIGHT...
...BUT I DO KNOW ONE THING.
EVEN IF YOU CONTINUE TO HATE YOUR FATHER...
...I WILL STILL LOVE YOU, HOKUTO.

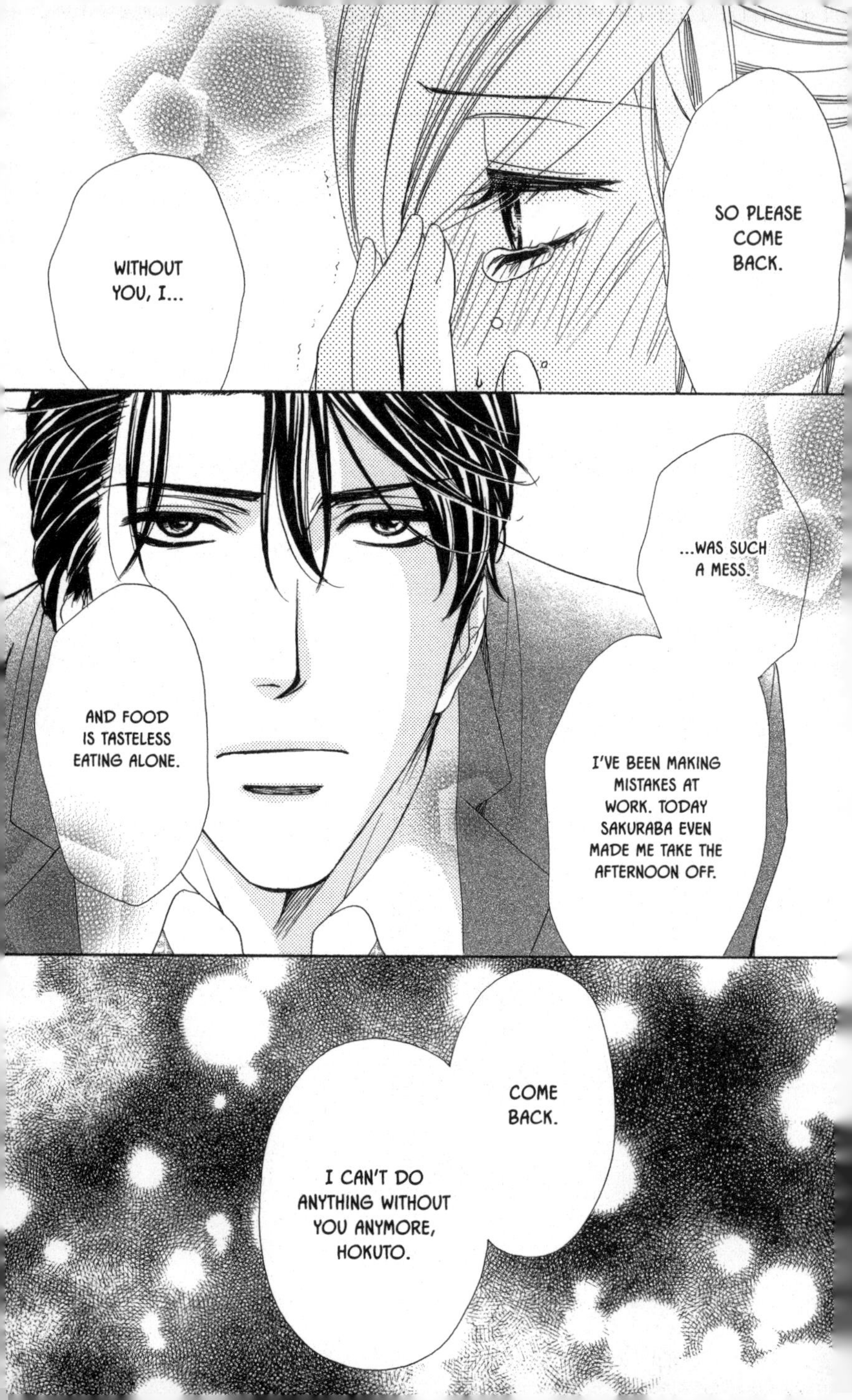
SO PLEASE COME BACK.
WITHOUT YOU, I...
...WAS SUCH A MESS.
I'VE BEEN MAKING MISTAKES AT WORK. TODAY SAKURABA EVEN MADE ME TAKE THE AFTERNOON OFF.
AND FOOD IS TASTELESS EATING ALONE.
COME BACK.
I CAN'T DO ANYTHING WITHOUT YOU ANYMORE, HOKUTO.

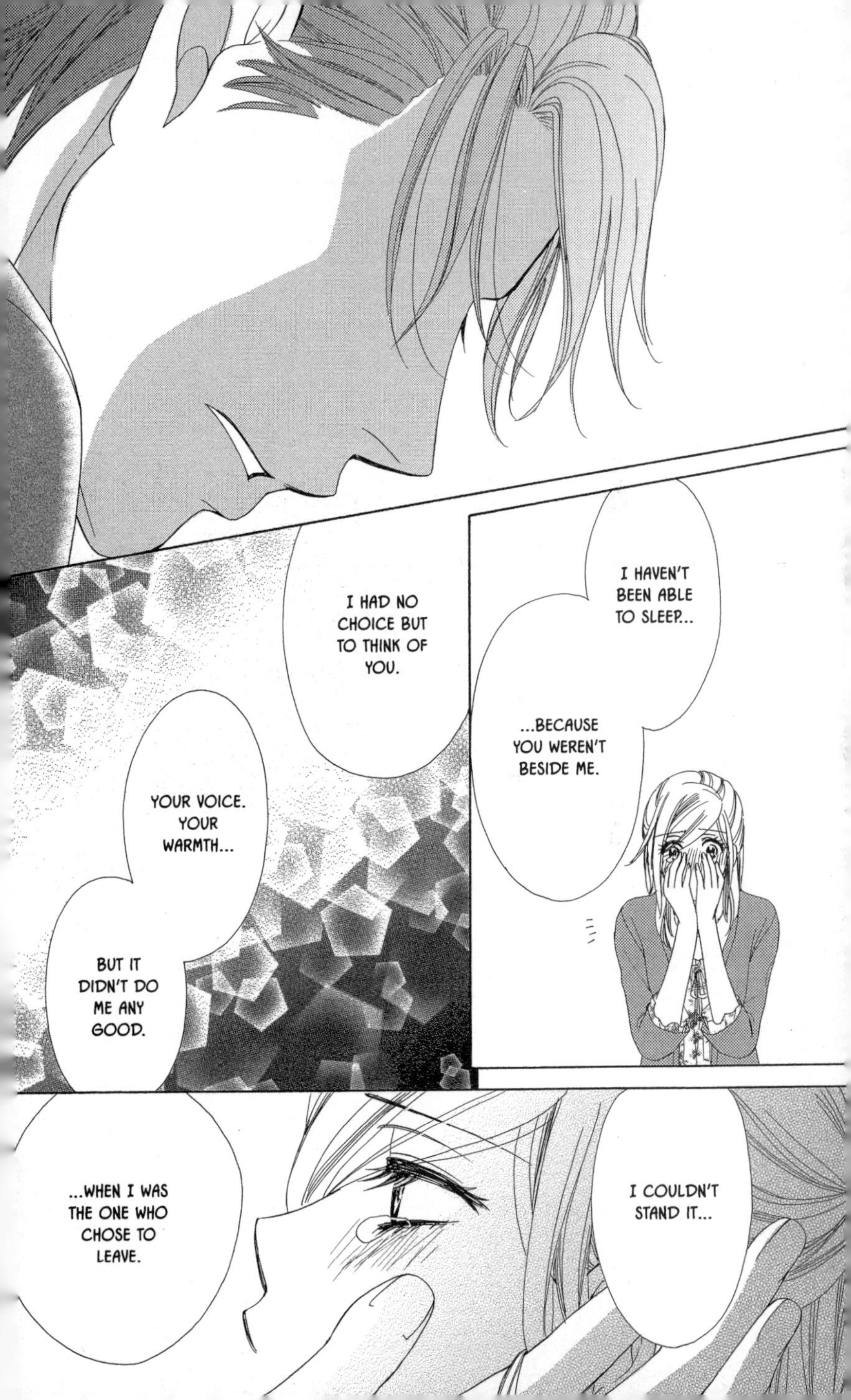
I HAVEN'T BEEN ABLE TO SLEEP...
...BECAUSE YOU WEREN'T BESIDE ME.
I HAD NO CHOICE BUT TO THINK OF YOU.
YOUR VOICE. YOUR WARMTH...
BUT IT DIDN'T DO ME ANY GOOD.
I COULDN'T STAND IT...
...WHEN I WAS THE ONE WHO CHOSE TO LEAVE.

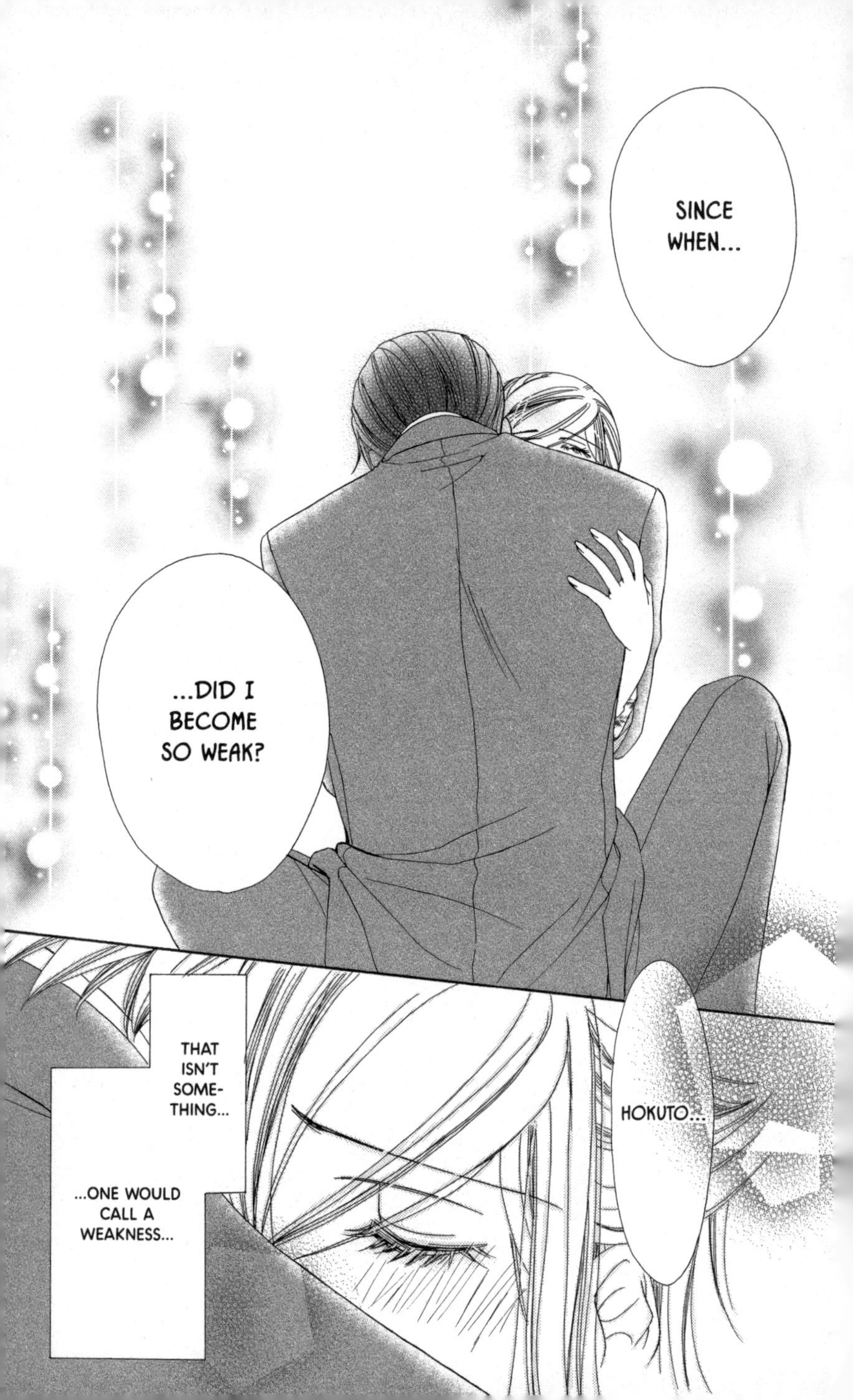
SINCE WHEN...
...DID I BECOME SO WEAK?
HOKUTO...
THAT ISN'T SOME-THING...
...ONE WOULD CALL A WEAKNESS...

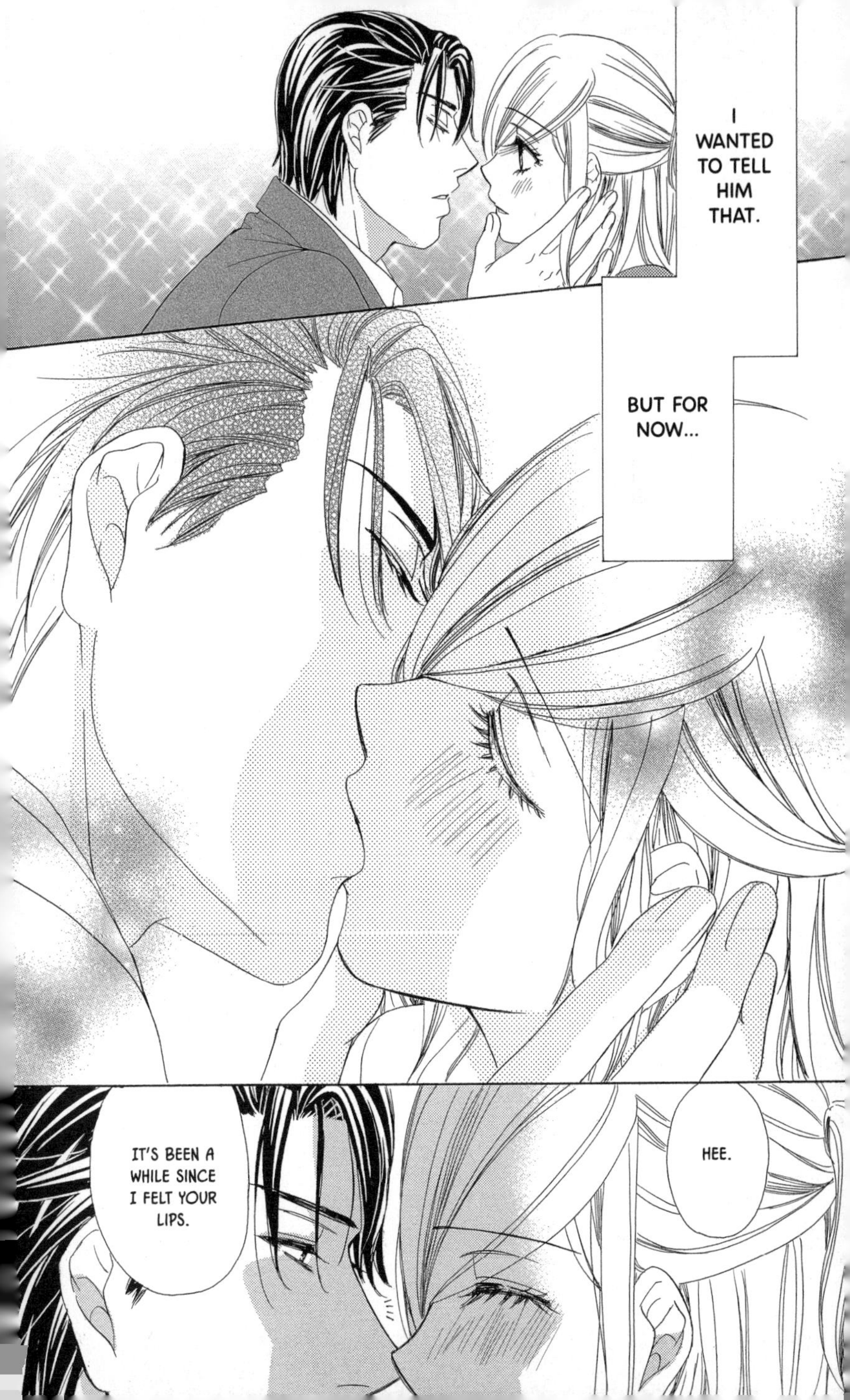
I WANTED TO TELL HIM THAT.
BUT FOR NOW...
HEE.
IT'S BEEN A WHILE SINCE I FELT YOUR LIPS.

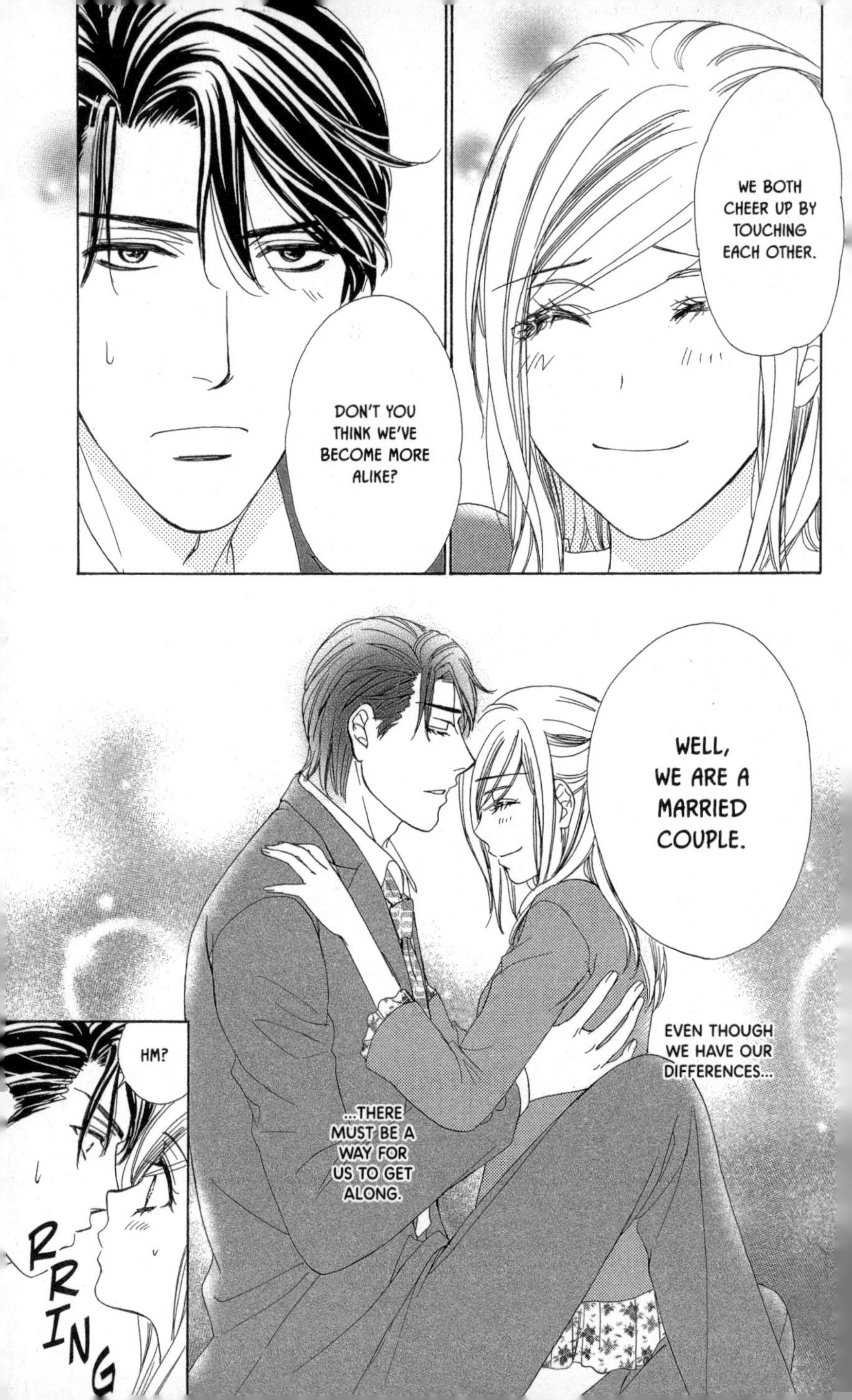
WE BOTH CHEER UP BY TOUCHING EACH OTHER.
DON'T YOU THINK WE'VE BECOME MORE ALIKE?
WELL, WE ARE A MARRIED COUPLE.
EVEN THOUGH WE HAVE OUR DIFFERENCES...
...THERE MUST BE A WAY FOR US TO GET ALONG.
HM?
RRING

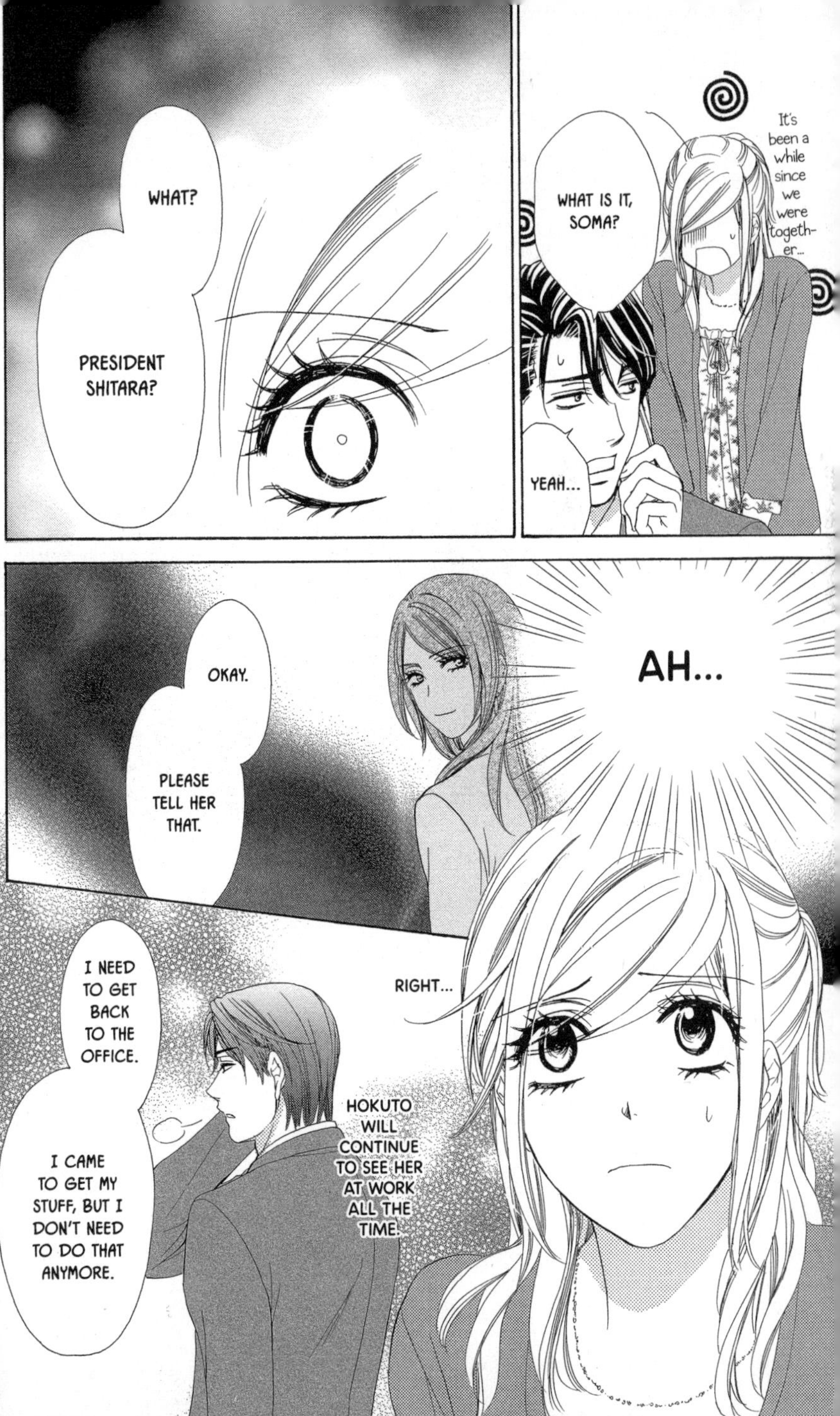
WHAT IS IT, SOMA?
It's been a while since we were togeth-er...
YEAH...
WHAT?
PRESIDENT SHITARA?
AH...
OKAY.
PLEASE TELL HER THAT.
RIGHT...
HOKUTO WILL CONTINUE TO SEE HER AT WORK ALL THE TIME.
I NEED TO GET BACK TO THE OFFICE.
I CAME TO GET MY STUFF, BUT I DON'T NEED TO DO THAT ANYMORE.

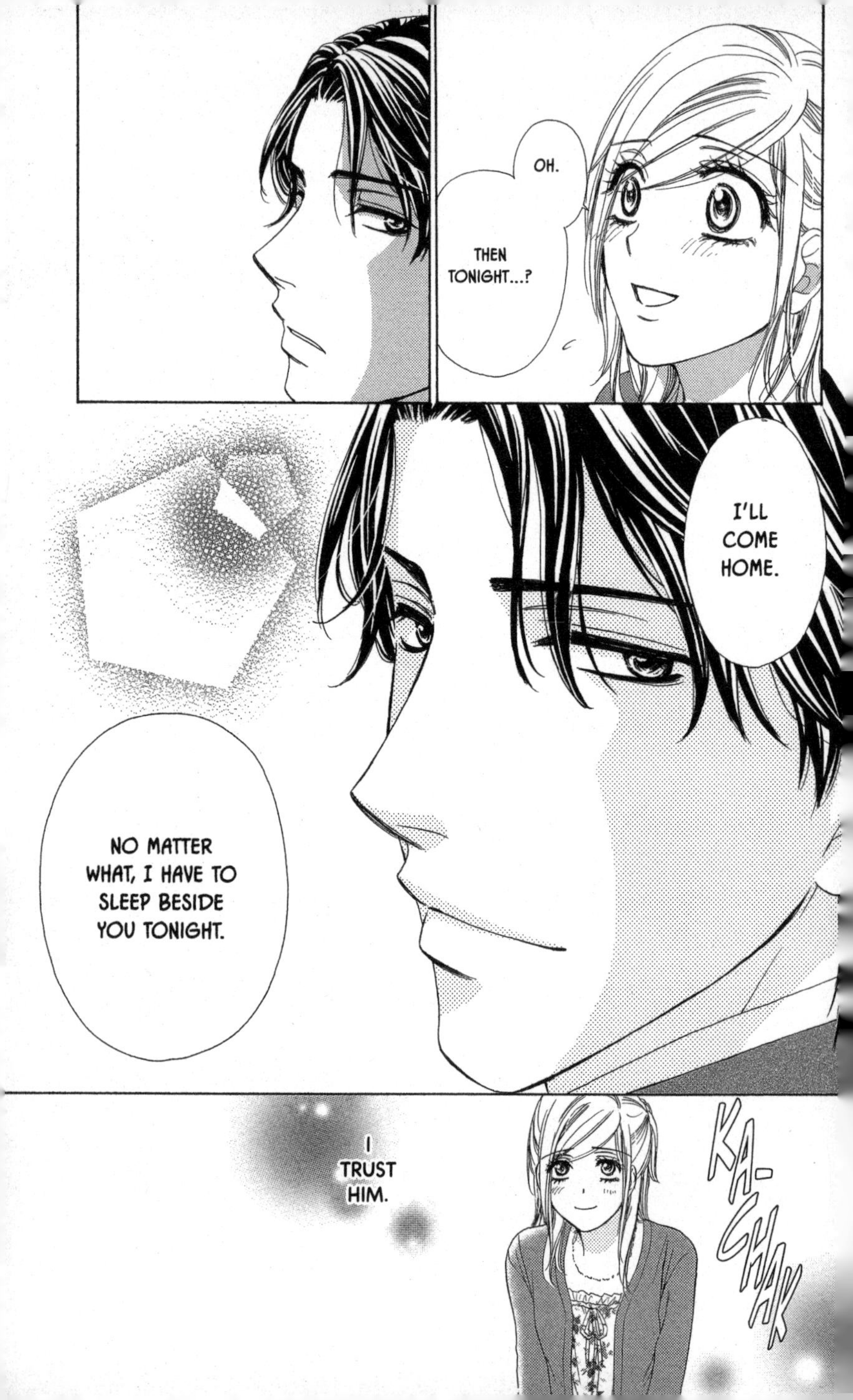
OH.
THEN TONIGHT...?
I'LL COME HOME.
NO MATTER WHAT, I HAVE TO SLEEP BESIDE YOU TONIGHT.
KA-CHAK
I TRUST HIM.

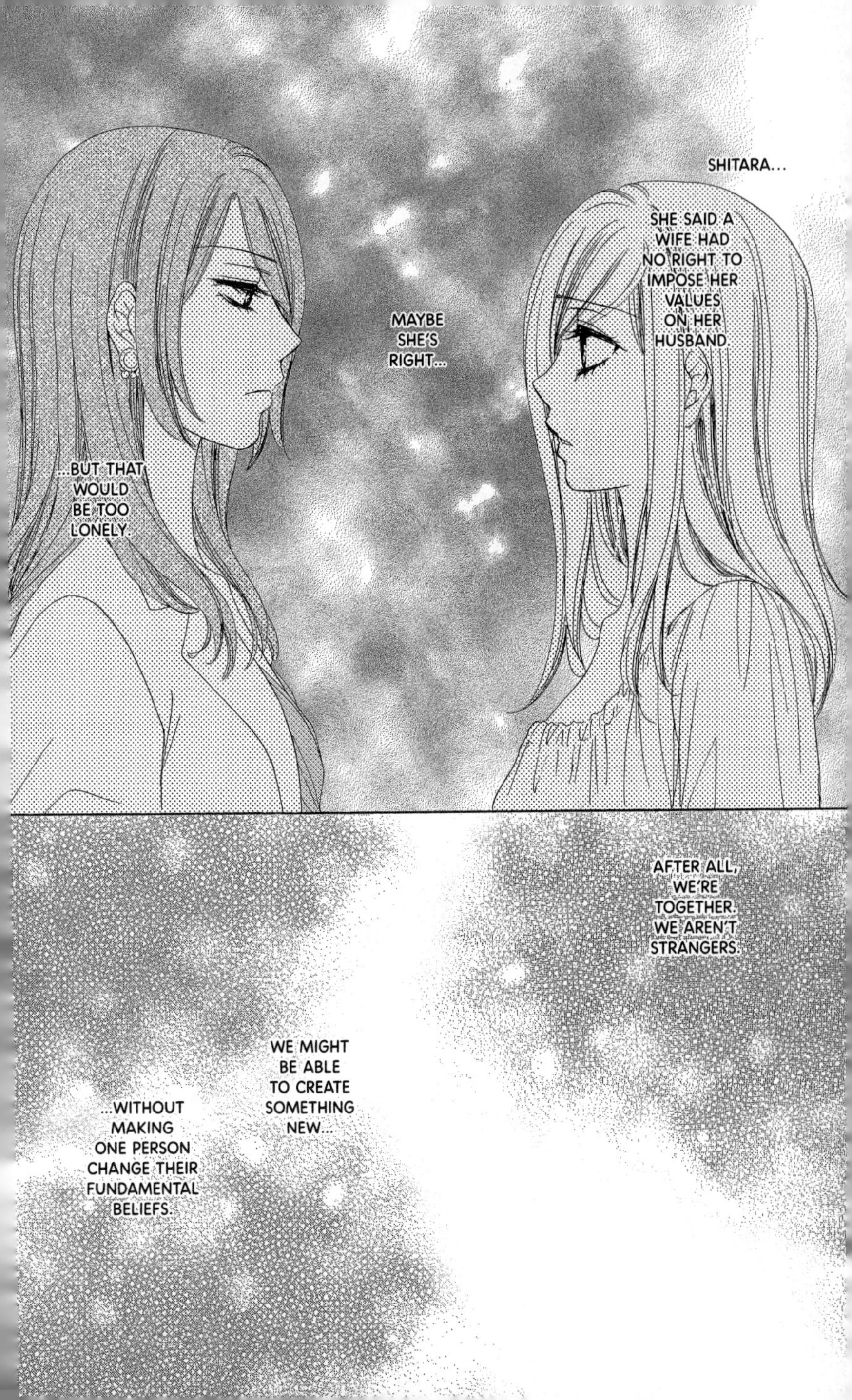
SHITARA...
SHE SAID A WIFE HAD NO RIGHT TO IMPOSE HER VALUES ON HER HUSBAND.
MAYBE SHE'S RIGHT...
...BUT THAT WOULD BE TOO LONELY.
AFTER ALL, WE'RE TOGETHER. WE AREN'T STRANGERS.
WE MIGHT BE ABLE TO CREATE SOMETHING NEW...
...WITHOUT MAKING ONE PERSON CHANGE THEIR FUNDAMENTAL BELIEFS.

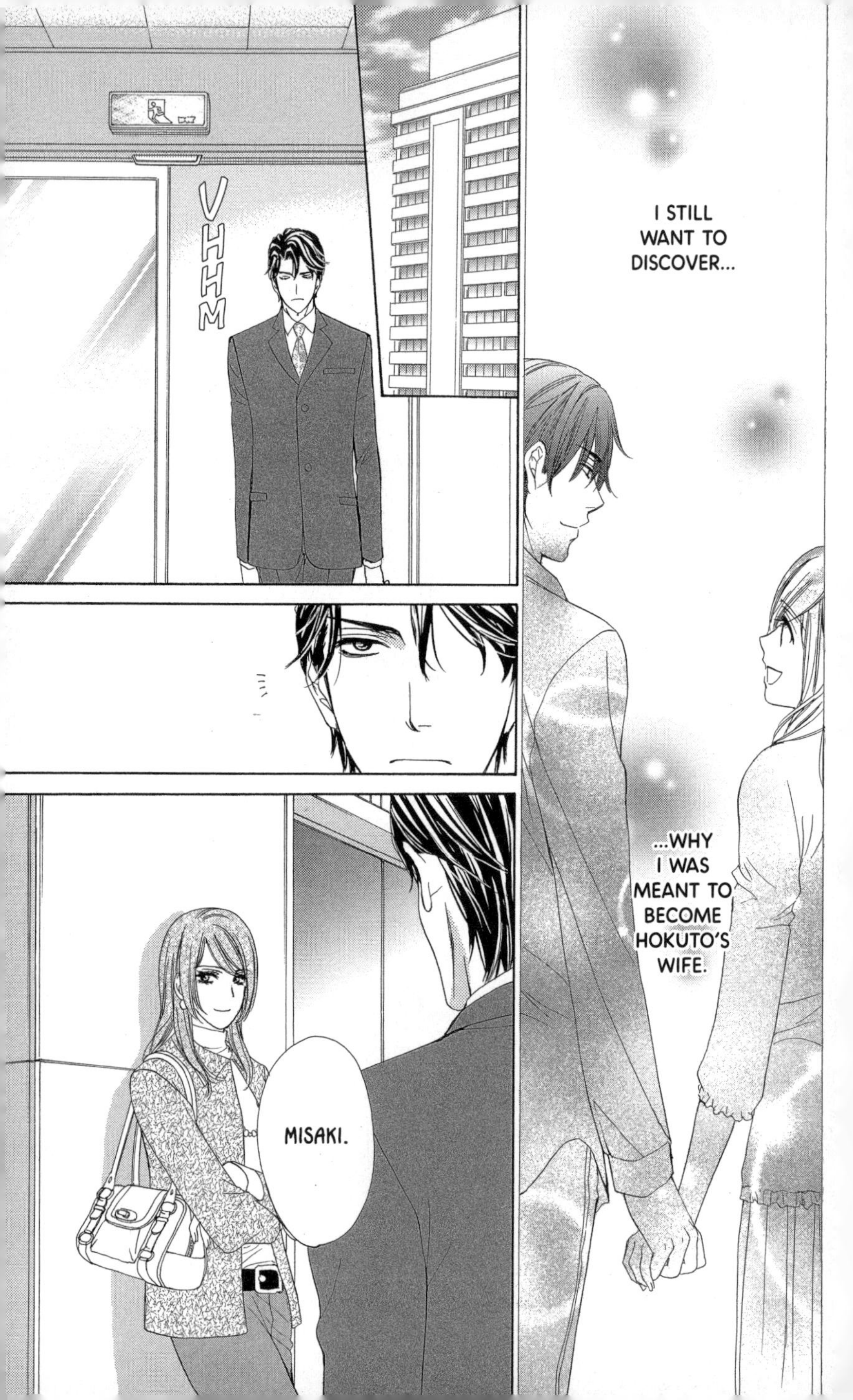
I STILL WANT TO DISCOVER...
...WHY I WAS MEANT TO BECOME HOKUTO'S WIFE.
VHHM
MISAKI.

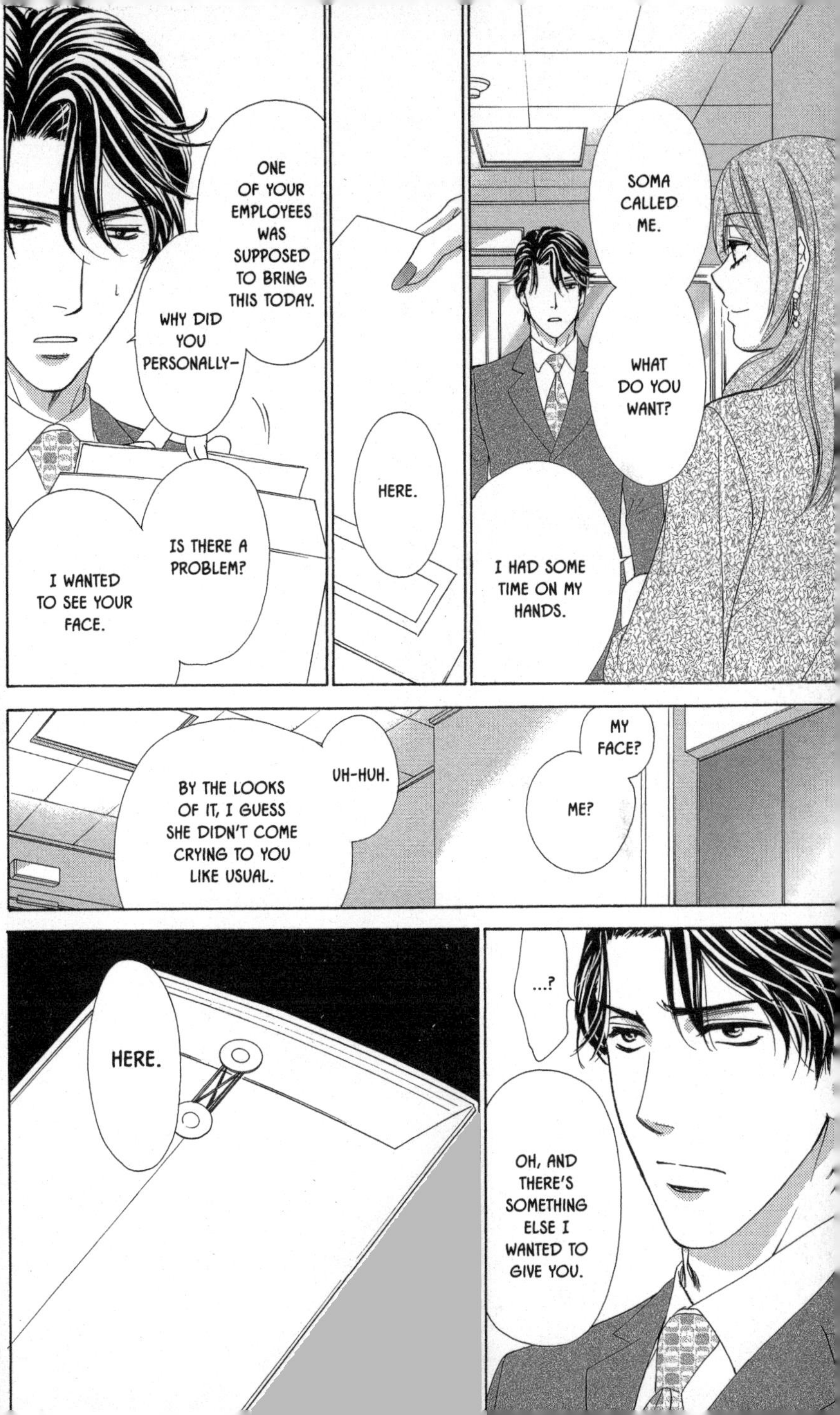
SOMA CALLED ME.
WHAT DO YOU WANT?
I HAD SOME TIME ON MY HANDS.
HERE.
ONE OF YOUR EMPLOYEES WAS SUPPOSED TO BRING THIS TODAY.
WHY DID YOU PERSONALLY—
IS THERE A PROBLEM?
I WANTED TO SEE YOUR FACE.
MY FACE?
ME?
UH-HUH.
BY THE LOOKS OF IT, I GUESS SHE DIDN'T COME CRYING TO YOU LIKE USUAL.
...?
OH, AND THERE'S SOMETHING ELSE I WANTED TO GIVE YOU.
HERE.

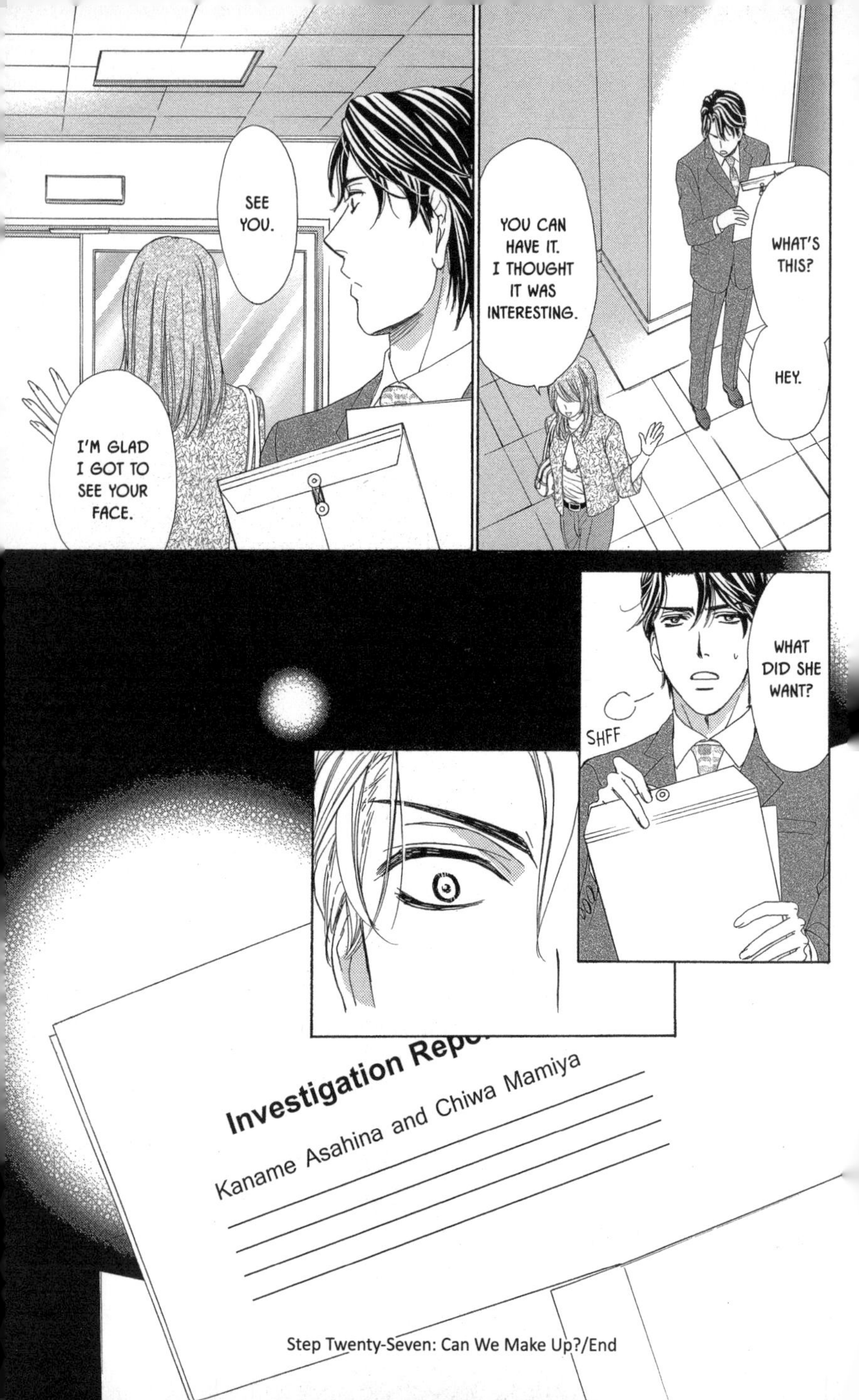
WHAT'S THIS?
HEY.
YOU CAN HAVE IT. I THOUGHT IT WAS INTERESTING.
SEE YOU.
I'M GLAD I GOT TO SEE YOUR FACE.
WHAT DID SHE WANT?
SHFF
Investigation Repo
Kaname Asahina and Chiwa Mamiya
Step Twenty-Seven: Can We Make Up?/End

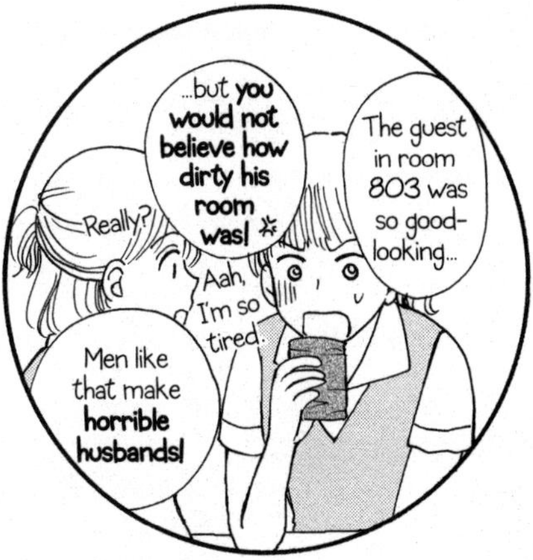
The guest in room 803 was so good-looking...
...but you would not believe how dirty his room was!
Really?
Aah, I'm so tired.
Men like that make horrible husbands!

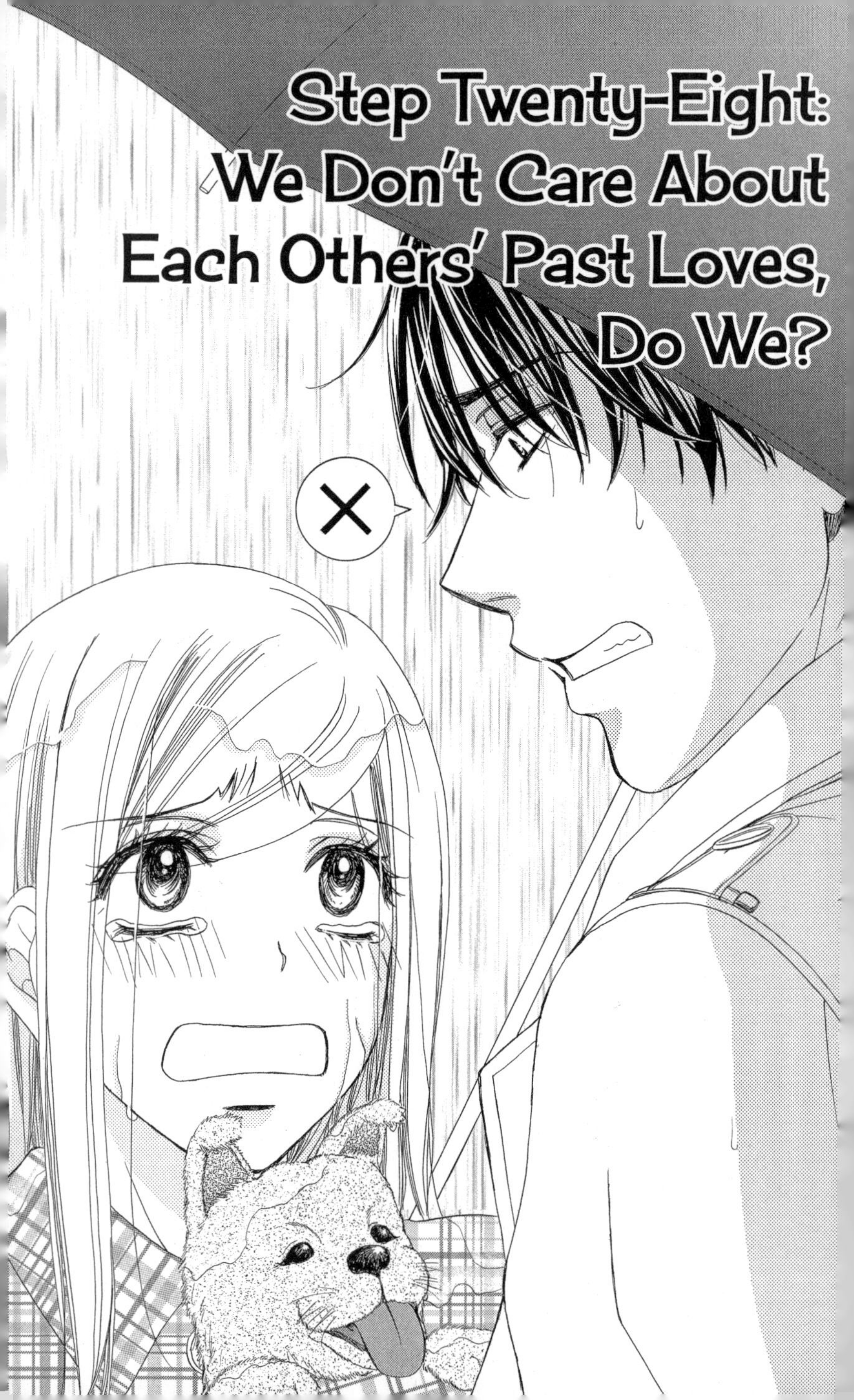
Step Twenty-Eight: We Don't Care About Each Others' Past Loves, Do We?
×

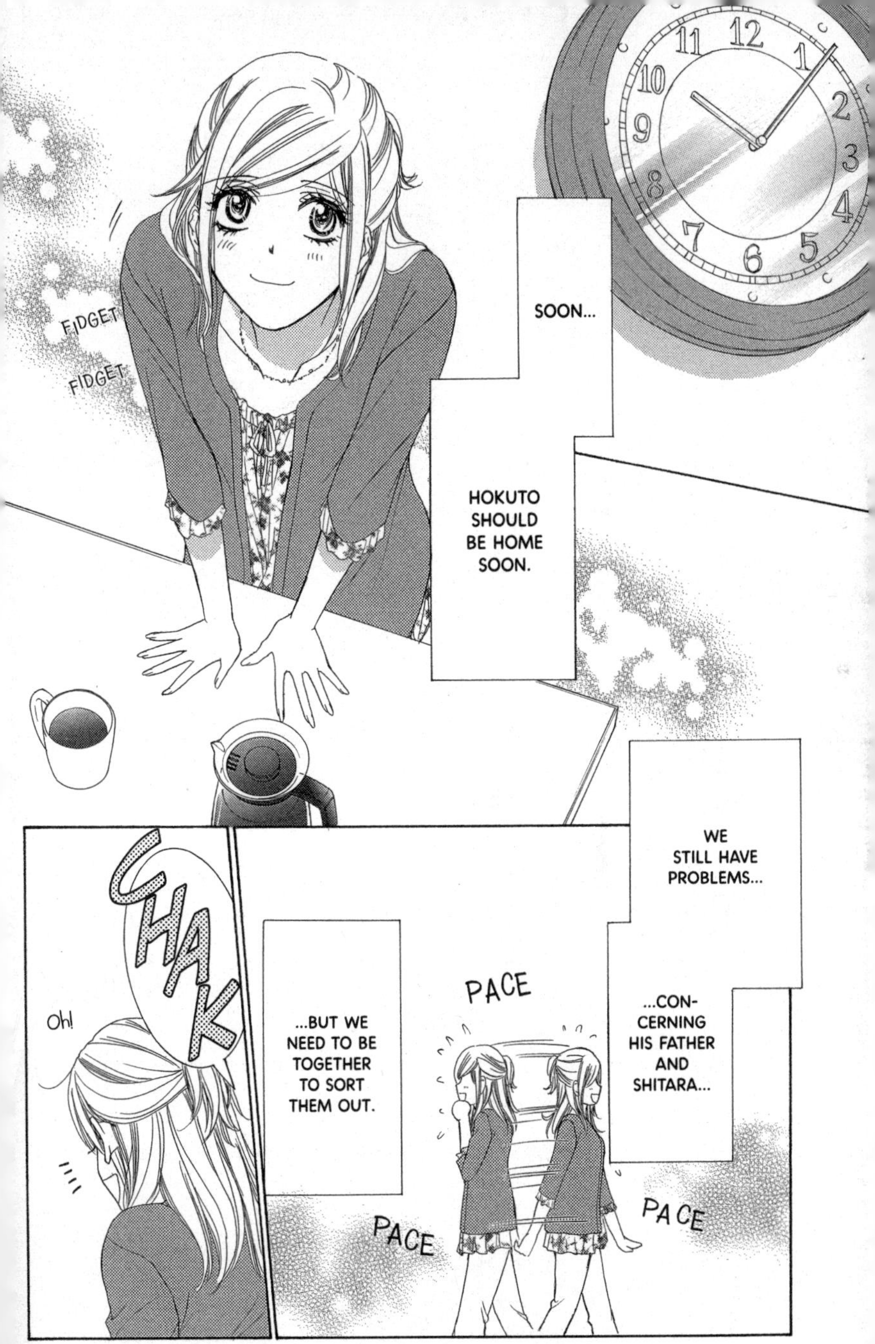
SOON...
HOKUTO SHOULD BE HOME SOON.
FIDGET
FIDGET
WE STILL HAVE PROBLEMS...
...CON-CERNING HIS FATHER AND SHITARA...
PACE
PACE
...BUT WE NEED TO BE TOGETHER TO SORT THEM OUT.
PACE
CHAK
Oh!

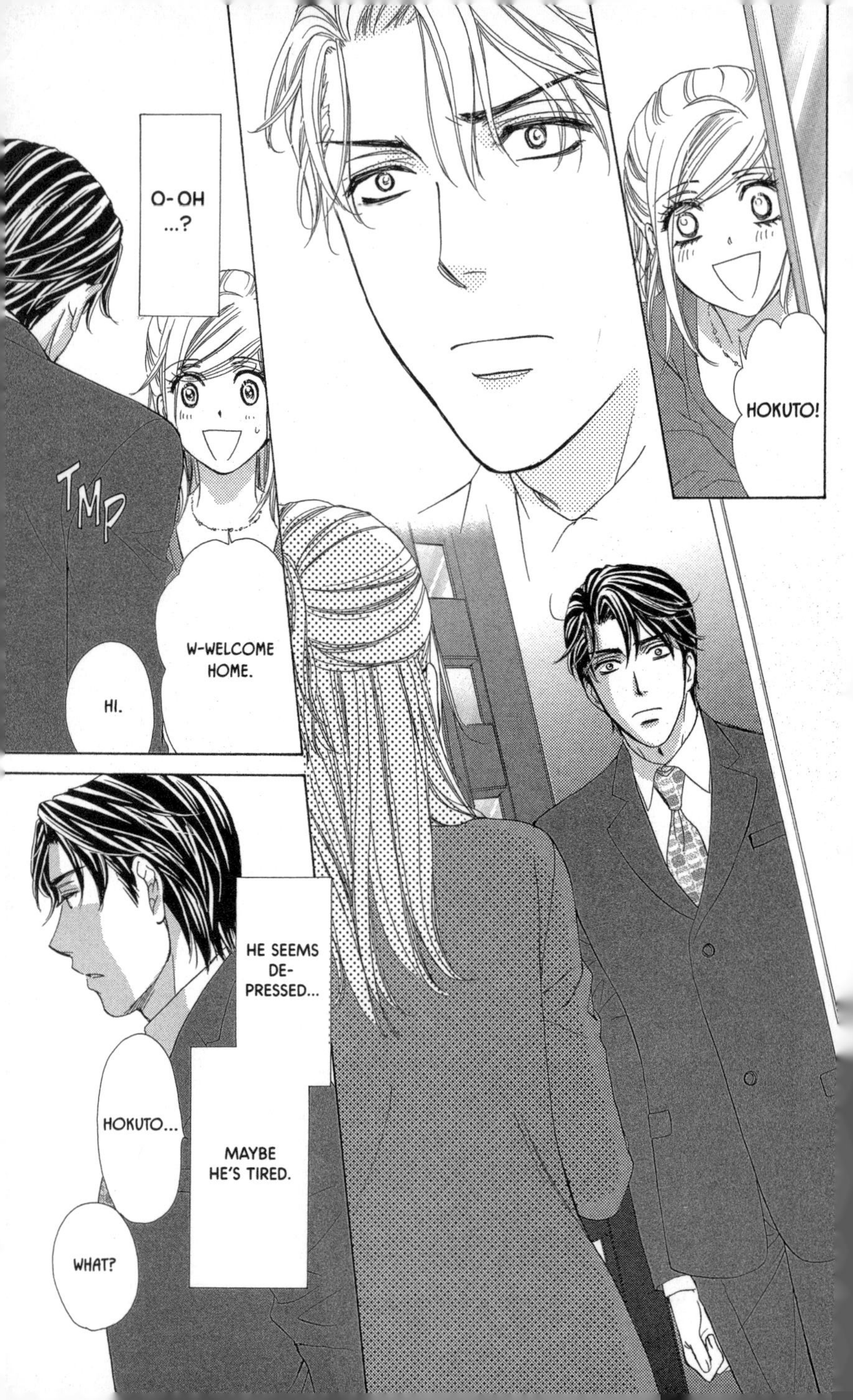
HOKUTO!
O-OH ...?
W-WELCOME HOME.
HI.
TMP
HE SEEMS DE-PRESSED...
MAYBE HE'S TIRED.
HOKUTO...
WHAT?

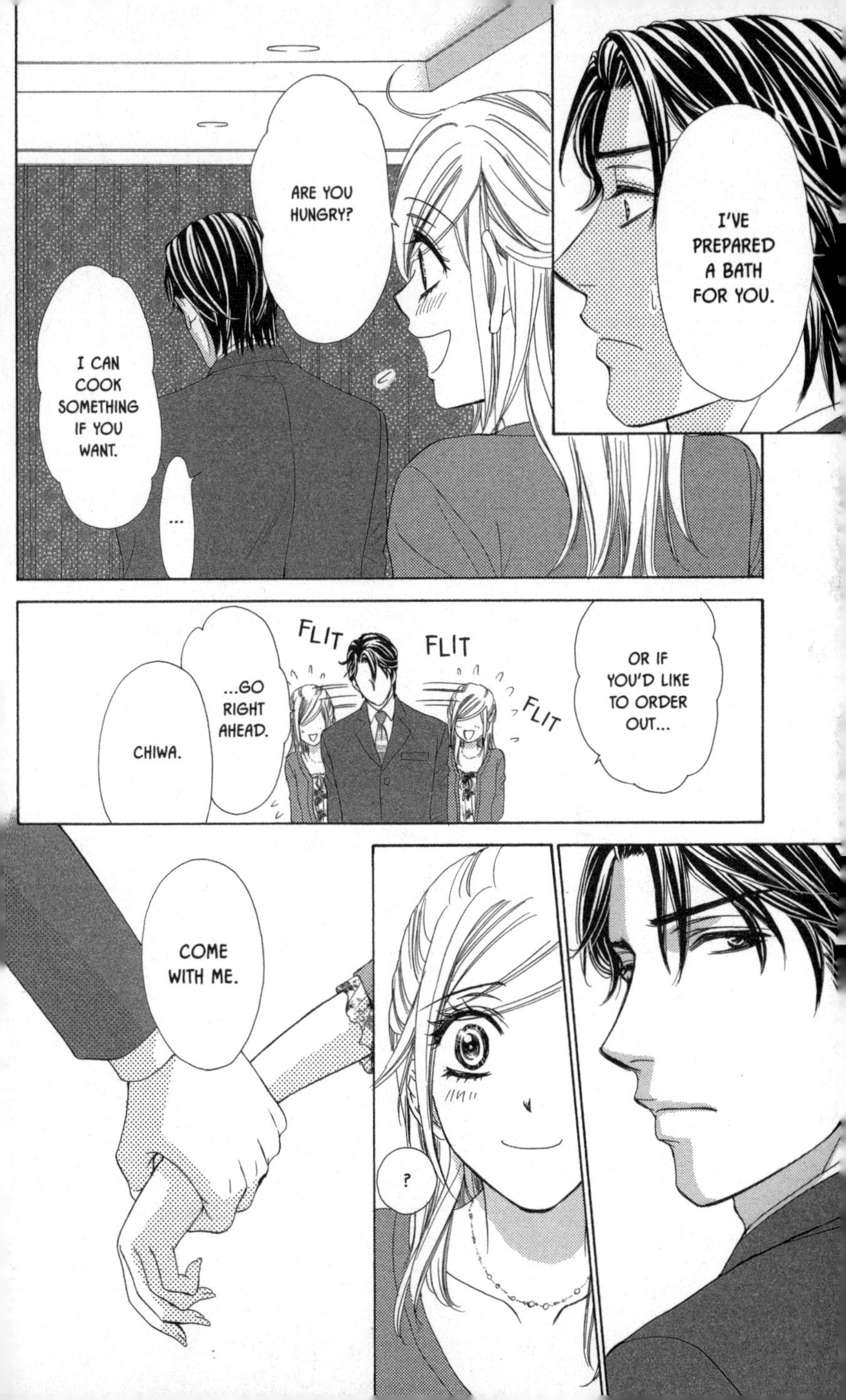
I'VE PREPARED A BATH FOR YOU.
ARE YOU HUNGRY?
I CAN COOK SOMETHING IF YOU WANT.
...
OR IF YOU'D LIKE TO ORDER OUT...
FLIT
FLIT
FLIT
...GO RIGHT AHEAD.
CHIWA.
?
COME WITH ME.

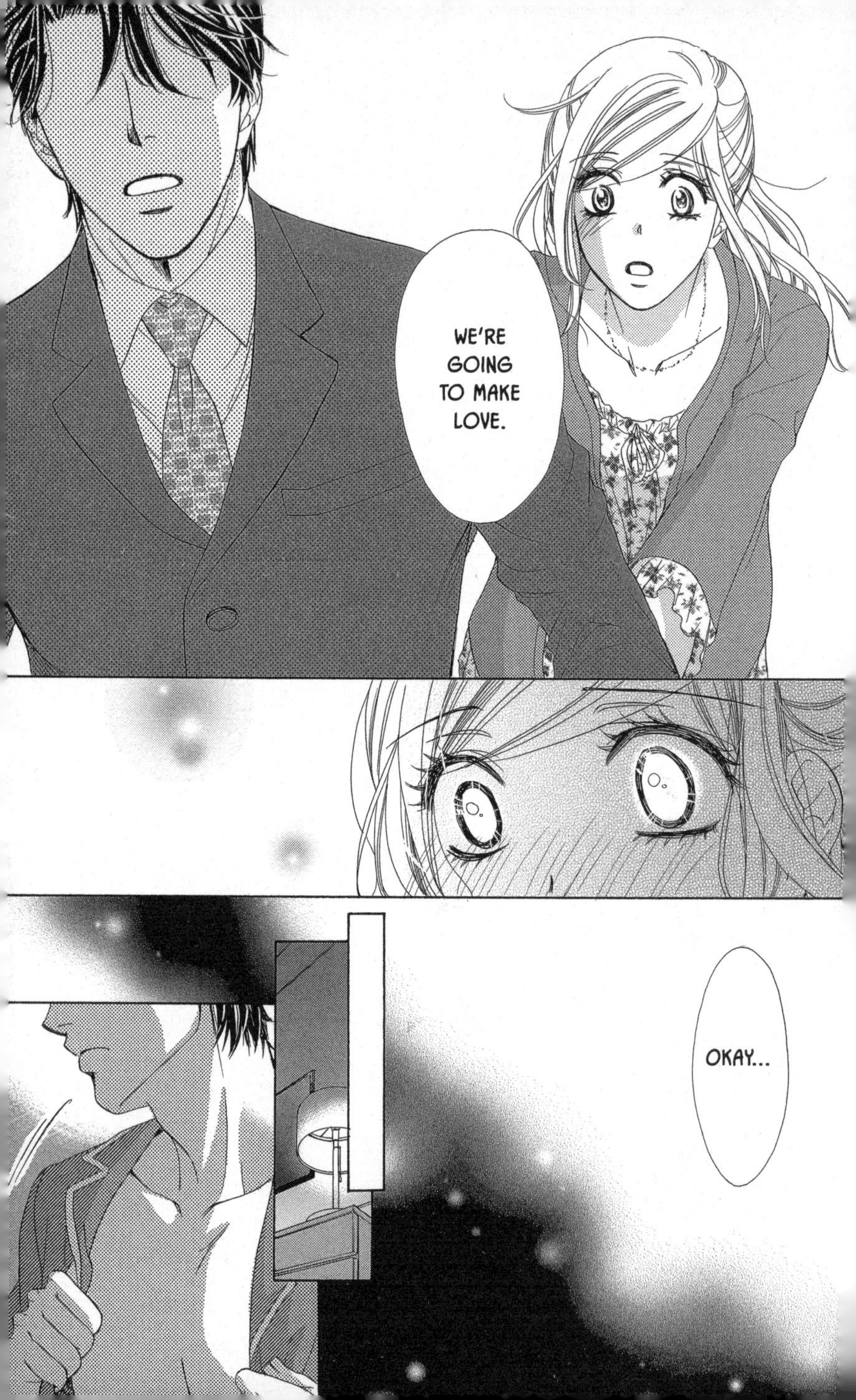
WE'RE GOING TO MAKE LOVE.
OKAY...

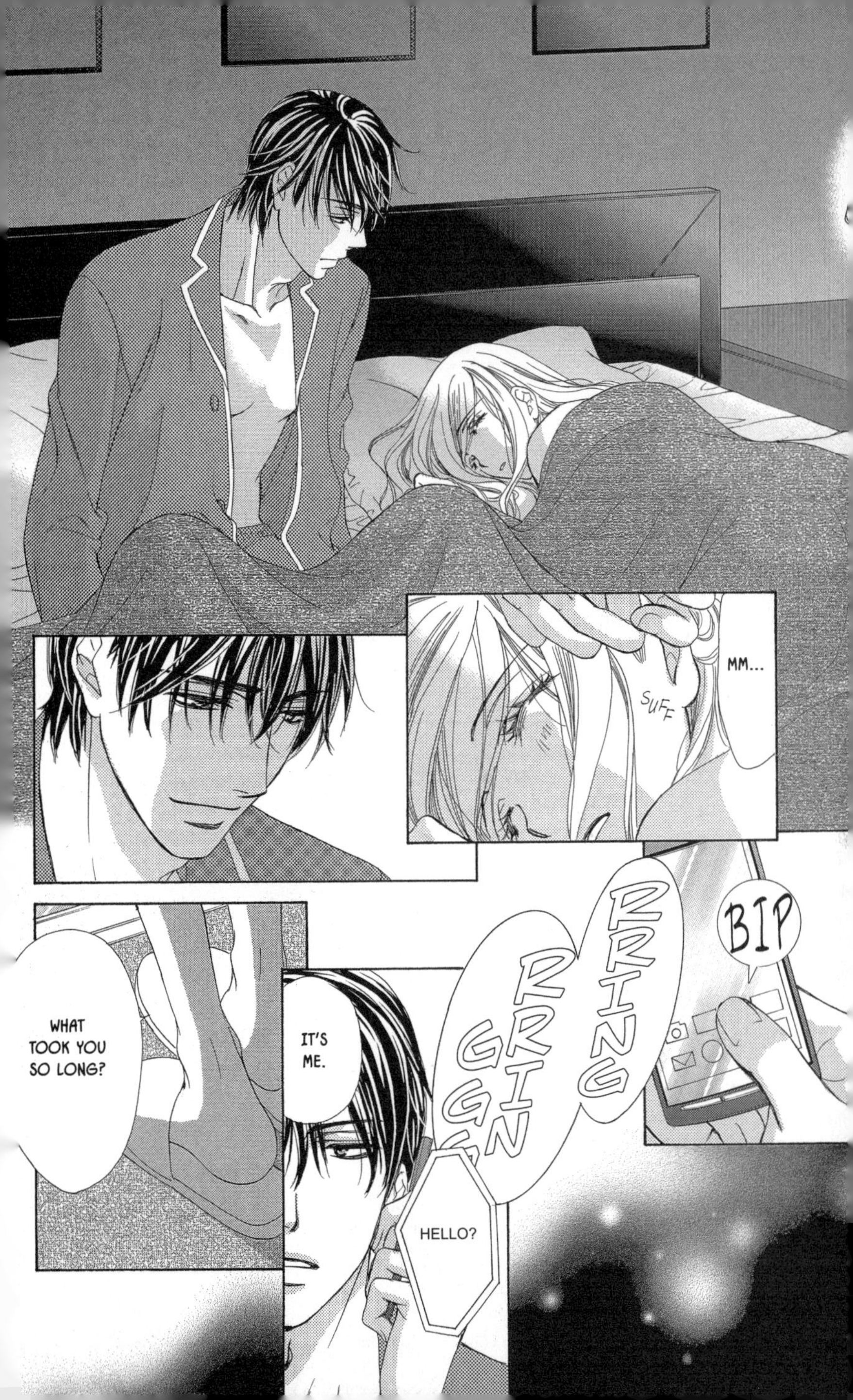

MM...
SUFF
BIP
RRING
GRING
IT'S ME.
HELLO?
WHAT TOOK YOU SO LONG?

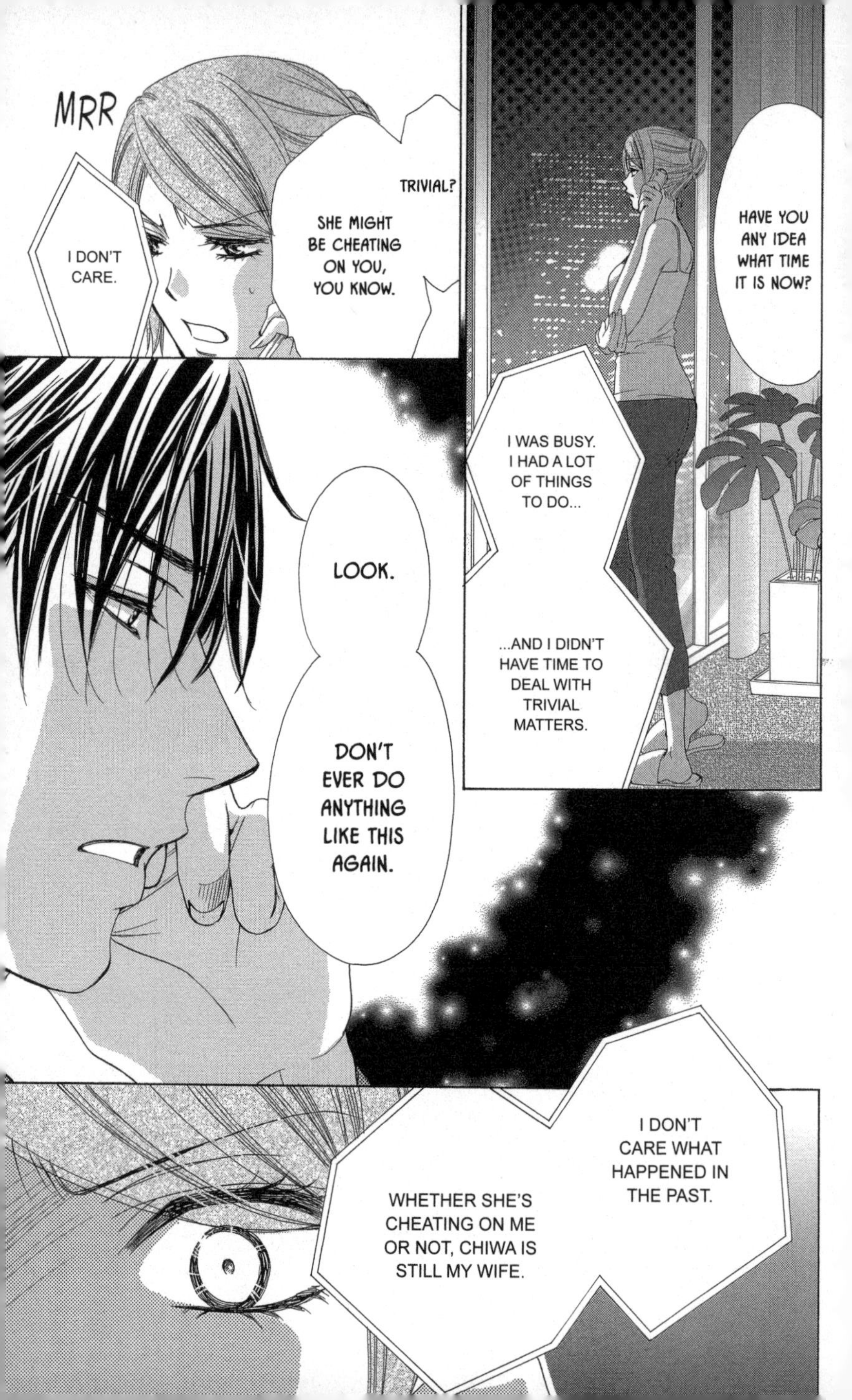
HAVE YOU ANY IDEA WHAT TIME IT IS NOW?
I WAS BUSY. I HAD A LOT OF THINGS TO DO...
...AND I DIDN'T HAVE TIME TO DEAL WITH TRIVIAL MATTERS.
TRIVIAL?
SHE MIGHT BE CHEATING ON YOU, YOU KNOW.
MRR
I DON'T CARE.
LOOK.
DON'T EVER DO ANYTHING LIKE THIS AGAIN.
I DON'T CARE WHAT HAPPENED IN THE PAST.
WHETHER SHE'S CHEATING ON ME OR NOT, CHIWA IS STILL MY WIFE.

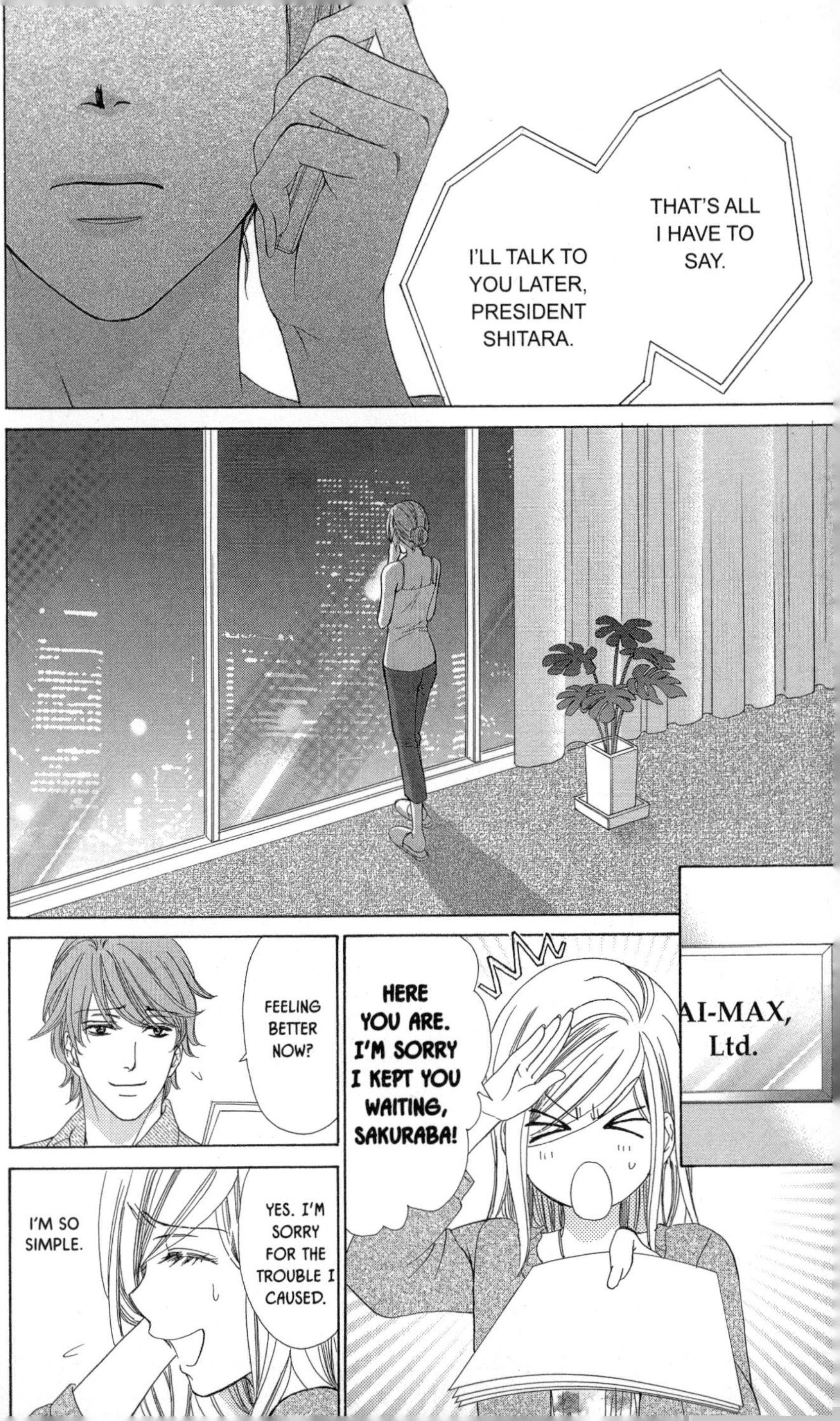
THAT'S ALL I HAVE TO SAY.
I'LL TALK TO YOU LATER, PRESIDENT SHITARA.
AI-MAX, Ltd.
HERE YOU ARE. I'M SORRY I KEPT YOU WAITING, SAKURABA!
FEELING BETTER NOW?
YES. I'M SORRY FOR THE TROUBLE I CAUSED.
I'M SO SIMPLE.

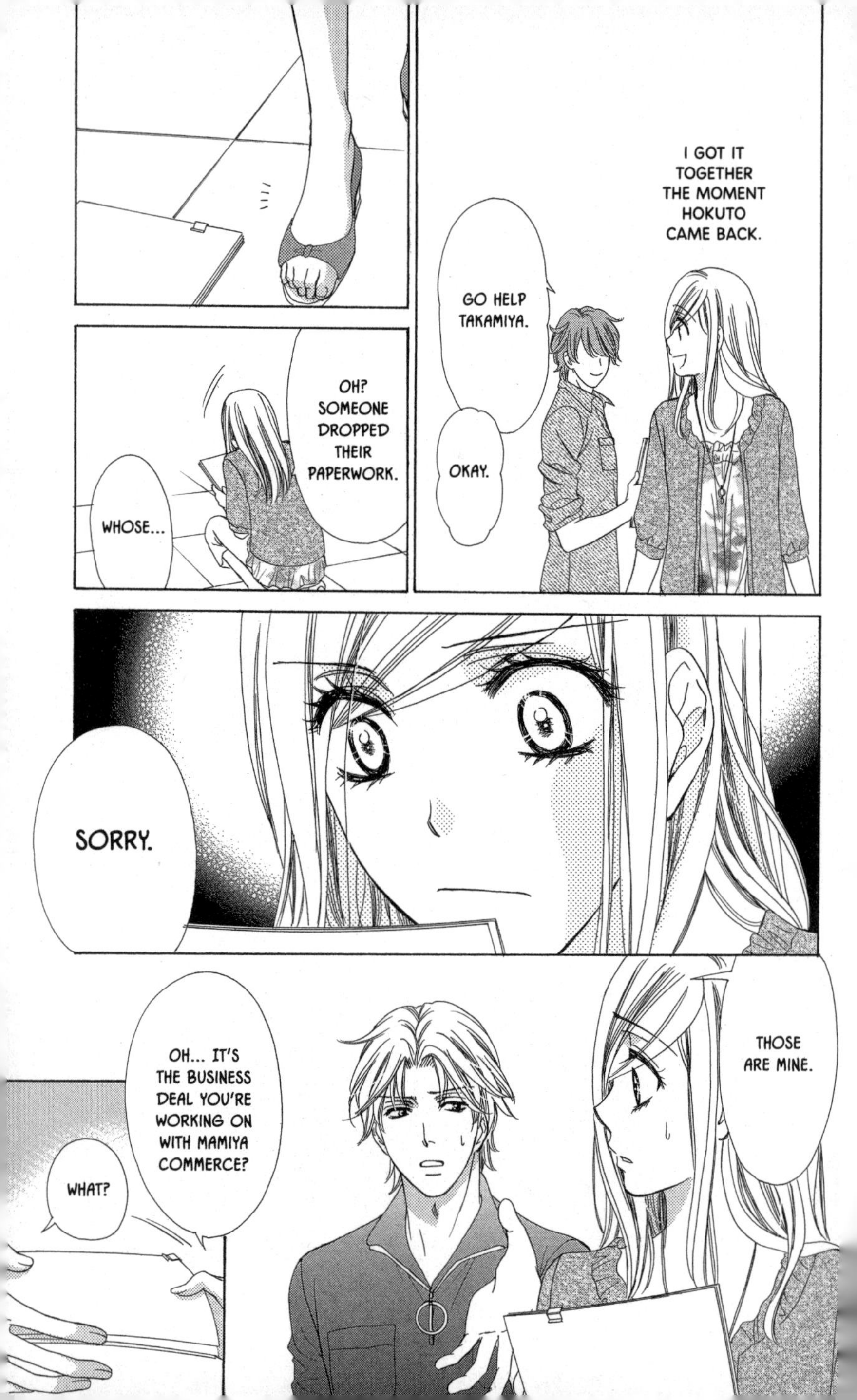
I GOT IT TOGETHER THE MOMENT HOKUTO CAME BACK.
GO HELP TAKAMIYA.
OKAY.
OH? SOMEONE DROPPED THEIR PAPERWORK.
WHOSE...
SORRY.
THOSE ARE MINE.
OH... IT'S THE BUSINESS DEAL YOU'RE WORKING ON WITH MAMIYA COMMERCE?
WHAT?

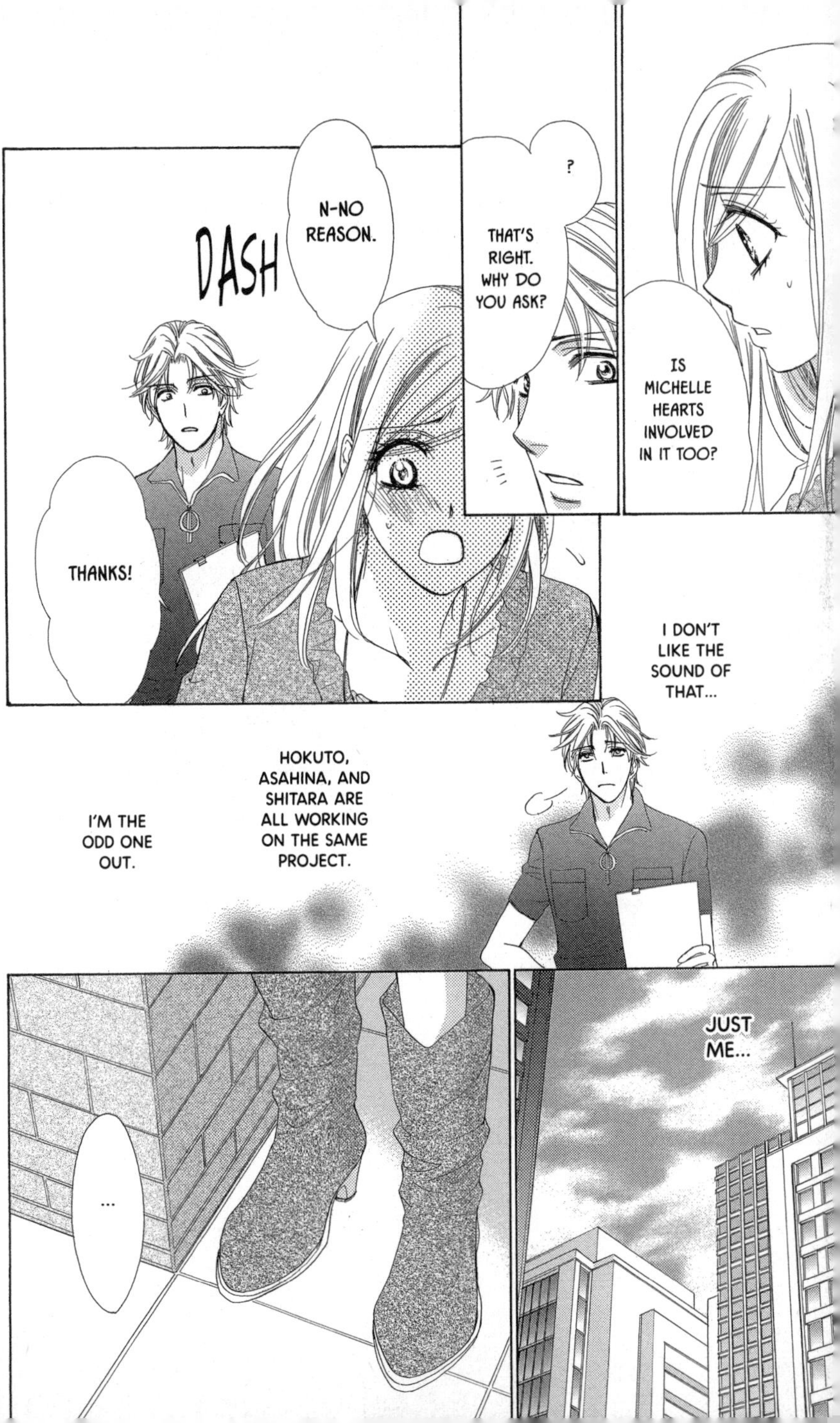
IS MICHELLE HEARTS INVOLVED IN IT TOO?
?
THAT'S RIGHT. WHY DO YOU ASK?
N-NO REASON.
DASH
THANKS!
I DON'T LIKE THE SOUND OF THAT...
HOKUTO, ASAHINA, AND SHITARA ARE ALL WORKING ON THE SAME PROJECT.
I'M THE ODD ONE OUT.
JUST ME...
...

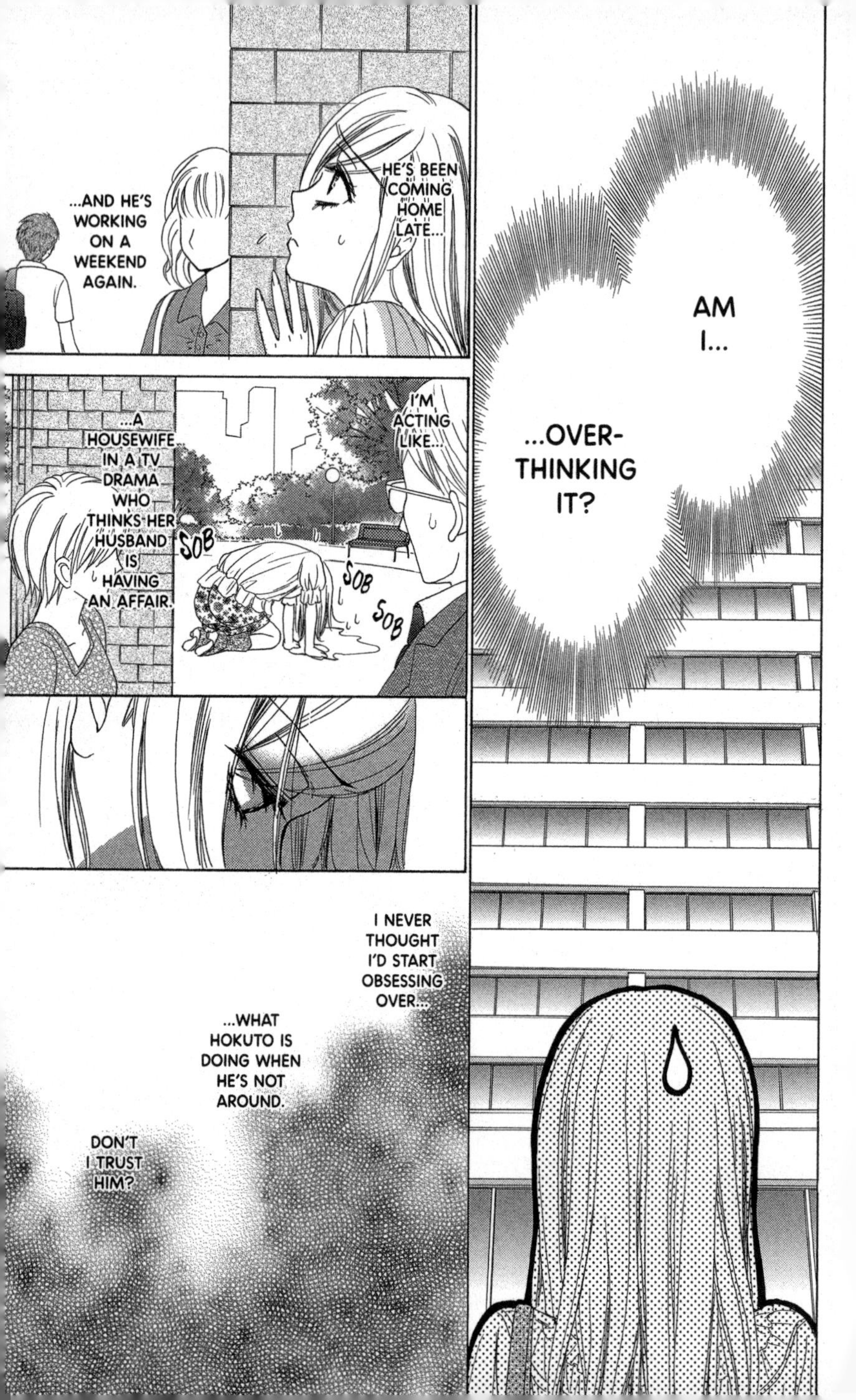
AM I...
...OVER-THINKING IT?
HE'S BEEN COMING HOME LATE...
...AND HE'S WORKING ON A WEEKEND AGAIN.
I'M ACTING LIKE...
...A HOUSEWIFE IN A TV DRAMA WHO THINKS HER HUSBAND IS HAVING AN AFFAIR.
SOB
SOB
SOB
I NEVER THOUGHT I'D START OBSESSING OVER...
...WHAT HOKUTO IS DOING WHEN HE'S NOT AROUND.
DON'T I TRUST HIM?

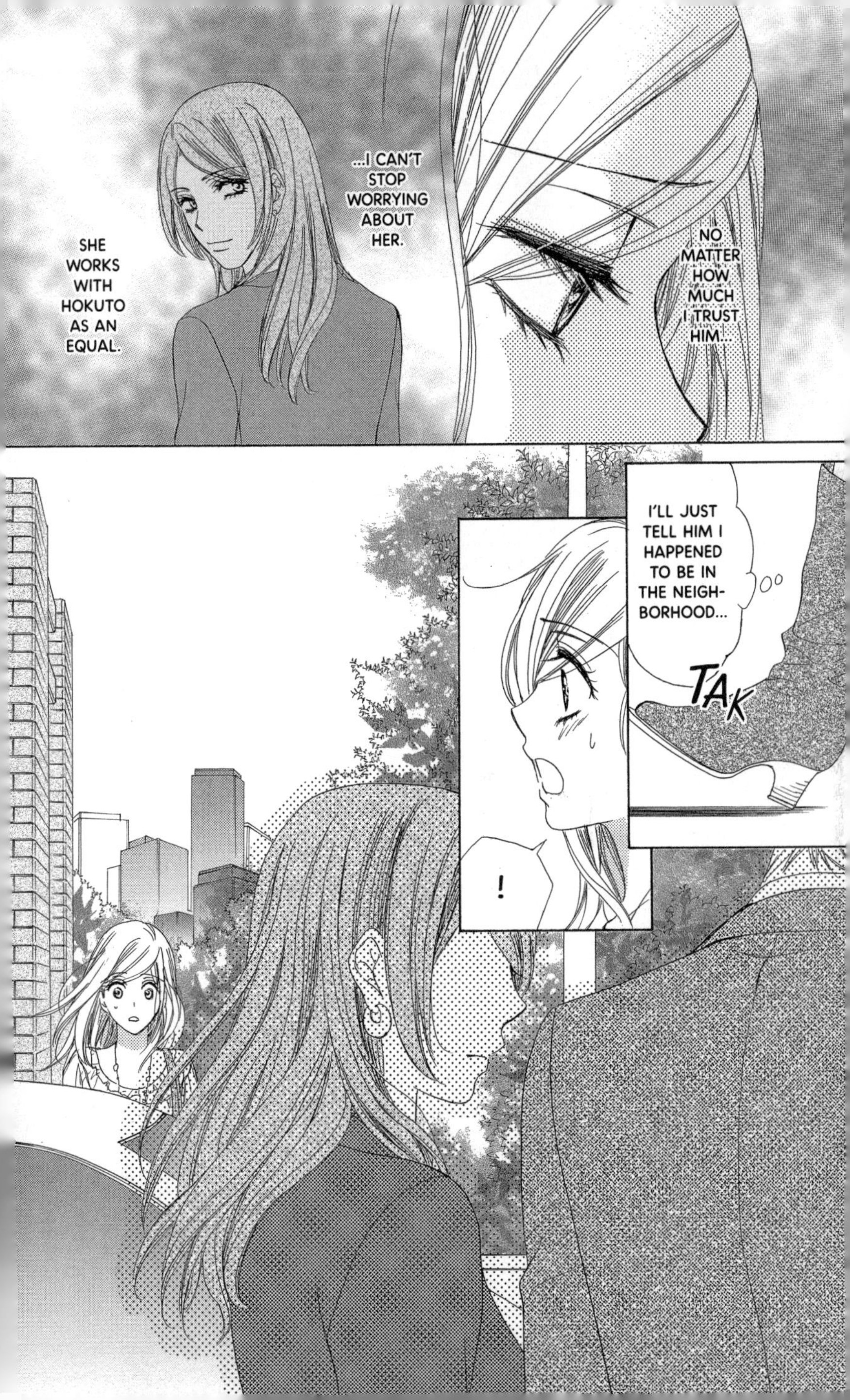
NO MATTER HOW MUCH I TRUST HIM...
...I CAN'T STOP WORRYING ABOUT HER.
SHE WORKS WITH HOKUTO AS AN EQUAL.
I'LL JUST TELL HIM I HAPPENED TO BE IN THE NEIGH-BORHOOD...
TAK
!

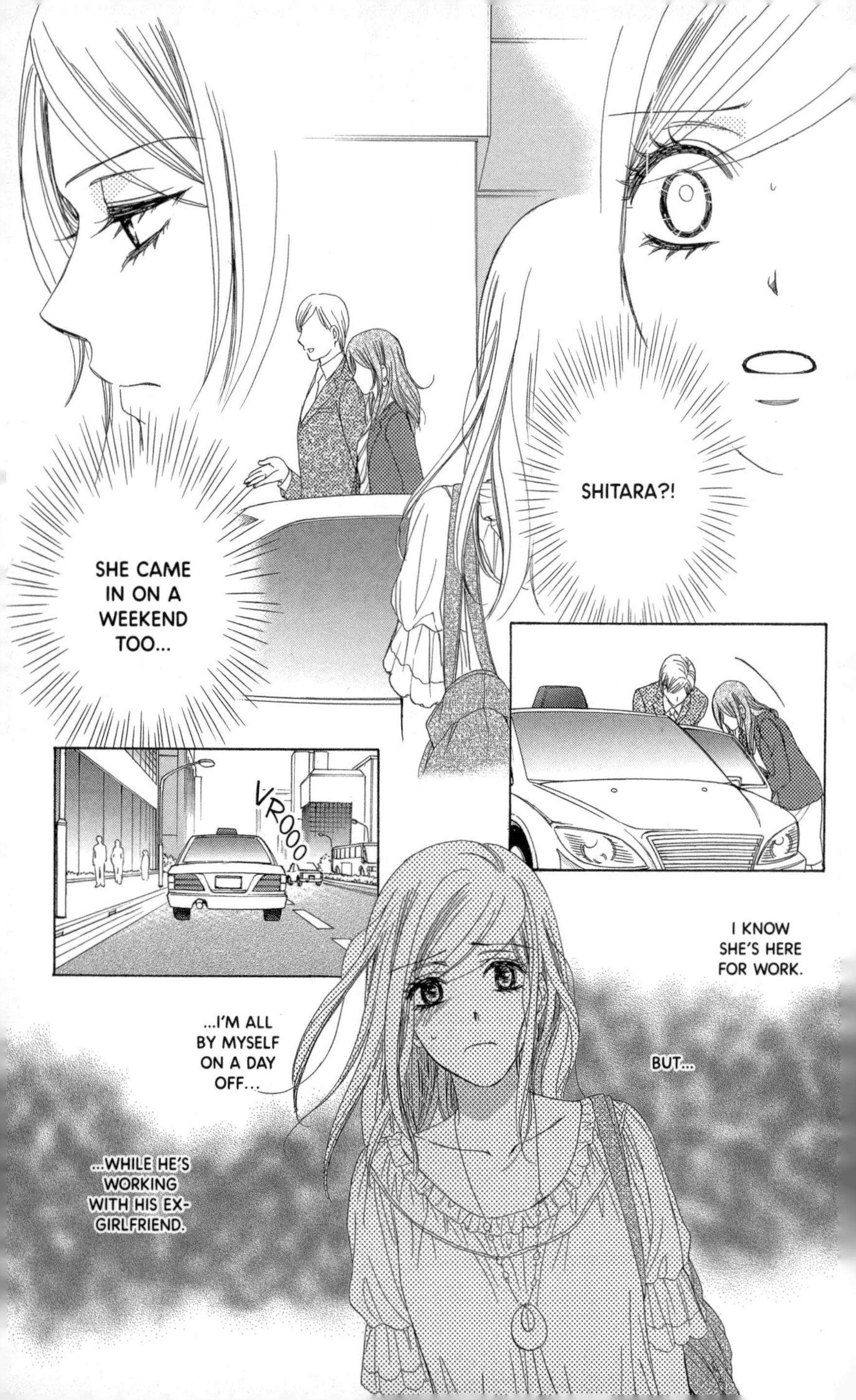
SHITARA?!
SHE CAME IN ON A WEEKEND TOO...
VROOO
I KNOW SHE'S HERE FOR WORK.
BUT...
...I'M ALL BY MYSELF ON A DAY OFF...
...WHILE HE'S WORKING WITH HIS EX-GIRLFRIEND.

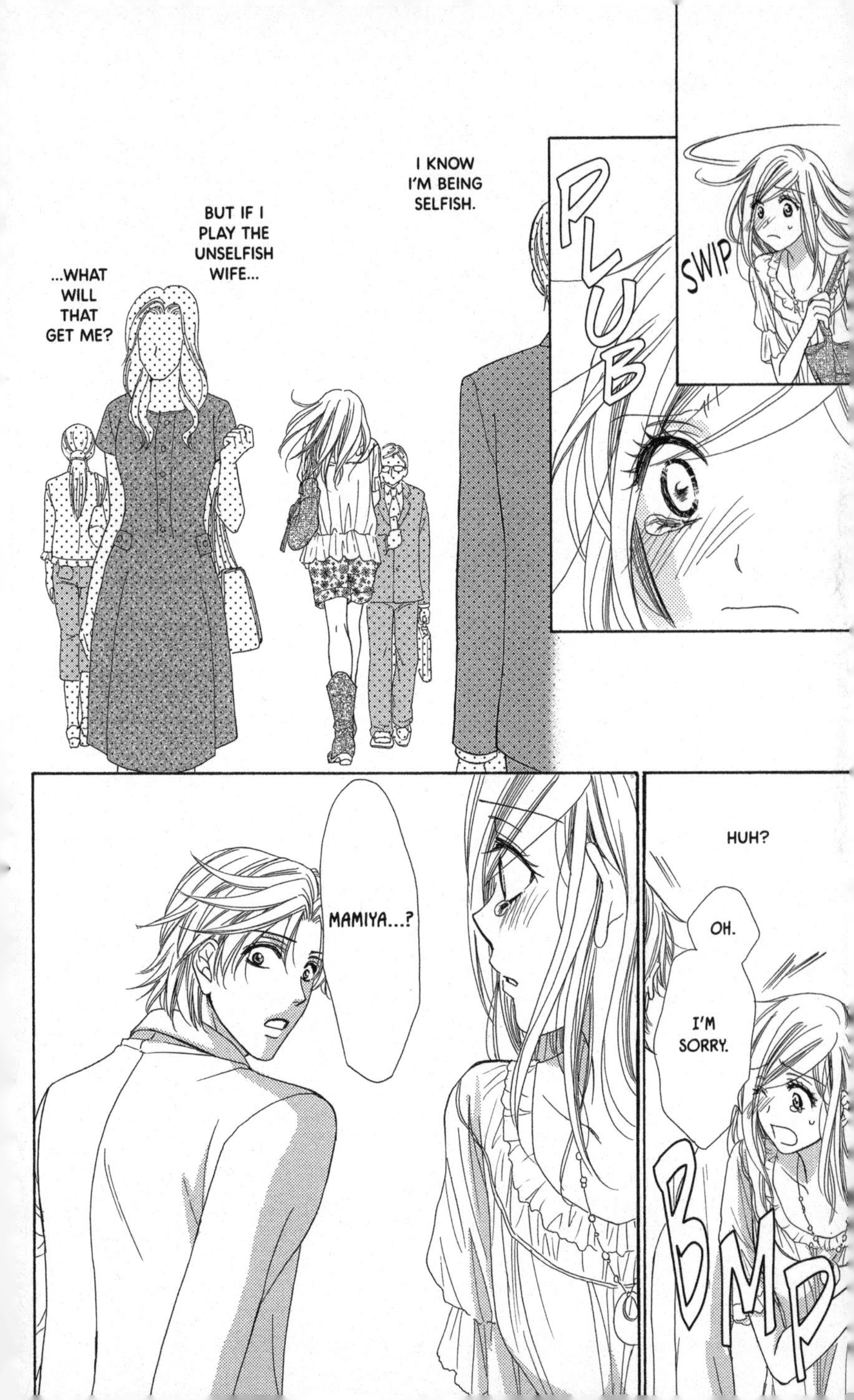
SWIP
PLUB
I KNOW I'M BEING SELFISH.
BUT IF I PLAY THE UNSELFISH WIFE...
...WHAT WILL THAT GET ME?
HUH?
OH.
I'M SORRY.
BMP
MAMIYA...?

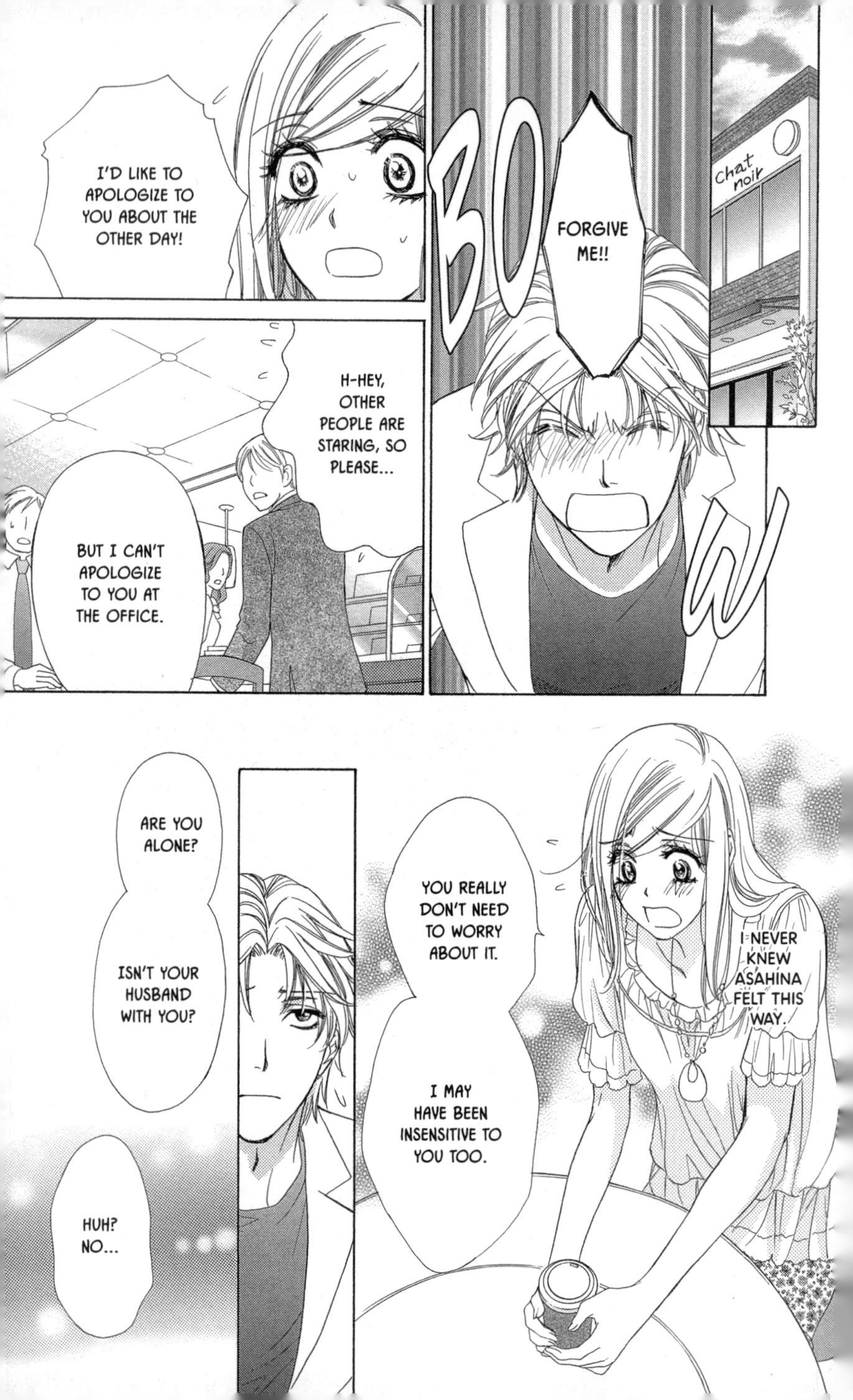
Chat noir
BOW
FORGIVE ME!!
I'D LIKE TO APOLOGIZE TO YOU ABOUT THE OTHER DAY!
H-HEY, OTHER PEOPLE ARE STARING, SO PLEASE...
BUT I CAN'T APOLOGIZE TO YOU AT THE OFFICE.
I NEVER KNEW ASAHINA FELT THIS WAY.
YOU REALLY DON'T NEED TO WORRY ABOUT IT.
I MAY HAVE BEEN INSENSITIVE TO YOU TOO.
ARE YOU ALONE?
ISN'T YOUR HUSBAND WITH YOU?
HUH? NO...

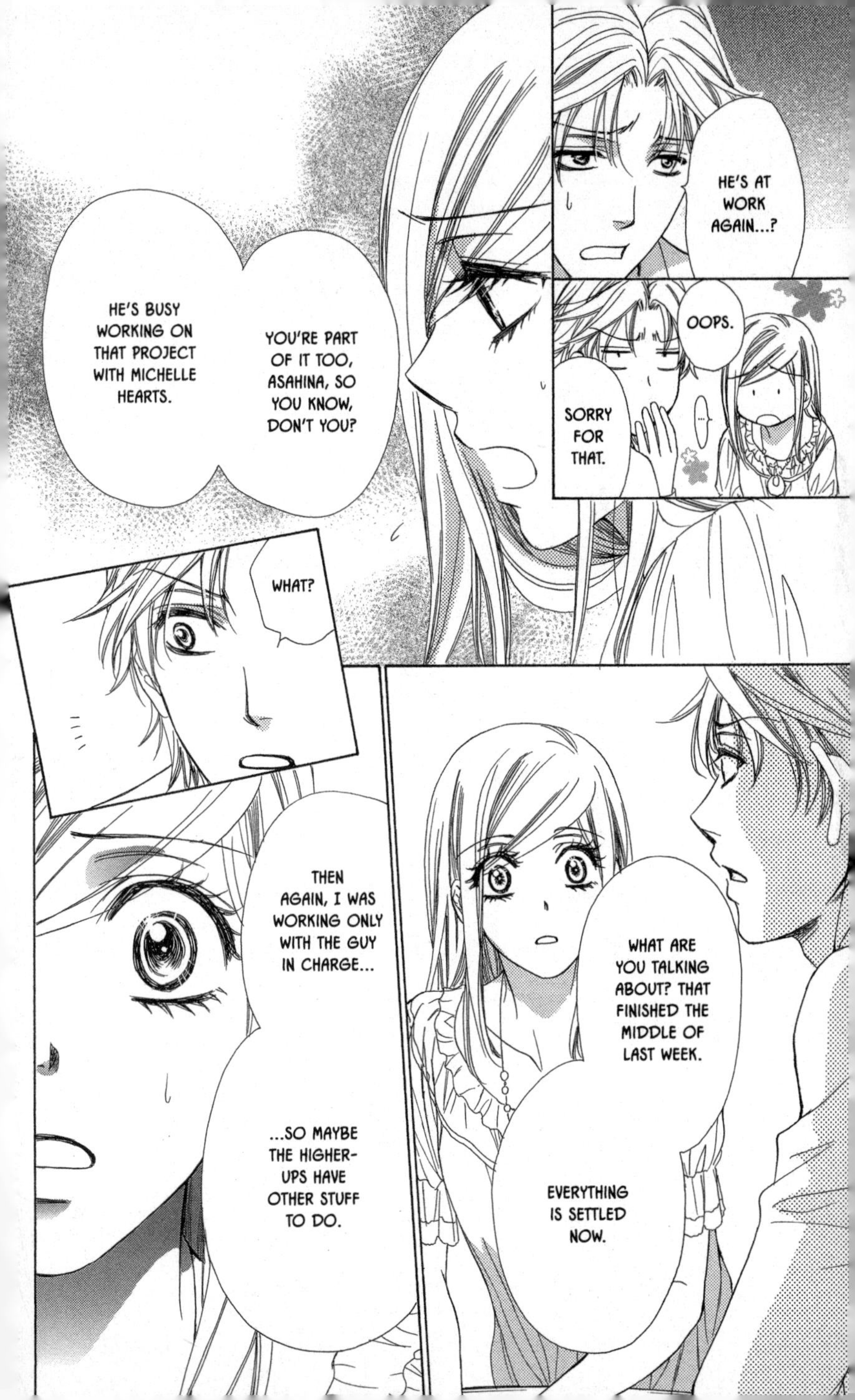
HE'S AT WORK AGAIN...?
OOPS.
SORRY FOR THAT.
...
HE'S BUSY WORKING ON THAT PROJECT WITH MICHELLE HEARTS.
YOU'RE PART OF IT TOO, ASAHINA, SO YOU KNOW, DON'T YOU?
WHAT?
WHAT ARE YOU TALKING ABOUT? THAT FINISHED THE MIDDLE OF LAST WEEK.
EVERYTHING IS SETTLED NOW.
THEN AGAIN, I WAS WORKING ONLY WITH THE GUY IN CHARGE...
...SO MAYBE THE HIGHER-UPS HAVE OTHER STUFF TO DO.

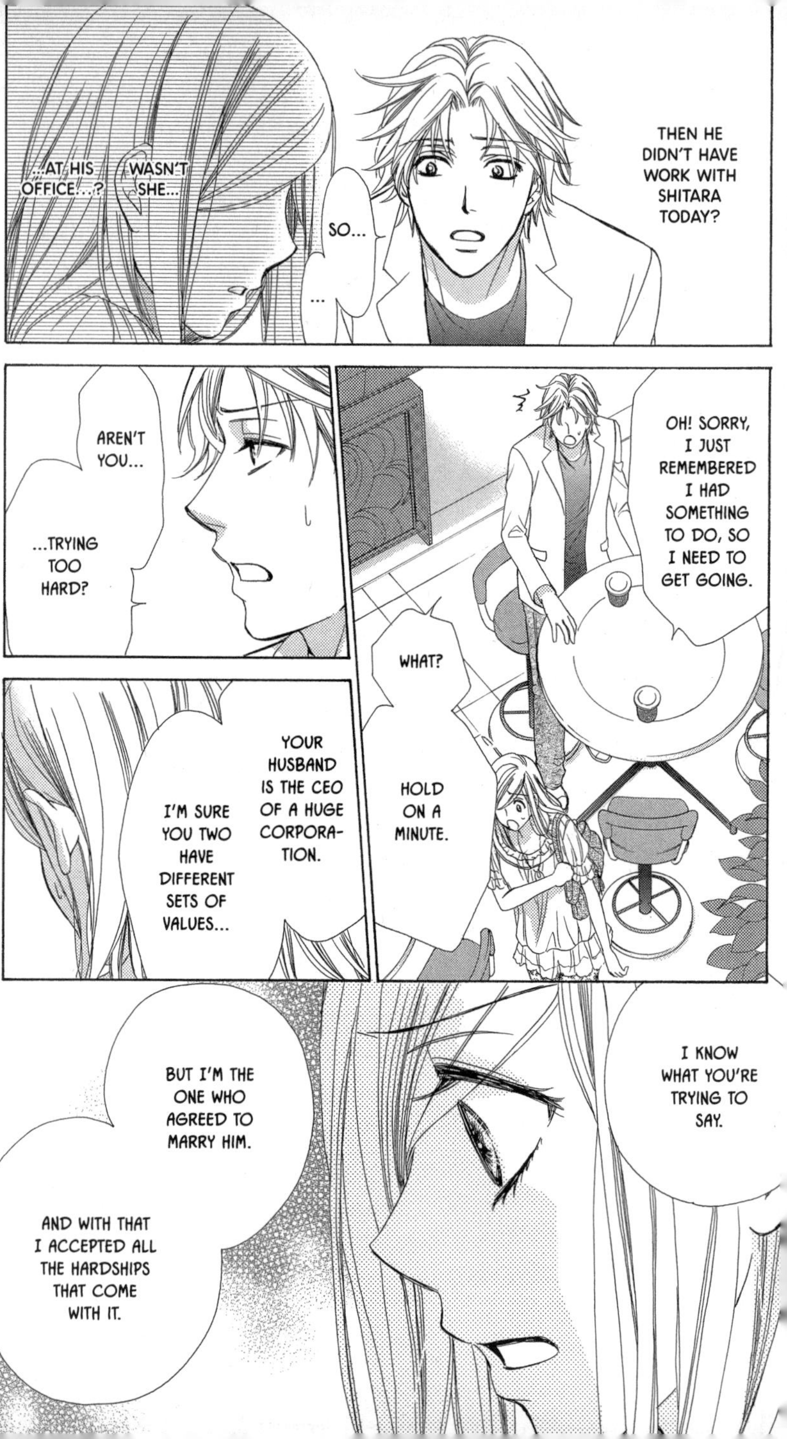
THEN HE DIDN'T HAVE WORK WITH SHITARA TODAY?
SO... ...
WASN'T SHE...
...AT HIS OFFICE...?
OH! SORRY, I JUST REMEMBERED I HAD SOMETHING TO DO, SO I NEED TO GET GOING.
WHAT? HOLD ON A MINUTE.
AREN'T YOU... ...TRYING TOO HARD?
YOUR HUSBAND IS THE CEO OF A HUGE CORPORATION.
I'M SURE YOU TWO HAVE DIFFERENT SETS OF VALUES...
I KNOW WHAT YOU'RE TRYING TO SAY.
BUT I'M THE ONE WHO AGREED TO MARRY HIM.
AND WITH THAT I ACCEPTED ALL THE HARDSHIPS THAT COME WITH IT.

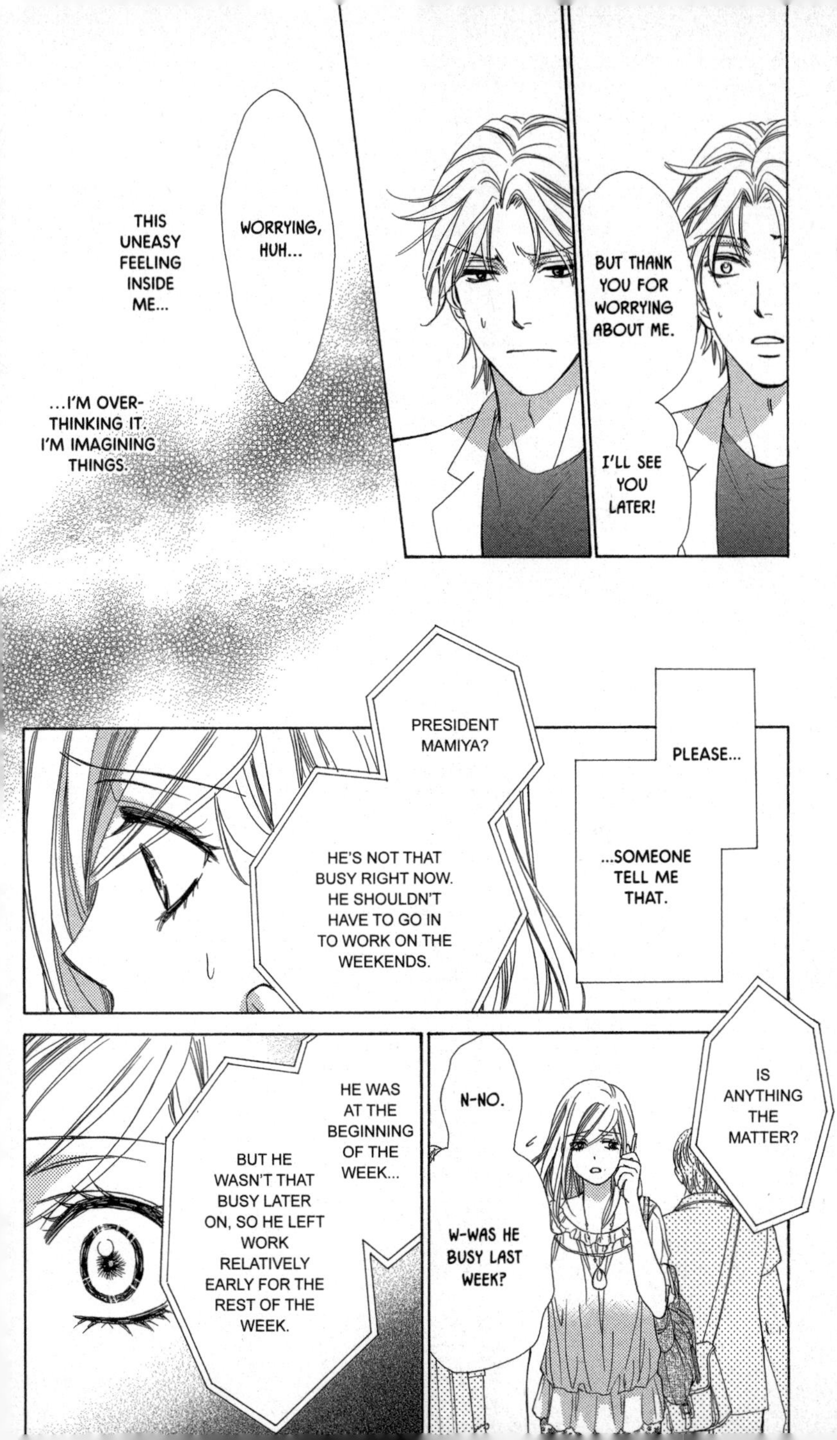
BUT THANK YOU FOR WORRYING ABOUT ME.
I'LL SEE YOU LATER!
WORRYING, HUH...
THIS UNEASY FEELING INSIDE ME...
...I'M OVER-THINKING IT. I'M IMAGINING THINGS.
PLEASE...
...SOMEONE TELL ME THAT.
PRESIDENT MAMIYA?
HE'S NOT THAT BUSY RIGHT NOW. HE SHOULDN'T HAVE TO GO IN TO WORK ON THE WEEKENDS.
IS ANYTHING THE MATTER?
N-NO.
W-WAS HE BUSY LAST WEEK?
HE WAS AT THE BEGINNING OF THE WEEK...
BUT HE WASN'T THAT BUSY LATER ON, SO HE LEFT WORK RELATIVELY EARLY FOR THE REST OF THE WEEK.

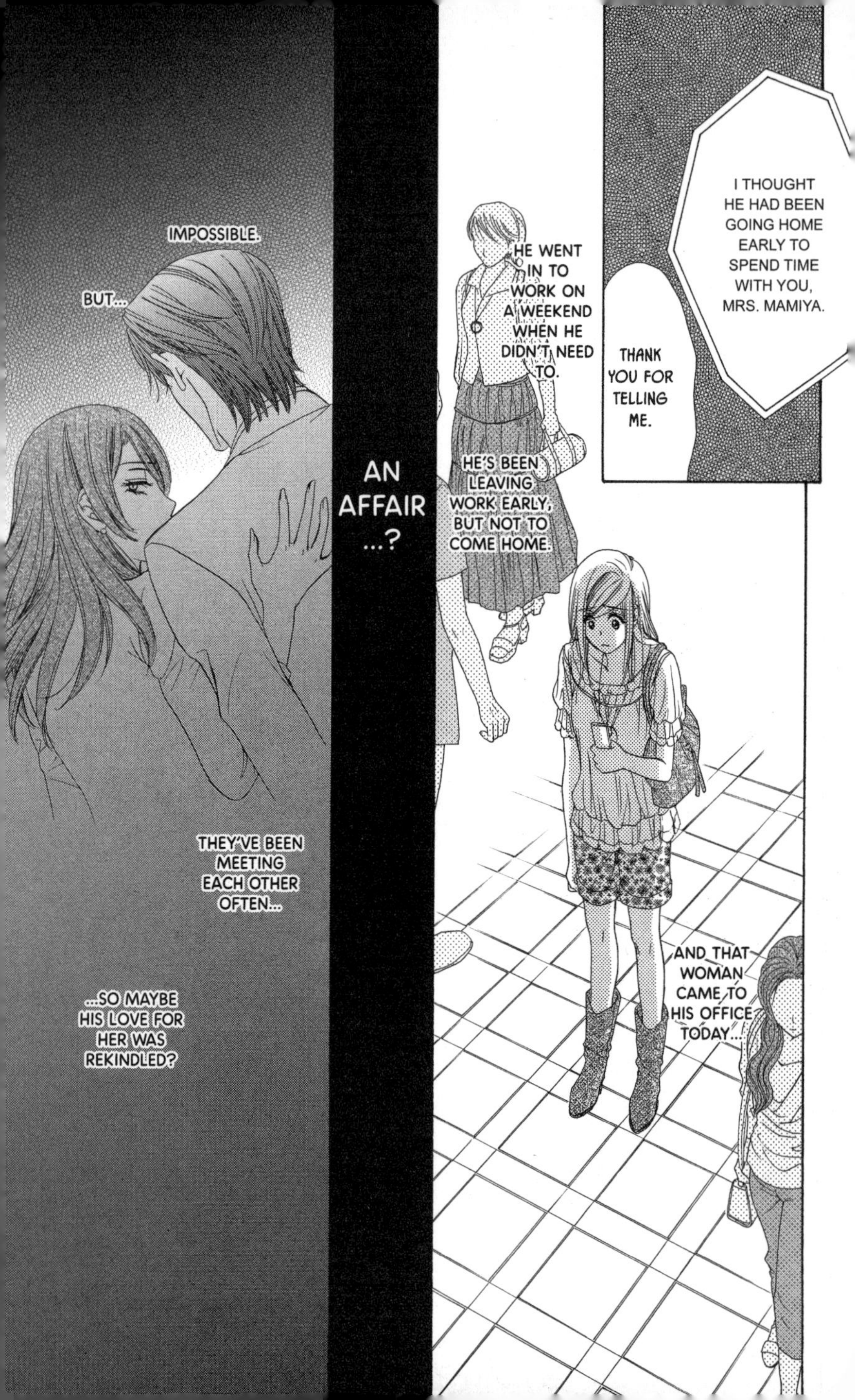
I THOUGHT HE HAD BEEN GOING HOME EARLY TO SPEND TIME WITH YOU, MRS. MAMIYA.
THANK YOU FOR TELLING ME.
HE WENT IN TO WORK ON A WEEKEND WHEN HE DIDN'T NEED TO.
HE'S BEEN LEAVING WORK EARLY, BUT NOT TO COME HOME.
AND THAT WOMAN CAME TO HIS OFFICE TODAY...
AN AFFAIR ...?
IMPOSSIBLE.
BUT...
THEY'VE BEEN MEETING EACH OTHER OFTEN...
...SO MAYBE HIS LOVE FOR HER WAS REKINDLED?

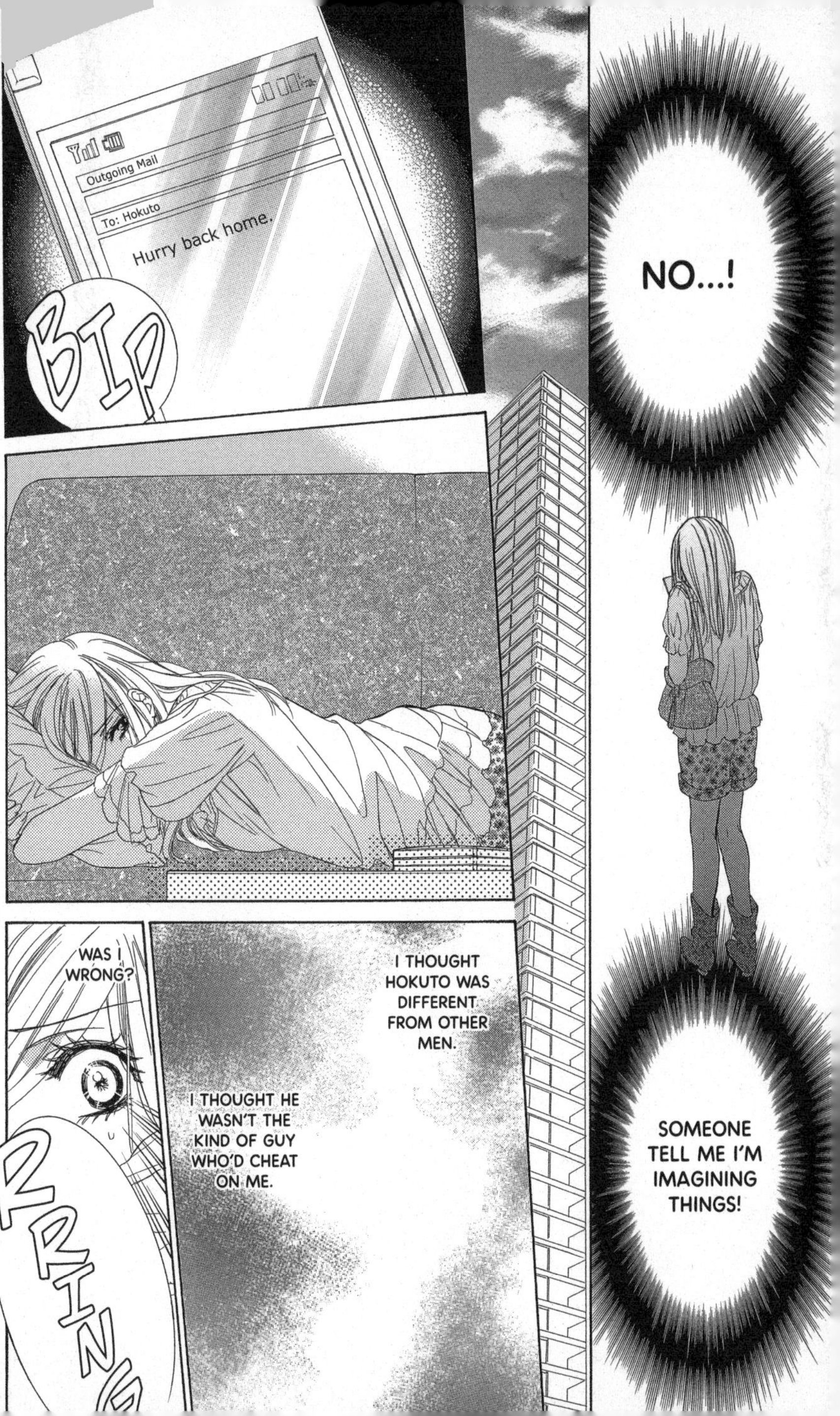
NO...!
SOMEONE TELL ME I'M IMAGINING THINGS!
Outgoing Mail
To: Hokuto
Hurry back home.
BIP
I THOUGHT HOKUTO WAS DIFFERENT FROM OTHER MEN.
I THOUGHT HE WASN'T THE KIND OF GUY WHO'D CHEAT ON ME.
WAS I WRONG?
RRING

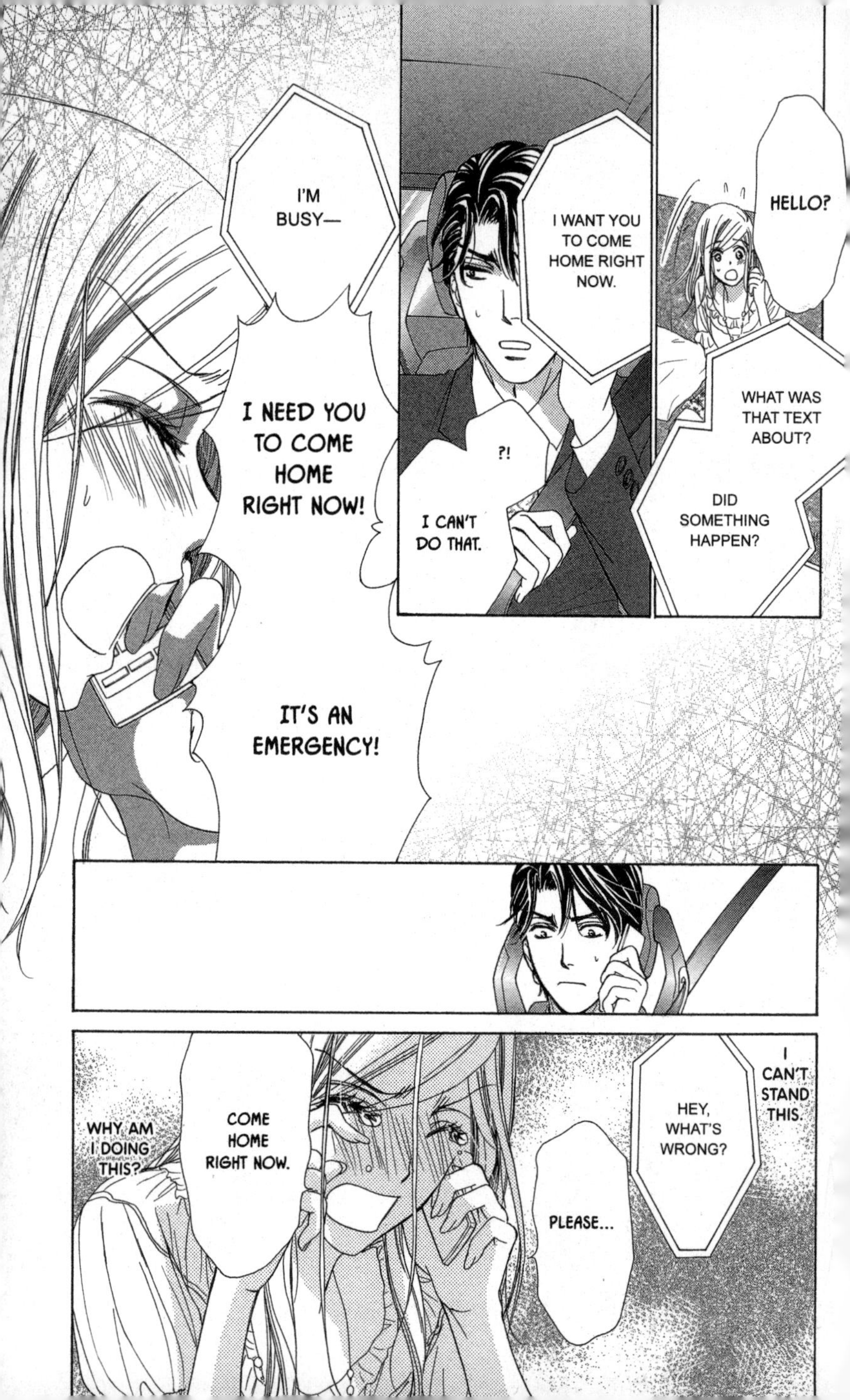
HELLO?
WHAT WAS THAT TEXT ABOUT?
DID SOMETHING HAPPEN?
I WANT YOU TO COME HOME RIGHT NOW.
?!
I CAN'T DO THAT.
I'M BUSY—
I NEED YOU TO COME HOME RIGHT NOW!
IT'S AN EMERGENCY!
I CAN'T STAND THIS.
HEY, WHAT'S WRONG?
PLEASE...
COME HOME RIGHT NOW.
WHY AM I DOING THIS?

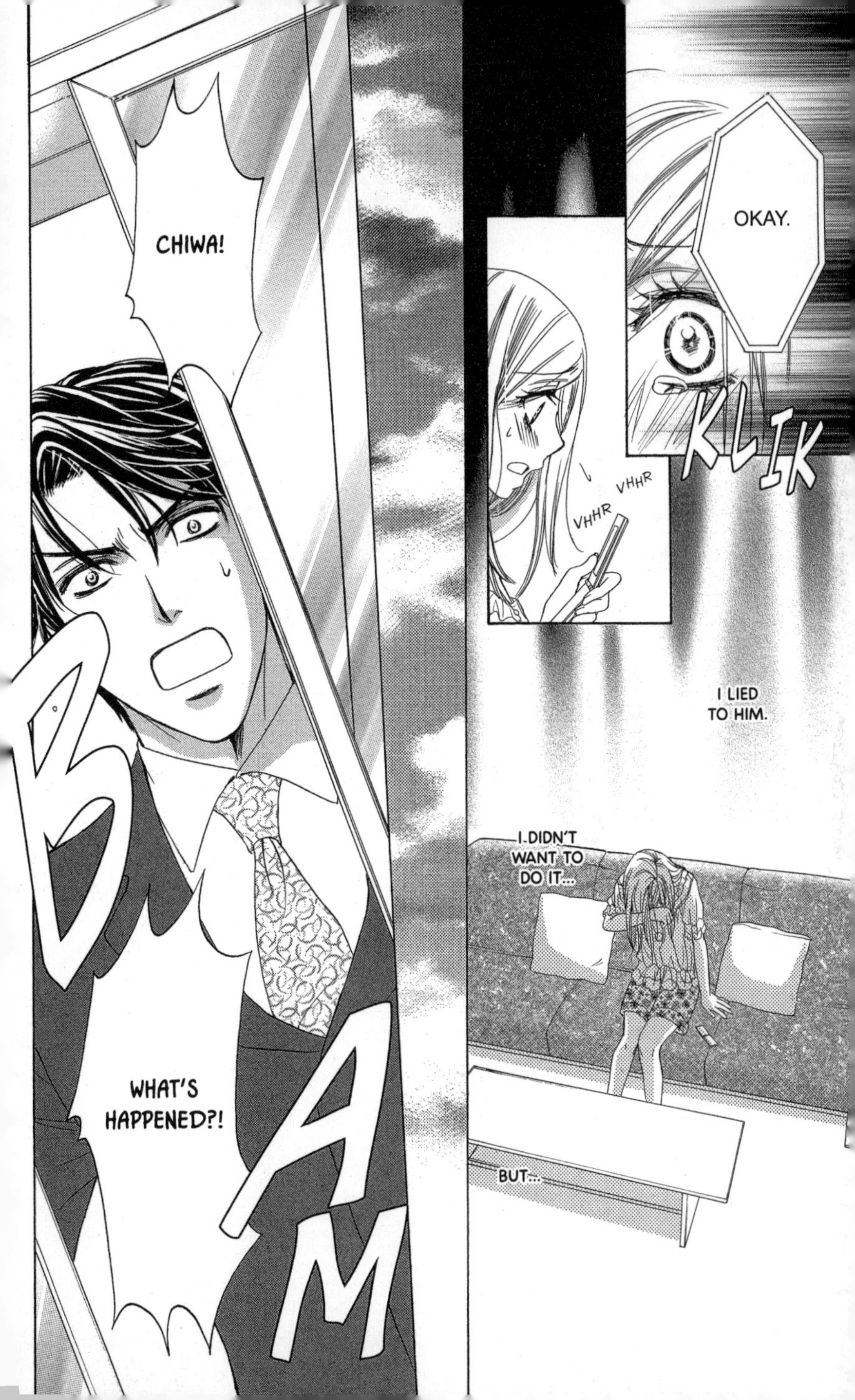
OKAY.
KLIK
VHHR VHHR
I LIED TO HIM.
I DIDN'T WANT TO DO IT...
BUT...
CHIWA!
BAM
WHAT'S HAPPENED?!

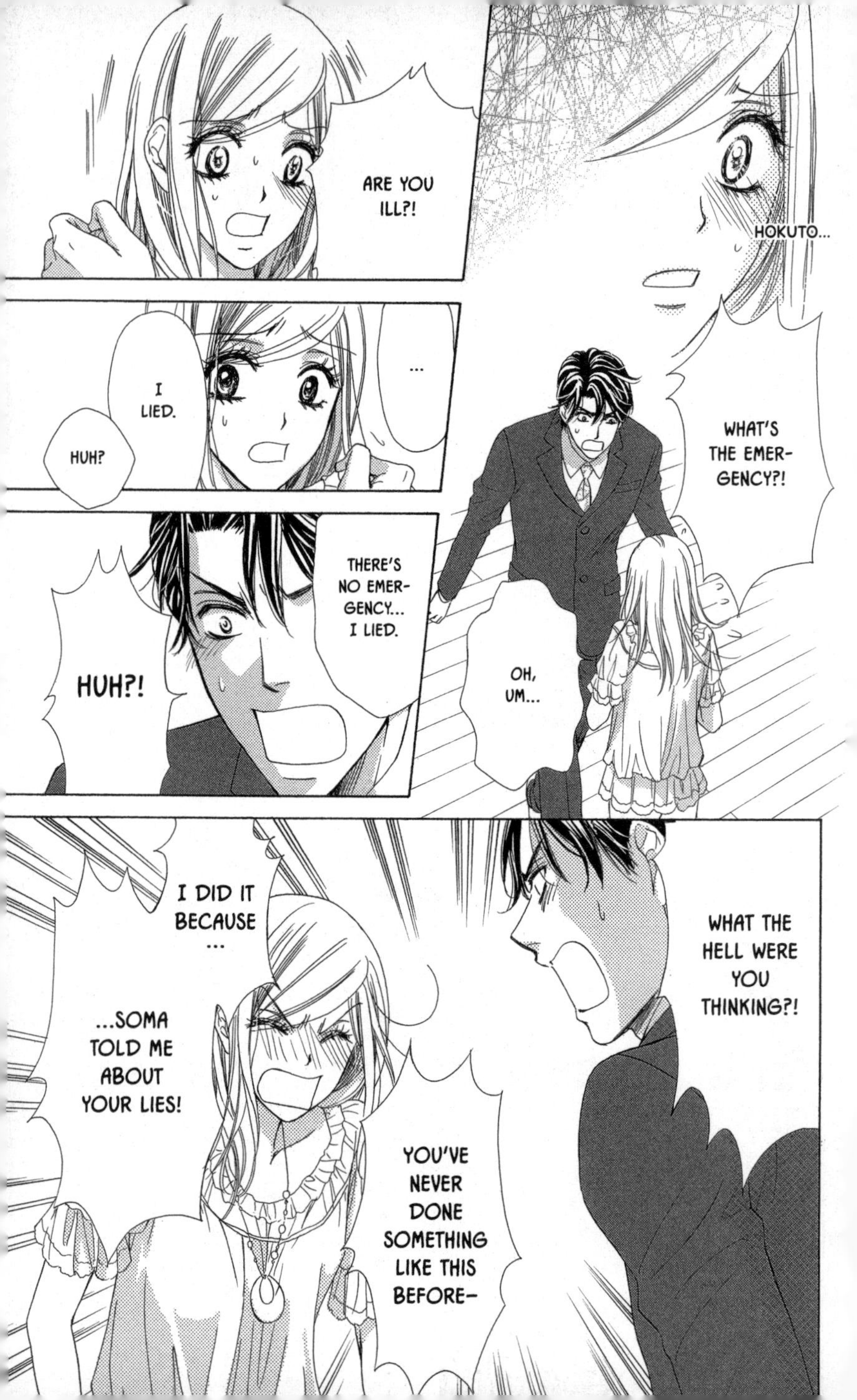
HOKUTO...
WHAT'S THE EMERGENCY?!
OH, UM...
ARE YOU ILL?!
...
I LIED.
HUH?
THERE'S NO EMERGENCY... I LIED.
HUH?!
WHAT THE HELL WERE YOU THINKING?!
YOU'VE NEVER DONE SOMETHING LIKE THIS BEFORE–
I DID IT BECAUSE ...
...SOMA TOLD ME ABOUT YOUR LIES!

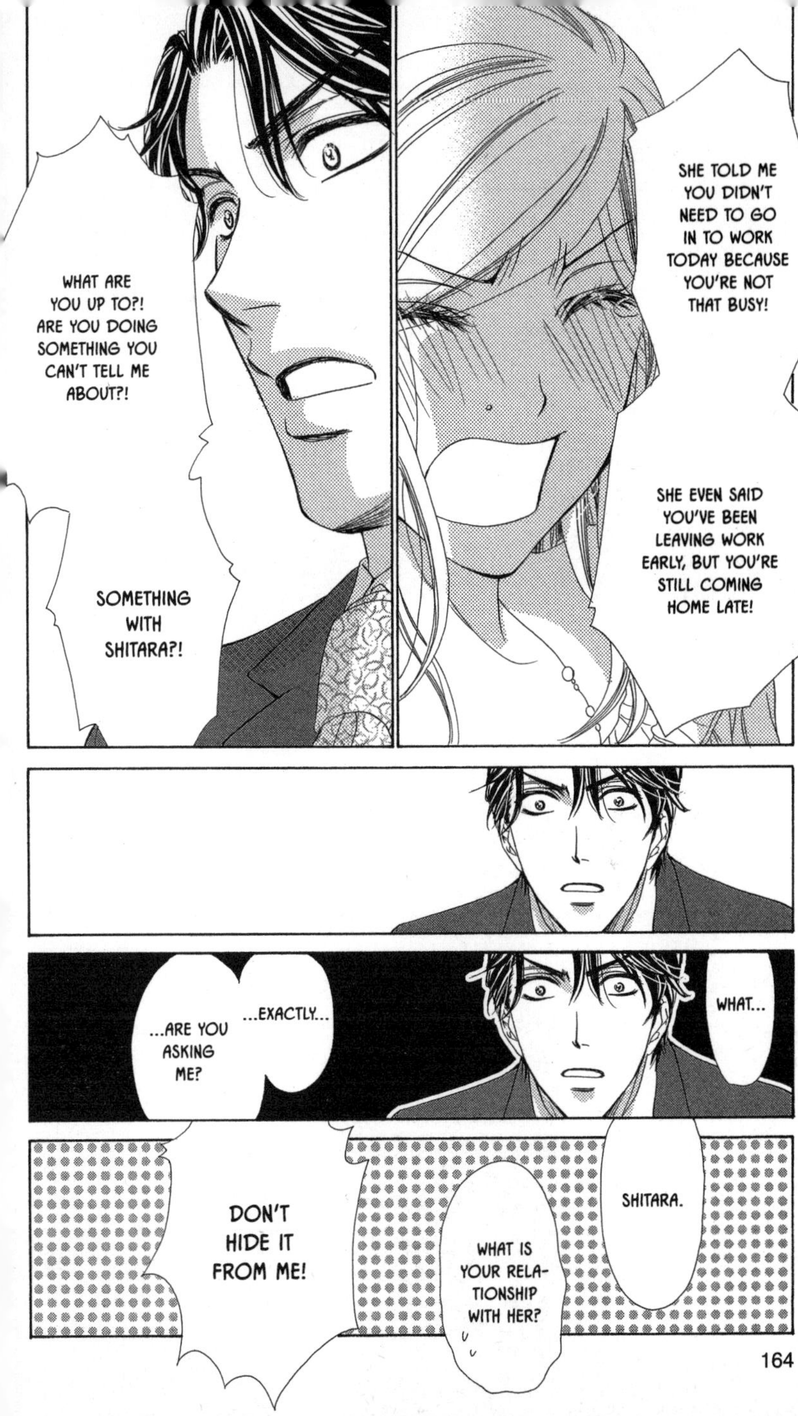
SHE TOLD ME YOU DIDN'T NEED TO GO IN TO WORK TODAY BECAUSE YOU'RE NOT THAT BUSY!
SHE EVEN SAID YOU'VE BEEN LEAVING WORK EARLY, BUT YOU'RE STILL COMING HOME LATE!
WHAT ARE YOU UP TO?! ARE YOU DOING SOMETHING YOU CAN'T TELL ME ABOUT?!
SOMETHING WITH SHITARA?!
WHAT...
...EXACTLY...
...ARE YOU ASKING ME?
SHITARA.
WHAT IS YOUR RELATIONSHIP WITH HER?
DON'T HIDE IT FROM ME!

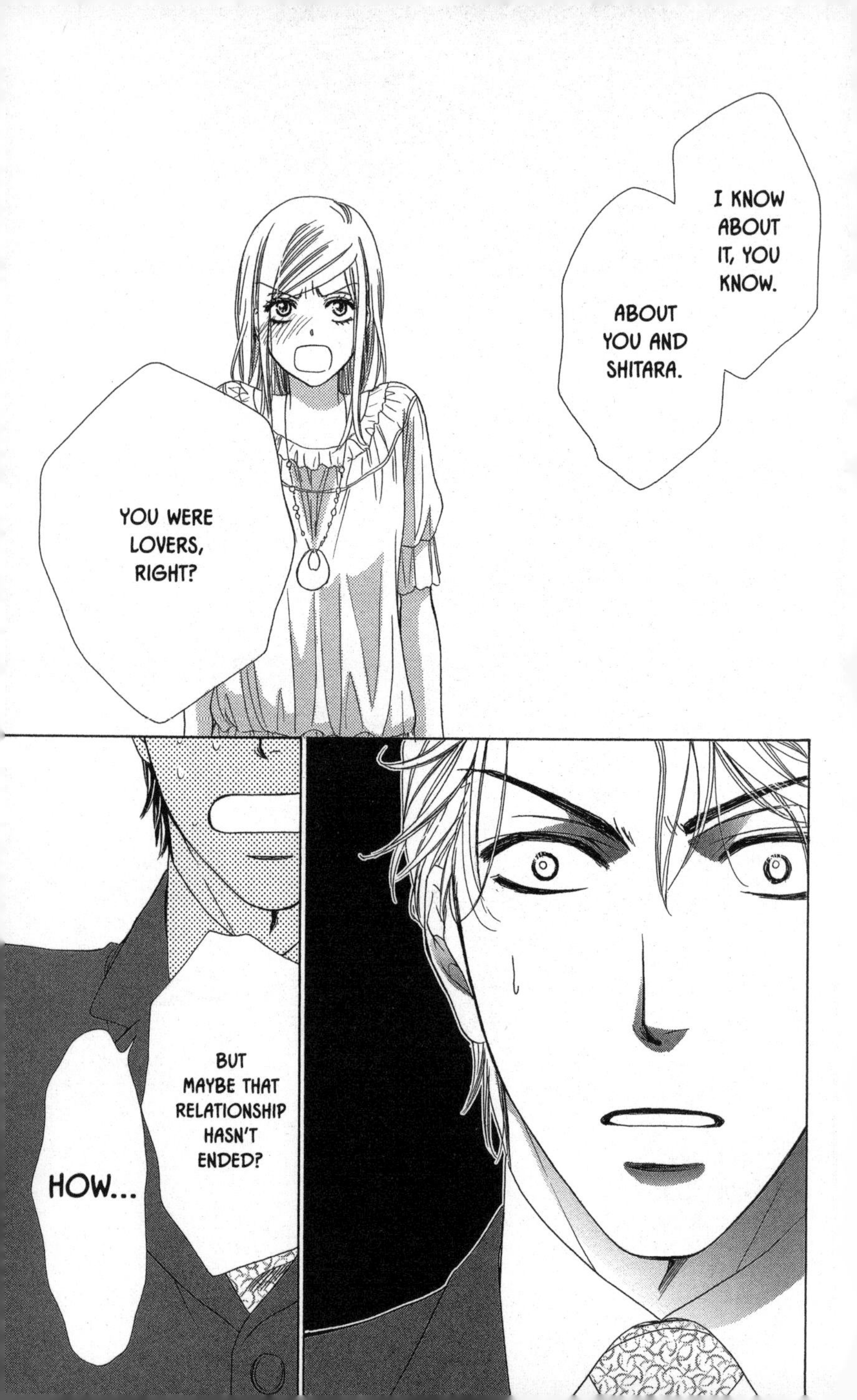
I KNOW ABOUT IT, YOU KNOW.
ABOUT YOU AND SHITARA.
YOU WERE LOVERS, RIGHT?
BUT MAYBE THAT RELATIONSHIP HASN'T ENDED?
HOW...

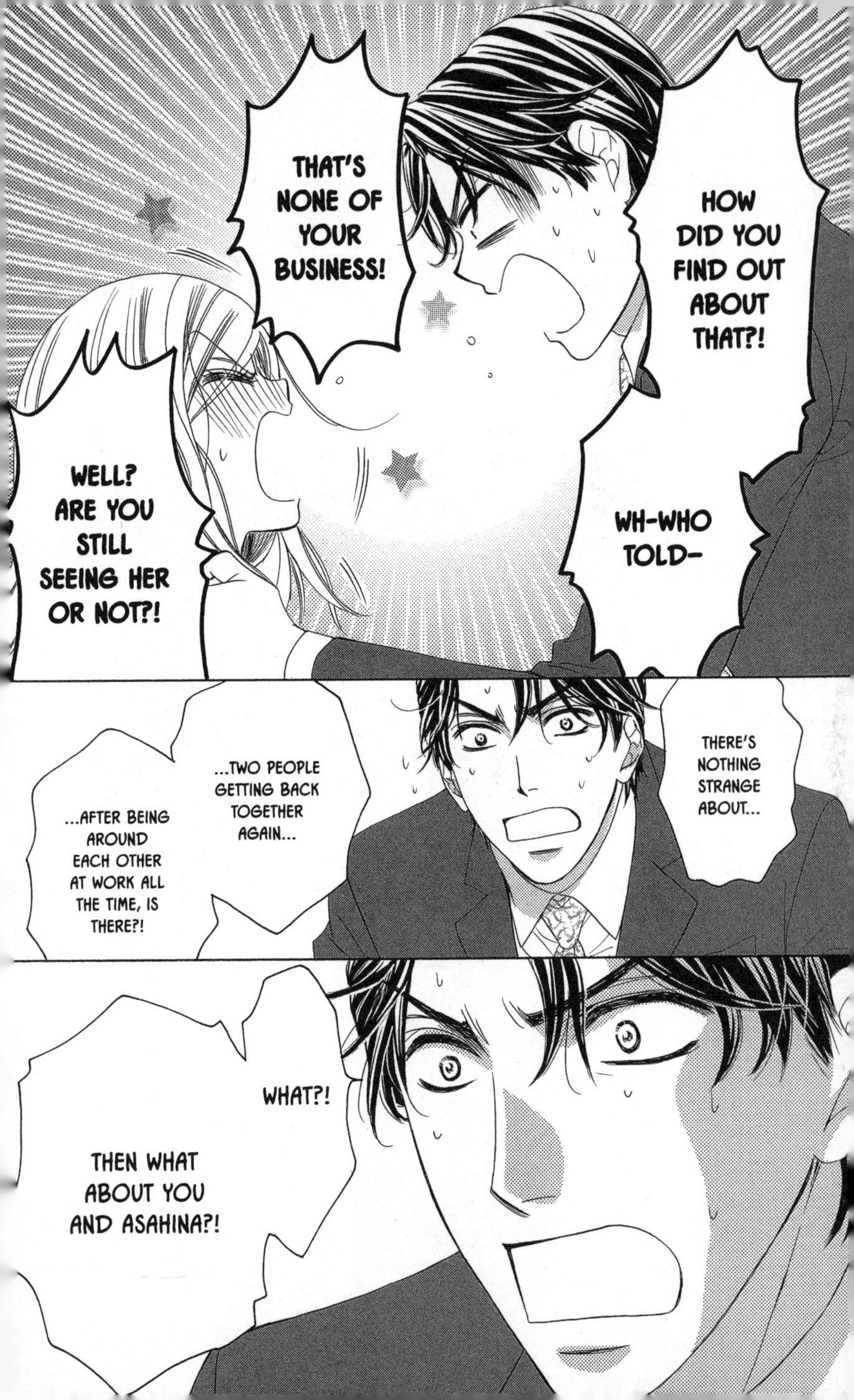
HOW DID YOU FIND OUT ABOUT THAT?!
WH-WHO TOLD-
THAT'S NONE OF YOUR BUSINESS!
WELL? ARE YOU STILL SEEING HER OR NOT?!
THERE'S NOTHING STRANGE ABOUT...
...TWO PEOPLE GETTING BACK TOGETHER AGAIN...
...AFTER BEING AROUND EACH OTHER AT WORK ALL THE TIME, IS THERE?!
WHAT?!
THEN WHAT ABOUT YOU AND ASAHINA?!

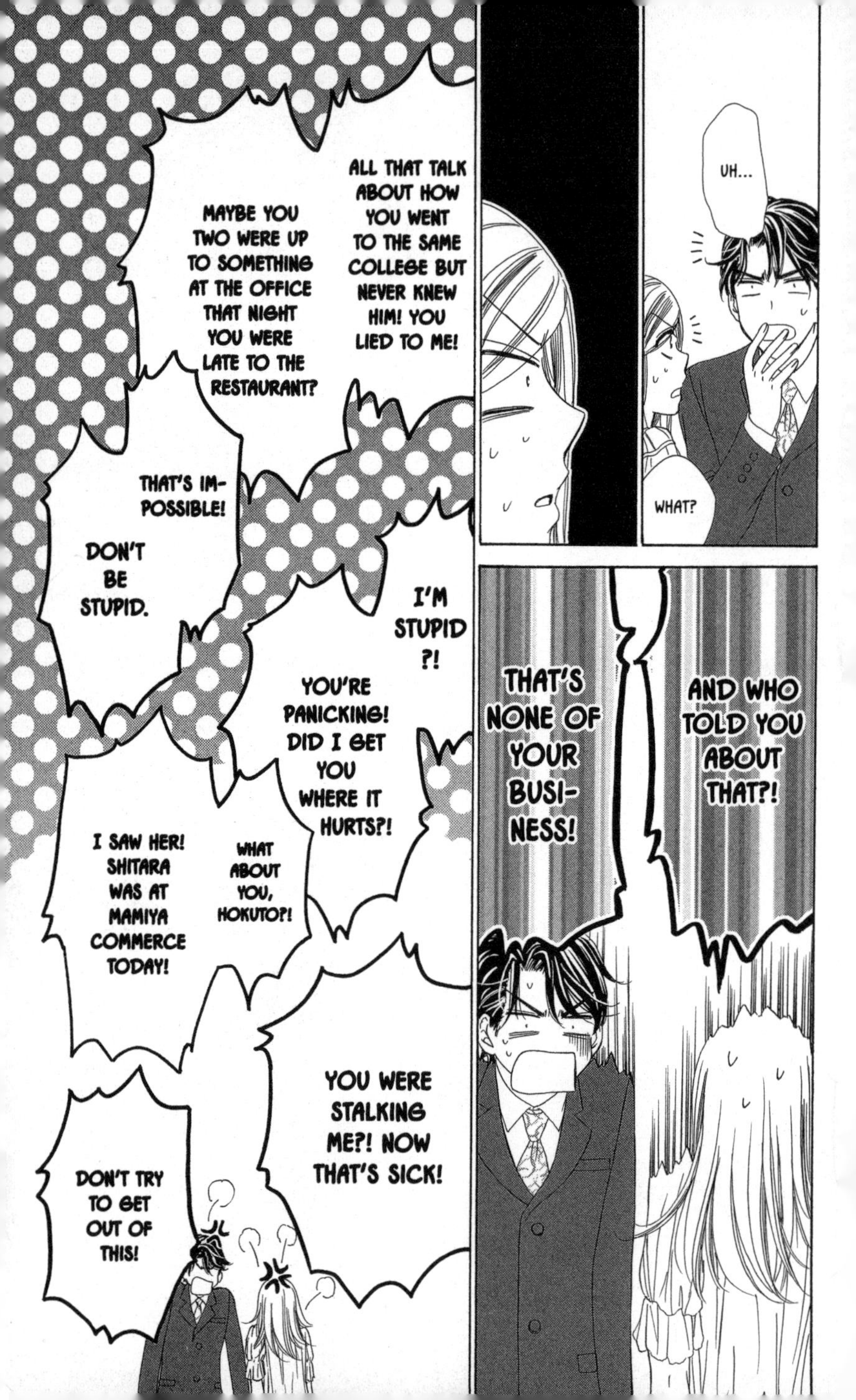
UH...
WHAT?
AND WHO TOLD YOU ABOUT THAT?!
THAT'S NONE OF YOUR BUSI-NESS!
ALL THAT TALK ABOUT HOW YOU WENT TO THE SAME COLLEGE BUT NEVER KNEW HIM! YOU LIED TO ME!
MAYBE YOU TWO WERE UP TO SOMETHING AT THE OFFICE THAT NIGHT YOU WERE LATE TO THE RESTAURANT?
I'M STUPID ?!
THAT'S IM-POSSIBLE!
DON'T BE STUPID.
YOU'RE PANICKING! DID I GET YOU WHERE IT HURTS?!
WHAT ABOUT YOU, HOKUTO?!
I SAW HER! SHITARA WAS AT MAMIYA COMMERCE TODAY!
YOU WERE STALKING ME?! NOW THAT'S SICK!
DON'T TRY TO GET OUT OF THIS!

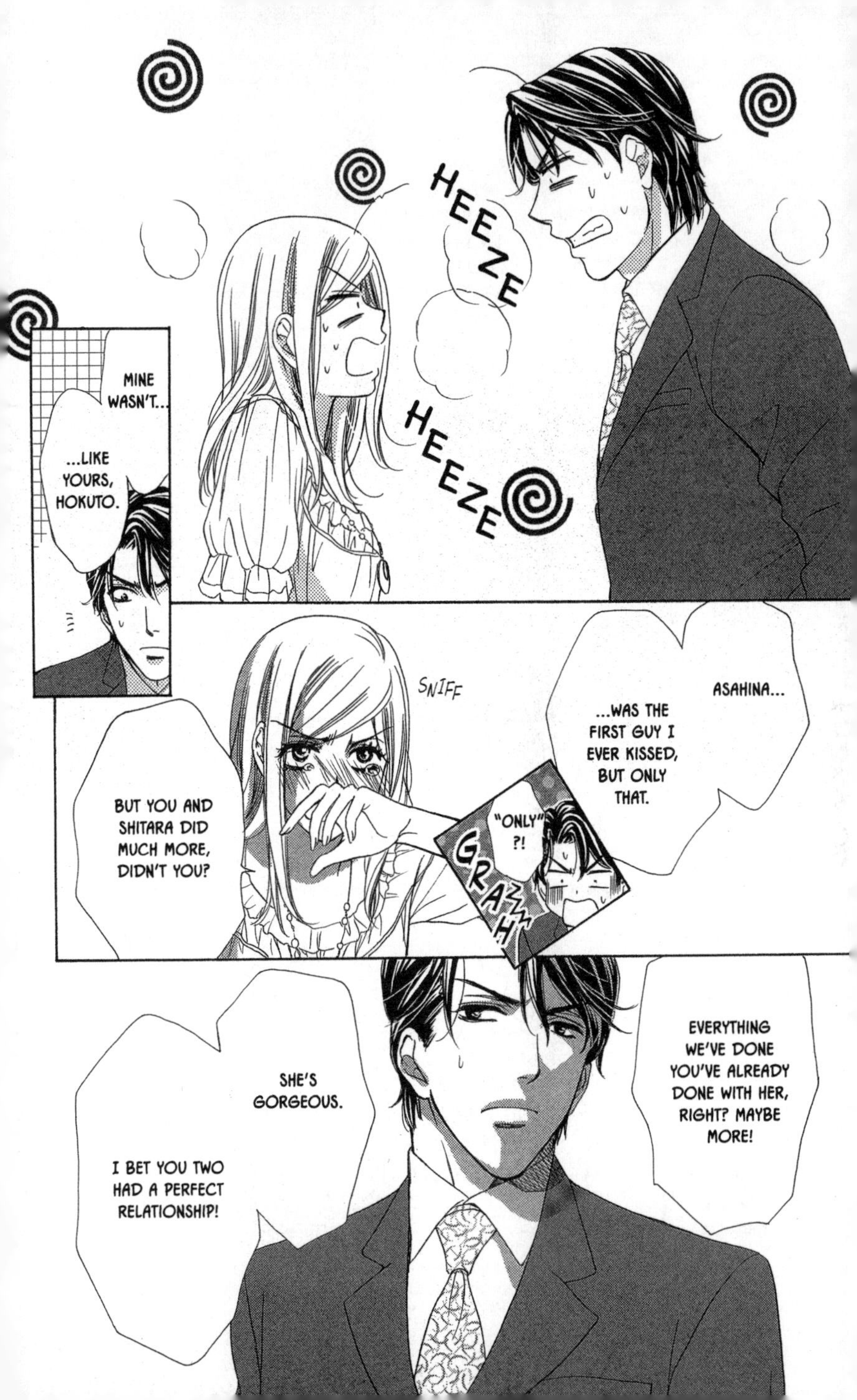
HEEZE
HEEZE
MINE WASN'T...
...LIKE YOURS, HOKUTO.
ASAHINA...
...WAS THE FIRST GUY I EVER KISSED, BUT ONLY THAT.
"ONLY" ?!
GRAZZH
SNIFF
BUT YOU AND SHITARA DID MUCH MORE, DIDN'T YOU?
EVERYTHING WE'VE DONE YOU'VE ALREADY DONE WITH HER, RIGHT? MAYBE MORE!
SHE'S GORGEOUS.
I BET YOU TWO HAD A PERFECT RELATIONSHIP!

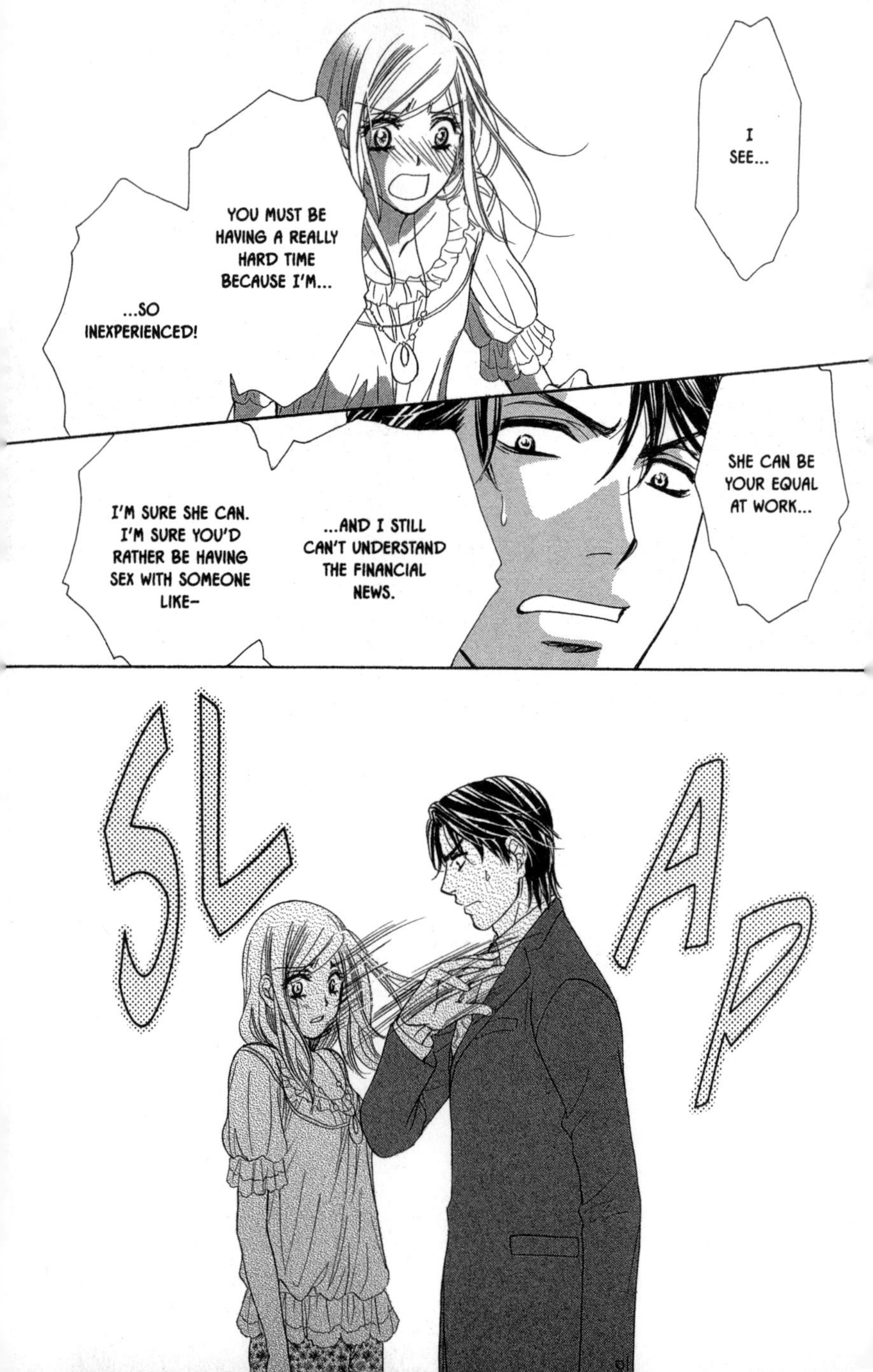
I SEE...
YOU MUST BE HAVING A REALLY HARD TIME BECAUSE I'M...
...SO INEXPERIENCED!
SHE CAN BE YOUR EQUAL AT WORK...
...AND I STILL CAN'T UNDERSTAND THE FINANCIAL NEWS.
I'M SURE SHE CAN. I'M SURE YOU'D RATHER BE HAVING SEX WITH SOMEONE LIKE–
SLAP

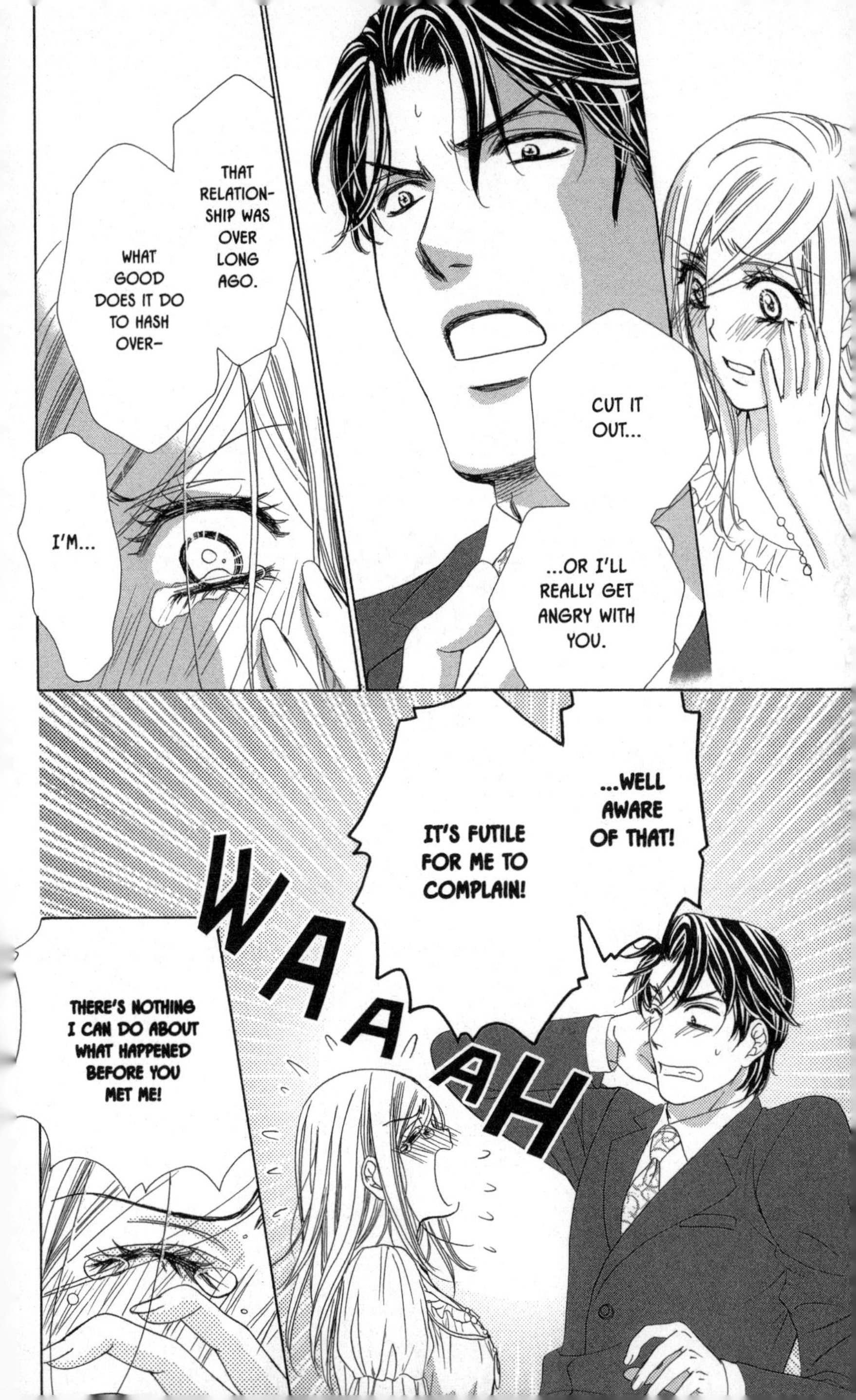
CUT IT OUT...
...OR I'LL REALLY GET ANGRY WITH YOU.
THAT RELATION-SHIP WAS OVER LONG AGO.
WHAT GOOD DOES IT DO TO HASH OVER–
I'M...
...WELL AWARE OF THAT!
IT'S FUTILE FOR ME TO COMPLAIN!
WAAAAH
THERE'S NOTHING I CAN DO ABOUT WHAT HAPPENED BEFORE YOU MET ME!

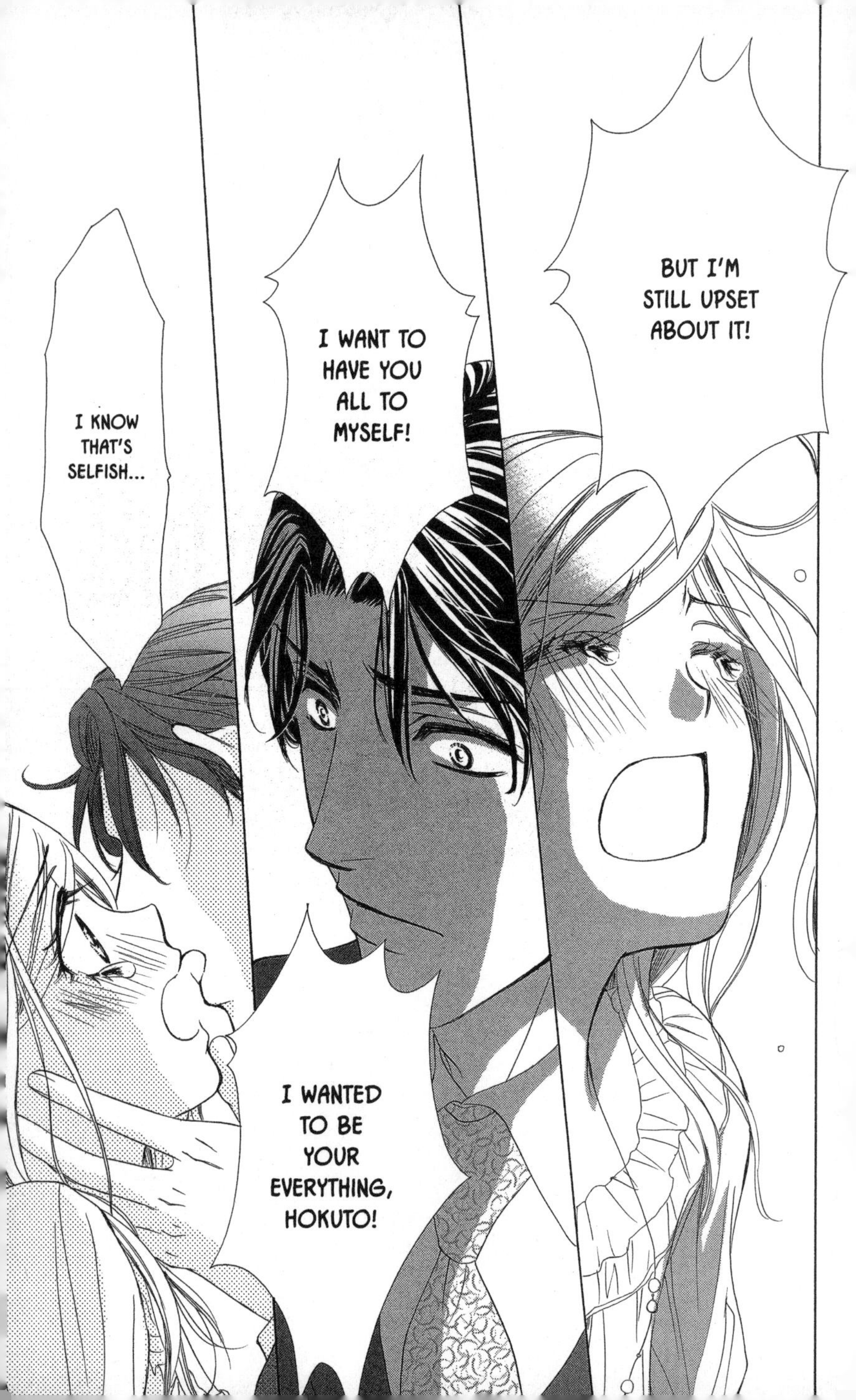
BUT I'M STILL UPSET ABOUT IT!
I WANT TO HAVE YOU ALL TO MYSELF!
I KNOW THAT'S SELFISH...
I WANTED TO BE YOUR EVERYTHING, HOKUTO!

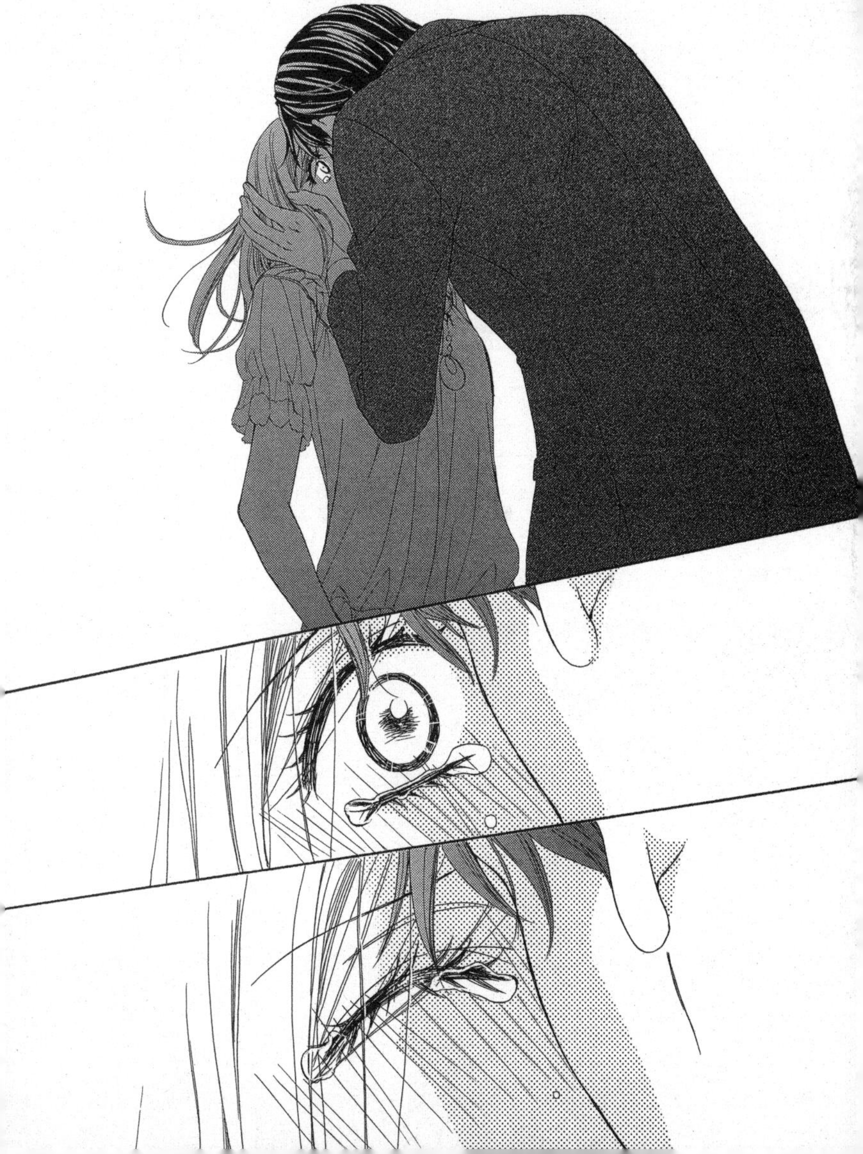

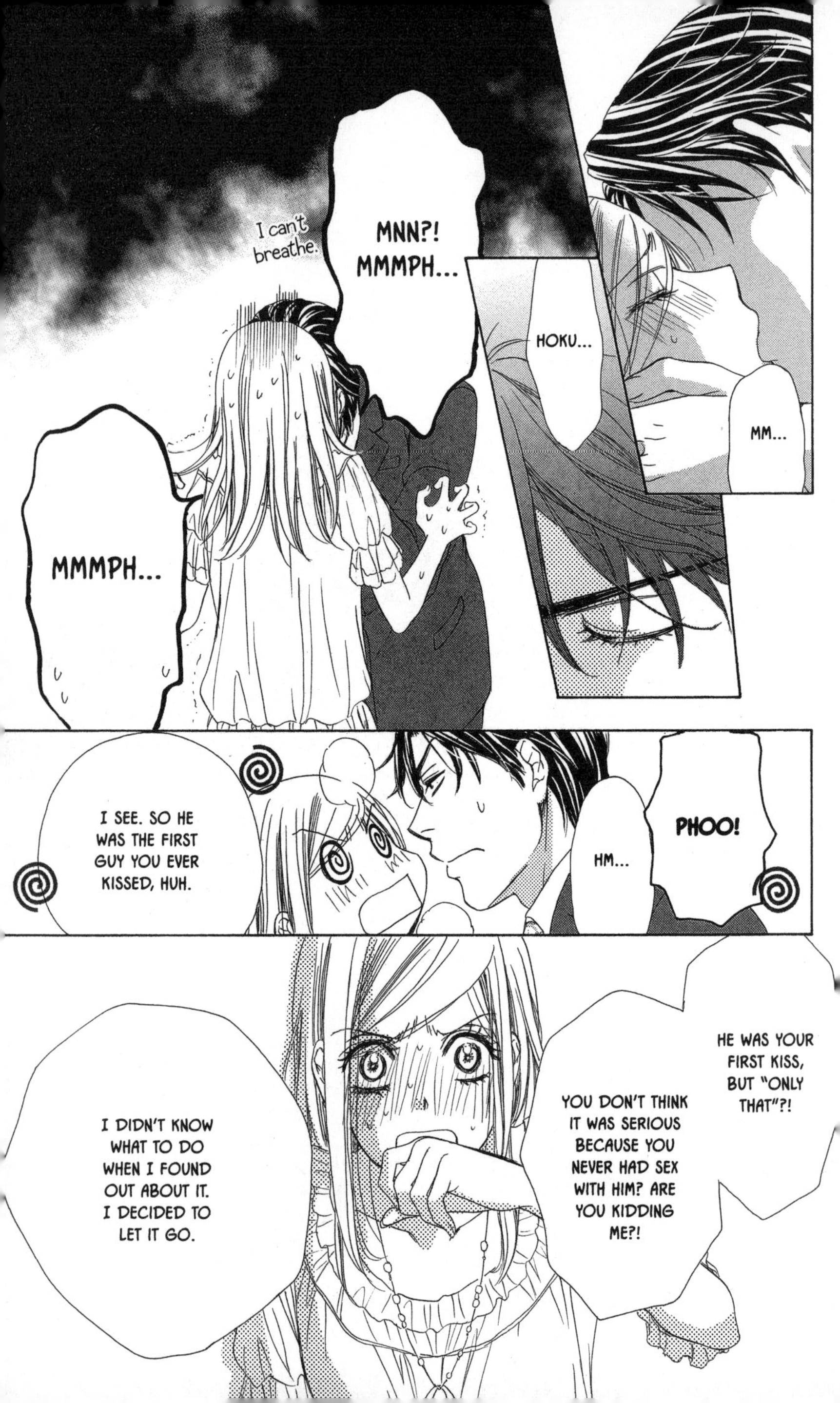
MM...
HOKU...
MNN?! MMMPH...
I can't breathe.
MMMPH...
PHOO!
HM...
I SEE. SO HE WAS THE FIRST GUY YOU EVER KISSED, HUH.
HE WAS YOUR FIRST KISS, BUT "ONLY THAT"?!
YOU DON'T THINK IT WAS SERIOUS BECAUSE YOU NEVER HAD SEX WITH HIM? ARE YOU KIDDING ME?!
I DIDN'T KNOW WHAT TO DO WHEN I FOUND OUT ABOUT IT. I DECIDED TO LET IT GO.

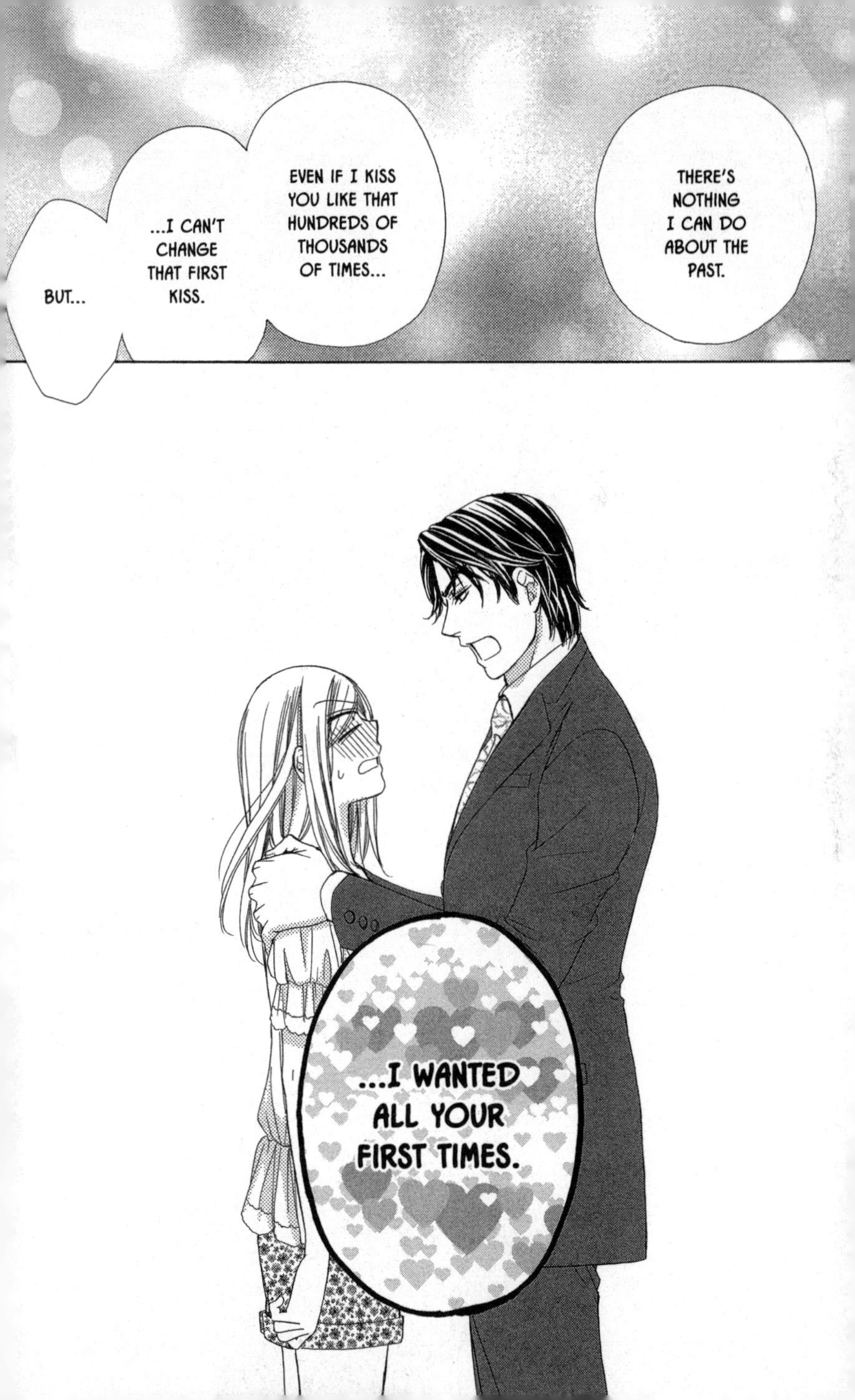
THERE'S NOTHING I CAN DO ABOUT THE PAST.
EVEN IF I KISS YOU LIKE THAT HUNDREDS OF THOUSANDS OF TIMES...
...I CAN'T CHANGE THAT FIRST KISS.
BUT...
...I WANTED ALL YOUR FIRST TIMES.

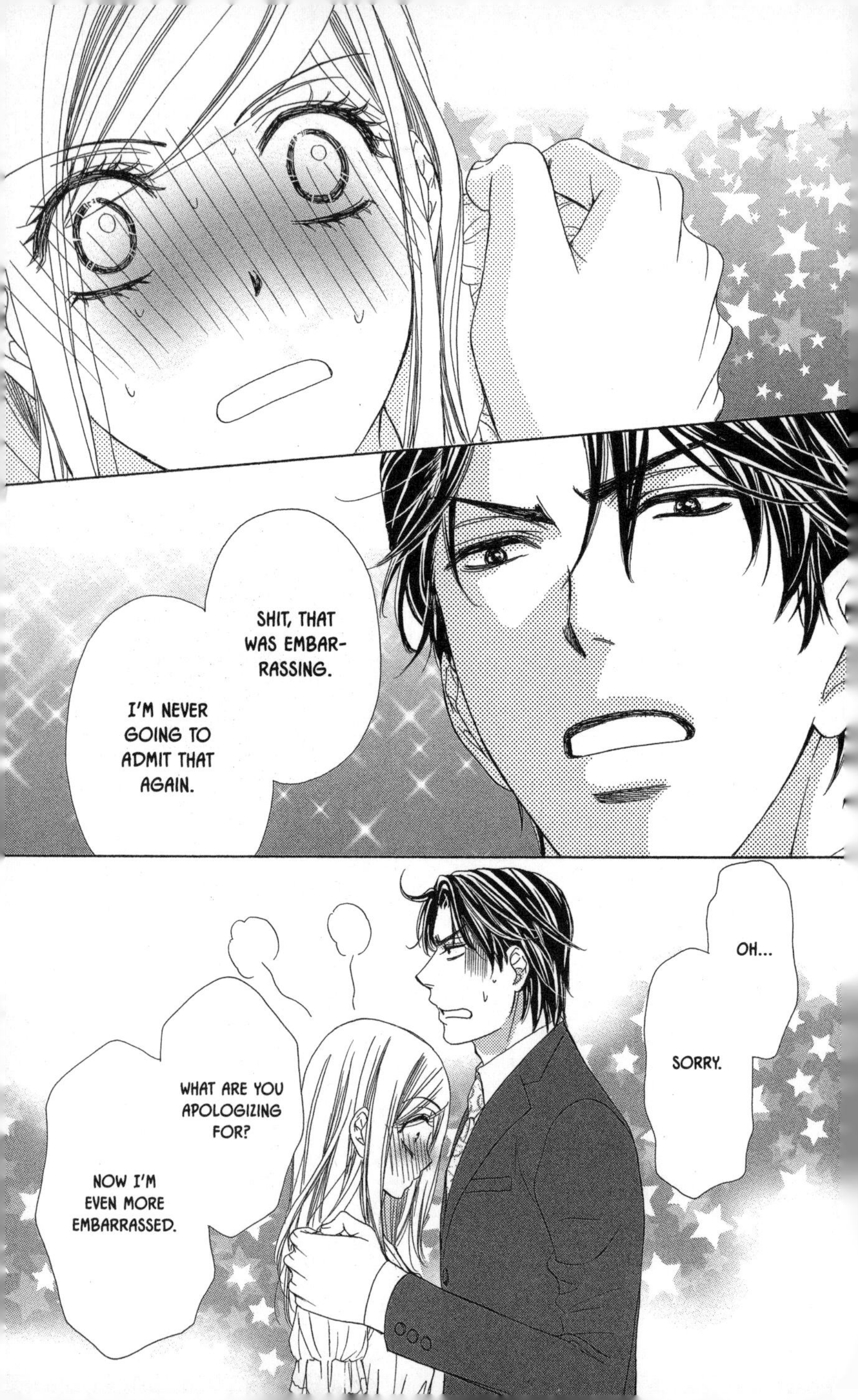
SHIT, THAT WAS EMBAR-RASSING.
I'M NEVER GOING TO ADMIT THAT AGAIN.
OH...
SORRY.
WHAT ARE YOU APOLOGIZING FOR?
NOW I'M EVEN MORE EMBARRASSED.

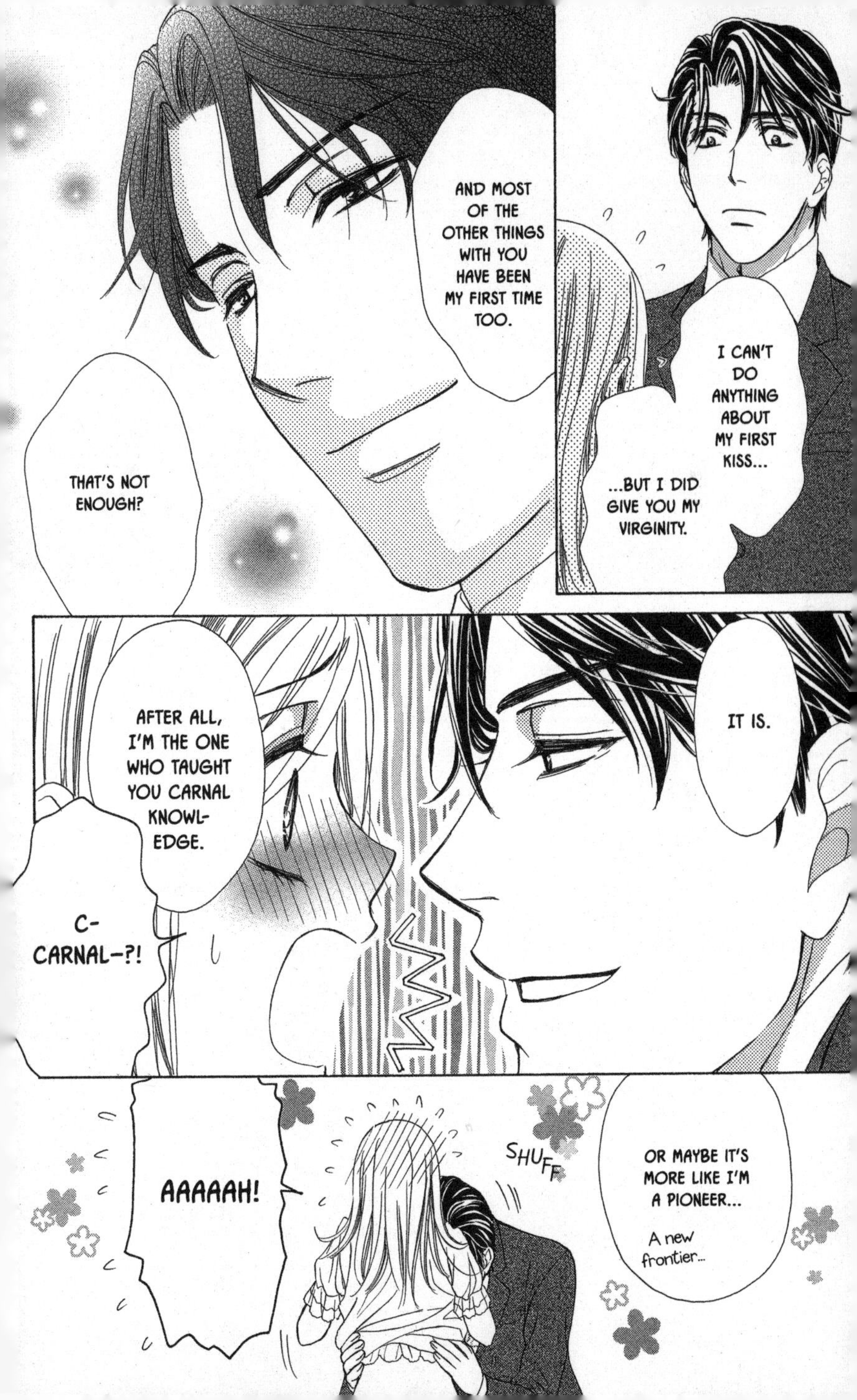
I CAN'T DO ANYTHING ABOUT MY FIRST KISS...
...BUT I DID GIVE YOU MY VIRGINITY.
AND MOST OF THE OTHER THINGS WITH YOU HAVE BEEN MY FIRST TIME TOO.
THAT'S NOT ENOUGH?
IT IS.
AFTER ALL, I'M THE ONE WHO TAUGHT YOU CARNAL KNOWL-EDGE.
C-CARNAL-?!
OR MAYBE IT'S MORE LIKE I'M A PIONEER...
A new frontier...
SHUFF
AAAAAH!

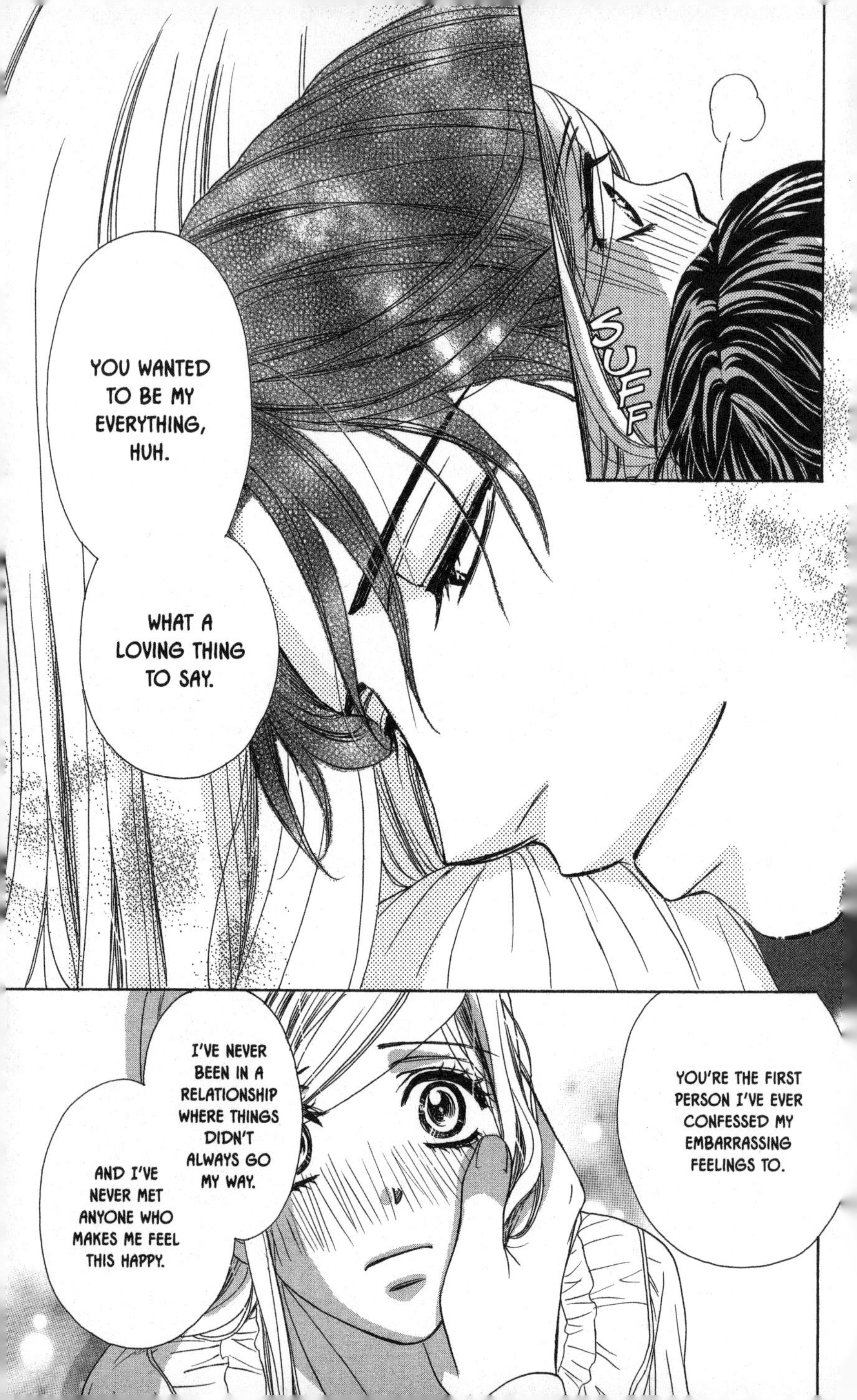
SUFF
YOU WANTED TO BE MY EVERYTHING, HUH.
WHAT A LOVING THING TO SAY.
YOU'RE THE FIRST PERSON I'VE EVER CONFESSED MY EMBARRASSING FEELINGS TO.
I'VE NEVER BEEN IN A RELATIONSHIP WHERE THINGS DIDN'T ALWAYS GO MY WAY.
AND I'VE NEVER MET ANYONE WHO MAKES ME FEEL THIS HAPPY.

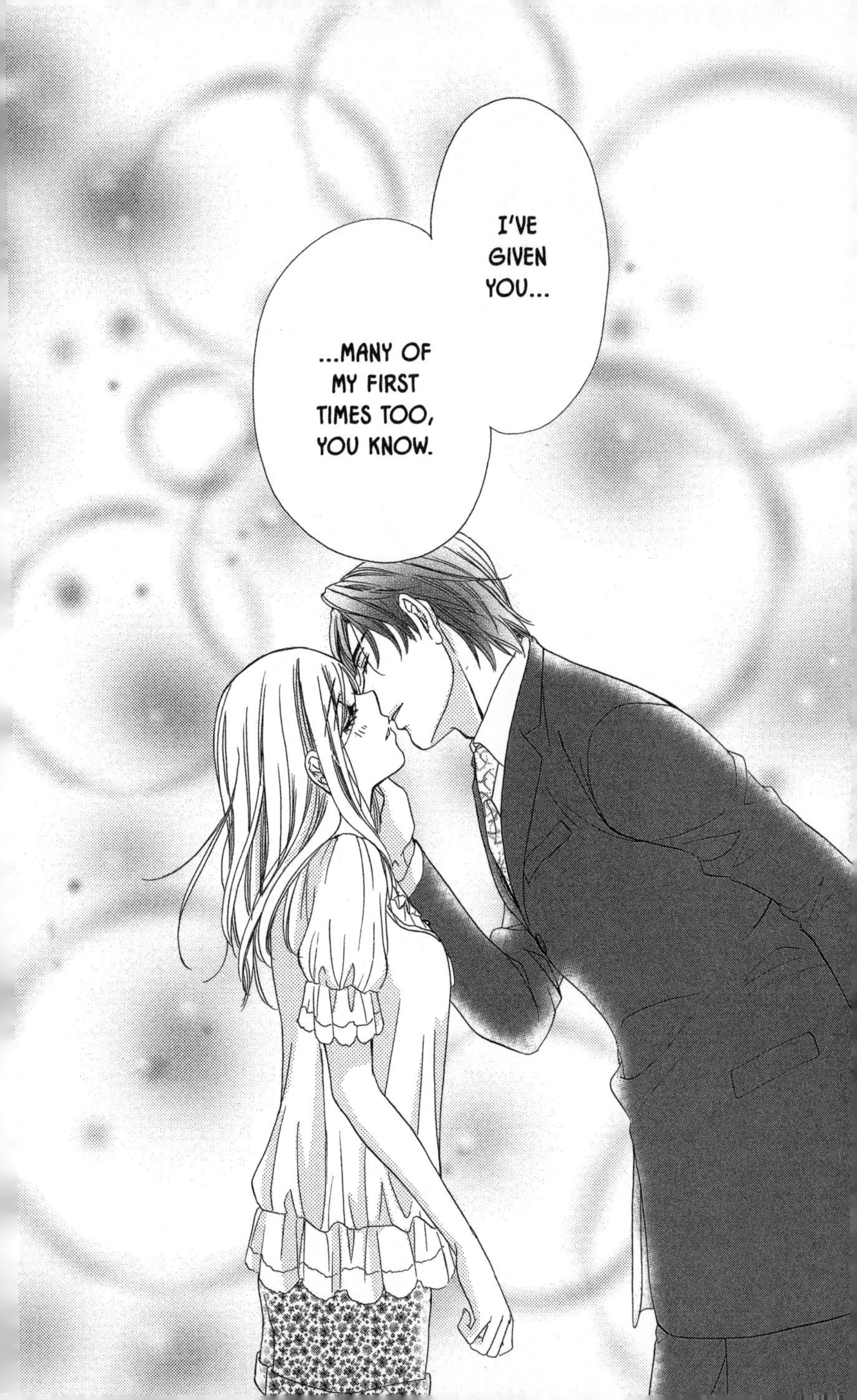
I'VE GIVEN YOU...
...MANY OF MY FIRST TIMES TOO, YOU KNOW.

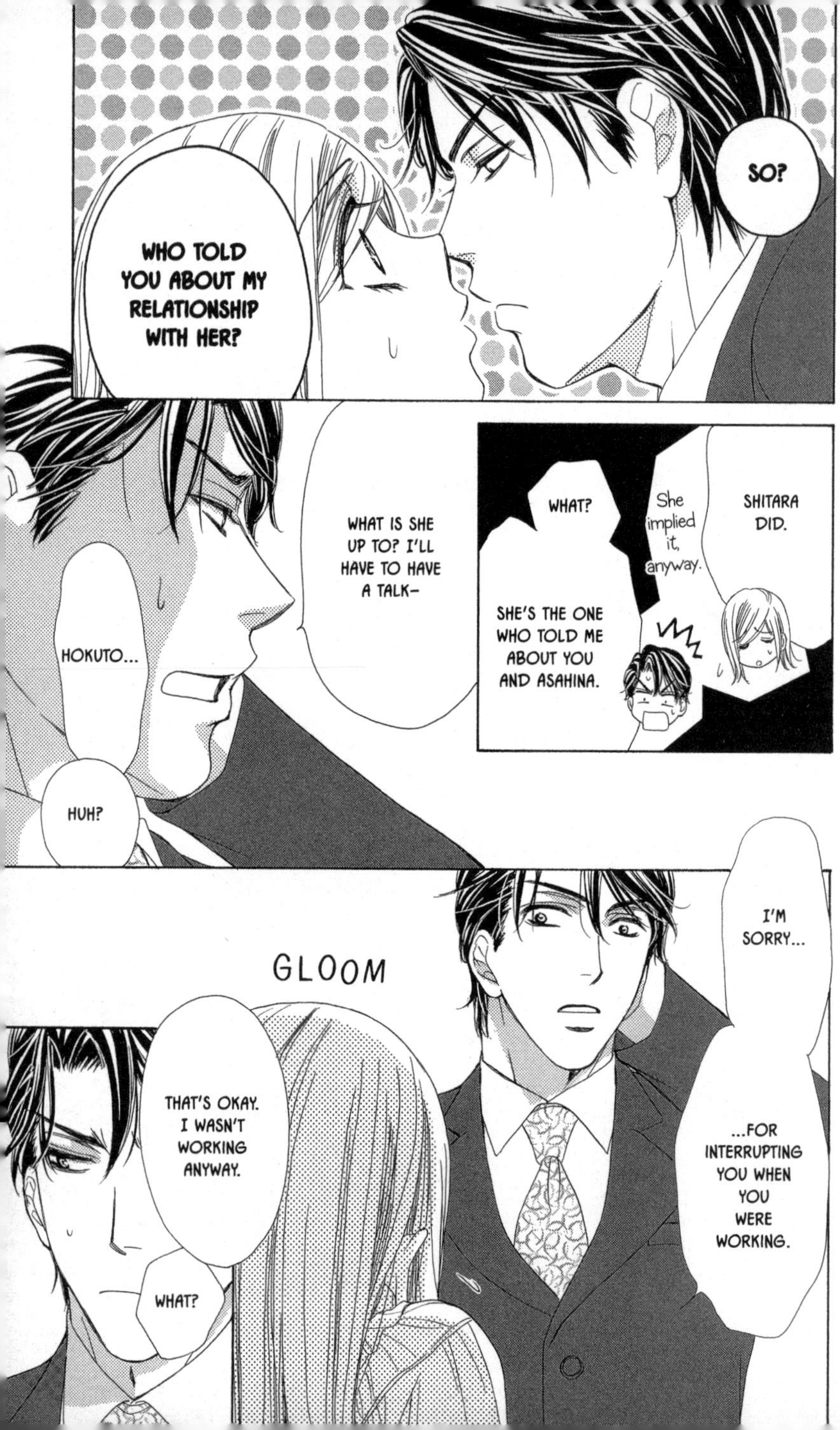
SO?
WHO TOLD YOU ABOUT MY RELATIONSHIP WITH HER?
SHITARA DID.
She implied it, anyway.
WHAT?
SHE'S THE ONE WHO TOLD ME ABOUT YOU AND ASAHINA.
WHAT IS SHE UP TO? I'LL HAVE TO HAVE A TALK–
HOKUTO...
HUH?
I'M SORRY...
...FOR INTERRUPTING YOU WHEN YOU WERE WORKING.
GLOOM
THAT'S OKAY. I WASN'T WORKING ANYWAY.
WHAT?

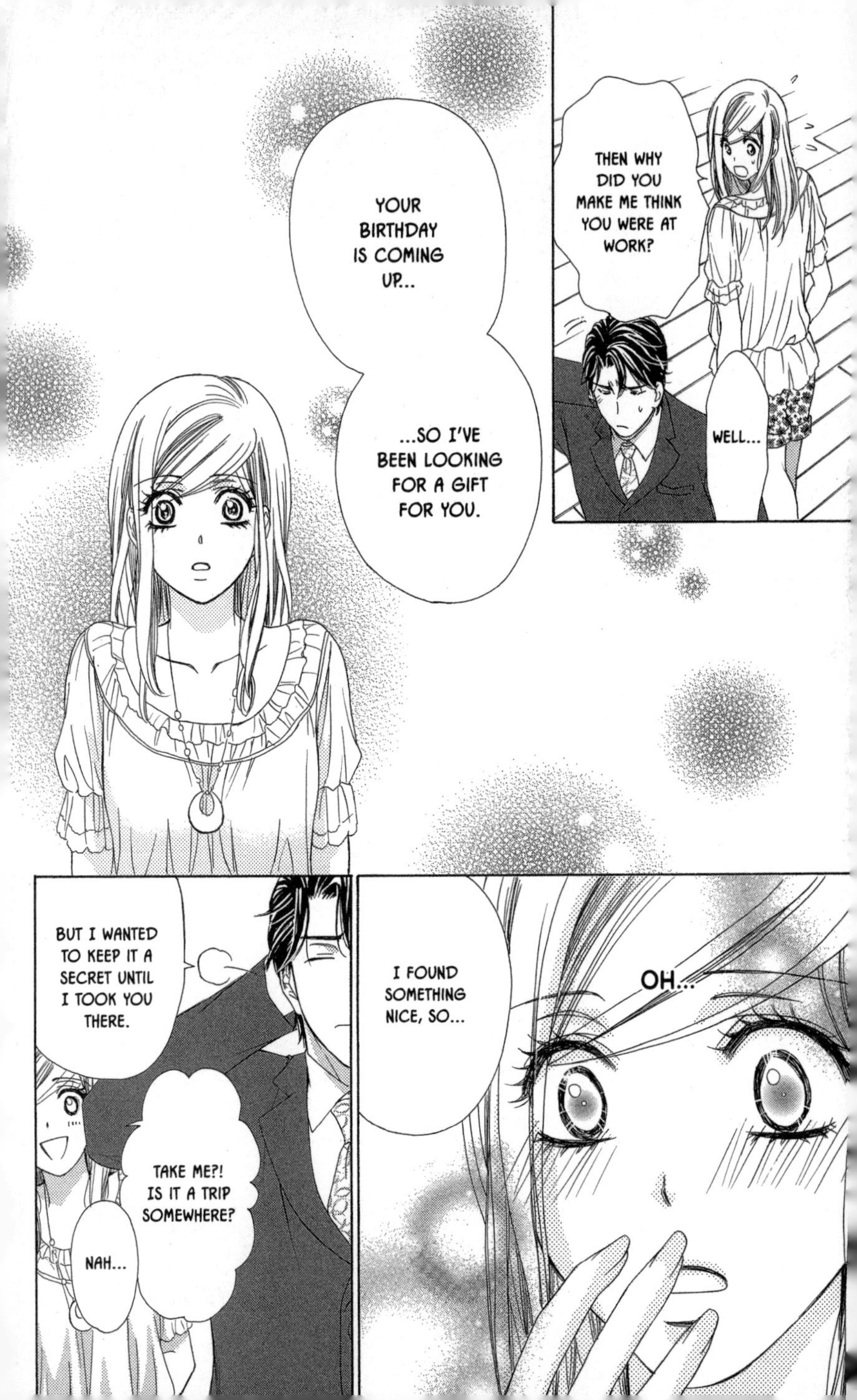
THEN WHY DID YOU MAKE ME THINK YOU WERE AT WORK?
WELL...
YOUR BIRTHDAY IS COMING UP...
...SO I'VE BEEN LOOKING FOR A GIFT FOR YOU.
I FOUND SOMETHING NICE, SO...
OH...
BUT I WANTED TO KEEP IT A SECRET UNTIL I TOOK YOU THERE.
TAKE ME?! IS IT A TRIP SOMEWHERE?
NAH...

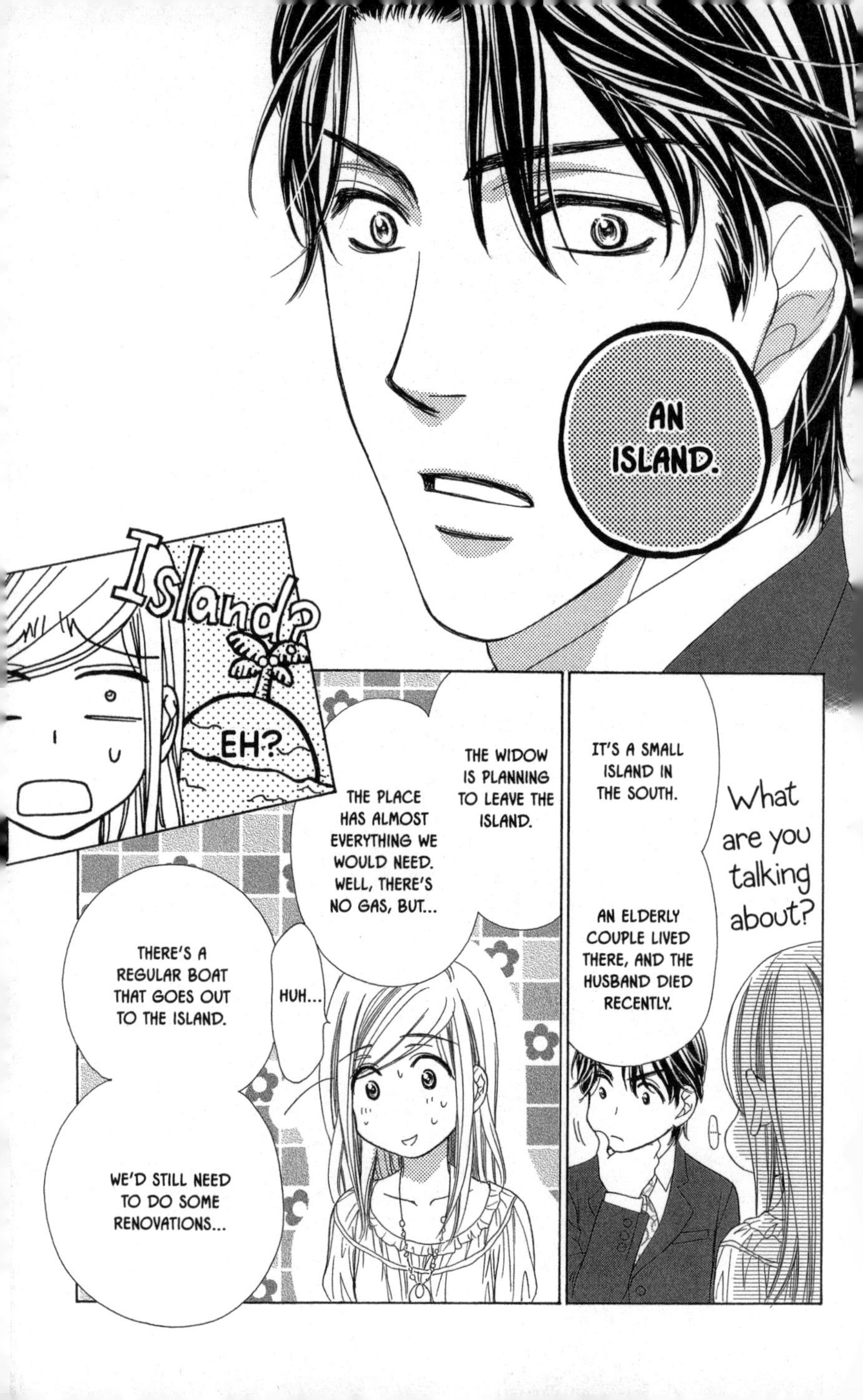
AN ISLAND.
Island?
EH?
What are you talking about?
IT'S A SMALL ISLAND IN THE SOUTH.
AN ELDERLY COUPLE LIVED THERE, AND THE HUSBAND DIED RECENTLY.
THE WIDOW IS PLANNING TO LEAVE THE ISLAND.
THE PLACE HAS ALMOST EVERYTHING WE WOULD NEED. WELL, THERE'S NO GAS, BUT...
HUH...
THERE'S A REGULAR BOAT THAT GOES OUT TO THE ISLAND.
WE'D STILL NEED TO DO SOME RENOVATIONS...

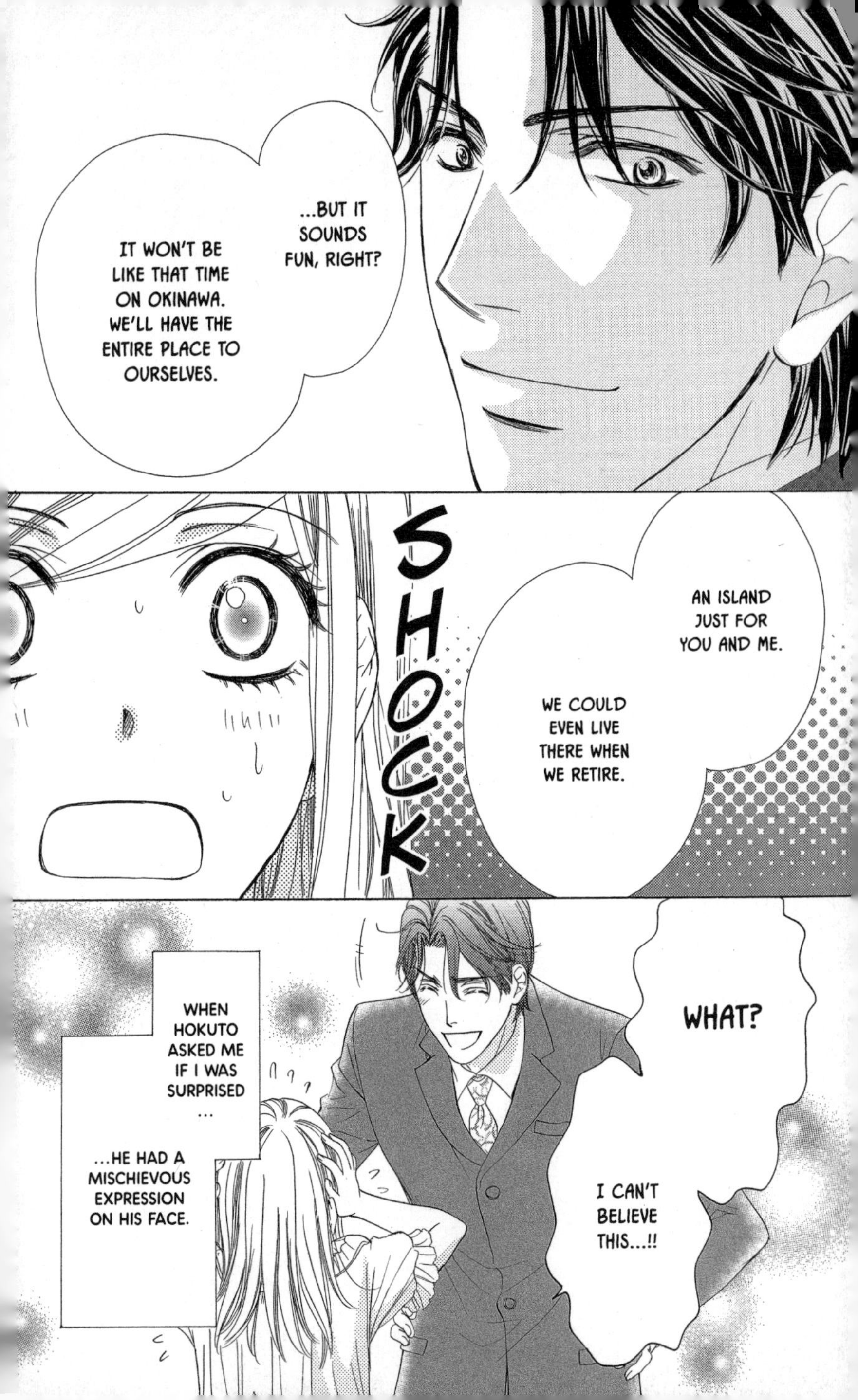
...BUT IT SOUNDS FUN, RIGHT?
IT WON'T BE LIKE THAT TIME ON OKINAWA. WE'LL HAVE THE ENTIRE PLACE TO OURSELVES.
AN ISLAND JUST FOR YOU AND ME.
WE COULD EVEN LIVE THERE WHEN WE RETIRE.
SHOCK
WHAT?
I CAN'T BELIEVE THIS...!!
WHEN HOKUTO ASKED ME IF I WAS SURPRISED...
...HE HAD A MISCHIEVOUS EXPRESSION ON HIS FACE.

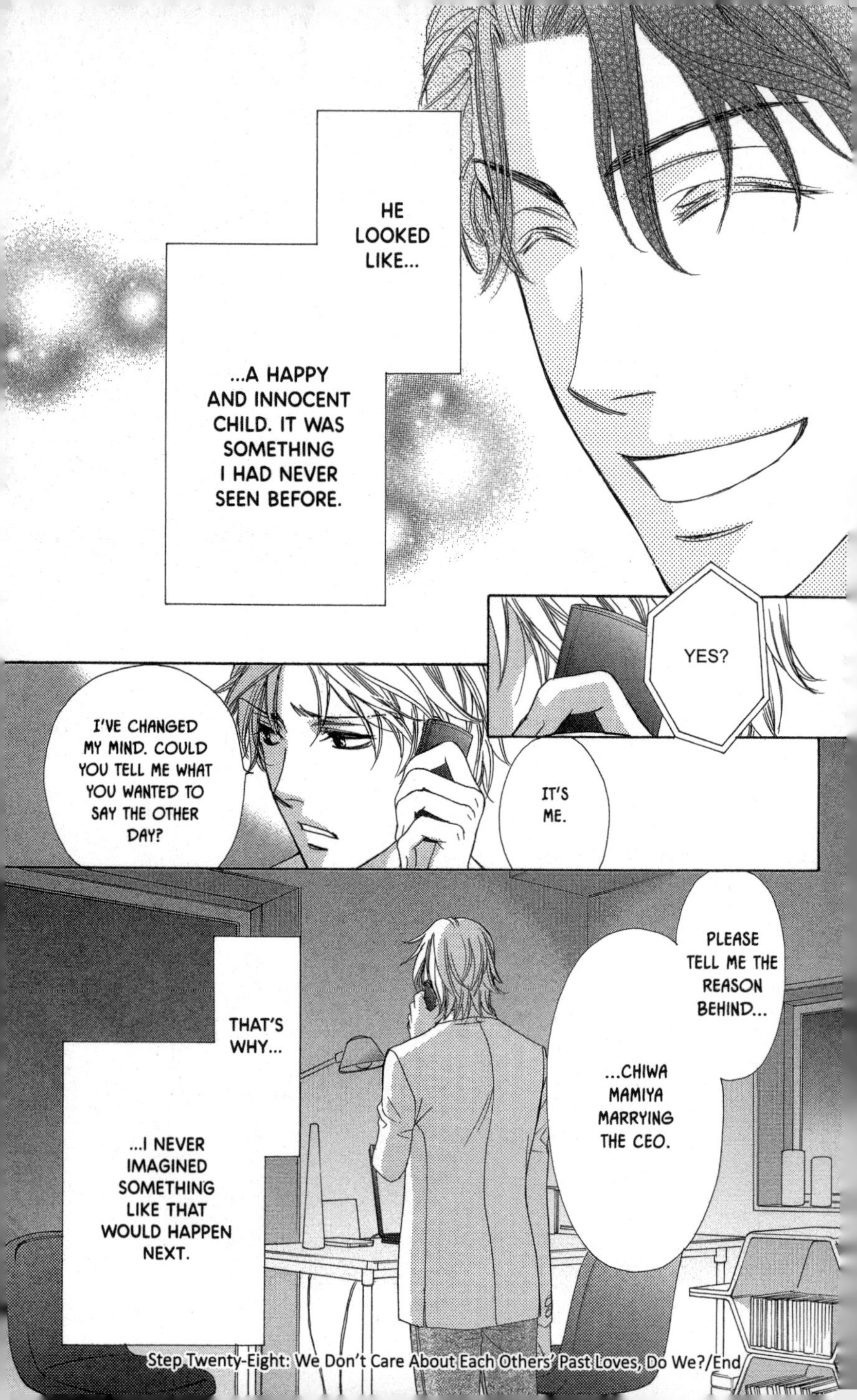
HE LOOKED LIKE...
...A HAPPY AND INNOCENT CHILD. IT WAS SOMETHING I HAD NEVER SEEN BEFORE.
YES?
IT'S ME.
I'VE CHANGED MY MIND. COULD YOU TELL ME WHAT YOU WANTED TO SAY THE OTHER DAY?
PLEASE TELL ME THE REASON BEHIND...
...CHIWA MAMIYA MARRYING THE CEO.
THAT'S WHY...
...I NEVER IMAGINED SOMETHING LIKE THAT WOULD HAPPEN NEXT.

Step Twenty-Eight: We Don't Care About Each Others' Past Loves, Do We?/End

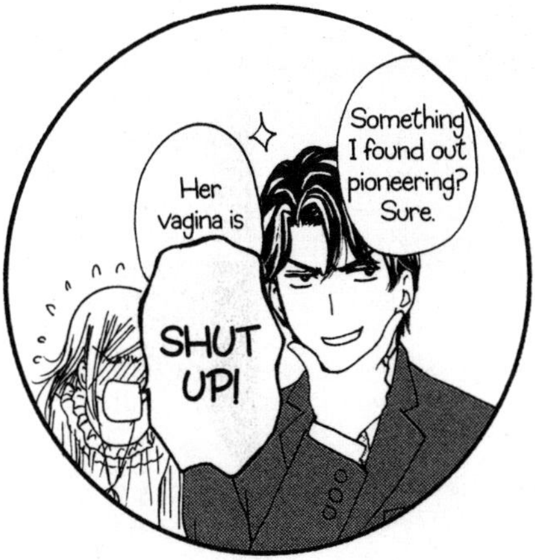
Something I found out pioneering? Sure.
Her vagina is
SHUT UP!

A GIRL'S DREAM

One day is twenty-four hours, but I wish I could increase the number of hours in a day to as many as I need... People have always told me I'm bad at managing my time. What must I do to be good at it? Is there a secret to it?

–Maki Enjoji

Maki Enjoji was born on December 8 in Tokyo. She made her debut with *Fu•Junai* (Wicked Pure Love). She currently works with *Petit Comics*. *Happy Marriage?!* is her fourth series.

Happy Marriage?!
Volume 7
Shojo Beat Edition

Story and Art by
Maki Enjoji

HAPIMARI - HAPPY MARRIAGE!? - Vol. 7
by Maki ENJOJI
© 2009 Maki ENJOJI
All rights reserved.
Original Japanese edition published by SHOGAKUKAN.
English translation rights in the United States of America, Canada, United
Kingdom, Ireland, Australia and New Zealand arranged with SHOGAKUKAN.

Translation/Tetsuichiro Miyaki
Adaptation/Nancy Thistlethwaite
Touch-up Art & Lettering/Inori Fukuda Trant
Design/Izumi Evers
Editor/Nancy Thistlethwaite

Printed in the U.S.A.

Published by VIZ Media, LLC
P.O. Box 77010
San Francisco, CA 94107

10 9 8 7 6 5 4 3 2 1
First printing, August 2014

www.viz.com   www.shojobeat.com

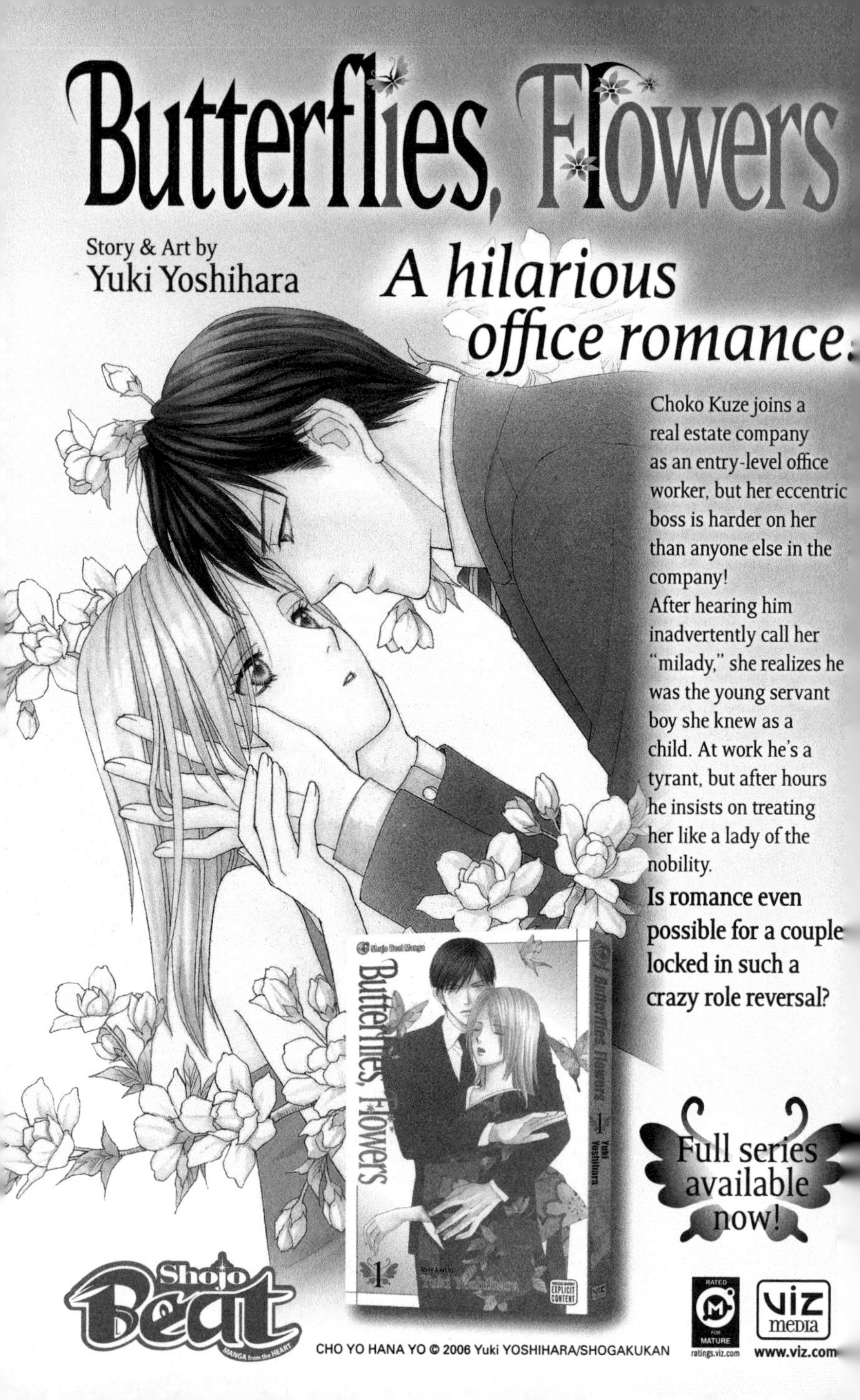
Butterflies, Flowers
Story & Art by
Yuki Yoshihara
A hilarious office romance.
Choko Kuze joins a real estate company as an entry-level office worker, but her eccentric boss is harder on her than anyone else in the company!
After hearing him inadvertently call her "milady," she realizes he was the young servant boy she knew as a child. At work he's a tyrant, but after hours he insists on treating her like a lady of the nobility.
Is romance even possible for a couple locked in such a crazy role reversal?
Full series available now!
Shojo Beat
MANGA from the HEART
Shojo Beat Manga
Butterflies, Flowers
1
Yuki Yoshihara
EXPLICIT CONTENT
RATED M FOR MATURE
ratings.viz.com
VIZ media
www.viz.com
CHO YO HANA YO © 2006 Yuki YOSHIHARA/SHOGAKUKAN

Kaya is accustomed to scheduling his "dinner dates" and working odd hours, but can she handle it when Kyohei's gaze turns her way?!

Midnight Secretary

Story & Art by Tomu Ohmi

Kaya Satozuka prides herself on being an excellent secretary and a consummate professional, so she doesn't even bat an eye when she's reassigned to the office of her company's difficult director, Kyohei Tohma. He's as prickly—and hot— as rumors paint him, but Kaya is unfazed...until she discovers that he's a vampire!!

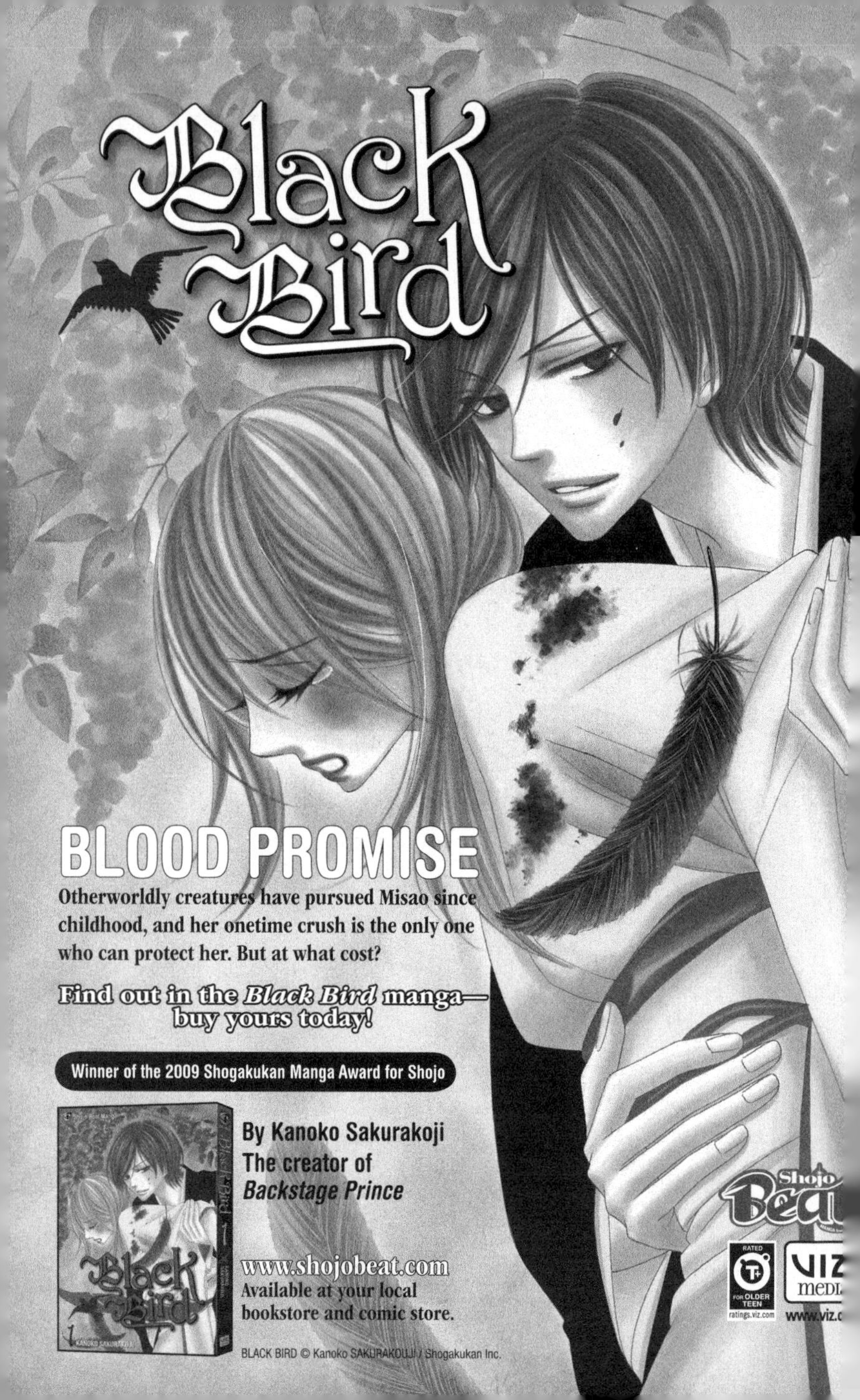
Black Bird
BLOOD PROMISE
Otherworldly creatures have pursued Misao since childhood, and her onetime crush is the only one who can protect her. But at what cost?
Find out in the *Black Bird* manga— buy yours today!
Winner of the 2009 Shogakukan Manga Award for Shojo
By Kanoko Sakurakoji
The creator of *Backstage Prince*
www.shojobeat.com
Available at your local bookstore and comic store.
RATED T+ FOR OLDER TEEN
ratings.viz.com
BLACK BIRD © Kanoko SAKURAKOUJI / Shogakukan Inc.

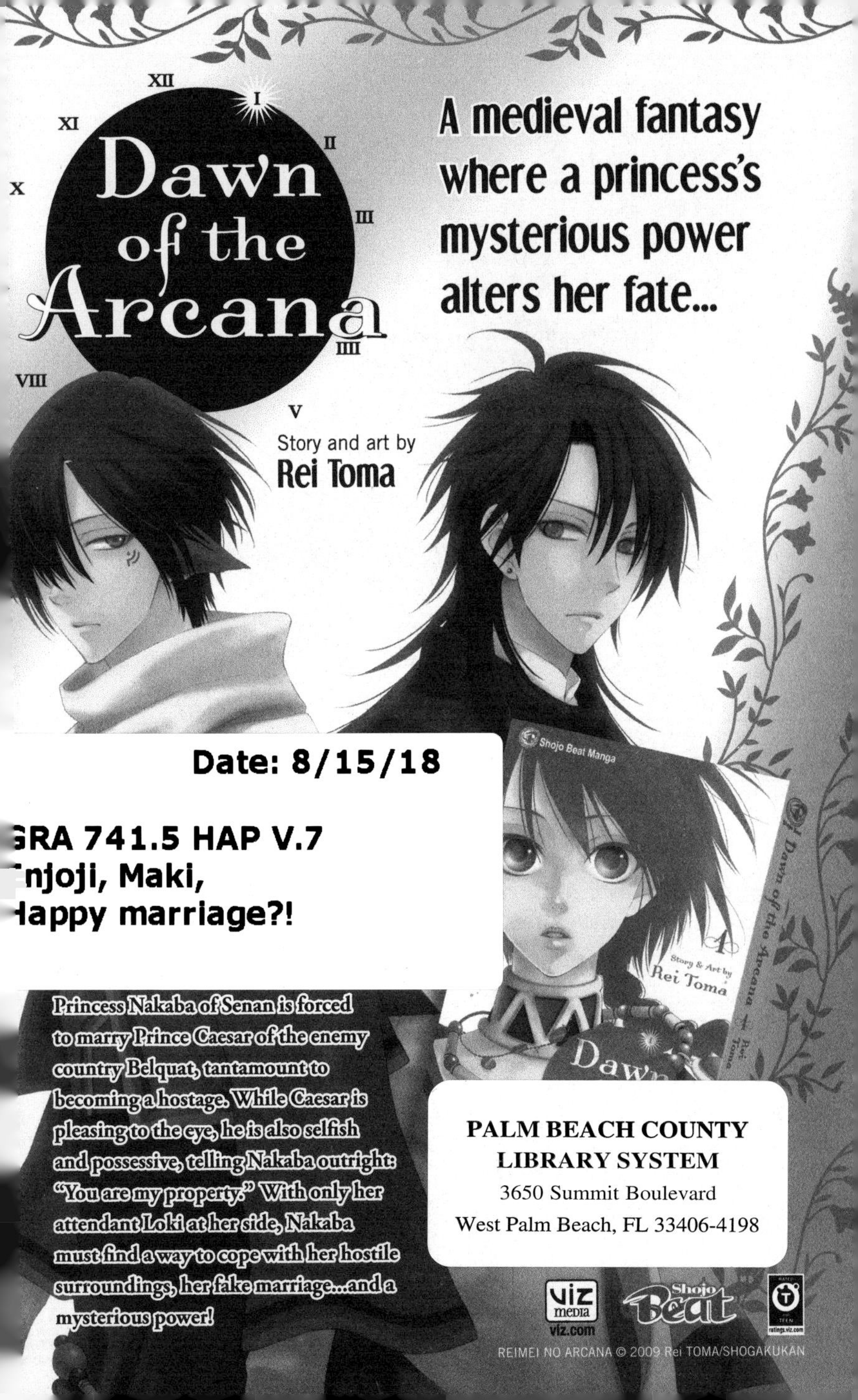
Dawn of the Arcana
A medieval fantasy where a princess's mysterious power alters her fate...
Story and art by Rei Toma
Shojo Beat Manga
Dawn of the Arcana 1
Story & Art by Rei Toma
Princess Nakaba of Senan is forced to marry Prince Caesar of the enemy country Belquat, tantamount to becoming a hostage. While Caesar is pleasing to the eye, he is also selfish and possessive, telling Nakaba outright: "You are my property." With only her attendant Loki at her side, Nakaba must find a way to cope with her hostile surroundings, her fake marriage...and a mysterious power!
VIZ media
viz.com
Shojo Beat
REIMEI NO ARCANA © 2009 Rei TOMA/SHOGAKUKAN

You may be reading the wrong way!

This book reads right to left to maintain the original presentation and art of the Japanese edition, so action, sound effects and word balloons are reversed. The diagram below shows how to follow the panels. Turn to the other side of the book to begin.

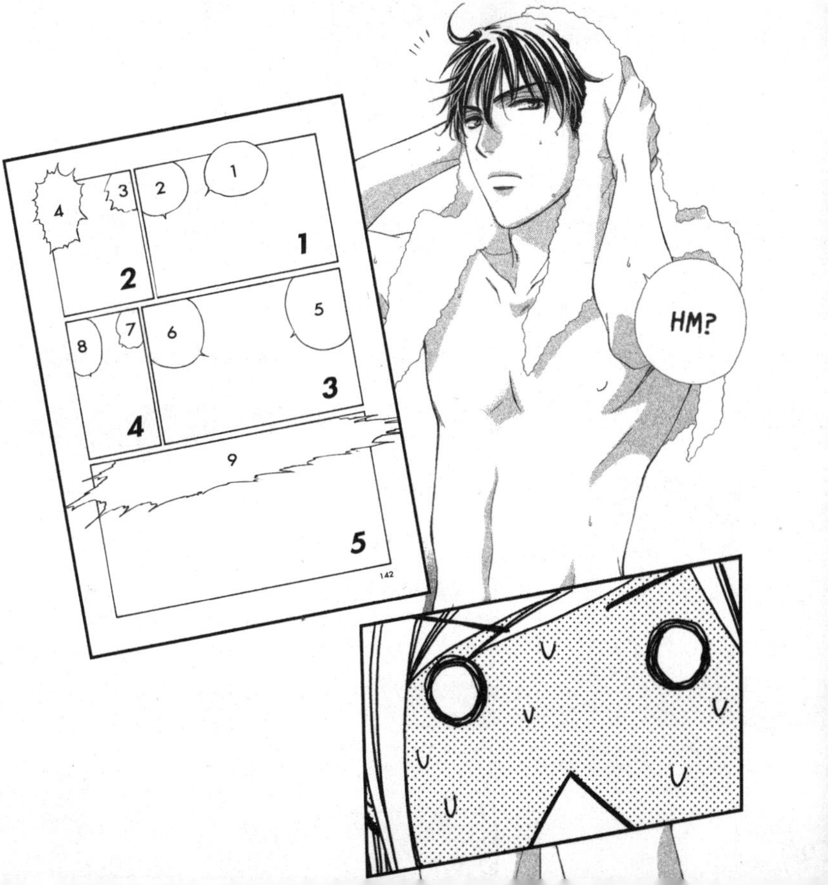
HM?
1
2
1
3
4
2
5
6
3
7
8
4
9
5
142